American History Made Simple

New, Revised Edition

Jack C. Estrin, M.A.
Revised by **Marilyn Miller**

Edited and prepared for publication by The Stonesong Press, Inc.

A MADE SIMPLE BOOK

DOUBLEDAY

NEW YORK   LONDON   TORONTO   SYDNEY   AUCKLAND

Edited and prepared for publication by The Stonesong Press, Inc.
Managing Editor: Sheree Bykofsky
Editor: Sarah Gold
Editorial Consultant: Dennis J. Maika
Design: Blackbirch Graphics, Inc.

A MADE SIMPLE BOOK

Published by Doubleday, a division of
Bantam Doubleday Dell Publishing Group, Inc.
666 Fifth Avenue, New York, New York 10103

MADE SIMPLE and DOUBLEDAY are trademarks of Doubleday,
a division of Bantam Doubleday Dell Publishing Group, Inc.

Copyright © 1991 by Doubleday, a division of Bantam Doubleday Dell Publishing Group, Inc.

Library of Congress Cataloging-in-Publication Data
Estrin, Jack C.
    American history made simple/Jack C. Estrin.—New, rev. ed./
  rev. by Marilyn Miller.
        p.   cm.
      A MADE SIMPLE BOOK
      Includes index.
      1. United States—History.   I. Miller, Marilyn (Marilyn Frances)
II. Title.
E178.E8   1991
973—dc20   90–22293
                                                        CIP

ISBN 0-385-41429-3

CONTENTS

CHAPTER ONE

The Discovery and Settlement of America

The date was October 12, 1492. It was about two o'clock in the morning, and a fierce storm was blowing. The lookout on the small Spanish ship *Pinta* was clinging to the mast when he saw something ahead, gleaming white in the moonlight. *"Tierra! Tierra!"* Roderigo de Triana shouted excitedly.

Triana had reason to be excited. The *Pinta* and its two companion ships, the *Nina* and the *Santa Maria*, had sailed more than 3,100 miles in 33 days without sighting land. Christopher Columbus, the master of the ships, had convinced Queen Isabella of Spain to finance the voyage to China, which the navigator estimated to be 3,000 miles across the Atlantic. If he was right, Spain would have a profitable and short trade route to the distant source of such highly prized oriental products as spices, perfumes, and fabrics.

The land Triana spied was not China (whose actual distance was over 10,000 nautical miles from Spain), but an island in the West Indies. When Columbus stepped ashore, he named the island San Salvador, or Holy Savior, in gratitude for having found land. Fourteen years later the great navigator was dead, unaware that he and his men had discovered a previously unknown continent. His voyage opened the door for the countries of Western Europe to exploit this vast New World.

Native American Civilizations

A Wide Range of Cultures. The new continent was not uninhabited. It is estimated that, in the year 1500, fifty to sixty million Native Americans lived there. One or two million of them inhabited what we now call the United States. The most advanced of their civilizations were in Mexico and Central America. The Incas of Peru and the Aztecs of Mexico had built large and beautiful cities. Mexico City, for example, was as big as Madrid, and, in the eyes of the Spanish conquistadors, as beautiful as Venice. Native Americans who lived in the territory to the north—now the United States and Canada—were technologically far less advanced. The various tribes in the Southwest and the Mississippi Valley survived mainly by farming, while those in the East also hunted and fished. Because living off the land was hard, tribal migration was common. Groups constantly moved on, searching for better hunting grounds or areas to grow crops like corn.

Contact Between Native Americans and Colonists. To the European colonizers, Native Americans—or Indians, as they called them—seemed vastly inferior beings, even savages. Although these prejudices tended to be racial in origin, they were not always so; some early colonists believed that the Indians they encountered were actually whites whose skin had darkened by excessive exposure to the sun. Also, because the Indians worshiped many gods instead of the Christian God, the Europeans regarded them as heathens whom they had to convert.

The cultures of whites and Indians clashed. To the Europeans, the Indians' lack of interest in acquiring worldly goods provided yet another reason to hold them in contempt. For example, Native Americans, believing that land should be owned communally, made no deeds or treaties to delineate tribal boundaries. The profound gulf between the two cultures was revealed by their different relationships to the land. While the Indians lived in harmony with their environment, the Europeans sought to change or control the natural world. While the various tribes led a nomadic existence, the colonists wanted to make permanent settlements.

The end result of these differences was that the Europeans exploited the Indians and exterminated them, partly through warfare. Huge numbers of Indians also died through the transmission of diseases the white men brought, such as measles, smallpox, and typhoid. It is estimated that some tribes lost 90 to 95 percent of their population during the first one hundred years of contact with Europeans.

European Settlements

The Colonizers. The three countries who best exploited Columbus's discovery were Spain, France, and England—the countries best equipped to generate the financial and military expenditures necessary for transatlantic exploration and settlement. The Dutch also tried initially to establish colonial claims. Each of their colonies in the New World had its own unique form of development.

Spanish Settlement. The first Spaniards to arrive in the New World were not colonists but conquistadors—men seeking gold, adventure, and the opportunity to convert the heathen to Catholicism. In the Treaty of Tordesillas (1494), arranged by Pope Alexander VI in Rome, Spain and Portugal divided the South American continent between themselves. Portugal, deciding to put her main efforts into Africa, claimed only Brazil, leaving the remaining territories to Spain.

In 1513 Juan Ponce de León became the first conquistador to land in North America. Six years later Hernán Cortés and six hundred followers sailed for Mexico, where they subdued the powerful Aztecs, ruled by Montezuma. Between 1539 and 1541 Hernando de Soto, looking for gold, discovered the Mississippi River, while Francisco Vasquez de Coronado trekked to Kansas and the Grand Canyon. A half century after Columbus's lookout sighted land, Spain had established an enormous empire in the New World; a larger empire, in fact, than it could govern.

After the conquistadors, Spain used the American colonies as a source of precious metals. To extract this wealth, the Spanish enslaved the Indians they had conquered who had offered fierce resistance. Huge amounts of gold and silver from the colonies poured into the king's coffers, but the mother country reinvested little in the New World. Poor leadership and costly colonial wars accelerated the Spanish decline, as did low immigration. One reason for the relative trickle of settlers was that Spanish colonies, such as St. Augustine in Florida, accepted only Roman Catholics. Thus, unlike the English colonies, they did not offer haven for people escaping religious persecution.

Spain controlled its colonies so tightly that immigrants could not expect much freedom. Spanish colonies had essentially the same system of political absolutism that prevailed at home. In addition, life in the colonies was economically unappealing. Grazing and agriculture failed to produce any significant surplus. The labor system, known as peonage (in effect, slavery) was inefficient; the home government hampered the colonies from engaging in free trade with self-defeating mercantilist restrictions; and the price of goods imported to the colonies was prohibitive because of high transportation charges and oppressive taxes. Manpower remained in short supply because immigrants were few. What Europeans would voyage from overseas to an unknown place where only a few gentry owned most of the sparsely watered land?

Spanish Contributions. Despite their use of American colonies primarily as a source of precious metals and their ruthless destruction of Indian cultures, the Spanish contributed greatly to American civilization. Their ceaseless exploration opened many pathways to the West. Spain also initiated the economic development of America; gold production gave all of Europe a specie base for expansion overseas. The Spanish also introduced many European, African, and Asian crops into the New World; they transplanted sheep, cattle, horses, and mules; and they located America's land and water resources.

Spanish missionaries spread Catholicism among Native Americans. Although they employed harsh measures to convert them, the missionaries also sometimes restrained the excessive brutality of Spanish governors.

The "oldest town in the United States," St. Augustine, was established in Florida by the Spanish in 1565. Colonists from Spain built houses, churches, hospitals, and monasteries. They influenced architecture in America. Even today, in the South and the Southwest, we still see the severe mission style, the use of stucco relief, the baroque style, and the ornate churrigueresque—all part of our Spanish heritage.

French Settlement. Although slower to colonize, the French, like the Spanish, dreamed of a huge empire in the New World. In 1608 Samuel de Champlain founded a settlement at Quebec. Because the French economy in Canada relied largely on the fur trade, these colonists, unlike their Spanish peers, cooperated with the Native Americans.

In 1673 Father Jacques Marquette journeyed down the Mississippi to the Gulf of Mexico. By the beginning of the eighteenth century, Louisiana was dotted with small French settlements, including New Orleans.

Yet the French, too, suffered setbacks to their dreams of empire. The settlements were underpopulated for many reasons. France restricted settlement to Roman Catholics; granted vast tracts to seigneurs (nobles) and subjected settlers to feudal conditions; extended French despotism to the regions; and hampered enterprise with rigid mercantilist regulations. Led by a king who was indifferent to the colonies, the government offered no inducement to its citizens to leave home and endure cold Canadian winters, sometimes hostile Indians, and limited economic opportunities.

Thus, by 1750 only fifty thousand French had ventured to the New World, most searching for fur. These rootless individuals, who often intermarried with Native Americans, offered France no permanent population base in the New World.

French Contributions. Like Spain, France bequeathed a cultural heritage to the American people. French books on philosophy, science, and engineering advanced knowledge in regions like New Orleans, St. Louis, St. Charles, and Mobile. French Jesuits spread their faith and schools in French-controlled territories. Long after they were expelled from the continent, the Jesuit influence lingered, in the laws of Louisiana and the customs and patois of the Creoles.

Dutch Settlement. Following the discovery of the Hudson River by Henry Hudson, in 1609, his sponsors, the Dutch East India Company, established two permanent settlements along the Hudson River: New Amsterdam (later Manhattan) and Fort Orange (later Albany). Although they successfully exploited the fur trade, these first Dutch settlers were unable to build up a permanent deposit of colonists. They were hampered by their feudal pattern of settlement ("the patroon system"), characterized by religious discrimination, political absolutism, and mercantilist restrictions.

Dutch Contributions. The Dutch influence has lingered in many aspects of American life: in place names (such as the Bronx, named for Jonas Bronck) and family names (such as Van Dam, Brandt); in the concept of public schools (the New Amsterdam Elementary School, founded in 1638 under Adam Roelantsen, was the oldest in America); in architecture (the brick gable and gambrel roof; the gutter; the multicolored planks, halfway doors, and high stoops); in the recreational sports of sleighing, skating, golfing, and bowling; and in holiday symbols and customs such as Santa Claus and Easter eggs.

English Settlement. Preoccupied with domestic and religious problems for much of the sixteenth century, the English turned their attention to colonizing the New World only in the century's last decades. The major religious concern of the English was their break with the Roman Catholic Church. In 1517 the German monk Martin Luther had publicly attacked the beliefs and practices of the Roman Catholic Church, and within a short time the Catholic monopoly of religious life that had endured since the Middle Ages no longer existed.

England was a fertile ground for the spread of the new religion, as its people deeply resented paying monies to churchmen, many of whom had grown greedy and corrupt. The catalyst for the English Reformation, King Henry VIII, had petitioned Pope Clement VII for a divorce. When the pontiff delayed answering his requests, Henry broke with Rome and, in 1534, was declared head of the Church of England. Having seized church lands and dissolved monasteries, he permitted these properties to be privately owned by Protestants, or followers of the new English church.

Only with the ascension of his daughter Elizabeth in 1558 did the religious turmoil initiated by Henry begin to abate. Elizabeth firmly established the Church of England as a unique church, blending both Catholic and Protestant elements. During her reign, nationalism and Protestantism slowly became entwined in the English mind.

In 1588 the smaller English navy defeated the mighty Spanish Armada, effectively ending Spain's supremacy as a European power. Emboldened by this victory, the Queen and her subjects began to look to the possibility of colonizing America. Among the most active supporters were the commercial classes, who had become influential and prosperous during her reign.

The first Englishman to attempt to colonize North America was Sir Humphrey Gilbert. In 1583 he sailed to Newfoundland with over two hundred settlers but did not establish a colony there, and on the voyage back to England, his ship sank.

Sir Walter Raleigh, Gilbert's half brother, next dispatched several expeditions to explore the eastern coast of North America, a region he diplomatically named Virginia in honor of the virgin queen.

In 1587 Raleigh sent a group of colonists, including women and children, to Roanoke Island, near the coast of North Carolina. Because of delays caused by the war with Spain, the English were unable to get a supply ship to the settlers until 1590. When the rescuers arrived, they found no colonists. Today we still do not know what happened to these men, women, and children.

The unfortunate end of these expeditions briefly discouraged English colonization. Financing for them had also come out of Raleigh's own pocket, and the cost far exceeded what any individual, no matter how wealthy, could bear. But what about royal aid? In 1584 Richard Hakluyt, who had published explorers' accounts of the Americas, wrote an essay advocating government support of colonization. The colonies would, he promised, provide a market for English wool and supply in return such raw products as wood. In the process, Hakluyt said, the settlers themselves would become rich. Elizabeth died in 1603 before acting on this issue.

Nevertheless, colonization did begin shortly thereafter, with financial support coming, not from the new king, James I, but from merchants seeking quick profits. Soon England was gripped by navigation fever. People were journeying all through Europe in search of new economic opportunities. Some left their villages to travel to cities. Others, who were more adventurous, immigrated to England from Ireland, and still others went to Holland to escape religious oppression. The boldest people went to the New World. Some were motivated more by religious reasons, others by the possibility of owning their own land. Another group consisted of ex-prisoners or extremely poor people who hoped to begin a new life abroad.

The individual stories varied, but all the settlers were thrust outward by the tumultuous religious and political controversies that marked 17th century England. In 1640 the conflict between the Stuart monarchs and Parliament erupted into civil war. Nine years later, Parliament beheaded King Charles I, and General Oliver Cromwell ruled England until his death in 1658. The Stuarts were soon restored to the throne (1660), but calm was not restored until the Glorious Revolution (1688), when the Catholic Stuarts were finally ousted and the Protestant William and Mary assumed the monarchy.

The Thirteen Colonies

The Tobacco Provinces: Virginia.   In 1607, after the failures of Gilbert and Raleigh to establish permanent colonies in Virginia, the London Company, a joint-stock company, sent one hundred settlers who founded Jamestown. This attempt succeeded through the efforts of Captain John Smith, who created a semblance of order; through the reinforcement of the settlement with immigrants and provisions (by 1622 about six thousand settlers had been sent); through the discovery by John Rolfe of the cure of tobacco, which the colonists then sold for profit in England; and, finally, through the wisdom of Sir Edwin Sandys, a stockholder in the London Company, who substituted private for communal ownership of farms.

Maryland.   Lord Baltimore received a charter from Charles I making him proprietor of the colony of Maryland. Baltimore hoped to profit financially from the colony, but he also wanted to found a haven for his Catholic co-religionists. To attract settlers, he permitted them to own their own farms and to have a say in local government. The success of this settlement (1634) was guaranteed when Baltimore opened his lands to settlement by Protestants (after protecting the Catholics with a Toleration Act) and when the colonists turned to the profitable production of corn, tobacco, and livestock.

The New England Colonies

Plymouth.   Plymouth was settled in 1620 by a group of Separatists (those "separated" from the Anglican Church) who had fled to Holland from Scrooby, England, to seek religious freedom. Financed by the Virginia Company, these "Pilgrims" sailed to the New World on the *Mayflower* under the leadership of their pastor, John Robinson, and their church elder, William Brewster. The approximately one hundred settlers landed at Plymouth.

The success of the Plymouth settlers was fostered by the captainship of Miles Standish, the wise governorship of William Bradford, the settlers' perseverance in discharging their debts to the businessmen who backed them, and peaceful and cooperative relations with the local Indians. In 1691 they were absorbed by their more powerful neighbor, Massachusetts.

Massachusetts.   Massachusetts Bay attracted some Puritan gentry, who in 1629 organized the Massachusetts Bay Company to finance a large-scale venture to America. These Puritans, who wanted to "purify" the elaborate structure and practices of the Church of England, were primarily interested in securing a safe refuge in the New World in the event that the religious climate in England became too hostile.

After receiving a royal charter that omitted naming a location for the annual meeting, the directors of the company decided to meet in the colony—a move that virtually freed them from the Crown's control. By itself this could not ensure the success of the venture. Between 1630 and 1640, however, persecution of Puritans in England increased. During this period nearly ten thousand of them migrated to Massachusetts Bay, where they founded Boston and several other towns.

These early colonists had an easier time than the settlers in Jamestown and Plymouth. The steady migration of newcomers helped, as did careful planning, under the commonsensical leadership of the elected governor, John Winthrop, and an elected legislature. The colony also benefitted from the fact that, in contrast to the settlers of Jamestown and Maryland, those of Massachusetts Bay came with their families. The whole enterprise, therefore, possessed a stability that was lacking in these other settlements.

Rhode Island. The Puritan system was not democratic, for only church members could vote or hold office. Colonist Roger Williams refused to accept the alliance between church and civil government. Hounded for these heretical beliefs, he fled Massachusetts in 1636 and organized a settlement in Providence, Rhode Island.

In 1638 he was joined by Anne Hutchinson and her followers, who had stirred up a hornet's nest in Massachusetts by preaching that those who possessed saving grace were not bound by the laws of the commonwealth or the rules of good behavior. Complete religious freedom, peaceful relations with neighboring Indians, a relatively democratic government, and economic prosperity ensured the success of the Rhode Island colony.

Connecticut. The Reverend Thomas Hooker also quarreled with Massachusetts's Puritan governors. In 1636 he left the colony to found Hartford. Others followed him and set up communities at Wethersfield, Windsor, Springfield, and New Haven. In 1662 the colony received a charter from Charles II, and later that year the towns were incorporated into the Connecticut Colony.

Maine and New Hampshire. The areas of Maine and New Hampshire were granted as proprietaries to Sir Fernando Gorges and Captain John Mason in 1623. Both made unsuccessful attempts to settle the territory. But people did join John Wheelright (a follower of Anne Hutchinson) when he moved into that area from Massachusetts. Massachusetts thereupon claimed Maine and New Hampshire. In 1680 New Hampshire shook loose from these claims and became a royal colony; Maine continued as a Massachusetts province until 1820.

The Middle Colonies

New York. In 1664 Charles II granted to his brother, the Duke of York, the land in the New World held by the Dutch—the entire area between Connecticut and Maryland. The Duke then dispatched a task force of four frigates to New Amsterdam, and the Dutch governor, Peter Stuyvesant, surrendered New Amsterdam to them without a fight. By 1668 the English possessed all the Dutch settlements. New Amsterdam became New York and, because the British did not interfere with the Dutch settlers, the colony continued its prosperous advance.

New Jersey.   In 1664 the Duke of York gave a generous portion of his proprietary grant to two favorites, Sir George Carteret and Lord Berkeley, which they divided into East and West Jersey. Because the two granted land to settlers on easy terms and established a system of local democratic government along with religious freedom, Puritan families from nearby New England and Rhode Island rapidly moved to the new colony. In 1702 Charles II united the two Jerseys into one royal colony.

Pennsylvania.   In exchange for a royal debt owed to his father, William Penn, a Quaker, received a grant of the land north of Maryland and west of the Delaware River to be called Pennsylvania. Penn wanted a haven in the New World for the universally persecuted Quakers, who believed every person received an "inner light" from the Holy Spirit. The colony was launched as a "holy experiment" in religious and political freedom. The Frame of Government (1682) and the Charter of Privileges (1701) granted complete freedom of religious worship and a government in which most of the power was lodged in a unicameral (one-house) legis-

lature. Penn treated the Indians fairly. His descriptions of the colony circulated throughout England, Ireland, and southern Germany, attracting many European immigrants, particularly Germans.

Delaware.   Penn bought Delaware from the Duke of York to protect the southern river approach to Pennsylvania. Although it possessed considerable local autonomy, Delaware remained a possession of Pennsylvania until the American Revolution.

The "Deep South" Colonies

North and South Carolina.   In 1663 Charles II granted to eight court favorites a charter for the land between Virginia and Florida. The charter established the Anglican Church, making it the official church, and placed restrictions on freedom of worship. The eight proprietors asked the famous English philosopher John Locke to draw up a model government. Called the "Grand Model," it was a fantastic array of carefully divided aristocracies. The plan was discarded as unworkable, and eventually a traditional plan of government was adopted.

The rapid spread of rice-planting in the south and free-farming in the north guaranteed the colony's success. When the proprietors surrendered their charter to the Crown in 1729, Charles II formally separated the two areas of settlement, and they became North and South Carolina.

Georgia.   In 1732 George II wanted a buffer state to protect British colonies from the Spanish in Florida. His interest converged with that of James Oglethorpe, who in the same year sought a proprietary grant to build a colony for London's debtors. The new settlement was to be a model community where no rum was swilled and no slaves toiled. In 1732 Oglethorpe secured his grant, but Georgia did not prosper. Few debtors migrated, landholdings were restricted to five hundred acres, black slaves were prohibited without other labor to substitute for them, and constant border warfare discouraged all but the hardiest. In 1751 the Crown received back the grant.

CHAPTER TWO

Colonial Foundations

In 1751 Dr. William Watson presented Benjamin Franklin's first scientific publication to the Royal Society of London. The slim volume described the Philadelphian's early experiments with electricity. "To give even the shortest account of all the experiments contained in Mr. Franklin's work," Watson remarked with admiration, "would exceed greatly the time allowed for these purposes by the Royal Society."

Franklin's experiments in electricity were remarkably consistent with the character of the man himself. Commonsensical, keenly observant, he exemplified the Enlightenment's attitude toward human inquiry. In his lifetime European intellectual and religious traditions were reinterpreted, not only by Franklin but by every variety of colonist, to suit the conditions of life in the New World.

Immigrants to a New World

The English Base. The mighty surge of the English into the colonies during the seventeenth and eighteenth centuries settled the cultural destiny of America. By 1790 there were over 2,500,000 British settlers, constituting 80 percent of the total colonial population. Their ascendancy set the cultural pattern that eventually absorbed all others. The English language became virtually universal, American universities were patterned after British ones, and the religious conflicts and settlements of the colonists reflected those of England. English ideas, practices, laws, and liberties were established everywhere. Yet many non-English tributaries also fed this broad cultural river.

Immigrants from Other Countries. Large numbers of immigrants speaking non-English tongues, practicing non-English faiths, and pursuing non-English ways poured into the colonies from Ireland, Scotland, France, Germany, Switzerland, and Scandinavia. Among the immigrants were also Jews from many lands. The customs these immigrants brought with them—their foods and fashions, songs and stories, habits and dress—were mostly modified after several generations by stronger trends from England, but their distinctiveness flavored the British heritage. America's historic mission of cultural absorption and fusion had begun.

Motives for Immigration. During the seventeenth century in Europe, many Germans fled the devastation of the Thirty Years War; the confiscations and terrors unleashed by Catholic princes against the Protestant religion and its followers; and the poverty they were condemned to, following the concentration of land and wealth into the hands of the few.

In France it was the wealthy Protestant Huguenots who fled. Under the Edict of Nantes, issued in 1598 by Henry IV, they enjoyed a measure of toleration. When it was revoked, in 1685, many Huguenots immigrated to New York, which was by then a British royal colony.

In the early eighteenth century the Scotch-Irish left North Ireland in droves to escape the British landlords who crippled their thriving cattle and woolen industries, tripled their rents, and excluded them from political office. The condition of the people of Southern Ireland was even worse, sending Irish Catholics in great numbers across the Atlantic to America. There they mixed with immigrants from Scotland who had suffered humiliation and defeat in an effort to preserve their independence and clan system; the expropriation of the lands had ruined them. Most of these newcomers settled in Pennsylvania. In southwestern Pennsylvania Swiss immigrants, who left their native land because of the lack of economic opportunity, mingled with German Quakers and other persecuted sects. And in parts

of Delaware and New Jersey, the Dutch, German, and Swedish outnumbered the English.

This mixture of ethnic groups worked, on the whole, amazingly well. The colonists, whatever their country of origin or religion, were linked by a desire for political freedom, the right to worship freely, a fluid class structure that would permit their children to advance in social status, and, above all, economic opportunity and security.

Colonial Free Enterprise

Early Obstacles to Free Enterprise. The colonists who descended on America relied on the free enterprise system to exploit its bountiful economic opportunities. Free enterprise meant private ownership of land and capital and the free use of both for private profit.

From the beginning serious obstacles impeded their efforts. First, the early settlements were usually corporate enterprises. Financed in their emigration by joint stock companies, the colonists had to work as company servants. They had to store their produce in a common hold, and their surplus was then shipped overseas for sale in Europe with no profit to them. Without incentive to produce a surplus, they produced none. As a result, the companies, deprived of profit, were compelled to sell or transfer land to individuals for private use. This change marked a vital turning point in American history.

The second obstacle was the Crown's granting of royal monopolies over the production or distribution of goods to individuals or companies. But colonists with small accumulations of capital ignored these monopolies and established private trading posts and private channels for the disposal of goods abroad.

Third, in certain areas, land granted to individuals was limited by feudal entailments such as quitrents (landlords' feudal fees) and primogeniture (inheritance of a father's entire property by the first-born son). Not until the end of the Revolutionary War were these restrictions permanently removed.

A final restriction to free enterprise existed in the mercantile regulations that served to exclude the colonists from certain occupations and to establish a single destination—Great Britain—for the flow of American goods abroad. Colonists, nevertheless, frequently found ways to evade these restrictions.

Free Enterprise in Agriculture. The huge stretches of arable soil in America held the promise of great wealth. To achieve it, the colonists had to develop a self-sustaining agriculture. Settlers who became landowners produced the basic cereals; raised poultry and hogs; herded cattle; cut down forests for building material, fuel, and tools; grew flax and wool for domestic manufacture; and concocted an impressive variety of alcoholic beverages. They accomplished this against fearful odds: clearing a planting area required backbreaking toil; existing tools were primitive; scattered fields and poor transport consumed precious time; and without adequate fertilizer, planting was primitive and wasteful. Additionally, colonial farmers frequently contended with pests, disease, and bad weather.

Even under the most favorable conditions, self-sustaining farming does not yield surplus for sale, and colonial farmers were forced to resort to cash crops. These were cultivated in every colonial area except New England, where the terrain proved too rocky. From the Middle, or "bread," Colonies of New York, New Jersey, Pennsylvania, and Connecticut flowed wheat, corn, flour, flax, and vegetables, supplemented by livestock, pork, and furs. From Virginia and Maryland, and, to a lesser extent, North Carolina, came the prime cash staple—tobacco. North Carolina also found sources of cash in tar, pitch, and turpentine. Rice and dye-producing indigo filled the coffers of South Carolina and Georgia.

Free Enterprise in Industry. Industrial enterprise was inevitable in a land so bountiful. Natural harbors, together with unlimited forests, produced a prosperous shipbuilding industry. Into northern shipyards poured planks, timbers, masts, pitch, turpentine, and barrel staves. Abundant iron deposits led to the construction of bloomeries and forges, which in turn produced nails, chains, hardware, and tools. The sea, too, provided a rich source for industrial enterprise. New England fishing fleets combed the Newfoundland Banks, then brought their catch home for curing in preparation for shipment to Spain and the Canary Islands. The whale's precious oil proved vital to the candle-making industry. Also of exceptional importance was the production of rum and whiskey, the pivot of an increasingly successful commercial venture.

Free Enterprise in Commerce. Colonies held a special place in the seventeenth-century theory of trade known as mercantilism. According to mercantilists, trade represented a means for the accumulation of gold and silver, which could be exchanged for anything. With luck, metal would be discovered and mined abroad; alternatively, it was necessary to maintain a favorable balance of international trade. If England sold more abroad than it imported, the balances would be paid for in gold.

To secure a favorable balance, England and the other western European countries discouraged imports by imposing prohibitive tariffs; encouraged exports by granting bounties (subsidies), patents, and monopolies; and constructed large merchant fleets and navies to protect them.

Colonies served a double purpose in this system. They provided England with essential raw materials, which otherwise would have to be bought from other countries, and also offered a large market for the goods manufactured in the mother country.

The Navigation Acts.   Between 1650 and 1696, England passed a series of Navigation Acts to encourage commerce. These laws were intended to direct the flow of colonial raw materials into England, develop England's merchant fleet, keep foreign goods and ships out of American ports, and bring money into the treasury. They legislated the following restrictions: The colonies could export certain "enumerated" articles (sugar, tobacco, cotton, ginger, dyestuffs, rice, molasses, naval stores, copper, and beaver skins) solely to the British empire and only in English ships manned by English crews.

Initially England did not rigidly enforce these laws, and the colonies ignored them.

But after 1660 enforcement became more efficient. The colonists nevertheless discovered many ways to evade them, such as smuggling and bribery. Yet, although the Navigation Acts hurt some colonists, such as tobacco planters (who had a surplus they could sell only in England), these measures had some positive effects. For example, they encouraged the shipbuilding industry (many English merchants purchased American-built vessels) and gave the colonists a guaranteed market for certain commodities, such as ginger. Additionally tariff duties were lower on colonial products vital to England's needs; the colonists received bounties; and many goods the mother country did not need— such as corn, wheat, and fish—could be shipped outside the empire. But Great Britain also maintained her favorable balance of trade against the colonies, and Americans suffered a continual shortage of gold and silver. Still, they were quite prosperous between 1650 and 1776.

One reason for American prosperity was that the colonists established lanes of commerce leading to a favorable trade balance. In the "triangular traffic," for example, they exported food to the West Indies for sugar, molasses, and gold. After the sugar and molasses were converted into rum, the rum was then shipped to Africa along with other products. There colonial ships were loaded with slaves, spices, and gold. This cargo went to the West Indies in exchange for more sugar, molasses, and gold.

When England declared the triangular traffic illegal and prohibited the colonies from issuing paper money to replace lost gold and silver, the problem of free enterprise in commerce ceased to be solely economic: it became also political.

The Labor Problem

Bonded Labor.   Free enterprise meant not only private ownership and private profit but the ability to employ labor. In the colonies it was easy for people to become entrepreneurs because only a small amount of capital was required. Despite high wages and virtual full employment, however, free hired hands were few in number, forcing employers to resort to forms of bonded labor.

Bonded labor fell into two groups: white servants and black slaves. Many whites seeking to come to America could not afford the voyage across the Atlantic. In exchange for transportation from Europe, indentured servants agreed to work for a fixed number of years. Most came to America voluntarily, but a large number of debtors, criminals, and paupers were sentenced to service in the colonies. Still others, usually children, were "spirited" (kidnapped) abroad and sold into service. The terms of service ranged from four to fourteen years. Since the colonies needed them, indentured servants generally received fair treatment. In certain colonies they could vote and exercise the rights of legal "persons" (they could sue, be sued, buy and sell). Yet they were not free: their physical movements were restricted, and they were subjected to severe punishment. After completing their service, most servants became landowners themselves.

Beginnings of Slavery.   The first black African slaves were sold by the Dutch to the Jamestown colonies in 1619. By the 1660s slavery was legal in Virginia. Most slaves worked on large southern plantations. In New England and the Middle Colonies they made up 10 percent of the population; even in Virginia slaves were in the minority. Until the late seventeenth century there were relatively few black slaves because of an adequate supply of white servants, who were also cheaper than slaves. This situation changed in the last quarter of the century when the flow of white servants dried up, and slaves became more easily available to the colonies.

Responses to Slavery.   How did whites react to slavery? One way of gauging their response is to note that settlers of all religious faiths bought and sold slaves. Even the Quakers owned them until Daniel Pastorius organized the Germantown, Pennsylvania, Brothers to protest the practice on the grounds that slavery contradicted Christian principle. This protest immediately caused the Quakers to forbid slavery and eventually, in 1776, to issue the first formal demand in America for its abolition.

The actions of the slaves in response to their situation varied, sometimes according to their status. For example, field hands generally had a harder time of it than household servants. Reactions ranged from indirect expressions of revolt, such as theft or "laziness," to running away, to outright rebellion, though this last was rare. The most serious slave revolt, the Stono Uprising, occurred in 1739 in South Carolina, when 150 blacks murdered several whites before being captured and punished. In response, harsh codes were adopted throughout the colonies that stripped slaves of all freedom of movement and virtually permitted a master to hang or bury alive a recalcitrant slave.

Persistence of Slavery. Why did slavery take hold in the colonies? Prejudice, ignorance, and economic self-interest may have been some of the original contributing factors, but gradually complex legal and social ties also bound together master and slave, until slavery became an integral part of the colonial mind and spirit.

The Odd Case of Bacon's Rebellion. Slaves were not the only ones in colonial society who revolted. In 1675 Indians began to attack outlying plantations in Virginia. When the royal governor, Sir William Berkeley, refused planters' requests that he retaliate, one of them decided to deal with the problem himself. The young planter, Nathaniel Bacon, raised an army of five hundred and led several attacks against the Indians, murdering some peaceful ones. He also burned Jamestown, forcing Berkeley to flee. Before English military aid arrived, Bacon died of dysentery in October 1676, and the rebellion soon ended. Berkeley returned to his post, but was recalled the next year. Unlike slave revolts, Bacon's Rebellion did not directly or indirectly seek to alter the social or economic order. Perhaps for this reason, it did not leave any lasting imprint on contemporaries.

Colonial Advances Toward Political Freedom

English Heritage. The ideal of political freedom was inbred in the seventeenth century Englishman. The charters under which the colonists settled usually guaranteed them the ''rights and liberties'' ac-

corded British subjects. To the colonists, these were not idle words.

Government meant a king with limited power, as defined by the Magna Carta, English Common Law, and a representative Parliament. The Magna Carta restricted the king's power by asserting that there was to be no taxation without consent of the taxed and no punishment without trial of the accused by his own peers. Common law further limited royal power by judicial protection of private property, the right to trial by jury, curbs against arbitrary arrest through insistence on proper warrant, and the ready grant of the writ of habeas corpus. Parliament limited royal control of the treasury. Indeed, it was during the first century of English settlement in America that the issue of Parliamentary control itself was settled.

A year after the Glorious Revolution of 1688, the new monarchs, William and Mary, accepted a Bill of Rights guaranteeing to every English subject the basic freedoms of speech, press, and assembly, as well as the right to fair trial. These were the rights of English people as the colonists understood them. Now they had to be adjusted to colonial conditions.

Patterns of Colonial Freedom. Colonial freedom began when the London Company granted the Jamestown colony a measure of home rule. First, the directors of the company appointed a governor. Then, in 1619, they set up a House of Burgesses composed of two elected representatives from each settlement to advise the governor. Its establishment marked the beginning of colonial home rule.

When James I revoked the company charter in 1624, he appointed a royal governor but permitted the colonists to keep their assembly. The powers of the House of Burgesses were quite extensive; it could make general laws, levy taxes, appropriate money for public purposes, and determine the salaries of the executives. The King also allowed it to maintain an agent in England to lobby for the colony's interest. This legislative model spread to all colonies. In these assemblies colonists learned the practical arts of government: voting, electioneering, framing legislation, and debating.

Democratic Advances.   The colonial assembly was a grant from above—the joint stock company, the proprietor, or the Crown. But when the Pilgrims devised the Mayflower Compact, they created a distinctly American concept of freedom. In their historic voyage across the stormy Atlantic, the colonists were blown off course, outside the jurisdiction of the London Company. Since they required some form of government, before disembarking the settlers drew up a compact pledging allegiance to the king and to any laws they themselves might agree on. Herein lay the principle of self-determination, the powerful idea that government must issue from the consent of the governed.

This idea took root in the colonies with many variations. In Connecticut it appeared in the Fundamental Orders (1639), the first written constitution in the New World, which defined consent as a specific, limited, and recorded grant of power. The Fundamental Orders also created a government for the valley towns that did not limit voting rights to church members. The idea of self-determination reappeared in the New England Town Meeting, a de-

vice for the administration of local affairs and for the election of members to the colonial assembly. At the Town Meeting all citizens gathered to make laws directly. The New England Town Meeting still represents the model of a "perfect" or "pure" democracy.

Barriers to Democracy.   Despite these notable and prophetic democratic advances, certain barriers to complete democracy existed in the colonies. One primary source of opposition was the King's Privy Council, appointed to make and execute law for the empire. One of the Privy Council's subcommittees, the Lords of Trade, exerted great influence over colonial affairs. In 1696 a new Board of Trade assumed and expanded the responsibilities of the Privy Council. It nominated colonial governors, as well as other officials, and reviewed laws enacted by colonial legislatures, recommending that those that conflicted with English policy not be put into effect.

The powerful colonial governors appointed by the Crown or the proprietor (except in Connecticut and Rhode Island) were another check on democracy. The governors selected minor officeholders, summoned and dismissed the colonial assemblies, and suggested legislation. They also had the power to veto laws passed by the colonial assemblies.

These assemblies, except in Pennsylvania, were composed of two houses. Usually appointed by the royal governors, members of the upper house advised the governors. Elected by voters (usually adult white male property owners), members of the lower house legislated on local affairs. In most of the colonies, the local legislature dominated, basically because it held the purse strings, even deciding on the governor's salary.

Although the Privy Council was supposed to set colonial policy, it did so individually for each colony. The Council had the power to annul specific laws passed by the colonial assemblies and to act as final arbiter of colonial disputes. It is estimated that the British government disallowed only about 5 percent of the laws it reviewed.

In sum, although legally London had great power, in practice it pretty much allowed the colonies to be in charge of their own affairs.

Religion and Society

Religion and Heresy. Many English citizens emigrated to the New World to worship freely themselves, not to establish freedom of worship for everybody.

This paradox may seem puzzling today, but it made sense in the seventeenth and eighteenth centuries, when many people believed that an unorthodox path to God represented a danger to the community. To protect the colonists against the risk of heresy, ministers and magistrates often attempted to bind the church to the state. Religious deviation thus became a political crime.

Established churches became the rule. In the South the Anglican church was legally established by the middle of the eighteenth century. In Virginia church attendance was required by law and heretics were banished; in Maryland, Catholics lost their voting rights in 1718; in the Carolinas, people of most faiths were not encouraged to settle. In New England, religious life was dominated by the Puritans. Only church members could vote or hold office. Yet by the 1630s applicants for church membership were rarely rejected. Although local magistrates, or civilian authorities, believed that they were responsible to God, ministers were not allowed to hold public office and so exerted their considerable power indirectly. Religious dissent was, nevertheless, not easily tolerated.

When Roger Williams opposed the connection between church and state, the magistrates in Massachusetts Bay banished him. In the same year, 1636, Anne Hutchinson was charged with defaming the clergy for arguing that those possessed of saving grace did not have to obey the law. (This was known as antinomianism.) At her trial she answered that these views were divinely inspired and that her own knowledge of God came from "immediate revelation." Feeling these beliefs represented a direct challenge to their own authority, the court banished Hutchinson from the commonwealth, and she and her followers departed for Rhode Island. In their refusal to accept some of the basic tenets of Puritan belief, Anne Hutchinson and Roger Williams represented a political and religious threat to the new colony.

The Salem Witch Trials. In 1692 the parish of Salem, Massachusetts, witnessed an outbreak of religious hysteria and fanaticism. The trouble started when several teenage girls began acting strangely. They initially accused three women of bewitching them, and a series of arrests followed. By summer one hundred and fifty people had been charged with witchcraft. The court convicted twenty-eight of them; nineteen eventually were hanged. Then, abruptly, the hysteria abated. A number of prominent ministers urged the governor to adjourn the court, which he did, and to forbid any more executions.

What caused the troubles in Salem? The community had a history of religious discord. In this atmosphere of bitterness and mistrust the accusations of the teenage girls caused a furor. A more stable community might have reacted differently.

Calvinism Puritan-Style. How did the Puritans justify their excesses? Puritanism was transplanted Calvinism, derived from the theology of John Calvin. According to his teachings, God arbitrarily chooses some people for election, or salvation, while consigning others to clerical damnation. He elects to save whom He will without regard to faith or good works.

When transplanted by the Puritans to America, Calvinism underwent modification. God's supremacy remained basic, but His arbitrariness was limited by covenants made with men. These covenants manifested themselves in the world: in the family, the state, and the church. The pious could discover them by close attendance to the Bible and the world of nature, as interpreted by the clergy.

The concept of covenant raised the dignity of human beings, although their end was still predestined. Within the church, the covenant appeared as a congregation, a union of the elect gathered in a church body that had to be small in size, self-constituted, independent of other churches, and not established by superior authority. An element of democracy thus is visible within the limits of election.

The Effects of the Enlightenment on Religion. During the eighteenth century, the new ideas of the Enlightenment traveled from Europe to America. Age of Reason philosophers replaced the idea of original sin with a benevolent God who gave human beings the power of reason, enabling them to understand the mechanical laws that operated nature and society. Through the use of reason, people could achieve perfection. Such views had an impact among the better-educated colonists. Some, like Benjamin Franklin, became Deists, celebrating God for the creations of the universe rather than for His power to interfere with human beings.

The Great Awakening. By the early eighteenth century, the colonies—even Massachusetts—were far less religiously fervent. Church attendance was no longer always enforced; in the South there were often not enough clergy to reach everyone; in New England, people complained about their ministers' boring sermons.

The Great Awakening of the 1740s changed all this, arousing in many colonists evangelical zeal and spiritual enthusiasm. George Whitefield, a young Anglican minister who arrived in Georgia in 1738, was the key figure in the revival of religious feelings. Touring the country, he urged the eager hordes who flocked to hear him to repent and be saved.

The most famous American-born revivalist was Jonathan Edwards. A fiery orator, Edwards delivered a stern Calvinist message by appealing to his listeners' emotions with vivid details of the torments of the damned.

Religion and Secular Life

New England Family Life. The strong religious impulse during colonial times extended far beyond the church, shaping many of the institutions we now consider primarily secular, such as the family. The family occupied a central place in Puritan society and theology. Ministers constantly warned their flocks that outside its shelter lay carnal temptation. The bonds tying together family members must be maintained; any loosening would make all covenants vulnerable. Just as God was the supreme authority in the universe, so father was the boss in the Puritan family. The economic and social well-being of the entire household, including servants, came under his domain. He even controlled any property his wife brought into the marriage.

The Puritan woman occupied a position subordinate to her husband. Her responsibilities were essentially domestic and included running the household smoothly, carrying for and educating the children, and in all matters acting like a loyal and obedient wife. Some women did, however, have lives outside home and family; for example, as teachers or shop workers. These women were usually widows, most of whom eventually remarried and returned to domestic life.

Puritan children occupied a position below their parents in the family hierarchy. From an early age they learned to be obedient, and to encourage this virtue, the rod was not spared. Like their parents, children were hardworking. Younger ones performed a variety of tasks. For example, girls sewed, while boys did outdoor chores. Older children were frequently sent out to be servants or apprentices. Despite their strict enforcement of discipline and a stern work ethic, Puritan parents permitted themselves to feel affection, even the tenderest concern, for their offspring.

Religion in the South. Religion played a more limited role in the colonial South, despite the legal establishment of the Anglican church by the middle of the eighteenth century. Ministers did not enjoy great prestige, partly because the English church sent mostly second-raters to fill southern pulpits. Moreover, once there, these men often failed to get along with their parishioners, who refused to treat ministers with the same reverence as their Puritan counterparts. As a result, many quit their ministries. Even with the weakness of the Anglican church, the southern colonies were generally intolerant of other religions. In 1619 Virginia dissenters lost the right to vote. With the establishment of the Anglican religion in 1602, Georgia denied Catholics their voting rights. In the Carolinas it turned out to be impossible to permit the immigration of people of all other faiths, including Jews and Quakers.

Religion and Education. American education was parochial in its inception, as colonists believed that the ability to read was necessary to learning Christianity. The first primary school and high school, mandated by the Massachusetts colonies, were public. In 1642 the General Court of Massachusetts ordered charity schools set up; and in 1647, it decreed that towns of fifty families must provide a teacher of reading and writing and that towns of one hundred families set up grammar schools to teach boys Latin and Greek. Even without the benefits of formal schooling, literacy among women (as well as men) rose in the colonies during the eighteenth century.

Higher Education.   For all practical purposes, colonial colleges were divinity schools. Harvard, the first institution of higher learning in America (1638), was founded—although the charter never mentioned it—to train Congregationalist ministers. The College of William and Mary (1693) was begun to produce Anglican ministers. Revivalists, too, established colleges of their own: the College of New Jersey (now Princeton), founded by New Light Churches in 1746; the College of Rhode Island (Brown), organized by Baptists in 1765; Queens College (Rutgers), created by the Dutch Reformed Church in 1766; and Dartmouth, founded by New Light Congregationalists in 1769. There were exceptions. Both the College of Philadelphia (The University of Pennsylvania) and Kings College (Columbia), founded during the 1750s, did not concentrate on training clergy. Educated Americans could quote European ideas, and intellectual life expanded beyond the domain of ministers. Lawyers and doctors now competed with ministers over who better understood the scientific and legal implications of the Enlightenment.

Religion and Literature.   The colonists' literary productivity was enormous, including theology, history, chronicles, and private journals. This voluminous writing remains a valuable storehouse of colonial culture, but, as literature, its value is notably less, for art was always subordinate to a religious message. There was no distinction between a poem and a sermon; both had to be useful, purposeful, and pious. The Puritan poet Edward Taylor made God's beauty and goodness the subject matter of his poetry.

Puritan literature did not probe human motives and emotions—what happened to the inner or outer person was simply proof of God's righteousness. After her husband left for England, Anne Bradstreet, one of the few Puritan poets, wrote, "Lord, let my eyes see once Again/Him whom thou gavest me,/ That wee [sic] together may sing Praise/For ever unto Thee." Only such a view could produce Michael Wigglesworth's "Day of Doom," really a Calvinist tract in verse.

Sermons.   Since no universal press existed, the pulpit served as one. Sermons explored political, social, and economic themes, even if they rarely deviated from their central theme: God's providence in a corrupt and sinful world. Despite these conventions, the sermon could rise to literary merit in the hands of a Cotton Mather or a Thomas Hooker or a Jonathan Edwards. These ministers powerfully dramatized the conflict between God and the forces of Satan. There are few pieces as alive as Edwards's "Sinners in the Hands of an Angry God," containing the famous sentence: "The God that holds you over the fire of hell, much as one holds a spider or some loathsome insect over the fire, abhors you."

History.   The goal of a Puritan historian like Cotton Mather was to show Christ's marvels in America, trace the hand of God in the course of events, and record the historic mission of the new Israelites in a new Canaan. Therefore, although much of the history of settlement is brilliantly recorded, the colonial chroniclers were hardly historians in the modern sense.

Secular Trends in Colonial Social and Intellectual Life

Life in the North.   In the eighteenth century the Middle Colonies contained the most diverse mix of peoples and lifestyles. Perhaps the most varied mix congregated in Pennsylvania, where, by 1750, Philadelphia, with a population of over eighteen thousand, had overtaken Boston as the largest colonial city. In Pennsylvania the thrifty and industrious Quaker merchants remained dominant, although Quakers no longer composed a majority. Yet, in contrast to Philadelphia's cosmopolitan atmosphere and mercantile activity, life on the colony's frontier was violent, as Indians and frontiersmen continually skirmished over land that the whites had seized from neighboring tribes.

The development of New York was slower than that of Pennsylvania, mainly because the Iroquois still controlled the interior while the Dutch landed gentry held enormous tracts of land in the Hudson Valley. Nevertheless, New York City—boasting a population of over fourteen thousand in 1750, an excellent harbor, and a cultivated environment—already attracted visitors from other colonies.

The landscape of Connecticut, Rhode Island, and Massachusetts was dotted by family farms and white clapboard Puritan churches. Newport, Rhode Island, was already favored as a vacation place by southern planters, while Boston was bustling and prosperous. Fishermen and whalers brought their catches to the city, which was also a center for shipbuilders and sailmakers. Boston merchants engaged in a lucrative trade with all the ports on the Atlantic. In contrast to the plainness of life that marked its earlier history, a wealthy class accustomed to a more elegant style of living was now evident. Outside of Boston rural New England villages proliferated, their most striking characteristic the relative absence of class and social distinctions among their inhabitants.

Life in the South.   The population of tidewater Virginia, Maryland, and parts of North Carolina was, in contrast to northern colonies, homogeneous; that is, it was comprised mostly of white English men and women. The Chesapeake planters cultivated tobacco, while land speculation was another focus of economic activity. They also kept closer ties with England than northerners did. Planters assiduously imitated the British aristocracy, importing fine furniture from the mother country and copying English designs. Recreational activities centered on racing horses, fox hunting, and large parties, often at the price of increasing debt.

Life was quite different in tidewater South Carolina. The only colony where blacks outnumbered whites, it most resembled the West Indian sugar colonies. Until about 1850, when indigo growing was encouraged (it was the source of a dye used in the English textile industry), the staple crop was rice. Divisions between the classes were sharp. At the top of this society were approximately two thousand plantation families. Below them were the poor whites, with a low literacy rate and a high degree of hostility toward the plantation barons. Fortunes were, however, more stable here than in the Chesapeake region, because rice and indigo prices seemed more resistant to fluctuation than tobacco prices. Also, while towns were slow to develop in the Chesapeake region, by the middle of the eighteenth century Charleston was the fourth largest city in the colonies.

By the eve of the American Revolution, the backcountry of the southern colonies had been deluged by settlers, about two hundred and fifty thousand of them. Hunting, trapping, and a mixed subsistence agriculture including the cultivation of cereals, fruits, meats, and hemp characterized the region.

Literature. The colonial atmosphere was not exclusively religious. Secularism—the concern with this world—appeared as a secondary strain. Travel literature, diaries of such observers as Samuel Sewall, Sarah Kemble Knight, and William Byrd, and an increasing number of essays faithfully rendered the people and customs of the era.

The Diffusion of Knowledge. The colonists of mid-eighteenth century America hungered for knowledge. New media of communication began to fill this need. In 1704 the Boston *News-Letter*—a four-page, two-column newspaper—appeared and almost immediately became the vehicle for news, opinion, and gossip. With the rise of newspapers a battle began for freedom of the press since the great issues of the day were becoming increasingly political.

A great victory for this freedom was won by Peter Zenger, editor of the New York *Weekly Journal,* who attacked the governor of New York in his editorial pages. In 1734 the governor responded by shutting down the paper and arresting Zenger for seditious libel. During the trial, the editor's lawyer, Andrew Hamilton, pleaded for "the cause of liberty—the liberty both of exposing and opposing arbitrary power by speaking and writing Truth." The jury acquitted Zenger.

The Fine Arts. No Puritan painter, or painter of Puritans, ever portrayed a nude. The dominant artistic theme was the Puritans themselves, completely robed and severely austere—as befit members of the elect.

Believing that they could neither gain proper training nor find the right subject matter in the colonies, some of the finest American artists—such as Robert Feke, Benjamin West, and John Singleton Copley—went abroad to study and work. Among the best artists, only Charles Willson Peale remained, painting in the realistic tradition with great vigor and mature craft.

American architecture was of necessity derivative of the major English styles. Utility determined style; but as the colonists became wealthier, they copied more elaborate modes. During the reign of George I, elegant homes modeled on English country houses began to be built. Owners filled these Georgian houses with furniture copied by native artisans from English design.

Science and the Enlightenment. The scientific spirit of the Enlightenment profoundly affected the New World. Among those most interested in the new science were the Puritans themselves. For them it posed no conflict with theology: God remained the architect of the universe and universal lawfulness offered testimony to his nature. Puritans minutely investigated the flora and fauna of the New World, collecting specimens and writing papers on botany and animal husbandry. Later, in the enlightened rational and scientific tradition, came the remarkable pioneering work of Dr. Benjamin Rush in mathematics and medicine; David Rittenhouse with the pendulum, thermometer, and mathematical instruments; and John Bartram, one of the foremost botanists of his day. Their work eventually led to the establishment of the first American scientific society, the American Philosophical Society, devoted to promoting the applied sciences, practical arts, and philosophy.

Benjamin Franklin: The "New Man." The new day produced the new man— symbolized in the life of Benjamin Franklin. The Philadelphian was equally effective as printer, editor, man of letters, inventor, scientist, philosopher, social theorist, diplomat, and cosmopolite. Franklin's inventions included a stove and a lightning rod. He founded the first liberal arts college in America and the first subscription library, launched the widely read *Poor Richard's Almanack,*

(1732–58), and wrote political pamphlets and letters. At his death he left behind him the unfinished *Autobiography.* In his political capacity he developed a plan of union for the colonies and helped create the Declaration of Independence and the Constitution.

The source and stimulus of Franklin's activities was an emergent America, sharing in the Age of Reason that dominated Europe intellectually. From it he derived his guiding concept that the Creator was basically benevolent—a "reasonable" God, whose creatures lived in a world of infinite possibilities. Human beings were full of faults, irrationalities and superstitions, but were infinitely perfectible. They needed only to develop the habits of thrift, industry, self-discipline, sobriety, and diligence to realize their potential.

By his own achievements Franklin demonstrated how this was entirely up to the individual. He, therefore, opposed all restraints on personal freedom and expression, whether by the state, as in mercantilism, or by other individuals, as in slavery.

But new man though he was, even Franklin's break with the past was incomplete. For example, he did not espouse the doctrine of the natural rights of man, distrusted complete democracy, opposed the rising commercial spirit, and advocated a "physiocratic" (agricultural) society. But even his inconsistencies made him the bridge from the age of colonial dependence to that of national independence.

CHAPTER THREE

The Factors in the American Revolution

On March 5, 1770, the late afternoon was turning to dusk. Outside the offices of the customshouse on Boston's King Street, a group of young boys and street toughs started to pelt a nearby patrol of Redcoats with rocks and snowballs. As the mob grew and became increasingly dangerous, the frightened troops opened fire, killing five colonists. The victims were instant martyrs in what became known as the Boston Massacre. With public rage mounting, the British removed the army to an island in Boston Harbor. Although the Crown acted quickly to calm tensions, the incident was only one of many on the road to the Revolutionary War.

The British Factor. The Glorious Revolution had resolved the seventeenth century conflict between the British aristocracy and the middle classes. Parliament emerged the ruler of the nation, and the landed nobility shared leadership with the mercantilists. Both groups wanted Parliament to protect and extend their profitable ventures in world trade. In these plans the colonial plantations in America held both menace and promise: the menace

was that their products could compete with English goods; the promise lay in the many opportunities they offered for speculation with surplus capital.

To eliminate the menace and to foster the promise, Parliament created a Board of Trade composed of landlords and businessmen to guide the parliamentary ministry and especially the colonial secretary (known as the Secretary of State for the Southern Department) in assisting British business. One problem for the new board was how to resolve the often-conflicting needs of English and colonial business. The colonies profited from worldwide trade, England from empire-wide trade; English landlords fattened on colonial quitrents, and Americans refused to pay them; colonists sought a limitation on the slave trade to prevent a glut on the slave market, while English traders endeavored to redouble the number of slaves imported; and colonial debtors wanted cheap paper money, while English creditors preferred stable, hard currency.

Open conflict was delayed between 1688 and 1763 because of Prime Minister Sir Robert Walpole's policy of "salutary neglect," which consisted of ignoring American violations of the Navigation Acts—this despite the many constitutional channels that existed for compelling colonial obedience (such as governor's veto, judicial review by the Privy Council, or King's veto). Salutary neglect occurred because colonial secretaries were frequently changed, corrupt politics was the order of the day, enforcement agents were unpaid or poorly paid, and confusion of authority existed in the matter of colonial control. But the day was approaching when England would begin to enforce the existing controls. When this occurred, crisis would be inevitable.

Colonial War. The coming of that climactic day was speeded up by the outbreak in 1689 of a series of "world wars" that deeply involved the American colonies. In these battles for control among empires, France and England were the major contestants and the North American continent a major site of warfare. In 1689 the English claimed the area of the thirteen colonies, while France asserted its authority over Canada and the Mississippi Valley. The French also sought control of the New England Colonies as a source of food and lumber.

The Anglo-French Conflict. Great Britain and the colonies focused their attention on the North and West. These regions offered fishing and fur, attractive settlement areas in the Ohio Valley, and the chance to break through the French encirclement. Even before the Anglo-French war in Europe, the English started to penetrate Canada and the Ohio Valley, organizing the Hudson Bay Company to capture the fur trade. In 1689 King William's War (named after England's new monarch, William III) began with a Canadian raid against New York and New England. The war ended with the Treaty of Ryswick (1697), which re-established the status quo of before the war. But in 1702 Queen Anne's War erupted and continued for twelve years. The Treaty of Utrecht (1713) compelled France to surrender to England the Hudson Bay area, Newfoundland, and Nova Scotia. But the treaty did not decide control of the West, including the Mississippi Valley. King George's War, begun in 1744, also failed to settle this matter. In the Treaty of Aix-la-Chapelle (1748), both sides returned the land they had won.

Even as the ink on the treaty dried, a final struggle was taking shape over the vast lands of the West, which the English colonies now sought to control. The French had certain military advantages: they held a line of powerful forts extending in an arc from Quebec to New Orleans; they possessed stronger land forces, brilliantly commanded; they were supported by an absolute and highly centralized government; and most of the Native American tribes were their allies.

The English, on the other hand, outnumbered the French and Indians by about 1.5 million to 90,000; possessed a more compact strategic position, which was easier both to defend and to transform into a radiating offense; held more protected supply lines because of their command of the seas; controlled the food-producing areas in North America; and had some extraordinary military capabilities of their own.

Realizing that the division of their American territory into thirteen separate colonies constituted a weakness, the British attempted to unify the colonies. In 1754 they invited the northern colonies to send delegates to Albany to consider unification and discuss relations with the Iroquois. At the conference, Benjamin Franklin suggested his so-called Albany Plan for colonial union. After initial enthusiasm it was rejected by the colonies (who worried they would lose their authority) and the English (who thought they would lose theirs).

The French and Indian War. The situation exploded in 1755 in the Ohio Valley, where the British sent troops under General Edward Braddock to destroy Fort Duquesne (Pittsburgh). The French ambushed and defeated Braddock and his Redcoats, retaining their firm grip on the Ohio Valley. Nearly a year later, England declared war on France. The ensuing conflict in North America was called the French and Indian War. (In Europe it was called the Seven Years' War.)

During the early years of war, French strength dominated. General Louis-Joseph de Montcalm captured two key British posts; all efforts to invade Canada failed; and the Indians, armed by France, waged bloody warfare along the frontiers. The tide turned when England's prime minister, William Pitt, strengthened the armed forces, which then overwhelmed the French Navy, disrupting communications between France and Canada. Two young English officers, Jeffrey Amherst and James Wolfe, were promoted to top commands. Wolfe launched the final thrust at Quebec in 1759. Both he and Montcalm died during the battle, but British victory there doomed Montreal, which was captured in 1760.

The thoroughly defeated French signed the Great Compromise (1763), as the Treaty of Paris was called, ceding to England all claims to Canada and the land east of the Mississippi River—except New Orleans. In a separate treaty, Spain, which had been France's ally, gained Louisiana (with New Orleans) and the French territory west of the Mississippi but ceded Florida to the British. Only two tiny fishing islands near Newfoundland, St. Pierre and Miquelon, remained in France's possession. Nor was this the full measure of her defeat. She was driven from India and from her lucrative slave-trading posts in Africa. The victorious English now stood astride four continents.

During the war colonial militia fought beside British troops, sometimes with more discipline than at other times. The triumphant end of the war stirred widespread enthusiasm for the English among colonists. On a more practical level, it helped train officers like the young George Washington, who did not forget the experience of fighting beside the British. (The inexperienced Washington was credited with striking the first blow against the enemy in 1754, when he and a small band of 150 men routed a French reconnaissance party southeast of where the Allegheny and Monongahela rivers join to form the Ohio.)

"Problem of Empire." England's "problem of empire" was now enormous. To acquire her new lands, she had spent huge sums on the military; the upkeep of these lands was clearly going to be extremely burdensome. Moreover, the empire included diverse peoples, with different customs, languages, and cultures. How could she shape them into some form of imperial unity? How much freedom could she permit the new lands? How would she be able to defend and police her global domain?

The Mercantilist Factor. By the end of the war, the American colonies, like England, were accumulating surpluses for investment; they, too, demanded an expanding economy for the profitable employment of money and citizens. But they were forced by the mercantilist system to seek to expand only in areas where British capital had not penetrated. In the South, where tobacco had virtually exhausted the land, planters turned to grain production and land speculation. American merchants competed for trade with the sugar and molasses plantations of the West Indies. Colonial capital might have gone into manufacturing, but restrictive legislation like the Iron Act of 1750 prevented the construction of rolling mills and steel furnaces. The end of the French and Indian War brought new hope to these investors. For example, rival land companies now competed for charters that would give them control over the Ohio Valley, the great prize of the war.

The Factor of the Western Lands. Before driving the French from North America, the English had encouraged westward settlement by the colonists. Not only was such expansion profitable for British (and American) land speculators, these lands could be used as a defensive buffer against the French. With France out of the way, the British now sought to exploit their advantage. At present English creditors were unable to pursue a debtor beyond the frontier. If England controlled the western area, this part of the debtor problem might be solved. But Pontiac's Rebellion in 1763 (a failed Native American uprising to push the whites back across the mountains) showed that westward movement now created a different kind of problem.

Still, Americans were eager to colonize the West. Rival companies fought to gain charters, while fur traders attempted to keep the lands free from settlers, who they imagined would destroy the sources of their income. The English began to believe that if westward movement went unchecked, the situation might get out of control.

The Proclamation of 1763. Pontiac's Rebellion made immediate the problem of the western lands. The English sent troops to protect the settlers and the Indians from each other. In 1763 a Royal Proclamation sealed off the lands west of the Appalachians from settlement. The proclamation angered many colonists by extinguishing the hopes of land speculators and the dreams of pioneers.

The "Aristocracy" Factor. Although America began as a western frontier of Europe, an area of escape from a closed European society, she had developed her own pattern of stratification as a result of the unequal accumulation of wealth. By 1763 the eastern seaboard had produced a colonial "aristocracy." Compared with that of the Old World, it was untitled and membership in it was extremely fluid; but the gentry did represent an elite that strove to maintain its control.

English traditions that fostered the development of such an elite were retained in the colonies. Feudal practices like entail, primogeniture, and quitrents still prevailed, as did imprisonment for debt and barbarous treatment of prisoners. Franchise, or the right to vote, was restricted by property and religious qualifications, and representation favored settled areas over frontier. Such practices obviously antagonized the unpropertied. Haunted by fear of a revolt of the lower classes, the propertied and powerful also felt that England was undermining them. Competing British capitalists were closing off investment opportunities; threats to enforce the Navigation Acts doomed a favorable balance of trade; and the burden of debt to British creditors had become tremendous.

The Factor of the Lower Classes.   The so-called lower classes represented a varied group—small farmers, shopkeepers, urban artisans, frontiersmen, indentured servants, and slaves. Each of these groups suffered in varying degrees under British rule—their greatest grievance was the direct taxes imposed on them by Parliament to help pay off the costs to England of protecting the American colonies—and in each, discontent grew.

The Frontier Factor. Perhaps the strongest unifying element among Americans was the frontier itself. Pressures on the eastern seaboard drove many established settlers to the edge of civilization—at that time, the Appalachian region—while new Scotch-Irish and German immigrants went there directly to avoid the settled communities of the East. The harsh environment produced a new type of American: the self-reliant individualist, scornful of privilege and class distinction. Such people pushed ever westward into the Mohawk, Shenandoah, and Susquehanna valleys, ignoring prohibitory law, proclamation, and court order, squatting without legal title when necessary—always in conflict with British land speculators.

Crisis and Unity

The Democratic Idea.   By 1763 the crisis between the colonies and Britain had begun to develop as the mother country intervened more in colonial affairs. John Adams was certainly right when he wrote: "The revolution was in the minds of the people, and the union of the colonies, before hostilities commenced. The revolution and union were gradually forming from the years 1760 to 1776." The "minds of the people" were repositories not only of grievances but of democratic sentiments and ideas planted during the long resistance to royal and clerical absolutism.

These ideas came from England and France, and consisted of a new democratic emphasis by Locke, Montesquieu, Voltaire, Rousseau, Adam Smith, and Beccaria. From Locke came the doctrine of the "natural rights" of human beings to life, liberty, and property; from Montesquieu, the relativity of government to time and place and the need for a separation of powers to prevent tyranny; from Voltaire, an assault against superstition; from Rousseau, a defense of revolution; from Smith, the great attack on mercantilism; from Beccaria, a philosophy of humanitarianism.

But specific steps taken by the Crown kindled the emotions of the colonists and brought their resistance into the open.

Grenville's Program. George Grenville, who became Prime Minister of England in 1763, was an honest though mediocre man, determined to raise money to support the greater costs involved in administering an expanded American empire. On visiting the colonies, he discovered what seemed to him to be shockingly dishonest practices: smuggling in defiance of the Navigation Acts; general disregard of British law; and inefficient, wasteful customs collection. He returned to England determined to remedy these conditions.

The Sugar Act of 1764. As a "just and necessary" measure to raise revenue for the defense of the colonies, Parliament passed a Sugar Act, levying new duties on sugar, wines, and other colonial imports. It lowered the duty on molasses (the chief item in the smuggling traffic) but arranged for its efficient collection.

Enforcement of Trade. To strengthen enforcement of the Navigation Acts and to end smuggling, Parliament declared that those accused of disobeying the Sugar Act be tried before British vice-admiralty courts. Such stricter enforcement caused Britain's income from import duties to rise dramatically.

The Quartering Act of 1765. In colonies where troops were stationed, local inhabitants were required to supply them with barracks or quarters, rations (such as salt and rum), and transport.

The Stamp Act of 1765. Duties in the form of stamps ranging from half-a-penny to ten pounds were placed on all legal and commercial documents, newspapers, pamphlets, and almanacs.

American Reaction to British Legislation. In analyzing Grenville's legislation, it is tempting to observe that the revolution was plotted in London and carried out in America. In any case, the colonists responded swiftly to the Stamp Act. First, the assemblies strongly protested this direct tax. According to them, Parliament had no legal right to tax the colonies; only the colonies could do that themselves. Then, in the urban areas, violence broke out as artisans and intellectual leaders organized into groups known as the Sons of Liberty. They intimidated would-be stamp collectors by tarring and feathering them, burning them in effigy, and wrecking their houses as well as those of customs officials. The result was that everyone disregarded the new law, because no British official could enforce it.

Worried by the violence, some opponents of the Stamp Act tried to appeal to reason. In October 1765 the colonies sent delegates to the Stamp Act Congress in New York. These representatives declared that people should not be taxed without "their own consent."

The Constitutional Debate. The fundamental question had been raised: What is the nature of true representation in a federal system such as that represented by a mother country and her colonies? The British view was that representation was "virtual," that is, a member of Parliament stood for all Englishmen. English law had the same validity in Scotland and Massachusetts as it did in England. Because they were corporations, colonies could be created and dissolved at will. Their legislatures were subject to the will of the King (and Parliament). In response, the colonists denied that an "imperial Parliament" existed. Laws, they held, derive their validity from enactment by representatives of the governed.

Beyond the constitutional debate lay a widening difference in viewpoint between England and America. The British felt that they had to show the Americans who was in charge.

The Repeal of the Stamp Act. Neither reason nor violence achieved the repeal of the Stamp taxes—but an effective colonial boycott of British goods did. English merchants, whose business losses were severe, petitioned Parliament for its repeal. The Stamp Act was rescinded in March 1766. Unwilling to appear weak, on the same day Parliament passed a Declaratory Act, reaffirming that the King and Parliament had the right to "make laws . . . of sufficient force and validity to bind the colonies and people of America . . . in all cases whatever." While Americans rejoiced over the repeal of the Stamp Act, they disliked heartily the act that accompanied it. The idea of parliamentary authority extending over them seemed totally unjust.

The Townshend Acts. The following year (1767) Chancellor of the Exchequer Charles Townshend, needing monies to cover the English budget, imposed indirect taxes, or duties, on glass, lead, tea, and paper exports to America. The Stamp Act scenario renewed itself but with re-

doubled violence. The colonies angrily rejected the distinction Townshend pushed, namely that it was an external, not an internal, tax; one, therefore, that only Parliament could levy.

The colonists reacted quickly. They reinstated a boycott of all English goods. Colonial women organized spinning bees to produce more American-made clothing. The Massachusetts General Courts circulated a letter to the other colonial legislatures stating that the Townshend Acts infringed the constitutional rights of Americans.

The Boston Massacre. In 1768 England stationed four thousand soldiers in Boston to quell any unrest. Their presence was a source of constant irritation to Bostonians. The inevitable clash occurred on March 5, 1770, in the Boston Massacre. Shortly afterward the new Prime Minister, Lord Charles North, sensibly recommended the repeal of the Townshend duties, except that on tea, and Parliament quickly followed his lead. An interlude of uneasy tranquility descended, as both sides drew back.

The Boston Tea Party. For Lord North English tea symbolized the power and prestige of Parliament. To Samuel Adams, the radical American propagandist and patriot, it was a symbol of tyranny and a standard for revolt. Time and circumstance favored Adams. The British East India Company was in serious financial straits. A three-pence duty on tea caused the colonists to boycott it. Parliament decided to intervene on the company's behalf. Although it retained the Townshend duty on tea, an export tax required for any shipment to the colonies was eliminated, making East India Company tea the cheapest the colonists could buy. Parliament, of course, was not simply being generous to the colonists; by its action the company would reap a nice profit.

The British may have correctly assumed most Americans would benefit by the plan, but they did not foresee that the colonists would view it as another attempt to tax them without representation. The colonists also believed that if they permitted Parliament to grant one company a monopoly on trade with America, it could distribute parts of colonial commerce to other companies. Meanwhile, the company's ships sailed for colonial ports. On their arrival in New York and Philadelphia, they were turned back by authorities before they could even unload.

In Boston Samuel Adams incited the Sons of Liberty to action. On the night of December 16, 1773, disguised as Indians, they rowed out to the ships and dumped the tea into the ocean—the episode renowned as the Boston Tea Party.

While Americans applauded the actions of the radicals, the British responded with rage. The colonists, they agreed, needed to be taught who was in charge. As George III said, "We must master them or totally leave them to themselves."

The Intolerable Acts of 1774. Parliament officially responded to the Boston Tea Party with the Coercive Acts, or as Americans called them, the Intolerable Acts. This legislation, which closed the Port of Boston until the dumped tea had been paid for, also virtually shut down the Massachusetts legislature; allowed trials of Englishmen for crimes committed in the colonies to be removed to England or Canada; and inflicted a new quartering

act on Bostonians. Soon four new regiments of Redcoats arrived to keep the peace. And George III appointed British General Thomas Gage as Governor of Massachusetts.

The Quebec Act of 1774. These unwise and unjust laws strengthened the influence of radicals such as Samuel Adams. Colonial indignation over the treatment of Massachusetts filled the air as protests thundered from legislature to pulpit. This was the moment England selected to promulgate the Quebec Act, which would resolve the western lands question, make some provision for Catholic French Canadians, and channel the fur trade to Montreal. The act stipulated that all territory south of what is now Canada to the Ohio and Mississippi rivers should be incorporated with the province of Quebec. It also provided for a centralized government to administer the region and granted French-speaking Catholics religious and political rights, including a significant role in local affairs.

Americans were outraged by what they saw as yet another denial of their rights—in this instance, the right of trading and settling in the western lands. The Anglo-American crisis reached the boiling point.

The First Continental Congress. Boston became the cause all Americans rallied behind. In June 1774 Massachusetts asked that each colony send delegates to a meeting to consider what common action the colonies should take in response to Britain.

The First Continental Congress convened in Philadelphia in September, with all colonies but Georgia sending delegates. In this historic meeting the radicals, led by Samuel Adams, carried the day, and the assembly passed a declaration of grievances and resolves. This declaration denounced British behavior toward the colonies and encouraged Americans to resist the Coercive Acts, forcibly if necessary. The delegates also established a Continental Association to organize the boycott of all British goods until the repeal of the Intolerable Acts.

The convening of the Continental Congress and the actions it took revealed that Americans, in their opposition to England's arrogance, were recognizing their common ground. Although the Congress called for another meeting if grievances persisted, some delegates believed that a reconciliation might still be possible. Britain's response quickly dashed these hopes.

"The Shot Heard Round the World." Before Congress reconvened, General Gage, now commander of all English soldiers in North America, ordered 700 of his best troops to confiscate military supplies that he believed were in Concord, Massachusetts. That night, April 18, 1775, the silversmith Paul Revere rode through the countryside, warning the colonists that the Redcoats were coming. On their arrival in Lexington, the troops found 70 minutemen (armed colonists) blocking their path to Concord. During a heated confrontation, a shot was fired, followed by more gunfire, and 8 minutemen fell dead or dying. The Redcoats then pushed on to Concord, where they met even greater resistance. After destroying some military supplies, they began a long and disastrous march to their Boston base. Along the way, minutemen opened fire, causing Gage to send 1,500 reinforce-

ments. After a day of armed confrontation, the British casualties numbered 273 and the American casualties 100. The Revolutionary War had officially begun.

The Second Continental Congress. When the Second Continental Congress convened in Philadelphia on May 10, 1775, the delegates remained divided, but events had escaped beyond their control. Their task was difficult: the Congress was without any legal or official status, but the crisis demanded action and unity.

The delegates met their destiny brilliantly. They organized the forces around Boston into the Continental Army, appointed George Washington as its commander in chief, created a navy, and commissioned merchant vessels to serve as privateers. They also purchased military supplies and issued paper currency.

Only one step was left: that of declaring themselves independent from Britain. Here the delegates hesitated. Why? Many of the people they represented were still moderates. Being English and all that it signified—love of King, pride in being part of the empire—was central to the identity of most colonists. Finally, England was a great empire; how could they defeat such a power?

The Birth of a Nation

From Hesitation to Decision. As it turned out, independence became an act of necessity, not choice. The unannounced war was spreading and the casualties mounting. In June Gage drove the colonial militia from Bunker Hill and Breed's Hill overlooking Boston. But while the Americans lost the Battle of Bunker Hill, they inflicted terrible losses on the Redcoats, causing the English to realize, for the first time, that the colonists might be a force to be reckoned with.

Then, in July, Washington took command of fourteen thousand troops. In December the British Navy blockaded American ports and seized seagoing American ships. And, in an action that enraged the colonists, Britain sent Hessian mercenaries to fight against them.

"Common Sense." Events, then, were pushing the Continental Congress toward a declaration of independence. At the crucial moment, in January 1776, came the publication of Thomas Paine's pamphlet *Common Sense*—a passionate and compelling cry for total independence. Paine attacked George III as the "Royal Brute of England" and asked the colonies to reject the idea of monarchy. The tract became an instant bestseller, converting moderates to the cause of independence.

The Declaration of Independence. On June 7, 1776, Richard Henry Lee moved, in the Continental Congress, "That these United Colonies are, and of right ought to be, Free and Independent States." The motion was not passed immediately. Congress first constituted a drafting committee, composed of Thomas Jefferson, John Adams, Benjamin Franklin, Roger Sherman, and Robert Livingston. Then, after a month of furious debate, the delegates passed Lee's motion on July 2. Two days later, on July 4, the Declaration of Independence, written by Thomas Jefferson and amended by Franklin and Adams,

was read and adopted with only minor changes.

Jefferson's Declaration consisted primarily of a long list of George III's "abuses and usurpations." But the document's fame lies in its general statement on the rights of people to revolt if their basic human rights are denied. "All men are created equal," Jefferson wrote, and "are endowed by their Creator with certain unalienable Rights, that among these are Life, Liberty and the pursuit of Happiness." Governments are formed "to secure these rights," and "whenever any Form of Government becomes destructive of these ends, it is the Right of the People to alter or to abolish it, and to institute new Government. . . ."

War and Peace

The Revolutionary War. At the start of the war, Washington possessed several advantages over the British. He was campaigning on familiar soil; not only were his men good marksmen, they were equipped with a superior rifle. The English army was inefficiently run; the British had to transport soldiers and supplies across the Atlantic; and their army's general staff did not adapt easily to the unconventional military tactics required in the New World.

With these advantages, why did victory not come sooner for the Americans? The reasons are numerous: enlistments were short-term; recruits expressed reluctance to fight away from home; the men lacked experience and many were poorly equipped (armed only with spears and tomahawks and without uniforms); large numbers of the colonists were either indifferent or opposed to the struggle; British forces almost always outnumbered Washington's; there was no navy, except on paper; and money shortages were continual.

Another problem was that many colonists remained loyal to the Crown and did not want to fight against England. These Loyalists, or Tories, came from all classes and areas. They probably constituted about one fifth of the colonial population. Patriots, or supporters of independence, confiscated their property, and it is estimated that 100,000 Loyalists went into exile during the war.

Early Disasters. The poor performance of Gage's men in Massachusetts prompted the King to replace him with Sir William Howe, who evacuated Boston and in August crossed from Staten Island to Brooklyn. In the Battle of Long Island (August 26, 1776), he defeated Washington's troops, driving them across the Hudson River to New Jersey. Howe's easy successes seemed to indicate that victory was within his grasp. In November and December Washington's army retreated across the Delaware River into Pennsylvania. American morale was at a low point. "These are times that try men's souls," wrote Tom Paine, attempting to rally the colonists.

But the Continental Army was hardly finished. The British had garrisons at a number of strategic points in New Jersey. In a surprise daybreak attack (December 25, 1776), the Americans captured 900 Hessians. Several days later the Continental Army won another victory at Princeton. Both armies then retired to their winter quarters, but these two battles, although militarily insignificant, restored American confidence.

Saratoga: The Turning Point. In the spring of 1777 the British formed a complex, three-pronged plan for the capture of New York. Two of the elements failed to materialize, and at Saratoga the Americans, under General Horatio Gates, outnumbered and outmaneuvered General John Burgoyne and his men descending from Canada. In October 1777, Burgoyne surrendered 5,800 men; his defeat marked a turning point in the war.

Diplomacy. The second phase of the war hinged on the diplomatic isolation of England. After the victory at Saratoga the French King Louis XVI recognized the United States, and, seizing the opportunity to avenge her defeat in the Seven Years' War and to weaken England, France authorized spending a million livres for weapons for the colonists. In 1788 France and America also agreed to recognize mutual conquests and not to sign separate peace treaties.

Yorktown and War's End. The new alliance offset many of England's initial advantages: the Americans now had a navy, making the British supply line across the Atlantic even more precarious; and Britain had to worry about a possible invasion of her own country. Supplies now poured into the colonies; foreign military leadership (including generals Kosciuszko and Lafayette) improved the quality of the army.

A series of maneuvers brought the British army into the South under the command of Lord Charles Cornwallis. With brilliant combined generalship by Washington and Nathaniel Greene, Cornwallis, who had pushed north into Virginia from the Carolinas, was encircled at Yorktown. After the French Navy under Admiral De Grasse cut off a possible escape to the sea, the British general surrendered his entire army of six thousand men (October 1781). The war was over, and the Americans had triumphed.

The Peace of Paris. Peace negotiations soon revealed the "marriage of convenience" that the Franco-American alliance had been. Each side now pursued its own advantage. After the American peace commissioners—Benjamin Franklin, John Jay, and John Adams—became convinced that France and Spain were negotiating privately to the disadvantage of the colonies, they secretly signed a preliminary peace treaty with England on September 3, 1783.

In the treaty England recognized the independence of the United States. The new nation's boundaries were set from the Atlantic Ocean to the Mississippi River and from the Great Lakes to the northern boundary of Florida. Both sides agreed that the Mississippi was to be open to British and American commerce. England granted the Americans fishing rights off Newfoundland; they could also now dry and cure their catch in Labrador and Nova Scotia. In return the Americans permitted English creditors to collect debts incurred before the war without legal impediment. The United States also promised that it would recommend to the state legislatures the restoration of Loyalist properties confiscated during the war. By clearly exploiting the rivalries between the European powers, the three American diplomats negotiated an excellent treaty for the new nation.

Postwar Democratic Advances. The mass exodus of propertied Loyalists during the war prepared the way for reforms in the new state governments. These governments resembled the old, except they were not imposed by England. State constitutions included bills of rights, provision for amendment, restriction of executive power, enlargement of the legislative power, election of governors whose powers were severely limited, short terms of office, and a system of checks and balances.

Democratic advance stopped short of removing religious and property qualifications for voting. Suffrage was nevertheless extended by dividing and selling small parcels of royal forest, proprietary holdings, and confiscated Loyalist estates to depressed farmers. With these changes all feudal vestiges—entail, primogeniture, and quitrents—were ended. Many states also lowered property requirements for voting. Since most white males already owned enough land to vote, however, this did not greatly extend voting rights.

With the Quebec Act eliminated, the western lands were also thrown open for speculation and settlement. A number of states moved toward a separation of church and state. Many of them also began to consider taking steps against slavery. Not only did the language of the Declaration of Independence conflict with it, but approximately five thousand blacks had served in the colonial forces. Thus, after 1780, northern states virtually abolished the institution, decreeing that slaves born before a certain date were to be freed on reaching their maturity. (The coming of the war had virtually halted the importation of slaves from Africa, and this remained nearly permanent.) Most of the southern states granted individual owners greater liberty in freeing slaves, and some, like James Madison, seized the opportunity. The South did not, however, abolish slavery, because it was economically disadvantageous to do so.

Other Reforms.   Other changes occurred in the aftermath of war. Wide reforms were instituted in prison practice. Some states limited the use of capital punishment to those convicted of murder. Others modified the length of imprisonment for debt. A number of state governments seized Loyalist property, although they did not then redistribute these lands to the poor.

Women After the War.   Because of the war, the position of women improved. While their husbands, fathers, and brothers went off to war, many women assumed the men's responsibilities, running farms and managing businesses. The raised expectations of women after the war, combined with the rise of egalitarian sentiments, led to a number of reforms. Women could obtain a divorce more easily, and female literacy rose as schools for girls were founded.

The Rise of Nationalism.   After the war, Americans increasingly began to see themselves as part of a national culture. The effects of this new nationalism were everywhere. Noah Webster's 1783 *Speller* described American spellings and usage. Painters and writers became enamored of patriotic themes. The artist John Trumbull depicted the great events of the war, such as the Battle of Bunker Hill, while Gilbert Stuart painted portraits of Americans. And poets like Philip Freneau glorified American revolutionary heroes.

This new national identity was eloquently revealed in a 1782 essay by St. John de Crèvecoeur, who asked, "What is the American, this new man?" Crèvecoeur answered, "He is either an European, or the descendant of an European, hence that strange mixture of blood, which you find in no other country. . . . Americans are the western pilgrims who are carrying along with them that great mass of arts, sciences, vigour, and industry which began long since in the East; they will finish the great circle."

CHAPTER FOUR

Confederation and Constitution

July and August of 1787 were hot in Philadelphia, but the delegates worked six days a week. The only break came when a committee on detail met to consolidate what had been accomplished since May, when the convention had begun. The other delegates used their time off to visit the countryside, fish, write letters, and dine out. Then, on September 17, the members signed the document they had created in less than four months: the Constitution of the United States. As the last delegates put pen to paper, Benjamin Franklin remarked that during the debates he had often looked at the president's chair, which had a painted sun on it, and wondered whether it was a rising or setting sun. But now, he said, he was sure it was rising.

The delegates dined together afterward for the last time at the City Tavern, and, according to Washington, "took a cordial leave of each other." The arduous work of the convention was done.

"The Critical Period": 1781–89

The Articles of Confederation. During the Second Continental Congress, John Dickinson headed a committee that drew up and submitted, in July 1776, a report on the "Articles of Confederation and Perpetual Union." After much debate on the issue of how to develop the western lands, the revised Articles were submitted to the states for ratification in November 1777 and became law in 1781.

One critical issue facing the new country was the balance of power between the individual states and the national government. The Articles, at least temporarily, resolved this issue of states' rights with the balance tilting toward the states. It created a unicameral legislature (Congress) composed of representatives chosen annually by the state legislatures. Each state was allotted one vote in Congress. In addition, the Congress's powers were severely limited. It had no power of taxation and could only obtain money by requesting a contribution from the states. If a state refused, Congress had to make do without its financial support. Prompted by bitter memories of mercantile exploitation, the Articles' framers also denied Congress the power to regulate commerce among states. The Articles did not provide for an independent executive or judiciary. Moreover, any amendments to the Articles required the consent of all thirteen states.

The Postwar Depression (1784–86). Americans thought their victory over England would restore prewar prosperity. But the opposite occurred. During the war, with English goods cut off, American wool-growing, mining, metal fabrication, and manufacturing industries had boomed. With the war over, England began to dump vast stores of accumulated surpluses on the American market, and people rushed to buy them. But while the new nation's imports soared, its exports dropped precipitously, mostly because of Britain's decision to keep American imports at a minimum. In this way England hoped to ease the depression at home and cripple her infant competitor. Thus, Parliament imposed a new duty on rice, thereby halving American exports of this product. In 1783 it again came down hard on the new country, preventing America from exporting meat, fish, and dairy products to the British West Indies. Other products could only be shipped to these islands if they arrived on English vessels.

American merchants and fishermen endured losses as a result of these policies, and the shipbuilding industry slumped. Public anxiety increased because of the perception that the country suffered from chronic financial problems. Many Americans attributed the depression to the lack of a strong central government.

In fact, the war itself was responsible for many of these difficulties. There was a huge war debt to be paid to domestic and foreign creditors. Soldiers had been promised a bonus of full pay for five years but had yet to be paid. State and federal currencies had depreciated disastrously; money needed to be raised in value and stabilized.

In 1781, when Congress asked the states for $11,000,000 to meet some of these obligations, it received only $1,500,000 from them. When the Nationalists—those who supported major constitutional reforms to save the Confederation by increasing the power of the federal government—led by Alexander Hamilton and James Madison, proposed an amendment to the Articles to permit Congress to levy a 5 percent tax on imports, Rhode Island killed the bill by exercising its constitutional right of veto. How could merchants do business with such a currency? How could business continue when the Articles of Confederation rendered the government helpless to remedy these conditions?

State Tariff Wars. The free flow of commerce was severely handicapped by artificial barriers that the central government, as established by the Articles, could not remove. Between 1780 and 1789 Pennsylvania enacted fifteen tariff laws; Virginia, twelve; Massachusetts, New York, and Maryland, seven each. The states were soon waging commercial war with one other. Some sought to attract British trade by lowering their tariffs. For example, after New York imposed a retaliatory tariff on English goods, Connecticut and New Jersey lowered theirs. New York then angrily extended its tariff to include those states. England became the beneficiary of these conflicts, entering into commercial treaties with the separate states. As a crowning reminder of the weakness of the central government, powerful Barbary pirates raided American ships (no longer protected by the British Navy) engaged in Mediterranean commerce.

As Creditors Saw It. The inability of mortgage holders and other creditors to collect debts, especially when forced to resort to local courts with biased juries, compounded the new nation's economic confusion. British and Loyalist creditors found it almost impossible to collect.

Views from Europe. The British response reflected the European attitude toward the brash upstart across the Atlantic—contempt, mixed with fear of the American democratic experiment. Proud and still smarting from its loss, England refused to return captive slaves and established military and trading posts on the Great Lakes. And England continued to incite the Indians against Americans on the frontier. At stake was the area's lucrative fur trade, which was still controlled by the British.

Spain likewise showed her contempt by ignoring the treaty line set for Florida (the thirty-first parallel). More seriously for Westerners trying to sell their goods in Europe, the Spanish closed the mouth of the Mississippi to American grain shipments bound for New Orleans.

The Jay-Gardoqui Treaty. Just as American creditor-owners had opposed the British imperial government during the war, they now were in conflict with their former allies, the debtor-farmers (who made up the majority of taxpayers). Thus, while debtors wanted paper money, lower taxes, and state laws delaying mortgage foreclosures, creditors demanded heavy taxes in gold or silver and strong enforcement of mortgage contracts. Two events in 1786 illuminated this conflict: one was the Jay-Gardoqui Treaty and the other was Shays' Rebellion.

On the one hand, western farmers had demanded that the Mississippi be opened to unrestricted shipment. On the other hand, seaboard commercial interests wanted a treaty to renew the influx of desperately needed Spanish gold specie. Congress sent John Jay, a supporter of the commercial forces, to Spain to negotiate a treaty with the Spanish representative, Don Diego de Gardoqui. In a treaty signed on August 3, 1786, with the permission of Congress, Jay bartered away the rights to the Mississippi in return for Spanish coinage. Angry outbursts from the West and the agrarian East, accompanied by violent threats of secession, caused Congress to end the negotiations.

Shays' Rebellion. To pay off the state debt, the Massachusetts legislature had levied a heavy tax of twenty pounds on each household with five people. The levy hit farmers especially hard; those failing to meet their debts had their farms foreclosed and often ended up in prison for debt. In the summer of 1786, armed debtors, under the leadership of the Revolutionary War veteran Daniel Shays, prevented a country courthouse from meeting to foreclose farms. Shays and his followers next marched on to Springfield, where the state militia easily crushed the rebellion. To some sensitive observers the events in

Massachusetts were troubling. "There are combustibles in every State which a spark might set a fire in," Washington observed afterward. Shays' Rebellion had been easily suppressed; but the conditions that caused it remained. The Nationalist reaction to Shays' Rebellion was intense. To them, the events in Massachusetts signaled the breakdown of law and order. Only true national government, they argued, could restore the country's equilibrium.

Settling the West. Following the war, settlers poured into the West. Seven states claimed this territory, Virginia most vigorously. The six states without claims insisted that it be ceded to the national government. They argued that no single state should have the power to control the West and its future development. Thus, the weak Congress came to possess a land area larger than the nation itself. The great question became, "How should this land be developed?" Thomas Jefferson's solution is a landmark in democratic history. Rejecting the eighteenth century practice of imperialistic domination, he instituted a standard for the democratic treatment of territories in the Ordinances of 1785 and 1787.

The Ordinance of 1785. The Land Ordinance of 1785 began a national policy of generous land grants at low prices. It provided for western lands to be divided into townships 6 miles square; every other township was to be subdivided into 36 sections of 640 acres (1 square mile) each, with one section in every township set aside for the support of schools. The land was auctioned off at a minimum price of one dollar an acre.

The Northwest Ordinance of 1787. The Ordinance of 1785 did not establish governments for the western lands. The Ordinance of 1787 remedied this omission. It stipulated that the Northwest Territory—"Ohio to Wisconsin"—be divided into from three to five states. The progress from dependency to equality was to occur in three stages: (1) A territory with fewer than five thousand free males was to be governed by a governor, secretary, and three judges appointed by Congress; (2) when a territory had five thousand free males above the age of twenty-one, voters could elect a House of Representatives and send a nonvoting representative to Congress; and (3) when a territory had sixty thousand free males, it could become a state. The new state had to be republican, that is, democratically governed, and no citizen could own slaves.

The Framing of the Constitution

Commerce and Conventions. In 1785 the first signs appeared that the nation was on the road to economic recovery, causing some practical men to seek to achieve what the Articles could not—better regulation of interstate commerce. The same year representatives from Virginia and Maryland suggested a national meeting to discuss uniform codes of commerce. Early in 1786 Virginia issued a formal call for such a convention to be held at Annapolis. When only five states responded, the delegates felt unable to proceed. Alexander Hamilton, one of the delegates most interested in centralizing the government, suggested calling another convention to meet at Philadelphia, a more central location, in May of 1787. His suggestion was adopted and passed on to the Confederation Congress, which, to save face, issued the call.

The call contained Hamilton's suggestion for an agenda—a meeting "for the sole and express purpose of revising the Articles of Confederation and reporting . . . such alterations . . . as shall . . . render the Federal Constitution adequate to the exigencies of Government and the preservation of the Union." In response all states but Rhode Island appointed delegates.

The Philadelphia Convention met formally in Independence Hall on May 25, 1787, with only twenty-five of the fifty-six delegates present. They elected George Washington as the convention's president. They also agreed to keep the proceedings secret so that no delegate would feel the need to curry public favor. Next, exceeding their instructions to revise the Articles of Confederation, they decided to frame a new form of government. One circumstance encouraging such boldness was that the convention could only recommend; the states had to ratify or reject any changes suggested.

The Founding Fathers.   The delegates at Philadelphia were men of substance and property: university presidents, professors, lawyers, planters, statesmen, judges, financiers, land speculators, and bondholders. Despite their experience, they were fairly young, usually in their early forties.

Among the delegates were George Washington, Benjamin Franklin, Robert Morris, James Madison, John Dickinson, and Alexander Hamilton. Madison has been called "Father of the Constitution" and

for good reason. He was an extraordinary scholar and a brilliant floor leader. Not only did he keep the only complete and official record of the speeches and proceedings of the Convention, he devised, before the delegates arrived, the framework for a new federal system.

Madison's Plan.   Madison's plan called for a bicameral (two-housed) national government: the lower house elected by the people; the upper house by the lower. Representation in both houses would be proportional to a state's population. The larger states, led by Virginia, supported this plan. The smaller states opposed the plan because they wanted to maintain the equal representation of each state mandated by the Articles of Confederation. They supported the plan proposed by William Patterson, of New Jersey. He suggested retaining a unicameral Congress based on the equality of states but enlarging Congress's powers and making its acts the supreme law of the land. On June 19 the delegates rejected the New Jersey Plan.

Compromise.   Should government representation be proportional to population or equal for each state? Should national power or that of the states prevail? The debate grew heated and seemed, to the delegates, to go on forever. Finally, the common desire for a strong central government brought the extremes toward moderation, and in mid-July the delegates agreed to what is called "The Compromise." The legislature would be bicameral; its lower branch, the House of Representatives, would be proportional to population and elected by the people, while its upper branch, the Senate, would contain an equal number of representatives from each of the states, with the state legislatures choosing its members. In this compromise the founders created the "federal principle."

Representation and Taxation. No sooner had this controversy been resolved when another arose. If each state was going to be taxed based on population, was population to include slaves? Northerners argued that slaves should be counted in deciding a state's share of males. Georgia and South Carolina disagreed, but said that they should be included in determining representation in the House of Representatives (although they could not vote). This vexing issue was resolved by the Three-Fifths Compromise, under which a slave was to be counted as three fifths of a person in apportioning both representatives and taxes. The delegates also voted for a clause making it illegal to abolish the slave trade before 1808. In this way they delayed deciding the issue of the African slave trade.

The Final Stages. On July 26 the Convention assigned a group of delegates to make a rough draft of the Constitution. All the delegates then discussed each article in the draft. During these debates they decided that the nation's president should be elected by an electoral college composed of prominent men chosen by the voters of each state. The number of electoral votes in a state would be equal to the number of its representatives and senators. The candidate receiving the second-highest vote in the electoral college was to become vice president. If no one received a majority of votes, the House of Representatives would choose the President, with each state permitted one vote.

The delegates also gave the president the right to nominate judges and other officials, to veto legislation (although a two-thirds majority of both houses could override his veto), and to command the armed forces. On September 17, 1787, thirty-nine delegates signed the Constitution of the United States.

The Constitution. The Constitution was indeed a "Great Compromise." On the one hand, it greatly expanded the powers of the central government. On the other hand, the states retained their independence. To prevent the misuse of power, the document contained a series of checks and balances. One example is the separation of the legislative, executive, and judicial sectors. Others are Congress's right to impeach members of the other branches, the President's veto on legislation, the Senate's power to approve judicial appointments, the House's right to declare war, and the President's control over the armed forces.

Ratification

Federalists and Anti-Federalists. People who favored the Constitution knew that ratification would be difficult. Their premonition proved correct. To be ratified, the Constitution had to be adopted by special state conventions. Even before it went through the trial of ratification, powerful figures like Patrick Henry and Samuel Adams raised their voices in opposition. Supporters of the document took to calling themselves Federalists, thereby suggesting they favored a confederation of states. Opponents of the Constitution were called by its supporters Anti-Federalists. Federalists were often well-to-do professionals, artisans, and merchants, while Anti-Federalists tended to be small farmers, less-educated and poorer. Yet many opponents of the Constitution were members of privileged groups, while many farmers supported it.

Anti-Federalist Arguments. Most of the opposition centered around fears that the Constitution sacrificed the independence of the states. Anti-Federalists argued that the document was illegal because it violated the delegates' express mandate to amend the Articles of Confederation. They also claimed that state sovereignty would be destroyed and that the Constitution was a private instrument for the protection of landed and mercantile property. For example, only the rich would be able to afford to hold office in large Congressional districts. Perhaps most disturbing to the opposition, the Constitution did not contain a Bill of Rights. Without one, the people possessed no protection against a tyrannical central ruling power. Their unalienable rights and liberties were clearly in jeopardy.

The Federalist Response. The Constitution was brilliantly defended by Madison, Hamilton, and Jay, who wrote eighty-five essays in favor of ratification for New York newspapers. These were later collected into a classic volume of political theory and commentary on the Constitution, called *The Federalist* (1788). The authors analyzed the legal implications of each clause of the document. For example, they argued that only a strong central govern-

ment could control the effects of factionalism. Opposition quieted after the Federalists pledged to add amendments guaranteeing individual civil rights immediately after ratification.

The Ratification Process. Delaware was the first to ratify, on December 7, 1787. Pennsylvania, New Jersey, Georgia, and Connecticut followed in rapid succession. The fight was bitter in influential Massachusetts, but on February 6, 1788, the delegates, by a vote of 187 to 168, ratified the Constitution. Maryland, South Carolina, and New Hampshire followed, to complete the nine states required to make the new government legal. But no union was possible in practice without New York or Virginia. Late in June 1788, Washington, Madison, and John Marshall finally prevailed by ten votes in the Virginia convention over Patrick Henry and George Mason. With Virginia in, New York fell into line. North Carolina and Rhode Island decided to ratify only after the first Congress threatened to treat them as foreign powers and punish them with discriminatory tariffs. After the Constitution's ratification, on June 8, 1789, James Madison proposed a series of amendments to the House of Representatives to protect individual liberties. Ten of his amendments were ratified on December 15, 1791. Together they were called The Bill of Rights.

A Government Is Launched. On July 2, 1788, Cyrus Griffin, President of the Confederation Congress, declared the new Constitution to be in effect. A little over two months later, on September 13, New York was fixed as the temporary capital of the national government. On April 6 the ballots of the presidential electors were counted. George Washington had been unanimously elected President with sixty-nine votes. John Adams, with thirty-four votes, became the Vice President. One of history's great democratic experiments now began.

CHAPTER FIVE

The Federalist Era

On April 30, 1789, George Washington stepped into a coach drawn by four horses to begin the ride from Philadelphia to New York. Along the route troops rode ahead of his carriage, and in New York City, crowds surrounded the procession as it wound its way to Federal Hall. There, in a small portico, Chancellor Livingston administered the oath of office to a grave Washington, who, after repeating it, kissed the Bible in his hands. "It is done!" Livingston exclaimed and then shouted, "Long live George Washington, President of the United States." In this way the Federalist era began.

Toward a National State

The Election of 1788. Because the political climate favored the Federalist cause, the elections of 1788 were hardly contested. Anti-Federalists generally did not seek office under the new government. Thus, those instrumental in framing the Constitution and in obtaining its ratification became senators and representatives.

Eleven of the founders of the country were senators. Other Federalists elected to the House of Representatives came under the expert leadership of James Madison. The presidency was in the hands of the presiding officer of the Constitutional Convention, now vested with the all-important power of appointments.

Washington as President. Washington was a strong, fair, cautious, and dignified president. Although he frequently consulted his department heads, he alone made the final decisions. His selections for department heads reveal his lack of partisanship. He picked two men of sharply differing political philosophies as key advisers: Jefferson for Secretary of State and Hamilton for Secretary of the Treasury.

Washington's caution showed in his scrupulous concern for the principle of the separation of powers. For example, he never proposed or fought for any legislation or campaigned for or against any congressional candidate during his two terms in office.

The Machinery of Government. The task before the first Congress was daunting—to set up the machinery of government and put it in motion. The legislature quickly created several executive departments—State, Treasury, and War—and established a federal court system by passing the Judiciary Act of 1789. The act provided for thirteen federal district courts to review decisions of the state courts; created three circuit courts of appeals; and set the number of Supreme Court justices at six. Washington named New York's John Jay as Chief Justice.

Economic Policies. Memories of the depression of 1784–86 stirred Congress to pass the Tariff Act of 1789, which set a 5 percent tariff on imports. Although the tariff brought in needed revenue, southern planters, who depended more on European goods than their northern neighbors, complained that it discriminated against them.

The "Unwritten Constitution." When Congress established the departments of State, Treasury, and War, it was setting a precedent. The Constitution had not provided for administrative departments or a cabinet to assist the president. To his cabinet, Washington named—besides Jefferson and Hamilton—General Henry Knox as Secretary of War and John Randolph of Virginia as Attorney General (a post created in the Judiciary Act). These appointments established an informal system of checks and balances among the presidential advisers, as Hamilton and Knox were ardent Federalists, while Jefferson and Randolph remained relatively lukewarm to these ideals.

The Achievement of Alexander Hamilton

Philosophy. Both during his lifetime and after his death, the brilliant, imaginative, and ambitious Hamilton stirred controversy. More than anyone else he inspired and directed the policies of the first administration. Yet, in contrast to many of his peers, he was not a product of the Enlightenment. Hamilton did not believe in the natural rights of man or in the inevitability of universal progress. Instead, he saw self-interest as the root of all human action. Each of the thirteen states, therefore, contained conflicting self-interest groups. Hamilton allowed that Americans must govern themselves but argued that for human society to exist at all a strong national government must arm itself with power to coerce people to restrain their bestial appetites.

Fearing the "turbulent" masses, Hamilton decided that the republic could survive and prosper only if the wealthy were persuaded that it was in their economic interest to back the central government. If the monied classes did decide to lend their support, the government and the entire country—even the common people—would benefit economically.

Hamilton's Financial Reform. America needed capital to develop its resources, but how could it attract investors without first repaying debts to foreigners and to its own citizens? Congress turned to Hamilton, as Secretary of the Treasury, to find a solution to this and other economic problems. In a series of reports to Congress, he developed a daringly innovative master plan. The first and second reports dealt with public credit, the third with the necessity for a national bank, and the fourth with manufacturing and the tariff. These reports were designed not only to restore public credit at home and abroad, but to guarantee the stability of the new government by winning the support of the wealthy.

The Public Debt. America's foreign debt, held chiefly by the French and the Dutch, amounted to $11,710,378, while its domestic debt surpassed $40,000,000. For a new government without a treasury, this was an immense sum. In his Report on the Public Credit, Hamilton proposed payment in full on a funding basis. He suggested recalling outstanding securities and issuing new bonds for them at the same face value. To ensure payment of interest and principal, he requested the creation of an untouchable sinking fund (a fund set up and accumulated by usually regular deposits to pay off a debt), customs revenues, and the sale of public lands. Finally, he asked that the national government assume responsibility for paying the remaining state debts.

The Debate over Hamilton's Plan. Albert Gallatin (later Jefferson's Secretary of the Treasury) led the opposition to Hamilton's program. Not only was the plan extravagant, he argued, it would benefit unscrupulous speculators in bonds instead of the original holders of the old securities, such as soldiers, merchants, and farmers. Hamilton was unmoved by counterproposals suggesting some form of divided payments. Speculators had paid the market value of the bonds and took the risks. They should be compensated.

Since it was impossible to identify many of the original holders, Congress eventually backed Hamilton. Some members, however, questioned the treasury secretary's motives, as his plan consciously curried the favor of the rich. Under his plan, speculators would have a field day.

Assumption of state debts caused the first major rift among the Federalists in Congress. The division was sectional. Citizens of New England held more than four fifths of the unpaid state debts, while the southern states had almost completely discharged theirs. Why, argued the South, should there be national taxation for the benefit of one section? Because of this strong opposition, the proposal suffered a temporary defeat on April 12, 1790. Hamilton now sought out Jefferson's and Madison's assistance, and they convinced some Southerners to switch their vote. In exchange, Hamilton agreed to support the southern plan to locate the new nation's capital on the Potomac River. Assumption of state debts became law, and the funding plan proved immensely successful. America's credit rating soared, and foreign capital soon flowed readily into the nation's coffers.

The Bank Proposal. Hamilton next proposed that Congress charter a national bank (one that was partly government-owned) permitted to open branches everywhere. The Bank of the United States would increase the capital necessary for economic expansion; provide the government with facilities for borrowing money and for collecting taxes; serve as a depository for government funds, and, most significantly, issue uniform and stable currency.

Madison and others in Congress fiercely protested Hamilton's plan. It would, they argued, mainly benefit the rich. For example, a small number of rich investors would receive the dividends from government monies in the bank belonging to all citizens. Opponents of the proposed bank also claimed that it was unconstitutional since that document did not contain any provision granting Congress the power to establish a bank. Despite the strong opposition, Congress passed the bill creating the Bank in February 1791.

The Doctrine of Implied Powers. Before he signed the bank measure, Washington asked his cabinet to submit opinions on its constitutionality. Attacking the measure on this basis, Jefferson developed the doctrine of the strict interpretation of the Constitution. The Congress could only do what the constitution specifically enumerated. The so-called "elastic clause," authorizing Congress to "pass all laws which shall be necessary and proper," needed to be interpreted literally (strictly); otherwise Congress would obtain "boundless" power. A bank, Jefferson contended, was clearly unnecessary; therefore, Congress had no power to authorize it. In response Hamilton developed the doctrine of implied powers. The Constitution granted Congress more power than it specified by saying it could enact "all necessary and proper" laws. Accepting Hamilton's loose interpretation, Washington signed the bill.

Like the funding plan, the Bank of the United States was a great success. People quickly accepted the new issues, and businesses discovered they could more easily raise capital for their enterprises. Even the Bank's success did not quiet fears about Hamilton's motives. The general public remained concerned that he wanted to turn power over to unscrupulous speculators.

The Excise Tax. To put his grand economic design into effect, Hamilton needed a new source of revenue. In his second report on public credit he recommended a tax on domestic distilled liquors. This was to be collected at the source, which was mainly in the backcountry of Pennsylvania, Virginia, North Carolina, and Maryland, where farmers found the shipment of grains too expensive to be profitable and therefore reduced their grain in bulk by converting it into spirits. Opponents denounced the proposed tax as odious, unequal, unpopular, and oppressive and threatened to prevent its collection. Nevertheless, a small excise tax on whiskey was passed in March 1791.

A little more than a year later the threat was translated into action. Those most affected (mainly western farmers) held a convention at Pittsburgh, where they drew up resolutions declaring their intention to use legal measures to obstruct collections. The governor refused to call out the militia to suppress this Whiskey Rebellion. Then, in the summer of 1794, a federal judge in Pennsylvania notified Washington that the courts were unable to enforce the law, and he responded by ordering thirteen thousand troops into the area. After a few arrests, the rebels scattered. Officials subsequently had no trouble collecting the tax. This show of force demonstrated that the central government would not permit any new Shays to defy it. But Washington's action was not entirely uncontroversial. Democratic-Republicans—congressional supporters of

Jefferson—charged that Hamilton was behind the decision, wanting to use the Army to intimidate them.

Coinage. Hamilton's proposals for a system of coinage were enacted in the Mint Act of 1792. The act established the $20 gold eagle, the half, and the quarter eagle; the silver dollar, half dollar, and quarter. A mint was set up to issue this uniform coinage.

Significance. Hamilton laid the foundation for the country's prosperity, strengthened the national government and increased its authority, and expanded the Constitution through his loose interpretation of it. Additionally, the growing rift between his ideas and Jefferson's led to be the creation of America's two-party system, a system that, like the Cabinet, was to become an indispensable feature of the unwritten constitution.

The Birth of Political Parties

Hamilton vs. Jefferson. During Washington's presidency, Jefferson and Hamilton frequently disagreed. Hamilton favored the rich, and Jefferson believed in the common people, by which he meant farmers and independent craftsmen. While both men owned slaves, Hamilton thought blacks were intellectually equal to whites, while Jefferson believed they were inferior. Jefferson saw English society as morally corrupt; Hamilton looked up to it as orderly and well governed. Hamilton advocated a strong central government; Jefferson argued that government was a necessary evil. Jefferson wanted America to be a nation of small farmers; Hamilton wanted a commercial society. The division between the two men grew gradually. Jefferson supported Hamilton's funding plan but opposed the creation of a national bank and tariffs to encourage manufacturers. Both these plans, he felt, benefitted the commercial interests and harmed farmers.

By 1791 Jefferson and Madison had gathered together like-minded politicians, such as Aaron Burr, James Monroe, and Dewitt Clinton. Standing for localism, strict interpretation of the Constitution, and democratic participation of the masses in government, these Democratic-Republicans, as they called themselves, attracted tobacco and cotton planters, small farmers, the urban dispossessed, artisans and laborers, frontier elements, states' rightists, and whiskey rebels.

With the aid of the vigorous *National Gazette* (edited by the poet-pamphleteer Philip Freneau), they publicized their views and attacked Hamilton's. Hamilton took up the challenge, using another newspaper, the *Gazette of the United States* (edited by John Fenno), to expound his views and attack Jefferson's. Hamilton's ideas attracted people who favored centralization, a loose interpretation of the Constitution, and aggressive capitalism. These included a solid core of merchants, manufacturers, financiers, lawyers, clergymen, and university men. These men eventually called themselves Federalists. The struggle over who would be the next president had begun.

The Election of 1792. But the full impact of the party division was not felt in the election of 1792 because Washington reluctantly decided to run again, mainly to delay the impending clash. Federalists and Democratic-Republicans supported him, and he was reelected unanimously. The Democratic-Republicans made a bid for the vice presidency with New York's Governor George Clinton, but they failed in this objective as John Adams, a Federalist, was elected Vice President; nor could they capture the Senate. They did, however, win the House of Representatives.

Foreign Policy Conflicts.   Just as domestic problems absorbed Washington's attention during his first administration, so foreign affairs dominated the second.

France.   In 1793 France could hardly be classified as an enemy; if anything, she was a friend, bound to the United States by treaties of alliance, commerce, and amity. The reasons for friendship between the two nations had actually multiplied. The American Republic was barely founded when, in 1789, the French nation erupted in a democratic revolution against a corrupt Louis XVI, ultimately dethroning and beheading him. The French acknowledged the inspiration of the American Revolution and in their Declaration of the Rights of Man echoed the noble "self-evident" truths of the Declaration of Independence.

The French Revolution was another cause for dispute between the Jeffersonians and the conservative supporters of Hamilton. The Democratic-Republicans cheered the Revolution on even after the Reign of Terror, while the Federalists condemned its increasingly violent course. A cautious Washington issued a proclamation of neutrality in April 1793, virtually repudiating the treaties with France, and endorsing a policy of neutrality.

Reasons for Neutrality.   The French not only engaged in a domestic revolution; they were at war with England, Austria, and Prussia. Hamilton forcefully stated the case for neutrality. War—especially with Great Britain—would be disastrous for the new nation, surrounded as it was by hostile powers. Britain was America's principal importer; tariffs on English imports yielded the chief source of the new nation's income and supported the entire structure of its financial and public credit programs. Even Jefferson agreed with Hamilton that America could not afford involvement in a European war.

Citizen Genêt.   Edmond Charles Genêt, a newly appointed minister of the French Republic, landed at Charleston, South Carolina, in April 1793, and promptly added to the confusion that attended Washington's proclamation of neutrality. Genêt had come to renew the amity treaty and to negotiate a commerce agreement. Fully persuaded that the proclamation meant nothing, he commissioned privateers, dispatched them to raid English vessels, and began to organize expeditions of Americans against Spanish and British territories in America. Washington received him with cool formality in mid-May. In August, after Genêt appealed to the American public and continued to commission privateers, the President asked France to recall the young man.

Genêt's brief ministry had serious consequences for America. During the crisis, Washington drew so close to Hamilton on the issue of French policy that Jefferson resigned as Secretary of State, making permanent the breach between the Federalists and the Democratic-Republicans.

England. Great Britain was America's best customer and most constant irritant. Although seven eighths of American trade was with England, no commercial treaty existed between the two countries. Instead of using the Genêt affair to advance its cause with America, Great Britain provoked American ire by systematically violating the Treaty of Paris, which had concluded the Revolutionary War. Redcoats occupied six forts on American soil in the area of Detroit. Now at war with France, England seized several hundred of the new nation's ships engaged in trade with the French West Indies. (France had also seized American vessels, but far fewer of them.) Such humiliating treatment provoked fury in the United States and aroused many of the old passions of the Revolution.

Jay's Treaty. Looking to avoid war, Washington sent Chief Justice John Jay to London with instructions to receive compensation for all American vessels seized, negotiate a commercial treaty, and gain acceptance of America's proclamation of neutrality. Unfortunately for Jay's mission, Hamilton had secretly informed the British Ambassador in America that, contrary to Jay's threat, the United States would never agree to join a neutral league of nations.

Nevertheless, Jay returned with a treaty. In it, England once again promised to withdraw from all United States' posts; compensate American shipowners for seized vessels; and permit American commerce with British possessions in the East Indies, Europe, and the continent of North America. Both nations granted each other "most favored nation" guarantees in the matter of tariffs. In return Jay agreed that the government of the United States would repay prewar debts to British merchants. The treaty, however, did nothing to restrict England from searching American ships and seizing sailors who might possibly be British, and omitted any mention of compensation for American slaves taken from the South by the British at the end of the Revolutionary War.

In Washington's words: ". . . the cry against the treaty was like that against a mad dog." Jay was burned in effigy, Hamilton was stoned, and the President himself was scornfully labelled the "stepfather of his country." The Senate debated the treaty for seven weeks before reluctantly approving it in June 1795. The House refused until Washington suggested that it was contemplating his impeachment. The public outcry caused the representatives to vote the necessary appropriations for fulfilling the treaty.

Spain. The most beneficial result of the Jay Treaty was its effect on Spanish-American relations. Spain feared that the treaty meant that England and the United States were going to attack its American possessions. These anxieties enabled Thomas Pinckney to conclude a treaty with Spain in October 1795, that did much to restore American pride, which had been humiliated by Jay's treaty. In the Treaty of San Lorenzo, Spain promised to control the Indians it had previously incited to violence; accept the thirty-first parallel as the southern boundary of the United States as established in the Treaty of Paris; permit free navigation of the Mississippi; and grant Americans the "right to deposit their goods" on Spanish soil without payment of duty.

The Indians.   The movement to settle the northwestern and southwestern territories of the United States' part of the Mississippi Valley was encouraged by several factors: the Land Ordinance of 1785 and the accompanying Northwest Ordinance; the payment of veterans' claims with western lands; the cheapness (one dollar per acre) of land (handicapped, however, by the requirement to purchase in 640-acre lots); and by the enterprising activities of new land companies at home and abroad. Settlement was hampered by defensive attacks of local Indian tribes—including the Chippewas, Miamis, Shawnees, and Ottawas—armed by the British, who still controlled the fur posts around the Great Lakes.

An apathetic Congress finally provided an army of two thousand under General Arthur St. Clair to subdue these hostile neighbors. St. Clair was disastrously defeated by the Miami Indians. Congress then sent out General Anthony Wayne with three regiments. His decisive victory in the Battle of Fallen Timbers (1794) compelled representatives of thirteen tribes to sign the Treaty of Greenville (1795), ceding virtually all the land that became Ohio to the United States.

By application of the same aggressive "foreign policy," the Cherokees, Creeks, Choctaws, Chickasaws, and their Spanish supporters were forced into similarly favorable treaties. These victories cleared the way for westward settlement, and a flood of newcomers poured into these areas. In 1796 Tennessee became a state, just four years after Kentucky. Quickly thereafter the Mississippi Territory was organized (1798), followed by Indiana.

The Decline of Federalist Power

Washington's Farewell Address: Premonition.   On September 17, 1796, an "address to his fellow citizens" written by Washington appeared in the *American Daily Advertiser*. The address contained two warnings. First, Americans must avoid political factionalism. Second, although the country had to develop foreign trade, it should avoid permanent alliances with other nations. The second of these warnings guided the nation's foreign policy for many years.

The Election of 1796.   The Federalist decline began with victory in the elections of 1796. After one of the most scurrilous campaigns in United States history—at its end many Federalists and Democratic-Republicans were not even speaking to each other—the Federalist John Adams was elected President, and a working majority of Federalists were chosen for the Congress. But during the campaign, Hamilton, who had resigned as Secretary of the Treasury, broke with the strong-minded Adams and sought to maneuver Thomas Pinckney into the presidency. Hamilton hoped by this strategy to be the behind-the-scenes president. When Adams retained Washington's cabinet—to do otherwise would have been perceived as questioning the judgment of the enormously popular ex-President—he knew that he was surrounding himself with Hamilton's henchmen.

Highly intelligent and learned, the new President also seemed to be cold and arrogant. Despite Adams's victory, the man of the hour was Jefferson, whose more attractive personality made him the center of attention. Since electors did not yet "vote the party," the Virginian had won the vice presidency. Although he and Adams got along, after a while the President did not consult Jefferson on any important issues.

The Undeclared War with France. Adams was convinced that America's existence depended on avoidance of war, yet events brought him to the brink of armed conflict almost immediately. Relations with France suffered rapid deterioration after the passage of the Jay Treaty. James Monroe, the Minister to France, had, in an excess of revolutionary fervor, promised that no such treaty would be concluded with England. (For his indiscretion, Monroe was recalled.)

The French felt the Jay Treaty was an open violation of the United States's treaties of alliance, commerce, and amity with them. They thereupon launched a series of retaliatory measures against American shipping vessels. To stop them, Adams dispatched three commissioners to negotiate a new treaty of commerce and amity.

The "XYZ" Affair. Of all the humiliations suffered by the infant republic none seemed worse than the French response to this mission. The French Foreign Minister—Charles-Maurice de Talleyrand—sent three delegates (designated in dispatches as X, Y, and Z) to approach the Americans, requesting that an enormous bribe be given to the French Directory for negotiating a settlement. The commissioners indignantly rejected this insulting offer. Adams informed Congress of the failure of the negotiations and submitted the commissioners' reports.

When the reports were made public, war fever rose to a great pitch as Federalists and Democratic-Republicans rallied to the slogan "Millions for defense but not one cent for tribute." The Hamiltonian wing of the Federalists attempted to propel the country into war. Wielding his influence in Congress and the Cabinet, Hamilton succeeded in having Washington appointed as commanding general and himself as second in command. Congress also created a Navy Department and repealed the treaties with France. A military force of ten thousand men was to be recruited, forty naval craft to be built, and merchant vessels armed. American privateers started attacking French ships. The Hamiltonian wing waited for the president's request for a declaration of war. The Republicans, on the other hand, hoped to avoid war with the French, whom they admired. They opposed any military appropriations and vehemently attacked Adams in their newspapers.

Unworried about his popularity, the President bided his time. When Talleyrand, who did not want to start a war, indicated that the French would receive a new commission with respect, the President appointed William Jans Murry to negotiate. After the Federalists tried to block the appointment, Adams threatened to resign. The threat worked, and Adams's delegation, now expanded to three, went to Paris.

By the time they arrived, Napoleon had come to power and was eager to consolidate his position by resolving foreign difficulties. In the Convention of 1800 he agreed to honor the treaties of alliance, commerce, and amity; pay indemnities for damaged ships and cargoes; and honor the principle that "free ships make free goods." A year later the Senate ratified the Convention. Adams won his peace, but there was no peace in the Federalist ranks.

The Alien and Sedition Acts.   The Federalists used the difficulties with France to crush the opposition, many of whom—like the Swiss Albert Gallatin—were recent immigrants. In the summer of 1798 they pushed through a number of bills known collectively as the Alien and Sedition Acts. The first measure, the Naturalization Act, raised the period of residence required for citizenship from five to fourteen years. The second measure, the Alien Act, provided for deportation of aliens who were dangerous to the peace and safety of the United States or who engaged in a "treasonable act or conspiracy" against the established government. The third measure, the Alien Enemies Act, authorized the President in the event of declared war to arrest, imprison, or banish aliens. These acts against aliens met with only moderate resistance.

Emboldened, the Federalists moved on to a fourth act, the Sedition Act, directed against the citizens of the United States. It declared the following acts to be high misdemeanors subject to fine and imprisonment: entering into unlawful combinations to oppose execution of the laws; preventing officers from performing duties; aiding insurrection or riot; participating in unlawful assembly or combination; and publishing any false, scandalous, or malicious writing that brought the United States Government, Congress, or the President into disrepute. Under the last of these provisions, the Federalists tried to silence the Democratic-Republican newspapers.

Ten opposition editors and printers were subsequently fined and imprisoned.

The Kentucky and Virginia Resolves. The Democratic-Republican counteroffensive began immediately. These laws, Jefferson objected, were vicious, despotic, and in violation of the First Amendment. He and Madison drew up a series of protest resolutions and had them introduced into the legislatures of Kentucky and Virginia.

Why the state legislatures? They were, Jefferson believed, the logical agencies for declaring a law unconstitutional. According to his theory, the Constitution is a compact among the states to delegate certain enumerated powers to the central government and to reserve all others to the states. Therefore, if the federal government assumes undelegated powers, its acts are void and of no force. As the central government cannot judge its own assumed powers, the parties to the compact—the states—have the right to judge infractions. Each state may nullify a law, Jefferson thought.

The Kentucky and Virginia Resolves called on all the states to declare the laws null and void. But the states did not respond to the resolves, and the laws remained in effect until they expired in 1801, the first year of Jefferson's presidency.

These resolves were not meant to be philosophical statements about states' rights. They were Jefferson's way of telling Americans that they could oust the Federalists from power by voting him into the presidency.

Finale: The Election of 1800.   The Federalists entered the election of 1800 an already-beaten party. Washington had died in 1799, and with him Federalist unity also died. The party was now divided between Hamilton and Adams.

The election was close, but the well-knit and disciplined Democratic-Republicans won the popular vote. When the electoral votes were counted, Jefferson and New York's Aaron Burr, the Democratic-Republican vice-presidential candidate, were tied, with seventy-three votes each. It was up to the House of Representatives to choose between them.

The Federalists threw their support to Burr—a corrupt and cynical politician—thereby deadlocking the election for thirty-five ballots. Finally, Hamilton, who despised Burr, decided that Jefferson was the safer candidate. Hamilton induced one of his congressional friends to abstain from voting, permitting Jefferson's election. Burr became Vice President.

Because of this deadlock, the Twelfth Amendment was drafted in 1803 and ratified the next year. It provided that the electoral college vote separately for president and vice president.

"Midnight Judges."   As far as the Federalists were concerned, the executive was lost; the Congress was lost; there remained the judiciary. Why not—Federalist strategists asked—fill this branch of the government with judges appointed for life who would check the "dangerous radicalism" of the Democratic-Republicans? Thus, the Judiciary Act of 1801 created sixteen new judgeships and a number of attorneys, marshalls, and clerks. Adams nominated Federalists for the posts, and the Senate confirmed them. The "lame ducks" (defeated candidates) had to act hurriedly before leaving office. Late in the night of March 3 (his term was to expire the next day), the President signed the commissions. One of the midnight appointments was John Marshall, as Chief Justice. The Federalists were to have the last word after all.

Although sometimes known as "the Revolution of 1800," the election of 1800 was not a revolution. Instead, it marked the peaceful transfer of power from Federalists to the Democratic-Republicans.

CHAPTER SIX

Jeffersonian Democratic-Republicanism

On May 14, 1804, a gang of men were busy loading three boats, a fifty-five-foot keelboat and two canoes. Army Lieutenant William Clark supervised the men, filling in for his superior, Captain Meriwether Lewis, who had gone to St. Louis on business. Finally, late in the afternoon, the boats slipped anchor and moved slowly upstream on the Missouri. That first night it rained, Clark recorded in his journal, and some provisions on the top of the open boats were wet. In this inauspicious way began one of the legendary expeditions in American history. Lewis and Clark's epic journey symbolized the optimistic westward expansion characteristic of the Jeffersonian era.

Theory and Practice

Time-Span. The election of Thomas Jefferson as President ushered in more than a quarter-century of Democratic-Republican rule. Jefferson served two terms (1801–09) and was succeeded by James Madison (1809–17), James Monroe (1817–

25), and John Quincy Adams (1825–29). With the exception of Madison's 1812 election and—in the ebbing years of Democratic-Republican strength—that of John Quincy Adams, no serious contest for presidential office developed. In 1820 Monroe, running unchallenged, received every electoral vote but one (thrown away to keep the honor of a unanimous election for Washington alone). Thus, a generation tested Jeffersonian ideals.

The long period of Democratic-Republican ascendancy seems to indicate the triumph of Jefferson over Hamilton. Nothing could be further from the truth. Had Hamilton not been killed by Aaron Burr in a duel (1804), he would have lived to see his policies and predictions fulfilled by the Democratic-Republicans.

Jefferson's First Inaugural Address. As March 4, 1801—the day of Jefferson's inauguration—approached, some Federalists worried that the president-elect was about to usher in an era of anarchy and atheism, partly because he was a defender of the French Revolution and subscribed to the philosophies of the Enlightenment. Hamilton was more sanguine. Jefferson was, he agreed, fanatic and crafty, persevering and unscrupulous, hypocritical and popularity-seeking; but "he is as likely as any man I know to temporize . . . and the probable result of such a temper is the preservation of systems."

Even the Federalists were reassured by the new President's address. Jefferson made a strong appeal for unity, social harmony, and balance between the rights of the majority and those of the minority. Reaching out in a spirit of unity to embrace the opposition, he declared that "every difference of opinion is not a difference of principle. . . . We are all Republicans—we are all Federalists." A good government, he stated, is one that is wise, and frugal, and restrains "men from injuring one another" and leaves them "otherwise free to regulate their own dispute."

Jefferson promised equal and exact justice for all whatever their political beliefs; "peace, commerce, and honest friendship, with all nations—entangling alliances with none" (an echo of Washington's Farewell Address); and full payment of the national debt.

The Democratic-Republican Government. Jefferson immediately set a new tone with his presidency. In contrast to Washington and Adams, he adopted a simplicity of manner in his official and public behavior: he received the British Ambassador in simple clothes and carpet slippers; visitors to the White House, no matter who they were, had to await their turn. The new President also quickly translated the promises of his inaugural address into actions. Albert Gallatin, his Swiss-born Secretary of the Treasury, viewed the national debt as a mortgage that had to be paid off to prevent a select few from becoming wealthier. To reduce the debt, the new government sharply cut military expenditures, shut some American embassies in Europe, and retired most of the nation's warships. In eleven years the Democratic-Republicans reduced the national debt by nearly $40 million.

The Assault on the Judiciary. Once in office Jefferson, who had been one of the chief opponents of those acts, allowed the Alien and Sedition laws to expire. Those imprisoned under them were set free and the fines imposed repaid. The partisan behavior of the Federalist judges who presided over sedition trials still rankled, as did the way in which the Federalists had used the Judiciary Act of 1801 to pack the new court positions with loyalists. In January 1802 the Democratic-Republican majority in Congress voted to repeal it. Jefferson ordered that the commissions for justices of the peace for the new District of Columbia be withheld.

***Marbury v. Madison* (1803).** William Marbury, one of these new commissioners, sued in the Supreme Court for a writ of *mandamus* (Latin for "We order"), requiring the new Secretary of State, James Madison, to grant him his commission. In ruling on this case, Chief Justice Marshall attempted to avoid a direct confrontation with Jefferson over Marbury's appointment, yet assert the independence of the judiciary from executive and legislative control. Although initiated by petty politics, the matter at issue was not petty, and Marshall's decision was a great one. While he denied Marbury's claim, the Chief Justice created a constitutional precedent that made the Supreme Court the final arbiter in constitutional matters and co-equal in power with the other branches of government.

Marshall decided the case without benefit of precedent, relying solely on logic. The Constitution, he reasoned, is the supreme law of the land and binds all who act under its name, including the Congress, which is a body with limited powers. Congress, therefore, is not sovereign, but rather the Constitution is. A Congressional measure then is not sovereign, but must be judged for its constitutionality, and the judges of the Supreme Court are appointed for this purpose. If an act of Congress exceeds its powers as assigned by the Constitution, it is unconstitutional and, therefore, void. In this case the clause was void, as the provision in the Judiciary Act of 1789 assigning to the Supreme Court the right to issue writs of mandamus was unconstitutional.

The immediate effects of this decision were that Marbury lost his job and Jefferson won his political point. It took years for the country to comprehend the revolutionary concept implicit in Marshall's decision—the right of judicial review of Congressional legislation, which has since become an essential feature of the "unwritten Constitution."

Jefferson's War against Federalist Judges. The *Marbury* decision spurred Jefferson on in his battle against Federalist judges. One way to reduce their ranks was through impeachment. First, the Senate voted to remove John Pickering, an insane New Hampshire judge. Next, Jefferson set his sights on a higher prize, the removal of Supreme Court Justice Samuel Chase, who had aroused the President's ire by the way he presided over some cases under the Alien and Sedition Acts. The Democratic-Republicans charged Chase with treasonous speech in attacking their policies. But although Chase may have been indiscreet, Congress found it difficult to conclude that he had committed the "high crimes and misdemeanors" the Constitution required for a judge's removal. He was acquitted, and Jefferson's ardor for attacking the Federalist-dominated judiciary abated.

Jefferson's Great Reversal

Pirates and Peace.   Jefferson may have preferred peace as a national policy, but the pasha of Tripoli refused to oblige. In 1801 the pasha raised the tribute the United States paid him to protect its ships against attacks by Tripoli's pirates. After Jefferson refused this demand, Tripoli declared war in May 1801. Jefferson ordered the several remaining ships of his navy to the Mediterranean. After four years of inconclusive warfare, the United States signed a treaty with Tripoli providing for reduced annual payments. (In 1815 all payments were stopped.) Jefferson had successfully concluded a small naval war without a real navy.

Purchase and Property.   The Tripolitan incident was relatively minor. But Spain's decision, in a secret treaty, to restore Louisiana to Napoleonic France was another matter. Jefferson was prepared to tolerate the presence of a relatively weak European power like Spain, but not that of a powerful, aggressive neighbor like France. What if France denied Americans their rights guaranteed by the Pinckney Treaty to navigate the Mississippi and to deposit goods at New Orleans? Jefferson's fears intensified on learning that Napoleon had sent an army of twenty-five thousand men to recapture Haiti from the Haitians.

A concerned president instructed Robert Livingston, his Minister to France, to obtain a renewal of the Pinckney terms and to arrange, if possible, for the purchase of a tract of land in the lower Mississippi area for use as a port. To reinforce Livingston, Jefferson sent James Monroe to Paris in 1803. Monroe carried even more specific instructions—he could offer from two to ten million dollars to purchase New Orleans and West Florida.

The Louisiana Purchase. The time was propitious for such an offer. French troops in Haiti had captured Toussaint L'Ouverture, the leader of the revolt, but the Haitians continued to resist against an army virtually decimated by yellow fever. Could a nation unable to hold an island command a continent? Moreover, his power consolidated at home, Napoleon looked toward a new assault on the continent and England. On April 11, 1803, Livingston received a proposal from France offering the sale of all of Louisiana; he was to name a price. The astonished minister managed to stall the negotiations until Monroe arrived. Early in May America purchased all of Louisiana for fifteen million dollars, or about three cents an acre.

Jefferson was delighted with his deal, but it presented him with some difficulties. How could a "strict constructionist" like himself purchase territory in the absence of specifically delegated power in the Constitution? To derive an implied power would confirm Hamilton's loose construction of the Constitution and negate the Tenth Amendment, which reserved undelegated powers to the states. Obviously an amendment was needed, and one was drafted; but to make the impatient Napoleon wait for adoption by three fourths of the states was too great a risk. Expressing his faith "that the good sense of the country will correct the evil of loose construction when it shall produce ill effects," the pragmatic Jefferson decided to "acquiesce with satisfaction," and Congress ratified the treaty.

Lewis and Clark. Early in 1803 Jefferson proposed a military-scientific expedition to explore the Louisiana Territory, and Congress appropriated $2,500 for this purpose. A group of men were organized under Jefferson's private secretary, Meriwether Lewis, and his second-in-command, William Clark, to explore the territory. After journeying up the Missouri, the expedition moved down the Columbia River to its mouth. On reaching the Pacific, the men returned by the same route. In 1806 they arrived at St. Louis. The President and the country were enthusiastic about the explorers' success. They returned with a wealth of scientific data, confirming Jefferson's faith in America's future economic well-being.

Sectional Stirrings. The purchase of Louisiana crowned Jefferson's first administration; a shared pride united the country, and he won reelection by an overwhelming margin. Jefferson was not, however, universally popular. Some extreme Democratic-Republicans felt that he had applied his "all Republicans—all Federalists" thesis too literally. South of the Mason-Dixon Line, Virginian John Randolph organized a group of dissidents known as Quids to oppose the President's nationalist tendencies. The Quids used the Yazoo Land Claims Case to make themselves known politically. In 1795 the Georgia legislature had awarded thirty-five million acres of land in the Yazoo River Valley (now Alabama and Mississippi) to four land companies for an incredibly low sum. It was subsequently disclosed that the shareholders of these companies included many Georgia legislators. Horrified by this corrupt deal, a new assembly rescinded the grant in 1796, but by then third parties had already purchased some of the land. Jefferson supported a bill offering the innocent buyers five million acres. Arguing that the government was condoning fraud, Randolph led his Quids in battle against the compromise bill and defeated it.

The Burr Conspiracy.   The secessionist schemes of Aaron Burr caused even greater trouble for Jefferson. A group of New England Federalists, known as the Essex Junto, hatched a scheme to secede from the Union and establish a Northern Confederacy, consisting of the New England states, New York, and New Jersey.

Disdained by Jefferson, Burr decided in 1804 to run for governor of New York. Even though he was a Democratic-Republican, Burr solicited the junto's support, which they gave him, believing that, if elected, he would bring New York into the Confederacy. Hamilton's successful opposition to this scheme cost him his life in a duel with Burr at Weehawken, New Jersey. New York and New Jersey indicted Burr for murder, and his political career was effectively over.

In his last weeks as vice president, Burr shifted his attention to the Southwest and plotted an expedition into Spanish territory. His ultimate goal seemed to be to separate the western states and territories from the United States. Burr was joined in this plot by James Wilkinson, whom Jefferson had appointed governor of the Louisiana Territory. In the summer of 1806 the two men put together a band of under one hundred men, who, under Burr's leadership, began to move down the Ohio River.

At this point Wilkinson found he did not have the heart to continue and revealed to Jefferson what was going on. Burr was captured in February 1807 and tried for treason. Chief Justice Marshall presided over the trial in the circuit court. Before it started, the furious Jefferson declared that Burr was definitely guilty, but his words had little effect on Marshall. Seeming to favor Burr, he applied a strict interpretation to the treason clause, and insisted on two witnesses to each overt act of treason. Burr had been too clever for that, and the jury quickly voted to acquit. The nation rested more easily when the former Vice President went into voluntary European exile to avoid going on trial for Hamilton's murder.

The War of 1812

The War Between England and France. In 1803 Napoleon began his war with England. America's peace, commerce, and diplomatic relations became entangled in this foreign struggle. Initially, because the two countries needed American goods, the conflict boosted the nation's economy. By the summer of 1805, however, Napoleon had conquered the armies of Europe, while England was left in control of the seas. The result was a military stalemate. The two nations next resorted to commercial warfare, each seeking to ruin the other's economy. Napoleon instituted a paper blockade of England, making all trade with her illegal. In 1806 the English retaliated by blockading European ports. Ships of neutral countries such as America could not trade in the blockaded area unless they secured British clearance and paid a customs duty. One result of this blockade was that the English continued to seize the American ships. Napoleon then declared that any vessel that submitted to England's demands had become English and subject to seizure by the French. Therefore, the French confiscated American vessels, too. Caught between the hostile powers, American commerce fell by two thirds.

Impressment. England intensified her impressment of British seamen on United States vessels into British service. What infuriated Americans was that the British did not only impress their own subjects, they also seized able-bodied Americans. Moreover, Americans claimed that naturalized English immigrants became Americans. The British government disputed this, saying if a man was born English, he died English. The situation was made worse because America's tiny navy could hardly defend its ships against the English harassment.

The Violation of Sovereignty. England treated American claims of sovereign rights contemptuously, as the *Chesapeake-Leopard* affair of 1807 showed. About eight miles off Norfolk, Virginia, a British frigate, H.M.S. *Leopard,* stopped an American frigate, the *Chesapeake,* demanding the right to search it for deserters. After the captain refused, the *Leopard* fired on the *Chesapeake,* killing three sailors and forcing its captain to surrender. The British removed the men they were looking for and permitted the *Chesapeake* to limp back to shore. Many Americans demanded war, but Jefferson realized his country was totally unprepared. He did what he could do and ordered British war vessels to leave American waters.

The Embargo Act. Jefferson knew he had to do more to stop the nation from being humiliated. In 1807 he sent a message to Congress proposing that United States ships be detained at port until England and France repealed their oppressive trade regulations and stopped seizing United States vessels. Congress responded and in the Embargo Act of 1808 forbade departure of all American merchant ships for foreign ports. Vessels engaged in the coastal trade were to post bonds to guarantee that their cargo would land on American shores. Foreign vessels might carry goods into, but not out of, the country.

The embargo policy failed miserably. American merchants schemed to avoid the act; foreign products were smuggled in on a large scale; legitimate trade fell disastrously; economic distress became widespread. In New England extremists suggested that the state assemblies nullify the act; in Congress it was mercilessly criticized by the Quids.

Then Napoleon made a complete mockery of the embargo by "enforcing" it. He ordered all American vessels entering the ports of France, Italy, and the Hanseatic towns seized on the grounds that, since the embargo was being effectively enforced by the United States, any American ships must really be camouflaged British vessels. On the day he left office, Jefferson signed the repeal of the embargo. His second term had supplied him with a bitter harvest.

James Madison.   The new President, the modest and conscientious James Madison, continued Jefferson's policy of peaceful coercion. Before Jefferson stepped down, Congress passed a Nonintercourse Act (1809) to replace the embargo. It provided that trade was to be resumed with all countries but England and France. If, however, either country stopped violating neutral trade, America would resume commercial relations with it. The act proved ineffective. Congress was forced to do a full turn, which it did in Macon's Bill Number 2 in 1810. The new law lifted all restrictions on trade with England and France, but if either country removed its restrictions, the embargo would be placed on the other. In a clever move, Napoleon declared that he would withdraw his restrictions in November 1810, if England also removed hers. Acting too quickly, Monroe closed American ports to English goods. He was then dismayed to learn that Napoleon had tricked him and that the French were confiscating American vessels arriving at their ports.

The final fiasco came when England, succumbing to the pressure of her own merchants (and impressed by the defeat of the British ship *Little Belt* by the American frigate *President*), repealed the Orders in Council (1812). Peaceful coercion had finally worked. But there was, in those days, no instantaneous communication. Ignorant of England's capitulation, the Americans declared war two days later.

The War Hawks.   Prompt communication might have made no difference. After all, Britain did not declare war; she merely provided the provocations. Some Americans, for reasons of their own, wanted war with England in any event. The war message of Madison listed the reasons for war: violation on the high seas of American sovereignty, confiscation of ships, illegal impressment and blockade, destruction of trade through Orders in Council, and incitement of Indians.

The United States had other reasons for entering into war. Congress now included a group of young, aggressive men from southern and western frontier areas who were members of the first generation never to have known British rule. Led by Henry Clay and John C. Calhoun, these intense nationalists and fiery patriots made every act of England against American commerce the occasion for a demand for war. Britain, they argued, must be eliminated from the continent; a second war for independence was necessary. To prove their point the War Hawks cited the uprising of the Shawnee chief Tecumseh and his brother, Tenskwatawa, known as the Prophet. These two had boldly organized a northwestern Indian confederacy to defy the latest of nine treaties (since that of 1795) compelling them to yield their land to American settlement. When the governor of the Indiana Territory, William Henry Harrison, destroyed their center at Tippecanoe, the shattered Indian forces retreated into British Canada. To most Westerners this retreat proved—incorrectly as it turned out—that English agents in Canada had incited the uprising. Such provocations would end if Canada were America's, the firebrands said! No wonder John Randolph baptized them the "War Hawks."

Madison, too, believed that by attacking Canada he might finally force England to respect American neutrality. He reasoned that cutting off Canadian shipments of food to the British West Indies would wreak havoc on sugar plantations there. Madison also agreed with the War Hawks that the agricultural depression in the West was caused by the loss of foreign markets as a result of the British blockade.

The War of 1812.

The United States was no better prepared for this "second war for independence" than she had been for the first. War required an army and a navy. Jefferson's retrenchment and peace policies had resulted in an army of seven thousand men, badly administered, badly commanded, and badly equipped. The nation also possessed a small navy, hardly capable of challenging the British fleet. To make the situation worse, Congress had permitted the Bank of the United States to expire (1811), leaving the country without a centralized financial administration. The government had to borrow money by public subscription. But New England, the financial center of the country, refused to subscribe to "Mr. Madison's War." The disaffection of the New England states was so extreme that they openly supplied the British troops with provisions, withdrew their militias from federal service, and sabotaged enlistments. The English did seem to have one weakness. The British in Canada numbered only about half a million, while the population of the United States was 7.5 million.

The Election of 1812.

The War of 1812 revealed an irony of American life. The peace-propagating Democratic-Republicans had plunged the nation into war, while the war-propagating Federalists wanted peace. This and other issues came to a head in the election of 1812. A faction of antiwar Democratic-Republicans nominated a strong peace candidate, DeWitt Clinton of New York, who was also supported by the Federalists. Clinton captured all northern states except for Vermont and Pennsylvania. But Madison, solidly supported by the South and the West, won.

The Hartford Convention.

The war dragged on for two and a half years, with the Federalists growing increasingly desperate. In their despair they met during 1814–15 at the Hartford Convention. From the text of Madison's Virginia and Kentucky Resolves they lifted the doctrine of state nullification, or interposition, and made it their own; they drew up resolutions and proposed constitutional amendments to restrict federal powers over conscription, taxation, declaration of war and embargo, regulation of interstate commerce, admission of new states—in other words, the repeal of everything that they had considered desirable when they were in power during the previous decade. This Convention proved to be the Federalists' last gasp. They ran one more candidate for the presidency in 1816 and then disappeared from American history.

1812.

American offensive actions in the year 1812 centered on Canada, which they sought to take by a three-pronged attack. In July General William Hull assembled 2,200 men to march against the Canadian positions facing Detroit. The campaign began inauspiciously with Hull losing his baggage train before the army got under way. The unlucky general entered Canada but was so obsessed with fear of encirclement that he retreated hastily to Detroit. When the British threatened Detroit, Hull succumbed to a new fear—of an Indian massacre—and surrendered the fort without firing a shot.

In the second part of the offensive, General Stephen van Rensselaer tried to move into Canada from Fort Niagara but was defeated by a larger British force. Van Rensselaer was depending on the arrival of reinforcements from the New York State militia. They finally arrived but then refused to fight outside state boundaries. The third prong of the American attack, led by General Henry Dearborn, met a similar refusal while marching to Montreal from Lake Champlain. The Canadian campaign was a complete fiasco. The first year of war would have been totally inglorious except for some naval successes by the tough and swift American frigates. The *Constitution* ("Old Ironsides"), under Isaac Hull, defeated the *Guerrière*, and, under William Bainbridge, the *Java;* John Paul Jones's *Wasp* defeated the British frigate *Frolic*, and Stephen Decatur's *United States* overcame the *Macedonian*. These victories, although incredible, had no decisive effect on the war.

1813. General William Henry Harrison and an army of ten thousand Kentuckians attempted to recapture Detroit. Harrison determined that he could not take it while a British squadron controlling Lake Erie threatened his line of communication. Captain Oliver Hazard Perry was assigned the task of clearing the lake. In September

Perry triumphed over the British ships. "We have met the enemy and they are ours," he reported. Their line of communication lost, the British evacuated Detroit. Immediately afterward Harrison fought a successful battle on the Thames River in lower Canada, destroying Tecumseh (who was killed in this battle) and his confederation. The British then captured Fort Niagara and burned Buffalo. For the brief remainder of the year, the war settled down to a series of border raids.

1814–15. The surrender of Napoleon in 1814 released British troops for an offensive in America. They planned a triple attack: one from Montreal along General Burgoyne's route, another from the south using the Creek Indians in a direct assault on New Orleans, and still another to capture the Chesapeake Bay area, destroying towns along the coast. This offensive fizzled. The northern descent was stopped by Captain Thomas Macdonough at Plattsburgh Bay on Lake Champlain. And southern forces under General Andrew Jackson soundly beat and scattered the Creeks. In the only English success, a force of four thousand sailed from Bermuda, landed in Maryland, then captured and burned Washington, D.C. The British next bombarded Fort McHenry "through the night." In the "dawn's early light" one anxious American observer, Francis Scott Key, saw that the "broad stripes and bright stars" were still flying. Inspired, he wrote "The Star-Spangled Banner," which later became the national anthem. But, then, unaware that the peace had been declared, Jackson defeated ten thousand British regulars at the famous Battle of New Orleans (January 1815). During the battle the English lost more than one fourth of their army, while Jackson lost only 21.

The Peace Treaty of Ghent. By the end of 1814 both sides were war-weary and their treasuries exhausted. The military situation was obviously at a stalemate. An American peace commission had traveled to Europe early in 1814 at the invitation of Lord Castlereagh. After a year of negotiation, England and the United States signed the Treaty of Ghent (December 1814). The treaty provided for a status quo ante bellum (a return to things as they were before the war) and the creation of commissions to settle outstanding boundary disputes. Yet despite the return to status quo, things were different. The end of the conflict in Europe meant that some of the original causes of the War of 1812 had been eliminated. For example, the English no longer needed to seize American sailors. The seas were free once again.

Evaluating the War

Some historians have evaluated the War of 1812 as "futile and unnecessary" or "stupid," resulting in "meaningless bloodshed." But although the country had done no better than hold its own against Great Britain, Americans chose to consider themselves victors and felt proud of their nation.

The conflict also served important national purposes for the United States. The ability to hold its own against Britain permanently established the country's international position. Interference by foreign powers with her national expansion ceased. More than any other nation, England recognized the new order and was disposed to permanently settle all outstanding difficulties that might lead to future war. The two former enemies now amicably resolved old disputes. In 1815 they signed a commercial convention withdrawing trade discriminations. The Rush-Bagot agreement (1817) provided for nearly complete demilitarization of the Great Lakes, a policy eventually extended across the entire Canadian-American frontier. A fisheries convention signed in the same year granted Americans permanent rights to fish along the coasts of Newfoundland and Labrador and to dry and cure their catch on unsettled shores. In 1818 the two countries drew a line across the forty-ninth parallel, establishing it as the northern boundary of the Louisiana Territory. They also peacefully settled a claims dispute over Oregon by agreeing to joint occupation for ten years.

In addition, the Battle of the Thames in the Northwest and the Battle of Horseshoe Bend in the Southwest cleared the Mississippi Valley of Native Americans. Freed of fear, settlers poured in unprecedented numbers into the territory. With peace established, many of these settlers were newcomers from Europe.

As the West expanded, the Northeast developed intensively. The Democratic-Republican policy of embargo and nonintercourse had destroyed American commerce and reduced foreign importation to a minimum. Capital, idle during the war, now sought new outlets for profitable investment. The obverse of the embargo policy was a unique system of absolute protection for potential manufacturers. Seizing on this advantage, states, counties, municipalities, and special societies offered attractive bounties for anyone willing to build factories. The War of 1812 thus helped to launch the American Industrial Revolution which was to transform the nation.

Finally, the war changed the Democratic-Republicans from dogmatic localists to confirmed nationalists. In the process they absorbed Federalism into their own program, making the existence of a Federalist party unnecessary. The Federalists also played a key role in their own demise. They had never supported the war, and some had actively undermined it. While the war dragged inconclusively on, their views were not unpopular, but after Jackson's great victory in New Orleans, the party's prestige plummeted.

CHAPTER SEVEN

Nationalism

"The nation has become tired of the follies of faction," the banker Nicholas Biddle said, commenting on the election of James Monroe as President in 1816. The new President, intelligent and principled, seemed to share these sentiments. In his inaugural address, he optimistically declared, "The American people . . . constitute one great family with a common interest." Not everybody agreed. In the House Henry Clay rose to respond to the new President's remarks. "Sir, I do not believe in this harmony," he said sarcastically, "this extinction of party spirit, which is spoken of. I do not believe that men have ceased to be men, or that they have abandoned those principles on which they have always acted hitherto."

Who was right? Monroe or Clay? During Monroe's presidency, events appeared to support his judgment, but then other forces began to stir, threatening the new sense of nationhood.

The Birth of Nationalism. American nationalism appeared in mature form only after the War of 1812. The American people came to see themselves as one, a united people without regard to section or regions or the vast distances that separated them. They identified themselves with the national community and felt that their nation was different from all others. Americans, they agreed, were different in the language they spoke, their origins, history, customs, and traditions; in their belief in the "common man," in the individual, in democracy, and in a free and classless society. And as Americans, they were now bound by obligations that flowed from habitation of a common soil and loyalty to a united nation, which they stood ready to defend with their lives. This sense of national pride led them to esteem individual Americans who established themselves in the world of science, ideas, or culture.

The "American System." The profound impact of nationalism on the history of the United States can be seen in the country's economic, political, and cultural life in the years following the War of 1812. Before the war each section—North, South, and West—examined national policies from the perspective of its local interests. Proposals for a protective tariff, national bank, and federal internal improvements caused dissension among competing sections. But now there was universal approval of Henry Clay's appeal for an "American System."

The key element in this program was a protective tariff, which was supposed to stimulate manufacturing in the North, thereby increasing demand for raw materials produced by western farmers. Western prosperity would in turn lead to increased consumption of eastern manufactured products, thus freeing the country from dependence upon European industry. To encourage new businesses and guarantee stability to existing ones, Clay suggested that another national bank be chartered.

The Second Bank.   There were good reasons for chartering a second Bank of the United States. The abandonment of the first Bank (1811) and the war had led the country to the brink of financial crisis. No longer curbed by a central bank, state banks proliferated, flooding the country with bank notes that declined in value as their number increased. Dollar bills with fluctuating values rendered normal business almost impossible, although for a short while farmer-debtors found them useful in discharging their debts cheaply. Earlier in their careers, Clay and John C. Calhoun, viewing the national scene through the eyes of many of their debtor constituents, had opposed a central bank. Now, in light of a nationalist perspective, they co-sponsored a bill to recharter the Bank. Although northern congressmen voted against the measure, those from every other region backed it, and the bill was passed in April 1816.

The new Bank, while similar in organization to its predecessor, was much larger and had triple the capitalization. Unfortunately, from 1816 to 1819, it adopted a "wildcat" method of banking: issuing bank notes with little regard to available reserves of gold and silver and making loans indiscriminately. Moreover, the Bank itself speculated on a phenomenal rise in the price of western lands.

In 1819 Nicholas Biddle became president of the Bank. Seeing that drastic measures were needed, he completely reorganized its policies, contracting note issues to conform with specie reserves and calling in the riskiest loans. Biddle's measures saved the Bank but, as some contemporaries said, ruined the people, for his stern policies brought hardship to borrowers. This retrenchment contributed to the Panic of 1819 (which lasted until 1823). As prices dropped sharply in response to Biddle's actions, many businesses went under, and banks repossessed land bought on credit.

The Tariff of 1816.   In an irony observed by some, the second Bank was the creation of Jeffersonian Democratic-Republicans. This was, however, a new Democratic-Republican Party, one inspired by a nationalist fervor that propelled Congress to pass a protective tariff. All sections of the country, except for New England, favored a high tariff. Many Northerners, injured by foreign competition, supported it. The majority of Southerners, influenced by the argument that a tariff would encourage the nation's economic self-sufficiency, backed it. And western farmers, who saw the workers in eastern factories as consumers of their raw materials, also stood behind it.

Westward Movement. Westward settlement was pivotal to the realization of the American System. Following the War of 1812, half a million people pushed into the Northwest Territory; the population of the Southwest rose from 40,000 in 1810 to 203,000 in 1820; an average of 20,000 Europeans immigrated annually to the United States and many of them went west; within a period of three years Indiana, Illinois, Mississippi, and Alabama were admitted into the Union as states.

To encourage westward movement, Congress began to consider more liberal land policies. The Land Ordinance of 1795 had fixed the price at $1 an acre and introduced an installment plan of two payments; but it also provided that 640 acres should be the minimum purchase. In 1800 Congress amended this law, increasing the number of installments to 4 and lowering the minimum purchase to 320 acres. Four years later the government again reduced the minimum purchase to 160 acres. After the panic in 1819 ruined many settlers who had purchased land on credit, Congress decreased land prices to $1.25 an acre; the minimum sale became 80 acres; unpaid-for land could be returned and paid-for land, kept. This generous legislation greatly encouraged the mass movement westward.

The sections differed over what to do about public lands. Westerners obviously wanted cheap land. But northern manufacturers were afraid that the attraction of inexpensive land in the West would lure workers from factories, while southern planters warned about possible competition from future cotton planters in the Southwest. In the face of western intransigence, both the North and the South were ready to compromise.

Internal Improvements. To satisfy insistent western demands to make the westward passage easier, Congress appropriated $7,000,000 in 1811 to construct the first national highway in the United States—the Cumberland Road. This undertaking had first been projected during Jefferson's administration, but war and intense objections from some states forced its temporary abandonment. Now, however, postwar nationalist sentiment overcame sectional differences.

In 1818 the first "National Road" was completed. It was 600 miles long, 60 feet wide, with a 20-foot macadamized strip down the middle, and ran from Cumberland, Maryland, to Wheeling, Virginia. By 1838 it extended to the Mississippi River at Vandalia, Illinois. But sectional quarrels hindered further federal road construction. Soon state governments encouraged private investors to build turnpikes, or toll roads. By 1825 these roads crisscrossed much of the Northeast. Yet the costs of transporting goods over them were high, and businessmen began seeking ways to improve water transportation.

Political Reflections of Nationalism

The Election of 1820. The issues of a national bank, a protective tariff, a liberal land policy, and internal improvements produced substantial unity within Democratic-Republican Party ranks. As the election of 1820 neared, it appeared that President James Monroe, the candidate chosen by that party's caucus, would be unopposed, since the Federalist Party had become extinct. The reliable Monroe thus received all the electoral votes except one cast for John Quincy Adams. Back in 1817 a Federalist newspaper, the Boston *Columbian Centinel*, had dubbed Monroe's first administration "The Era of Good Feelings," and in his second, Monroe attempted to ensure that this optimism would persist.

Judicial Nationalism: John Marshall. The spirit of Hamiltonian nationalism survived in the person of John Marshall, Chief Justice of the United States Supreme Court from 1801 to 1835. Through the Marshall court's crucial decisions, the property-centered concepts of the American Enlightenment of the eighteenth century passed over into the capitalistic individualism of the nineteenth. His primary goal was to establish a strong centralized government based on the protection of property against all assaults. He therefore opposed states' rights, which he considered the chief threat to union, and disliked democracy, which he considered the chief threat to property.

Expanding the Contract Clause. To protect property against confiscation, the Constitution had forbidden states to enact any law that would impair the obligation of a contract. A member of the Revolutionary generation, Marshall vividly remembered the days when the British arbitrarily seized colonial property. In *Fletcher v. Peck* (1810), he ruled that if a state made a land grant and then rescinded it, the state was violating a contract and the rescinding act was void. In *New Jersey v. Wilson* (1812), he held that if a state exempted someone from taxation, this was a contract and any later act taxing the exemptee was void; in *Dartmouth College*

v. Woodward (1819), he maintained that if a state legislature transferred control of a university to a more representative board of trustees by repudiating a grant to a less representative board, the transfer was void.

Extending Appellate Jurisdiction. There was some question whether the federal court could review decisions of the highest state courts. In other words, if a conflict developed between the state and the national government, which was the final arbiter? Article III of the Constitution and the Judiciary Act of 1789 had established the supremacy of the federal government. Virginia challenged this supremacy in two cases (*Martin v. Hunter's Lessee* and *Cohens v. Virginia*). In rendering the Court's decision, Marshall argued that uniform maintenance of constitutionality required a single system of courts; that the Constitution had placed limits upon the state's sovereignty; and that, since the Constitution is the "supreme law of the land," the national judiciary must prevail in any conflict of authority.

The Democratic-Republicans bitterly objected to these decisions, contending that Marshall had, in effect, amended the Constitution, and used the power of the Supreme Court in an irresponsible and tyrannical way. Moreover, what check was there, except by the long and difficult process of amendment, on the Court's assumption of power? Marshall was not noticeably disturbed by these arguments.

Implied Powers and the National Supremacy. Marshall reached the climax of his politico-legal reasoning in *McCulloch v. Maryland* (1819), a case that arose from the dispute concerning the second

Bank. In 1819 the Bank was being widely blamed for the depression. States began to retaliate by levying discriminatory taxes on it. Maryland had levied such a tax, and other states would probably follow her example unless the Court ruled against her. Marshall did just that, deciding that the Bank was constitutional because many of the powers specifically granted to Congress implied it. Having established the Bank's legality, he then argued Maryland's tax was illegal, for "the power to tax involves the power to destroy." This decision strengthened the implied powers of Congress (the so-called "loose interpretation" of the Constitution).

Commerce, Broadly Interpreted. The arrival of the steamboat on the interior lakes and rivers caused a temporary recurrence of the interstate chaos that had prevailed under the Articles of Confederation. States vied with each other in granting to favored companies exclusive privileges of navigation in inland waters. Robert Livingston had secured such an exclusive right from the state of New York and transferred it to Aaron Ogden, a former state senator and governor of New Jersey. Consequently Ogden retained the exclusive privilege of steam navigation between New York and New Jersey. Thomas Gibbons, who possessed a federal coasting license, challenged the monopoly. In *Gibbons v. Ogden* (1824), the Chief Justice, in his opinion in favor of Gibbons, defined commerce as "every species of commercial intercourse" and stated that the power of Congress over interstate commerce "is supreme; and the law of the state . . . must yield to it."

The Development of a Nationalist Foreign Policy

Expansion and Elimination. By 1820 the American foreign policy of isolation had become fixed. The War of 1812, America's geographic isolation, the need to exploit the continent, and the position it held as a minor power—all combined to convince the nation of the soundness of Washington's advice to avoid foreign entanglements. Moreover, the purchase of Louisiana and the seizure of West Florida in 1813 suggested an expansionist twist to this doctrine: eliminate potential enemies from the continent by land purchases, if they could be persuaded to sell.

Florida was the first target of American expansionists following the war. After the United States annexed West Florida, East Florida became the next prize, especially to Georgians living along the Georgia-Florida boundary. They complained of periodic raids by Indians and that runaway slaves and cattle rustlers found sanctuary in Eastern Florida. In 1818 President Monroe ordered General Andrew Jackson to oust the raiding Seminole Indians from American lands. In the course of his "policing" duties, Jackson invaded Eastern Florida, raided the Spanish archives in Pensacola, and court-martialed and executed two British subjects who had been trading with the Indians.

Jackson's actions made Spain acutely aware of her vulnerability. Weakened by the successful revolt of her Latin American colonies under the leadership of Simon Bolívar, she agreed to negotiate the sale of Eastern Florida to the United States, if in return the boundary between Spanish

Mexico and the Louisiana Territory could be pushed as far east as possible.

Spain could only obtain part of what she wanted. The Transcontinental Treaty of 1819 guaranteed Spanish claims to the land below the forty-second parallel. In exchange Spain surrendered claims to the territory north of the line to the United States. But England also claimed this territory, preventing expansion of the United States to the Pacific.

The Monroe Doctrine: Get Out and Stay Out

The Quadruple Alliance. The doctrine of nationalist isolation was crowned by the Monroe Doctrine. Behind its proclamation lay a complicated foreign situation. In Europe, Austria, Prussia, and Russia had constituted themselves a "holy alliance" to maintain the status quo; that is, to put down any attempt at revolution aimed at changing the existing state of affairs. France joined with them in an effort to regain the international prestige she had lost with the overthrow of Napoleon I. Spain now appealed to the Holy Alliance for help in regaining her lost Latin American colonies. After the Florida treaty, the United States had begun to recognize the independence of Spain's former colonies; now the country was faced with the possibility of a European invasion of the Western Hemisphere to restore the new Latin American republics to Spain.

Russia. At about the same time Russia extended her claim to the West Coast of North America to the 51st parallel, which brought her within the Oregon Territory.

Additionally, she closed all the surrounding waters to commercial shipping. Secretary of State John Quincy Adams notified the Russian government that "the American continents are no longer subjects for any new colonial establishments." Since they did not intend to colonize the region, the Russians signed a treaty in 1824 with America. In it Russia agreed to relinquish all claims to territory below the present southern boundary of Alaska (54°40' North latitude) and to lift all restrictions on commercial shipping.

England. England regarded Spain's loss as her gain; she now was in a position to win the trade of Latin America. The English, therefore, threatened to recognize the independence of the new republics if intervention were attempted. In 1823 England's foreign minister, George Canning, proposed to the United States that the two nations issue a joint statement opposing French intervention.

Secretary of State John Quincy Adams recommended that the United States refuse the English offer. Skeptical of Canning's intentions, he realized that, with or without America, England would act to prevent intervention; why then become a "cockboat in the wake of a British man-of-war." Adams was convinced, with true nationalist fervor, that the United States must act alone and create an "American System" in the Western Hemisphere.

The Monroe Doctrine. The President agreed with Adams, and in his annual message to Congress in December 1823 announced an American doctrine for the Western Hemisphere: the American continents were no longer subjects in future colonization by any European powers. As the European and American systems are "essentially different" and separate, the United States would consider any attempt to extend the European system into the Western Hemisphere "the manifestation of an unfriendly disposition" and, therefore, a threat to the nation's "peace and safety." The United States would not interfere with any existing colonies or in Europe's internal affairs; nor would she take part in European wars. Europe and Latin America ignored these remarks, but Americans were proud of the independence implied by Monroe's words.

Cultural Nationalism

Early European Influences. American culture around 1800 was still essentially derivative. In architecture, Charles Bulfinch, Thomas Jefferson, Pierre-Charles l'Enfant (who planned the District of Columbia), Benjamin Latrobe, William Strickland, and Robert Mills started a Greco-Roman Revival. First intended for state buildings, the vogue spread, until columns, pediments, friezes, rotundas, vaulting, domes, and other features of ancient architecture adorned even private homes. Similarly, American painters generally imitated English and French masters in subject matter and style.

The same trend was discernible in literature, which was dominated by imitations of popular English sentimental novels (soap opera–like tales of seduction and abandonment), or gothics (mystery tales featuring rattling chains and ghosts), or picaresque novels (with shifting scenes and rogue-heroes). Most American poetry was modeled after the great English verse of the eighteenth century.

Literature: The First American Triumph. The first real nationalist breakthrough in the arts was in literature in the works of Washington Irving, James Fenimore Cooper, and William Cullen Bryant. Although Irving imitated English style, he explored such American subjects as the "noble" Indian savage, the Dutch legends of the Hudson Valley, and the history of New York. Even if Irving recorded American customs only to lampoon them, still he saw them as subject matter worthy of a writer's attention.

Irving was praised by writers of the caliber of Sir Walter Scott and Lord Byron, yet Cooper was the nation's first important novelist. In his work we see the attempt to exploit American life for artistic purposes. Harvey Birch, the hero of *The Spy*, is an in-depth portrait of an American patriot during the Revolutionary War. And in Natty Bumppo, known as Leatherstocking, Cooper created a new American image—the pioneer who loves freedom and the natural world and who, with quiet heroism, faces ever westward.

What Irving and Cooper were accomplishing in fiction, Bryant was striving for in poetry. His poem "Thanatopsis" is significant for its American setting. Instead of using such English symbols as the nightingale, the yew, and the celandine, Bryant employed American elements: the bobolink, the waterfowl, and the pine.

First Stirrings of an American Art. Despite continued reliance on Europe, some American artists began to grope for independence from European culture. In painting, John Vanderlyn became notorious by exhibiting a nude "Ariadne." Thomas Doughty, Thomas Cole, and Asher Brown Durand successfully launched a school of landscape painting that featured idyllic and pastoral scenes of the Hudson River Valley and the Catskill and Adirondack mountains. Henry Sargent and Henry Inman began to create genre paintings, depicting people performing characteristically American activities such as whittling, barn-dancing, and eel-spearing. An outgrowth of genre painting, Currier and Ives prints also represented American events.

Sectionalism

But all was not well. The Bank Bill of 1816 passed the House of Representatives by a vote of eighty to seventy-two, proof of widespread opposition to the measure. Sizable numbers of southern representatives also voted against the Tariff of 1816, because it made imported goods so much more costly for their region and invited foreign buyers to retaliate against cotton planters. Calhoun argued that the South should develop its own industries, but the planters resisted. Nationalism was thus opposed by a strong counterforce: Sectionalism.

The Basis of Sectionalism. Despite a perception of common nationhood, Americans considered themselves different from one another. Sectionalism was a sense of belonging to a local community—with distinct accent, origin, history, customs, and traditions, pursuing a different way of life from other locales—and a corresponding loyalty to the state, not the nation. A common economic interest cemented each community: one section was bound to cotton production produced on plantations by slave labor; another to wheat produc-

tion produced on small freehold farms by free labor; a third to household manufactures or factory production or commerce, and so forth. Pride in cultural achievement enhanced the sense of sectionalism; all Southerners, for example, hailed an artist if he was from their region (being an American artist was less important). Local pride was the commanding sentiment.

The Missouri Dispute. One critical issue where sectional fears surfaced concerned admission of Missouri as a state into the Union. By 1819 the territory had qualified for statehood under the terms of the Northwest Ordinance. A committee of the House recommended favorable action on the admission request. There was, however, one ominous problem: because many of its settlers were slave owners, Missouri would enter the Union as a slave state. Congressman James Tallmadge of New York rose to amend the bill of admission: "That the further introduction of slavery or involuntary servitude be prohibited . . . and that all children born within the said state, after the admission thereof into the Union, shall be free at the age of twenty-five years." This amendment split the nation into two camps—slave states and free states. The House voted to accept the Tallmadge amendment, the Senate then defeated it. Missouri's statehood remained unresolved until the next Congress.

In December 1819, when the new Congress met, the issue was immediately raised. Northerners protested that, under the Three-Fifths Compromise, the new slave states would be overrepresented in Congress. An application by the people of Maine for statehood offered a possible way out of the impasse. In a compromise offered by Senator Jesse B. Thomas of Illinois, Maine and Missouri were linked: Maine would enter as a free state, while Missouri would be a slave state. A second amendment prohibiting slavery in the Louisiana Territory north of latitude 36° 30' was also passed.

With the achievement of this precarious balance, the country could return to national considerations. But the struggle over Missouri aroused both the North and the South to sectional self-consciousness. Reflecting the fury of the debate, Jefferson wrote: "This momentous question, like a fire bell in the night, awakened and filled me with terror."

Colonization of Freed Slaves.   The Missouri dispute showed that the issue of slavery was far from settled. In the years following the Revolution, the institution of slavery was actually revitalized. Even many of the Revolutionary generation, who had been inspired by libertarian ideals such as the equality of man, were more concerned with property rights than with the freedom of slaves. The idea of legally compelling slave owners to give up their slaves was not really considered.

In the 1780s some Americans had begun to suggest that colonizing freed slaves in the West or in Africa might offer a solution to the problem. The colonization movement was divided into two parts: one, led by black Americans, reflected an embryonic black nationalism; the other, led by whites, contained a mixture of idealists, people who hated the idea of living beside blacks, and pragmatists who thought that both races would profit economically from separation.

In 1817 the idea of colonization peaked with the founding of the American Colonization Society. This primarily white organization purchased land in Africa and established it as the Republic of Liberia. During its existence the Society managed to send only six thousand blacks to Africa. One of the major reasons for the lack of success of the colonization movement was the cotton boom early in the nineteenth century. Because of it, planters needed more labor and talk of colonization died out.

Another effect of the South's increasing reliance on cotton was the beginning of the interstate slave trade. Slaves were moved from the upper South (where there was a surplus of them) to the cotton plantations of the deep South. At first this traffic was informally organized, but as the need for slaves increased, it expanded and became more structured.

The Election of 1824.   The nation's turmoil registered in the election of 1824. Five "favorite son" candidates contended for three sections. Monroe's Secretary of the Treasury, William Crawford, and the coldly intelligent John C. Calhoun vied for southern support; the colorful Henry Clay and the legendary Andrew Jackson for western support; while John Quincy Adams was unopposed in his bid for the northern and middle states.

During the campaign Calhoun withdrew, announcing that he supported Jackson and accepting in return the offer of the vice presidency. The electoral count gave Jackson ninety-nine votes, Adams eighty-four, Crawford forty-one, and Clay thirty-seven. Since there was no majority, the vote went to the House of Representatives. There Clay threw his support to Adams. An immediate outcry followed, with one Philadelphia newspaper publishing an anonymous letter that charged a corrupt bargain between Adams and Clay. The House nevertheless voted, and Adams defeated Jackson, thirteen states to seven. Adams appointed Clay as Secretary of State and the Jacksonian-controlled House began an investigation of the "corrupt bargain"; no evidence was found. But this did not matter to Jackson, who felt he had been cheated out of the presidency.

The Unremarkable Administration of J. Q. Adams.   Although he was an able and honest man, John Quincy Adams's administration yielded no great achievements. In his first annual message, the new President projected a golden dream: federal road and canal construction; a national university; a national astronomical observatory; standardization of weights and measures; exploration of the West; and laws to promote agriculture, commerce, manufacturing, the arts, sciences, and literature. A decade earlier these proposals would have elicited a sympathetic hearing; now they became the victims of sectional and party politics. Nor did Adams's political ineptitude help in winning over Congress or the people.

As each of the President's proposals was offered to Congress, a coalition of supporters of Jackson, Calhoun, and Crawford defeated it. Although Adams served four years, it was Jackson's activities that attracted the most attention.

The "Tariff of Abominations."   In 1828 Congress debated a new tariff. Northern manufacturers and western farmers favored a higher tariff, while the cotton-growing South opposed it. After anguished consideration, Vice President Calhoun led the outcry against the tariff, which he felt would economically devastate not only his native South Carolina, but the entire South.

After the tariff became law, Calhoun wrote an essay, "The South Carolina Exposition and Protest," declaring that he was no longer a champion of the philosophy of nationalism. This tariff, Calhoun asserted, was discriminatory. But what mattered most was that the South had been made a permanent minority in the nation and was now completely at the mercy of a permanent and hostile majority. The Constitution provided checks on tyrannical majorities by placing the ultimate sovereignty in the states. Congress enjoyed only a limited sovereignty. If it exceeded its sovereign rights, the states must provide the remedy. Thus, if a state convention decided an act of Congress was unconstitutional, it could, by interposing its authority, nullify the act inside the state.

Calhoun's argument—that one state could set aside the national will as represented by Congress—struck an ominous note. Perhaps the glue of nationalism that had kept the nation together was cracking.

CHAPTER EIGHT

The Age of Andrew Jackson

On March 4, 1828, a man on a white horse rode to the White House. As he passed along Pennsylvania Avenue, the crowds of people who had descended on Washington followed him. Reaching the White House, they pushed inside and fought their way toward the long tables laden with orange punch and ice cream. They trampled mud over valuable rugs and smashed china and glasses. Friends had to rescue the man from his adoring hordes.

Washington had never witnessed anything like it. Andrew Jackson had just been inaugurated, and the ordinary citizens who elected him had come to see and touch their hero.

Democracy

The Term *Democracy*. While nationalism and sectionalism contended, a third great force was developing. During the 1820s and 1830s Americans began to use the word *democracy* to describe their way of life. The ideals of a democratic society resided in Jefferson's words in the Declaration of Independence, that "all men are created equal." But Americans sensed a difference between Jefferson's sentiments and those symbolized by the election and presidency of Andrew Jackson. While Jefferson believed in the rights of ordinary citizens, he assumed that they would choose those who were superior (the cultural elite) to govern them; in contrast, Jacksonian democracy saw the common men themselves as leaders. This elevation of the ordinary citizen was partly influenced by the new western states where people saw self-made men rise to power and influence. Therefore, Westerners believed that everyone enjoyed equal opportunity to become what he or she wanted. One area where these democratic ideas effected change was voting rights.

The Idea of Democracy. The democratization of American society was visible during this period in the expansion of suffrage and the rise of mass political parties. As early as 1807, New Jersey abolished tax qualifications for voting. Between 1812 and 1821, six western states entered the Union with constitutions providing for universal, white, male suffrage, and, in a wave of constitutional revisions between 1816 and 1821, four eastern states followed suit.

With the vote secured, further victories followed: religious qualifications were eliminated; representation was reapportioned according to population, not taxpayers; the choice of presidential electors in most states was transferred from state legislatures to the people; and the number of elective offices was increased. In national politics, parties no longer nominated presidential candidates through congressional caucuses after 1828. Following the pattern set by the anti-Masonic party in 1831, the more democratic system of national party nominating conventions was substituted. Political democracy, for white males, had become a fact.

Machine Politics. The rise of a new voting bloc transformed political activity. Now that they had to cope with the people, politicians needed a new type of organization to get out the vote. In response to this need, there arose the party machine headed by the political boss who derived power from his command of patronage. Observing this change, New York politician William Murray remarked, "to the victors belong the spoils." Men such as Murray spoke a new popular kind of political oratory—some critics contended it was demagoguery—in their efforts to win constituents.

Jackson as a Symbol. In the election of 1828, Jackson's political organization used innovative techniques, such as large public rallies, barbecues, and picnics to rally voters around the candidate. His campaign managers were able to make

voters see him as the epitome of the frontier democrat, a rough-and-ready warrior ready to fight against all privilege. Propagandists recited proudly the events of his brawling career: enlistment in the Revolutionary War at thirteen, mutilation and capture by the British, gambling on horses and cockfights, military victories during the War of 1812, rugged defiance of international law in Florida and roughhouse tactics in Tennessee politics. The incumbent Adams, they contended, was just the opposite: intellectual, aristocratic, ill at ease among ordinary citizens.

The legend was only one side of a complex personality. Born in the Carolina backwoods, Jackson was a newly arrived gentleman-aristocrat, but once he arrived he adopted the mien and manner of the gentry. He was a prosperous slaveholder and businessman and, until bankrupted, a creditor who had consistently sided with the "haves" against the "have-nots" on the frontier. He became dignified, courtly, and sentimental—a proper country gentleman, the owner of a Tennessee plantation, the Hermitage. Since these traits constituted political handicaps, Jackson's campaign managers carefully concealed them from public view.

Yet the real Jackson did symbolize many American ideals. He was generous, natural, patriotic, strongly moralistic, and an admirer of pretty women. In short, like Washington, he was a "man's man," a victorious general but a gentleman, too. Because of these characteristics, Jackson's appeal cut across sectional and class distinctions. Both the western farmer and the urban banker voted for him.

Coalition. With the nomination of Jackson, there appeared for the first time in

American politics a coalition organized around a powerful personality with broad appeal. By their organizing strategies, the men who formed this coalition laid the foundation for the Democratic Party—the first modern political party. Their success showed that only a national effort by a unified organization composed of various factions could capture the presidency.

The leaders of the national campaign were Vice President Calhoun, who represented the South and its advocacy of states' rights; Martin Van Buren, the tactful senator from New York who dominated state politics through a political machine known as the Albany Regency; and two Kentucky editors, Francis P. Blair and Amos Kendall, who tried to garner western support for Jackson. Personalities, not issues, dominated the campaign. The war of words became so rough that Adams's supporters even attacked Jackson's wife, accusing her of bigamy and adultery. The Jackson organization responded by contending that Mrs. Adams had been an illegitimate child. Jackson won by a comfortable but not overwhelming majority.

The Spoils System. The new President had a violent temper and a long memory for insults. In power at last, he decided to pay back the opposition who had assassinated his character and that of his wife during the bitter campaign. His predecessor, John Quincy Adams, had refused to use his executive powers to hire or remove people for political reasons. But Jackson, thirsting for revenge, fired many officeholders and replaced them with his own followers. This was the beginning of the so-called "Spoils System."

Jackson was the first president to defend such politically motivated appointments.

There was no place in American democracy, he contended, for a permanent bureaucracy. People who have held positions for a long time are "apt to acquire a habit of looking with indifference upon the public interest." Moreover, duties of public office are so simple that many "men of intelligence" may perform them. According to Jackson, the ordinary citizen could perform in government as well as the expert.

Coalition and Cabinet. The Cabinet had to serve the new coalition. With an eye to reconciling northern and southern supporters, Jackson appointed Van Buren as Secretary of State and divided the rest of the posts among relative unknowns from other regions. This practice marked another sharp departure from tradition. Previous presidents had enlisted men of recognized stature for their cabinets. Jackson also relied less on the Cabinet than his predecessors, using them primarily as advisers, not policy setters. To reduce their influence even more, he discontinued the presidential practice of holding regular Cabinet meetings and instead sought outside guidance. An unofficial "Kitchen Cabinet" composed of party leaders and journalists wrote his state papers, planned strategy, and kept alive his public image.

The First Break in the Coalition. The Calhoun forces representing the southern aristocracy were the weakest link in Jackson's coalition. Serving as his vice president, Calhoun studied carefully the character of the new President. In his role as president of the Senate, Calhoun saw Jackson powerfully assert the independence of the executive by resisting congressional checks and balances.

Conflict with Congress developed early as Jackson tried to force appointments through the Senate. In contrast to previous Presidents, who had used the veto sparingly, he wielded it like a club. With each veto message, Jackson spread the doctrine that his own energetic and self-assertive will was the "people's will." Calhoun also made note of the frequent cartoons dubbing Jackson "King Andrew I" and the mounting impeachment threats.

The two men had an implicit understanding that Calhoun was to be the presidential nominee in 1832. Now Jackson held his silence, even though the Kitchen Cabinet had begun maneuvering for a second term. Any opposition, Calhoun knew, had to move cautiously as the people loved the President.

It was Jackson, however, who forced the break. On learning that, in 1818, Calhoun had proposed he be court-martialed for invading Florida, Jackson publicly ended their friendship by purging his cabinet of the Vice President's supporters. Calhoun resigned and was reelected to the Senate where he would be better able to oppose the President.

The Policies of Andrew Jackson

The Webster-Hayne Debate. The main problems facing Jackson when he became President were the tariff and the western lands. Jackson cautiously suggested that after the federal debt was paid off, the government might distribute surplus revenues among the states. Westerners who wanted to lower the price of western lands to encourage emigration opposed this idea. They felt that, without the surplus,

the government would be unable to afford to lower land prices. The issue came to a head in January 1830 when Senator Samuel Foot of Connecticut proposed to limit land sales for a time. Senator Thomas Hart Benton of Missouri accused Foot of being part of a conspiracy to impede westward settlement; this was, Benton charged, a plot by New England manufacturers to keep cheap labor in the East. Robert Y. Hayne of South Carolina supported Benton, suggesting a South-West alliance, based on low tariffs and cheap lands. Daniel Webster of Massachusetts, a formidable orator, then rose to accuse South Carolina of encouraging disunion. Hayne answered Webster by an eloquent defense of the states' rights doctrine.

Webster, a famous constitutional lawyer, responded by arguing incisively that the Constitution was "the people's Constitution, the people's government, made for the people, and answerable to the people." One nation could not have many masters. Only those who made the Union—the people—could dissolve it. Talk of secession was talk of treason; any effort to disrupt the Union would be met with force. In their debate, Webster not only demolished Hayne's arguments, he prevented any alliance between the West and the South.

Jackson and the Debate. Jackson followed closely the Webster-Hayne debate. Calhoun's press, hoping that Jackson would defend South Carolina's position, began to campaign for the President to take a stand on the issue of states' rights. In fact, although Jackson was a Southerner and had frequently defended states' rights, he was opposed to the idea that states could nullify federal laws. In the Deep South, Old Hickory's popularity had mounted with his decisive handling of the Indian problem. He had fought two wars (the Black Hawk and Seminole wars), and during his presidency the government concluded more than ninety treaties with the tribes, each one pushing the Indians further west. The Deep South benefitted from Jackson's land grabs and was duly grateful. He was confident that he possessed the popular support to challenge Calhoun.

The issue came to a climax on April 13, 1830, at the Jefferson Day Dinner. His eyes squarely on Calhoun, Jackson offered a toast: "Our Federal *Union:* It must be preserved!" Calhoun rose and replied: "The Union, next to our liberty, most dear."

The Nullification Crisis. In 1832 a combination of New Englanders and Northwesterners pushed through a tariff that, although lower than that of 1828, was still substantially protective. South Carolina, more committed than ever to slavery and afraid that the federal government might act against it, called a state convention in November 1832. The convention resolved that the tariffs of 1828 and 1832 were "null, void, and no law, nor binding upon this State, its officers, or citizens." The delegates then forbade federal officers to collect tariffs in South Carolina after February 1, 1833. This was the challenge: nullification—and failing that, secession.

Jackson reacted quickly. First, he requested that Congress lower the tariff. Then he called on South Carolina to act moderately. Next he asked Congress for the power to use force to collect the duties and denounced the act of nullification, thus rallying the nationalists to his side. In response Congress passed the Force Bill, giving Jackson the military powers he requested. South Carolina found herself isolated (the other southern states had rejected the idea of nullification) and became eager to look for a way out of the impasse. Thus Calhoun and Clay joined together to shape a compromise tariff, which Congress passed in March 1833. Jackson emerged the hero from this confusion, and national harmony was preserved.

Jackson vs. the Bank. Jackson's most dramatic display of executive power was his successful battle against the Bank of the United States. More than any other incident, it revealed his genius as a political antagonist, if not, perhaps, as a sound economist. Brilliantly managed by its president, Nicholas Biddle, the central bank had regained the public's confidence by checking the "wildcat" tendencies of the local state banks. When the local banks overissued notes or credit, Biddle insisted that they pay their debts in specie and he suggested that new loans be suspended until uncollected ones were repaid. In its own banking practice, the Bank was a model of conservatism. It collected its debts, and when they could not be paid, foreclosed on mortgages held as securities.

While this was sound banking practice (many state banks supported Biddle's policies), Biddle's policies had their detractors, including those who were foreclosed, most of them Westerners. Some bankers, too, disliked Biddle's restraint, which they felt ultimately limited their projects. Other Americans simply distrusted paper money. When Jackson became President, he was already suspicious of the idea of banks and paper money. He also believed that branches of the Bank may have secretly lent their support to Adams in the presidential campaign. Aware of Jackson's attitude, Biddle worried about the renewal of the Bank's charter in 1836. To gain some support, Biddle offered generous loans to congressmen and journalists; Webster and Clay became his unofficial advisers.

They supported a renewal of the Bank's charter in 1832 to force the hand of Jackson before the presidential election of the same year. The two politicians reasoned that if Jackson vetoed the Bank Bill, he had chosen the unpopular side of the issue and the people would vote him out of office. The bill, they believed, might even make Clay President. Biddle reluctantly agreed. Congress passed the recharter in July 1832, and Jackson immediately vetoed it.

Upsetting Webster and Clay's predictions, Jackson's veto message earned him even greater popularity. Some of the Bank's powers, he remarked, were unconstitutional. The Bank was a dangerous monopoly with almost exclusive control of domestic and foreign exchange. The present bill would make the "rich richer and the potent more powerful."

The Election of 1832.   Besides being a referendum on Jackson, the election of 1832 was significant in other ways. It was the first in which parties held nominating conventions. The National Republicans, a party composed of opponents to Jackson, met and nominated Henry Clay. They also set a precedent by adopting a party platform condemning Jackson's stand on the Bank and the Supreme Court and endorsing once again the "American System." The Democrats then nominated Jackson, with Martin Van Buren as his running mate. The President's selection of his fol-

lower initially threatened the coalition. Jackson responded by insisting that the New Yorker be nominated by a two-thirds vote. (Democrats continued this precedent, the two-thirds rule, until 1936.)

The party adopted no platform, feeling that Jackson's strong stands in office sufficiently identified him to voters. This view proved correct, as he won an impressive victory over Clay, defeating the Kentuckian by 219 electoral votes to 49. Jackson now believed he had a popular mandate to destroy the Bank. Shortly after his second term began, he ordered his new Secretary of the Treasury, Roger B. Taney, to withdraw government deposits after September 15, 1833. Taney deposited new federal receipts in seven state banks.

A Hollow Victory.   Jackson had scored a great political victory, but one with serious economic consequences. The flow of federal funds into the state banks, or "pet" banks as opponents called them, and the distribution of a federal treasury surplus to state areas released a wave of reckless speculation. "Wildcat" loans, mounting inflation, and unsecured indebtedness followed. Eastern manufacturers were unable to supply inflationary needs, and imports poured in from overseas to drain the country of specie (foreign debts had to be paid in gold). As specie became short, foreign investors withdrew credit; local investors sought to cash in their holdings; and the banks began to contract their loans and to call in their outstanding obligations. Having no other alternative, Jackson issued his Specie Circular (1836), stipulating that land offices accept only gold and silver in payment for public land. A rush on the banks resulted, forcing them to suspend specie payments in the spring of 1837. A deflationary collapse began: land values disintegrated, businesses closed, and agricultural products accumulated. By the time the panic reached its peak, Jackson's term had ended.

Post-Jacksonian Government

Van Buren.   Jackson retired from office in 1837, but not from battle. In the election of 1836, he had thrown his tremendous influence behind Van Buren for President. The Democrats still commanded the allegiance of small western farmers, backcountry southern planters, and seaboard workers, but wealthier and more influential groups had departed the coalition. They joined the Jackson opposition, who now called themselves "Whigs" as a symbol of revolt against his "monarchical" tendencies. The Whig ranks were made up of Clay's supporters of the American System, Calhoun's states'-rightists, pro-Bank men, large southern planters, and northern industrialists.

The opposition, it became increasingly apparent, was more anti-Jackson than anything else. They could not agree on a single presidential candidate and offered instead a number of candidates in an effort to send the election to the House of Representatives. This strategy failed, and Van Buren was elected. His running mate, Richard M. Johnson, did not secure a majority in the electoral college, and for the first and only time in American history the Senate of the United States chose the Vice President. (Johnson won.)

Van Buren assumed office at the beginning of the short-lived Panic of 1837. He was, of course, not responsible for the crisis, nor for the depression that followed it in 1839. He did not do much, however, to help the situation, because he was committed to a policy of laissez-faire—government nonintervention. Still Van Buren did try to separate federal funds from state banks. He proposed an Independent Treasury Act to construct government-owned vaults as depositories for federal revenues. Because of fierce Whig opposition, the act did not pass Congress until 1840.

The Whig Coalition.   Van Buren was skillful and intelligent but colorless. His lack of personality did not help him in his bid for reelection in 1840, but the main reasons why he lost were the depression, which lasted until 1843, and the superior organization of the Whigs.

They had learned much from Jackson. Now they, too, selected a general for president, William Henry Harrison. As their vice-presidential candidate they chose John Tyler of Virginia, thus balancing North and South in one ticket. Copying Jackson's strategy in his first successful campaign, the Whig candidates avoided taking a stand on the issues of the day. They centered their attack on the aristocratic pretensions of Van Buren and converted their own aristocrat, Harrison, into a "log-cabin and hard-cider" candidate. Recalling Harrison's destruction of Tecumseh's headquarters at Tippecanoe in 1811, they exploited slogans like "Tippecanoe and Tyler too" and "Van, Van is a used-up man."

The Whig campaign was distinguished by abuse, evasion, irrelevancy, and misrepresentation. Van Buren tried to run on his record, but the people did not pay much attention. The Whigs won overwhelmingly in the electoral college over both the Democrats and a third party, the Liberty Party.

Harrison's Brief Presidency. Harrison achieved no more in office than selecting a cabinet; for all but two positions, he chose Clay supporters. Then, one month after his inauguration, the President died of pneumonia and was succeeded by John Tyler (he was the first Vice President to succeed to the presidency).

The country could not know it, but Harrison's death marked a fateful turning point—future events would carry America toward the Civil War.

CHAPTER NINE

The Maturing of the Nation

In Buffalo, New York, Governor DeWitt Clinton and many dignitaries gathered to celebrate the great event. Then a fleet of ships carried the governor and his retinue along the route. When they arrived in New York City, it seemed as if the entire population had come out to watch the boats. As part of the festivities, water from Lake Erie was poured into the Atlantic. Eight years after work on it had begun, the Erie Canal was completed.

This great engineering feat, along with other daring inventions and innovations, not only encouraged the development of the sections but eventually brought about vast socioeconomic changes in the entire society.

Population. The growth of United States population in the first half of the nineteenth century was phenomenal. Natural increase and immigration swelled the population from 5.3 million in 1800 to more than 23 million in 1850. While average annual immigration in the first quarter of the century was 10,000, it rose to 60,000 by 1832 and to 100,000 by 1842. Between 1845 and 1860 the influx was extremely high because of crop failure in Europe, famine in Ireland, and political upheaval following the French Revolution of 1848. Most of the immigrants who streamed into the country were German and Irish, but large numbers of English and Scandinavians came, too.

Only one-tenth of the immigrants went South. Most obviously could not afford to buy lands and slaves for cotton production, nor compete as labor against them. So by 1860 the South, with half the land area of the United States, contained only one third of the nation's population.

The Northeast and Northwest, based on free labor in agriculture and industry, shared the remaining two thirds of the population about equally. With the more prosperous newcomers lured westward, those who stayed behind usually settled in the East, finding work in factories. Of the immigrants, the Irish were among the poorest and tended to take the lowest-paying jobs in eastern cities. Packed into urban slums, the Irish, along with the Jews, encountered prejudice by native-born Americans.

Once settled, immigrants adopted the manners and mores of their section: they became Westerners, or Northerners, or, more rarely, Southerners. Their needs and demands became those of their section.

The West

Western Settlement. Farmers headed west in the face of great hazards and at great personal cost. It is difficult for us today to appreciate the hardships of travel in Conestoga wagons or on canal and river boats; of wheels registering every rut in the crude roads or dragging at a snail's pace through endless prairie. Pioneering was no romance: it entailed cutting a clearing out of timberland and river bottoms; acclimating to unknown and extreme weather conditions; and solving problems of seed-gathering. It also meant primitive methods of sowing, planting, and harvesting; transporting goods to distant centers; establishing communities from nothing. The miracle is that it was done and done quickly. How was the settlement of the West accomplished?

By the 1820s the hazards of travel were gradually reduced as steamboats transported people over inland canals and western rivers like the Mississippi and the Ohio. In 1830 transportation took a giant leap forward as railroads began to operate. During the period between 1810 and 1840 eight new states entered the Union.

The greatest waves of westward movement coincided with the height of American prosperity; hence, farmers were able to realize quick cash returns. The steamboat and the railroad permitted western farmers and eastern manufacturers to en-

gage in a profitable two-way commerce. Now western farmers could cheaply transport their crops like wheat, corn, and cured meat to the Northeast and, through New Orleans, to the South. In return eastern manufacturers sent textiles, shoes, and hats westward.

Western expansion was also aided by the government's policy of ruthless elimination of Native Americans, which heightened the sense of security among those interested in settling out west.

The Policy of Indian Removals. As a military commander after the War of 1812, Jackson had forced the Indians to sign treaties surrendering huge tracts of territory in Florida, Alabama, and Texas. The idea of forced removal of the Indians to areas west of the Mississippi originated in these treaties signed between 1815 and 1820.

Jackson was convinced of the benefit of such a policy to white society. In a formal message to Congress he argued that removal "will place a dense and civilized population in large tracts of country now occupied by a few savage hunters. By opening the whole territory between the Tennessee on the north and Louisiana on the south to the settlement of the whites will incalculably strengthen the southwestern frontier. . . . It will relieve the whole State of Mississippi and the western part of Alabama of Indian occupancy, and enable those States to advance rapidly in population, wealth, and power."

The Indians, then, stood in the way of westward expansion. In the same address Jackson justified his policy by asserting that they, too, would be better off far from "immediate contact with settlements of whites." Such a separation would "free them from the power of the States; enable them to pursue happiness in their own way and under their own rude institutions; will retard the progress of decay, which is lessening their numbers, and perhaps cause them gradually, under the influence of the Government and through the influence of good counsels, to cast off their savage habits and become a interesting, civilized, and Christian community."

The Creeks and the Cherokees.   Two of the worst examples of the cruelty of this policy involved the Creeks and the Cherokees. In 1826 the governor of Georgia had ordered a survey of Creek lands. President Adams threatened to use federal troops to prevent the survey, but the governor refused to back down. Under such pressure, the Creeks decided to remove themselves to Oklahoma, or Indian country as it was called. Many of them failed to survive the journey, and those who did were unable to adjust to the new and often harsh western climate.

The Cherokee situation proved equally dismal. More than most tribes, they had tried to adjust to the ways of white civilization. They established farms, adopted a constitution, and built schools and factories. In 1827 the Cherokees decided to form an independent state, or a "state within a state," in Georgia. In response Georgia nullified all federal Indian laws and ordered the seizure of Cherokee lands. In *Worchester v. Georgia* (1832), the Supreme Court stated that the Cherokee nation was a legitimate nation where "the laws of Georgia can have no force and which the citizens of Georgia have no right to enter" without Cherokee consent. Georgia defied this decision, continuing to seize the tribe's land without interference from the

federal government. After one faction of the Cherokees signed a treaty of removal in 1835, the entire tribe's fate was sealed. In 1838, supervised by federal troops, Cherokees from Georgia, Alabama, Tennessee, and North Carolina were removed to Oklahoma. They were forced to march under such terrible conditions that of the 14,000 who began the trek, only 1,200 survived. The infamous journey became known as the "Trail of Tears."

The Seminoles.   Although the Chickasaw and Choctaw Indians in Alabama and Mississippi had agreed to migrate westward to Oklahoma, the Seminoles of Florida refused to obey the removal treaty of 1832. Instead, beginning in 1835, a few hundred warriors fought federal troops in Florida's swamps and Everglades. At the end of seven years of guerrilla war (on which the government spent $50 million), most of the tribe had been removed to Oklahoma. With the defeat of the Seminoles, millions of acres of land came into white hands.

New Inventions.   A number of technological advances also helped western farmers to ease the problems caused by a shortage of labor. New inventions included John Deere's steel plow (which easily cut through tough prairie sod), Cyrus McCormick's reaper (which first cut and then deposited a swath of grain on a platform), the seed drill, and the horse-drawn threshing machine. Increased efficiency reduced costs of production per unit acre. For example, with the reaper, one worker could cut seven times as much wheat as with a scythe. Throughout this middle period, farm prices rose steadily. Since transportation remained competitive, shipping rates were reasonable.

Fairly steady national and international markets absorbed production. England, for example, became a very good customer after she repealed The Corn Laws, or tariffs on grain.

The Significance of the West.   The existence in the West of undeveloped land was a major influence in the growth of America, providing for a time almost boundless economic opportunity. Wealthy speculators often bought up the best land, holding it for sale or rental. Farmers who could raise the necessary money to go west, clear the ground, and plant several crops gravitated toward the more fertile areas. Other regions offered considerable opportunity to make money raising cattle or tapping abundant mineral resources. Opportunities existed in lumbering and in construction of roads, canals, and railroads. Almost all Westerners were linked by the common desire to become successful businessmen, to produce marketable commodities at a profit.

Settlers and Squatters. Since 1796 Westerners had pressed for cheaper land to be sold in smaller parcels. After the Panic of 1819, the government lowered the price of an acre to $1.25. By requiring payment in cash, it hoped to avert another panic and financial ruin for those who might have wished to purchase land on credit. This change in land policy, however, favored speculators over farmers. Many farmers, possessing little capital, were forced by speculators to buy at inflated prices or to borrow unless they preferred renting (and they almost never did). One alternative was to "squat" on the land—that is, to settle in some outlying region without purchase. Under these conditions eviction was inevitable, but the squatters fought back. Asserting that they had the right to buy the land they had worked at $1.25 per acre, they turned to the national government for relief.

In response to their demands, Congress passed the Pre-Emption Act of 1841. It permitted a squatter to select 160 acres of the public domain and at a later date (after he had a chance to farm it) to purchase the land with a cash settlement. Public auction of the land would be deferred to that date. Even this arrangement presented some problem for small farmers, for those unable to raise the money had to borrow at high interest rates.

From their viewpoint, then, there was only one solution—free land. The cry for free homesteads became so insistent that political parties could no longer afford to ignore them.

Land Speculators. The West attracted surplus investment funds from land companies that could buy up lots ranging from five thousand to one hundred thousand acres. Land speculators were tremendously significant in the settlement of this section. Long before the settlers reached their destination, speculators had parceled out choice locations and surveyed them. Moreover, the speculators exerted much pressure on the state and federal governments to finance or in other ways encourage the building of canals, railroads, plank roads, and river improvements to facilitate westward passage for producers and goods. Since they purchased so much of the land with wildcat bank notes, speculators also became outlets for the banks. In sum, these men were trailblazers, necessary to the nation's expansion, but their impact was temporary.

Extractive Wealth. Of more permanence (though in the pre–Civil War period, of less significance) was the western wealth resulting from fur trading and mining. The great pioneer in the fur trade was John Jacob Astor, who organized the industry on a vast scale. Astor first linked America to the Oregon Territory by way of St. Louis and the Columbia River, subdued the Indians by employing them in the fur trade, and carved the first pathway to the West. The fur trade proved too uncertain, though, and Astor invested his profits instead in Manhattan real estate.

More secure sources of future wealth were the iron, silver, lead, and zinc deposits. Mining and smelting of metals attracted eastern capital and encouraged railroad construction. After the discovery of gold in 1848 in the Sacramento Valley, the population of California swelled from ten thousand to one hundred thousand in two years. But gold did not establish great fortunes until organized companies began to dig for it. Instead, wealth in the gold areas initially came from the "accessories" to the hunt for the precious metal—transport, trade, food supplies, mining tools, furnishings, construction, gambling, and so forth. The peddler, the shopkeeper, and the retail merchant were the chief beneficiaries of the Gold Rush of '48.

Expansionism: Manifest Destiny. Western settlers were not known to respect boundaries; the land "out there" exerted a constant allure, and the problem of who owned it was of secondary importance. Frontier pressure had caused the vast territory of Louisiana and the Floridas to come into American hands; land hunger had converted the War Hawks into agrarian imperialists. The same hunger had led settlers to swarm into Texas and pushed them—after losing the Battle of the Alamo (1836) against an army led by Mexico's president Antonio López de Santa Anna—to declare their independence and become a Republic. Two hundred years of westward expansion had also led Americans to Missouri and Iowa.

Now in the 1840s propagandists started to speak of the nation's manifest destiny to expand until it possessed the entire continent including Mexico and Canada. From the West especially came constant pressure for possession of the immense terrain beyond Texas, ruled by a weak Mexican government; for the removal of the English from Oregon; and for the annexation of Texas.

Internal Commerce. Investment capital in the 1830s was inevitably attracted to road and canal construction in the northern and western states. Roads were financed mainly by joint stock companies that received exclusive franchises to build, improve, maintain, and repair them.

These private companies derived their profits from tolls, whose rates were set by the states. Because of this, investors were reluctant to build in less-populated areas and demanded government subsidies for such ventures. But sectional conflicts prevented the possibility of federal subsidies. Bowing to this reality, presidents Madison, Monroe, and Jackson successively vetoed bills for internal improvement. In their place, the states themselves eagerly offered financial support, as towns and cities pressed for improved communication with their neighbors. Some states even built their own turnpikes, operating them as public enterprises.

Turnpikes greatly helped the development of commerce. On these roads certain goods, such as clothing from New England's textile mills and shoes from eastern factories, could pass westward. Such shipping was expensive, however.

Until the introduction of railroads, it was impossible to transport bulk products overland. They went instead by water. River traffic had remained slight as long as transport of goods depended upon the keelboat and flatboat. In 1807 Robert Fulton produced the first workable steamboat, the *Clermont*. The steamer's capacity and speed soon resulted in a tremendous increase in river traffic, especially profiting the Mississippi Valley. In the early 1830s, for example, produce streamed down to New Orleans: receipts for these goods totaled about $26 million; by 1850 they amounted to $108 million, making New Orleans one of the world's great ports. River traffic had the considerable advantages of "no tolls to pay, no work animals to take care of, and no bad inns at which to put up." But because the great midwestern rivers did not flow into the Atlantic, it became clear that an artificial waterway had to be cut between the Midwest and the East. The Appalachian Mountains presented a formidable obstacle to such a plan.

The Erie Canal. New York State was aware that it possessed in the Mohawk Valley a favorable route to the West if it could be converted into a water route from the upper Hudson River to Lake Erie. A great advantage was that the land rose no more than 570 feet above the Hudson along the projected route.

The distance to be covered was 363 miles, a huge project by contemporary standards, as the longest canal was then less than 28 miles. The engineers Benjamin Wright and James Geddes were undaunted. They gathered together a number of extremely able men (indeed, some have argued that the Erie Canal was the nation's first engineering school). Begun near Albany in 1817, the canal did not reach its end point at Buffalo until 1825. When completed it climbed by a series of locks to the entrance into the Mohawk Valley.

Few projects undertaken in America encountered greater natural obstacles and public hostility. The canal would have been abandoned many times but for the vision and courage of New York's Mayor DeWitt Clinton, first in proposing the project and then in pressing it forward. (By the time it was completed, he was governor.)

The cost to New York State was about $7,500,000, which it soon recovered, for the canal was immediately successful. The canal reduced the time for shipping freight by two thirds and lowered freight costs from about $100 a ton to $10. A number of cities and towns along the route, such as Buffalo, Syracuse, and Rochester, profited enormously. New York City's preeminence as the nation's greatest port of entry and financial center was cemented, since most European exports headed for the West landed at New York City and from there were shipped to their destinations over the canal.

The canal also made possible the influx of western grains to the East and forced a radical shift in eastern farming (from grain production to truck-and-dairy farming). It encouraged westward migration by creating a major passageway and also reduced considerably the cost of this migration. It stimulated banking, warehousing, and manufacturing, which in turn served as additional outlets for surplus capital. And it started a national canal construction boom during the 1820s and 1830s.

Much of this construction occurred in the West. For example, Ohio built the Ohio and Erie Canal linking the Ohio River to Cleveland so that farmers could transport produce directly to the East. Unfortunately the zeal of western canal enthusiasts caused them to overbuild. The result was that there simply wasn't enough traffic to pay for the new canals. State debts mounted so dangerously that default and repudiation inevitably followed. In 1841–42, nine states stopped payment of interest on canal bonds; and when this was followed by repudiation of $40 million, profits were wiped out completely. Besides, by 1850 the railroad had emerged as an invincible competitor.

Railroads.   The railroads initially functioned as feeders for canals. The first railroad to begin operation was the Baltimore and Ohio in 1830. Despite its potential, railroad use developed slowly. Between 1830 and 1850 only nine thousand miles of track were laid. Private capital showed mild interest, leaving the states to supply most of the building funds. The problems involved in railroad construction seemed almost insurmountable. Cast iron proved a poor material to bear the weight of the train; bridge engineering remained in a primitive stage; no standard gauge was used; sparks and cinders constituted a menace to safety; and engines had insufficient power to carry heavy loads over inclines.

The lower cost of shipping goods on canal boats also stopped shippers from switching to railroads. Additionally, certain states, such as New York, which had constructed canal systems, did not want to help fund a competitive mode of transportation. Land companies nevertheless began to pressure the government to construct "trunk lines" into the West at its own expense. Much of the support for private investment in railroads came from town, county, and state governments, which not only loaned money to private investors—mainly local businessmen, merchants, and farmers—but invested in their stock.

In his Maysville Veto, Jackson had set a precedent against federal aid to an intrastate project, and this in turn limited the possibility of railroad expansion. But, railroad supporters argued, private capital might be induced to invest in an interstate railroad if the government would make land grants along the route and permit investors full use (for timber, minerals, depot sites, etc.) of that land. The federal government did eventually offer such land grants.

As a result, between 1850 and 1860 twenty thousand miles of track were laid. Because of these policies, during the 1840s and 1850s railroads began to take away much of the freight business from canals, forcing many of the latter to fail. By 1860 railroad tracks crisscrossed every state east of the Mississippi.

The development of railroads profoundly affected American life. First, by vigorously advertising their lands and selling farm sites cheaply, land-grant railroads attracted many settlers to the areas along their routes, which in turn stimulated agricultural expansion. Second, the access to world markets that the railroads provided encouraged farmers to increase their output.

The railroads also benefitted other industries. For example, the demand for iron rails hastened the development of a domestic iron manufacture. Additionally, railroads encouraged the growth and prosperity of many American cities. The "iron horse," as Native Americans called it, stimulated the economy of eastern seaports. Because of competition with canals and with each other, the railroads sharply cut both commercial and passenger rates for all modes of transport. Everyone gained: The East received more and cheaper goods from the West, and the Illinois farmer had a huge market for wheat. The railroads used their profits to build feeder lines, which opened even more lands to agriculture development.

Clipper Ships. The first clipper ships were built in the 1840s. From the late 1840s to the Civil War, these swift, beautiful, American-designed sailing vessels crossed the oceans at unheard-of speeds: one clipper made it across the Atlantic in two weeks. But most of these ships were used on the longer runs around Cape Horn to California and the Far East. The reign of the clippers was, however, brief. Their designers had sacrificed cargo space for speed, forcing owners to charge higher rates than most shippers could afford. By around 1851 the English steamboat, with its greater cargo capacity, was sufficiently improved to enable it to withstand voyages in rough seas. Once this happened, steamers captured most of the first-class

freight and most of the passengers crossing the Atlantic.

For the first time since colonial days, American shipbuilders and owners were at a disadvantage. Not only were steamers able to carry more goods, more cheaply; but, built of iron, they were stronger and easier to maintain than the wooden clippers. One reason for the low shipping costs was that the British government made substantial subsidies to steamship builders. Although Congress tried to compete by offering subsidies to the American shipping industry, this assistance had little effect, for most of it was inefficiently allocated. Moreover, while American lumber was cheap, the British metallurgical industry was far ahead of its American rival.

The result of this competition, improved technology, and government subsidy was that shipping rates plummeted. Among the beneficiaries of these lower rates were people emigrating from Europe to America. Although the crowded and unsanitary conditions on American cargo vessels caused many of the immigrants to die during the voyage, this cheap means of transportation enabled thousands to enter the country.

As American transatlantic shipping declined, so did the fishing and whaling industries. This decline was hastened by a change in the European diet. Many people were beginning to replace their fish with meat and to substitute coal, oil, and gas for whale oil.

The Transformation of America

Factors in Industrial Growth. The first turning point in American history was the creation and consolidation of an independent nation founded on written law and the idea of democracy; the second was the transformation of America from an agrarian-commercial-mercantile nation to an industrial one.

Industrial capitalism rested on many economic pillars: a factory system employing division of labor and power-driven automatic machinery; the free use of capital for short- and long-term needs; continuous production; employment of a labor force wholly dependent on wages. Out of this combination of factors mass production for a national and international market emerged. The maturing of industrial capitalism was slow as other forms were tried and found wanting.

The Household System. From the nation's earliest days, manufacturing existed in the United States—chiefly on a household basis. Wives and daughters produced crude linsey-woolsey textiles by spinning wheel and hand loom; husbands and sons hammered and carved tools, utensils, and furniture. Gradually an increasing separation developed between those who were farmers producing for market and those who manufactured as specialists—blacksmiths, leather workers, cabinetmakers, millers, and so forth. These manufacturers were in reality working people using their homes as shops. Merchant capitalists provided them with quantities of raw materials, collected and paid for the finished wares, then distributed them. This system, universally known as the "domestic" or "putting out" system of manufacturing, was an intermediate stage in the development of industrial capitalism.

The Industrial Revolution. The Panic of 1837 had wiped out large amounts of commercial and mercantile capital, thus delaying industrialization. Progress had also been hampered because capital was dispersed over too many mercantile and commercial ventures and labor over too large a terrain. Moreover, British competition acted as a constant depressant on American industrialization. The inspiration to invest in industry came, nevertheless, from England, where invention, capital accumulation, available labor supplies, and resources had caused industrial production to mature. Finally, by 1840, conditions within the United States made it ripe, too, for an industrial leap forward.

Technology. Impressive advances were made in New England textile production. Between 1813 and 1850, a trio of Boston merchants built a number of large textile factories. By means of the power loom, these factories for the first time combined the processes of spinning and weaving under one roof, making it possible to produce cloth from fiber in a single factory. Production was speeded by automatic machinery. Labor was specialized—laborers were spinners or weavers and so on—and workers, organized by departments, received cash wages. Output was standardized, cost accounting was introduced, and buying and selling were systematized.

The three merchants built their first mill in Waltham, Massachusetts. Its enormous success inspired the cities of Lowell, Lawrence, and Manchester to follow suit. These factories owed much of this success to their reliance on the "ladies of the loom," or young, female, native-born laborers. So desirable were these jobs that women flocked from all over New England to the mills, where they earned between $2.50 and $3.25 for a seventy-hour week.

Half of these wages went for room and board at company-run boardinghouses. Although the hours were long, the pace inside the mills was fairly slow, and the women had energy after work to join sewing circles, attend lectures, and even edit their own literary magazines. But by the 1830s many of them had left the textile factories to become teachers or clerks.

New technology encouraged the spread of mass production. Eli Whitney's invention of the cotton gin spurred other inventors. Elias Howe invented the sewing machine, and William Kelly independently discovered the Bessemer process of decarbonizing ore with air blast. Whitney dramatically advanced industrialization one more step when, in producing an order for rifles, he elaborated a system of standardization of parts and interchangeable mechanisms. The iron industry kept apace, developing a method for the cheap use of anthracite coal in the smelting process, permitting Americans to compete with low-cost British coke production.

Newborn industries, at least initially, had to locate near their sources of supply, but the development of cheap and rapid transportation permitted factories to select the most profitable locations. The government, too, aided industrial development by passing tariff protections. Finally the discovery of gold in California gave the country exportable specie, which industrialists used to buy machines and machine parts abroad.

Despite the development of industry, however, pre–Civil War America was still an agricultural society, although farmers, too, benefitted from technological advances such as the mechanical reaper, which produced savings in time, labor, and cost.

Corporations. The development of the corporation greatly aided the growth of industrialism by providing the substantial capital investment necessary for mechanization. Before 1801 relatively few corporations had been chartered by the states, and only a few of these were manufacturers. The general attitude was one of mistrust. Even businessmen believed that corporations were monopolistic, corrupt, and hostile to the American spirit of free enterprise. Gradually this attitude changed, as people saw the usefulness of corporations in bringing together the large amount of capital needed to construct a transportation system and to organize banks. Corporations then began to multiply.

Labor. The influx of a cheap labor supply through immigration after 1845 naturally encouraged industrial expansion. Prior to this, factory workers had mainly consisted of women and children (at the time, most people did not see child labor as harmful) willing to accept low wages and seeking supplementary income for their families. Because male labor was scarce, men's wages were high.

The new immigrants, mostly male and Irish, offered a labor supply of primary, family-supporting wage earners. Factory owners promptly took advantage of the needy workers. They lowered wages, lengthened working hours, and put more pressure on workers to produce. The worsening of on-the-job conditions led to increased attempts to organize labor. But legal restrictions, inexperienced leadership, and the continuous stream of Irish immigrants hobbled these efforts. Also, for many immigrant workers, bad as these conditions were, they represented an improvement over their previous life. Thus, by 1860, a new working class had been created, composed mostly of male immigrants laboring at low wages under miserable conditions. But by their presence in such large numbers, they accelerated the Industrial Revolution in America.

Finally, such a revolution would have been impossible without the acumen and toughness of the first industrial capitalists and their families: the Lowells, Jacksons, Appletons, Lawrences, Dwights, Browns, Phelpses, and Du Ponts. They fought against foreign competition, endured sudden economic collapse, picked themselves up and made new starts. Theirs was an industrial frontier, and they, too, broke new ground.

The South

The Plantation Economy. Five characteristics distinguished the plantation economy: it was essentially a single-crop (cotton), cash-crop system; it employed labor for most of the year; the labor was done by slaves and, therefore, had to produce enough both to maintain the labor force and to provide a profit for owners; and it required cultivating as much land as possible to realize the maximum cash return. But it was not Southerners who controlled the marketing of cotton. Instead, the financial center of the Cotton Kingdom was New York City—the location of the banks, shipping, insurance, and brokerage companies involved in its distribution.

In the long run such an economy militated against the widespread accumulation of wealth. The plantation system wasted soil resources and tended to discourage small but necessary economies; large money returns encouraged great extravagance; the planter was normally a debtor because of his drive to expand his holdings; income tended to be concentrated in a tiny percentage of the population and therefore contributed to a general state of impoverishment; and finally, it made an adequate labor force unavailable to smaller planters and doomed them to permanent low status and general stagnation.

Slaveholding Society. Southern society was sharply pyramided. At the apex stood fewer than 2,500 planters who held 100 slaves or more. In an intermediary position was a group of about 45,000 planters with 20 slaves or more. In 1860 only one fourth of Southerners were members of slave-owning families. Even in the Deep South, where most plantations were located, 75 percent of the population were "poor whites" with no important stake in the plantation system.

Planters. Most of the owners of large plantations did not descend from colonial gentry but were self-made men. A large percentage were originally businessmen who used their capital to buy plantations. Plantation owners did not live a life of leisure. Certainly, they were assisted by their factors, agents who sold the crop and gave advances against future sales, and by their overseers—but owners had to keep a sharp watch over the market, slaves, and land.

If the large planters were hard workers more often than not, their families lived more genteelly. Social life revolved around hunting, card-playing, visiting, horse racing. Many of the men allotted some of their time to politics. Sons were expected to become lawyers or join the army, daughters to learn the appropriate social graces and skills—like speaking French and playing the piano—and wives to be the gracious lady of the house.

Southern women were placed on a pedestal and treated chivalrously by their men. Yet this outward appearance was somewhat misleading, as even being mistress of a large plantation was a demanding and complicated job. Nevertheless, the myth of southern women as helpless creatures needing the protection of gallant men subtly constricted the life of these women perhaps even more than that of their northern counterparts.

Relation between Planters and Slaves.
Most planters believed themselves to be kindly and paternal caretakers of "childlike" slaves. But how did they actually treat their slaves? In general, slaves received food, clothing, and shelter adequate to sustain life. But planters cared for their slaves mainly out of self-interest. Slaves were valuable property. If an owner wanted to remain prosperous, he had to treat his slaves well enough so that they could work hard and have many children. The reason children were so important was that, after 1808, slave importation was banned. If there was to be a next generation, then slaves would have to reproduce themselves.

Perhaps some planters did own several slaves—usually house servants—for whom they had some affection. Yet most field hands rarely encountered their master, who left the business of dealing with them to his overseer. To keep these slaves obedient, overseers commonly whipped those guilty of some real or imagined infraction and threatened to separate them

from family or friends by selling them away. In the presence of an abusive master or overseer—one who raped the women or tortured the men—slaves had no legal protection, as they were considered property.

Smaller Slaveholders. In contrast to the owners of large plantations, small slaveholders lived in simple houses and had harder lives. Because they possessed a small number of slaves, these owners had more intimate, but not necessarily easier, relations with them. If the master was bad, life for slaves could be terrible and terrifying. If the master was good, it might be better than on the large plantations.

Yeoman Farmers. Yeoman farmers came next on the social scale. Most were self-reliant and lived in the backcountry, rarely encountering slavery. They usually raised subsistence crops like corn, but most of their money came from raising livestock. Although they neither owned slaves, nor depended on them economically, most yeoman farmers supported the institution. They did so primarily out of fear and dislike for blacks. They feared that freed slaves would compete with them for jobs. Perhaps they also worried that their own status would be jeopardized by freed slaves.

Poor Whites. At the bottom of the white social and economic hierarchy were the utterly despised and depressed "sandhillers," "crackers," and "clayeaters" grubbing a bare subsistence from pine barrens and sandy coastal plains. They, too, despised the slaves, although their contact with them was minimal. Like the yeoman farmers they feared that their status and access to jobs would be diminished if they had to compete with freed slaves.

Thus, whether slave owner or not, nearly every white Southerner was psychologically bound to the slave system. From birth whites were taught to perceive the world as divided in two, white and black; the richest and the poorest white Southerners believed that every white was superior to and the ruler of every black. With this indoctrinated view, whites bound themselves to and then bled for a system that doomed most of them to near poverty, to severely limited economic opportunity, to unfair labor competition and a declining economy.

Slaves. Most slaves lived and worked on plantations as field hands. A minority secured favored service as domestics, while some herded cattle and others performed household labor (carpentry, masonry, smithing, shoemaking, spinning, and weaving).

Whenever they could, slaves demonstrated their desire for freedom and hatred of their enslavement. Their most strident form of resistance was open rebellion. Between 1800 and 1831 a number of slaves showed a willingness to risk their lives for freedom by joining in revolts. In 1822 Denmark Vesey, a former slave, planned a conspiracy to free the slave population and take over Charleston, South Carolina. When the plan became known, thirty-seven slaves were executed. Of actual revolts, the most disturbing to slave owners was that organized by Nat Turner in Virginia in 1831, in which fifty-seven whites died.

Less dramatic than the leaders of revolts but sometimes more effective in achieving freedom were the runaways who, if successful, served as a beacon for every slave left behind. Thousands of slaves sought freedom in this manner. Owners used bloodhounds to track them down. Most runaways were captured and were subjected to brutal beatings. Yet many escapees made it to swamps or other remote areas, where they hid, sometimes for years.

Engaging in less overt resistance, many blacks defended themselves against the trauma of slavery through a mixture of passive resistance (working slowly and inefficiently), sabotage (petty thievery, breaking tools), apparent accommodation, and subterfuge (faking illness or injury).

Slave Families. Although slaves were not permitted by law to marry, most lived in monogamous relationships. Slave families tended to be close, despite, or because of, the difficulties of their existence. Thousands of slaves after emancipation spent their lives searching for spouses or children from whom they had been forcibly separated. Kinship among slaves usually extended beyond the family to outsiders. Slaves who had been separated from their families and sent to a distant plantation were usually adopted by a new family. And in a very real sense, all the slaves on a plantation belonged to the same extended family, or community. The feeling of community was probably the major reason that slavery did not break the black spirit.

The Role of Black Religion. One powerful way slaves achieved a sense of community was through the practice of their religion. Although slaves who had been exposed to Christianity sometimes attended white churches or Sunday services on large plantations, they practiced their own form of religion, often secretly at night, outside of white scrutiny. At these gatherings, led by black preachers, slaves sang, shouted, and danced, mixing African religious beliefs and customs (such as chanting) with Christianity (preachers emphasized sin and damnation). In their sermons and songs they directly asserted their right to freedom. One popular theme was the arrival into the Promised land.

Besides offering them hope for release from bondage, communal religion provided slaves with a sense of inner worth in comparison with whites, who they believed were damned for their treatment of blacks. Moreover, this religion empowered slaves because they could create through it a world outside of white control. Thus, although black religion did not preach overt resistance to slavery, it encouraged internal resistance and resolve by increasing self-esteem and creating a sense of community.

Slave Culture.   The slaves also told each other stories, which allowed them to pass on their Afro-American folk tradition and to share the many sorrows and few joys of a life in bondage. These stories were often subtle expressions of resistance. Some described how a clever slave fooled the master. Others were allegories of the master-slave relationship. Thus, in the famous Bre'r Rabbit stories, the rabbit consistently outwits the bigger, stronger animal.

The Southern "Defense" of Slavery.
White Southerners preferred to argue slavery on its economic merits. It was, they proclaimed, an efficient system.

"King Cotton" remained the bulwark of American national and taxable wealth; the economy of the North itself depended on the production of cotton by slaves. Slavery, as practiced in the South, was, they argued, a thousand times more humane than northern "wage-slavery" under which workers labored long hours in factories under often miserable and hazardous conditions for pitiful wages.

But try as they might, Southerners could not long avoid the moral implications of the purchase and sale of other people. They cast about to prove the fundamental inequality of human beings; they brought in Biblical testimony to show that God sanctioned slavery; they argued that slaves were "child-people," held by their masters as wards. The slave system was paternalistic, and the master acted with complete humanity toward his "children"—gave them dignified employment, provided them with basic necessities, cared for them in illness, trained them in civilized decencies, and attended to their religious needs. Northerners might shout "democracy"; but no political system was exclusively right. Southerners also pointed to the glories of ancient Greece to justify the slave basis of their society.

The white Southerner saw himself as a moral aristocrat acting on a code of honor (derived from the medieval chivalric code) whose precepts were courage, generosity, noblesse oblige, and the glorification of women. What more noble purpose could slaves serve than to support this system with their labor?

The Economic Dilemma.   Despite the white South's defiant defense of their "peculiar institution," the plantation system was not doing well by the 1840s. Planters constantly faced the necessity of cutting costs to augment profits. The greatest single cost was the fixed, immobile investment in slaves; but there were other unvoidable costs such as freight, commissions, mortgage and interest payments, property maintenance, and acquisition of new land.

After 1840 these costs began to rise significantly. The discovery of gold in California precipitated a monetary inflation that increased land values; sharp competition for a limited number of slaves drove prices upward; prices also rose on manufactured goods. Why, then, didn't planters boost their own prices accordingly? They couldn't because the fluctuating world market determined the price of cotton.

The only alternative was a reduction in costs. The price of slaves could be reduced if Congress were persuaded to repeal the law preventing importation from abroad; the costs of manufactured goods could be lowered if Congress abolished tariffs; rent costs could be reduced if the government opened up cheap lands; commissions and interest costs could be lowered if a way could be found to break the stranglehold of northern bankers.

These were some of the needs that dictated the sectional demands of the antebellum South.

CHAPTER TEN

Religious, Intellectual, and Social Ferment

"Our farm is a sweet spot," Sophia Willard Dana Ripley wrote to a friend in the summer of 1840. Ripley confessed that even "my lonely hours have been bright ones, and in this tranquil retreat I have found that entire separation from worldly care and rest to the spirit which I knew was in waiting for me somewhere." Ripley was writing from Brook Farm, near Roxbury, Massachusetts. The desire to escape from an increasingly industrial American society began to be expressed during the second quarter of the nineteenth century in the emergence of a number of utopian communities such as Ripley's "sweet spot."

The age of Jackson and the years up to the Civil War gave rise to a wide variety of religious, social, and intellectual reform movements. These reformers were initially interested in individual reforms but gradually broadened their scope to include correcting the ills of the entire society.

The Second Great Awakening

Southern Revivalism. One of the major influences on the reform movement began earlier. The Second Great Awakening arose in the 1790s along the southern frontier. Fearful of a spread of "infidelity," or excessive worldliness and loss of faith, dissenting groups like the Methodists and Baptists organized camp meetings. So popular were these intensely emotional gatherings that they became for Southerners and Midwesterners an integral part of religious life. An essential feature of every meeting was the conversion of nonbelievers. For the most part, frontier revivalism concentrated on individual salvation, and it did not lead directly to a reawakening of social conscience.

Northern Revivalism. Reformist tendencies were more apparent in the North, where, alarmed at the spread of liberal religious attitudes inspired by the Enlightenment, Congregational and Presbyterian ministers preached a less stern form of evangelical Calvinism. Yale's Timothy Dwight and Lyman Beecher focused on God's "disinterested benevolence."

During the late 1820s a more radical form of revivalism began to be preached by Charles Grandison Finney in upstate New York. Finney told his listeners that, if redeemed, they could be as free from sin as God Himself. Finney also "worked up" his audiences by having all-night meetings, soliciting personal testimonies, and encouraging the singing of hymns. His methods worked remarkably well; after Finney preached in a town, the number of conversions increased dramatically.

The hysteria Finney produced in his audiences at first distressed Beecher and his followers. Their concerns diminished when they saw that his tactics did not simply produce momentary excitement but contributed to the development of active churches.

The Changing Family. Evangelism deeply affected family life. It encouraged men to respect a good Christian woman. The ideal wife was such a person and was believed to possess greater spirituality. Thus she was now permitted to exert greater influence over her husband and within the family itself. This influence was particularly important in child-rearing, which came to be viewed as preparation for a Christian life. For women this transfer of power meant that the most of their time and energy were devoted to domestic duties. If a middle-class wife and mother wanted (and had the time) to pursue any other activity, she was criticized. Woman's place was in the home on a pedestal. (Of course, other factors explained the new power of women. Since men increasingly worked outside of the home, they needed to delegate some of their domestic authority to their wives.)

Historians have called this new notion of women's role the "cult of domesticity," or the "cult of True Womanhood." The ideal wife—a creature of morality and virtue—made the home a wholesome environment, exercising her influence by loving nurturance of husband and children.

The evangelical emphasis on feelings also promoted another change in family life. The influence of parents on their children's choice of mates declined as young people more frequently married for love.

Revivalism and Reform. Revivalism in the North affected more than religion and the institution of the family. It also inspired a great upsurge of organizations involved with social reform. Converts organized themselves into voluntary associations to eradicate sin and purify society according to their interpretation of Christ's desire. Armed with evangelical zeal, most of the members of these organizations came from the middle class. Some of the associations they formed dealt with local issues, such as housing and care for orphans. The operation of others, such as the American Bible Society, which distributed Bibles in the West, were more far-flung. The activities of these associations sometimes led to crusades to eradicate sinful practices such as prostitution, gambling, and the drinking of alcoholic beverages.

The Temperance Crusade. The most successful evangelical reform movement was the temperance crusade. In the 1820s

Americans—even women and young people—consumed more alcohol than ever before, partly because of the availability of cheap whiskey. To persuade people to "sign the pledge" not to consume liquor, a group of clergymen founded the American Temperance Union in 1826. The society distributed pamphlets, sponsored essay contests, and sent out teachers to reveal to the multitudes the evils of alcohol.

A million people became members of the temperance movement. Throughout the 1830s the consumption of hard liquor vastly decreased. By the early 1840s the reformers had pressured many states to limit strictly licensing of, and impose high taxes on, alcoholic beverages.

From Reformation to Transformation

Utopia. During this period, many individuals driven by religious, spiritual, or humanistic ideals became full-time reformers. The most radical of these founded experimental communities to test their ideas on a small scale.

Some radicals regarded the whole reform movement as mere patchwork, covering a basically unworkable system. Social evil resulted from competition among individuals. The greatest evil lay in existing inequalities among Americans. If people would stop competing, these reformers argued, they could merge their private selves into the collectivity and create a utopia on earth.

It was obviously impossible to immediately transform American society into utopia. But what if a small band of initiates, of inspired men and women, found some corner they could withdraw to and built there a perfect community? Would not such a community become a magnet, attracting all people of good will, and eventually lead the way to a complete reorganization of society? Fueled by these kinds of visions and by either religious or humanistic sentiments, or both, a number of utopian seers established such model communities.

Mormonism. Many sects arose claiming a special road to salvation based upon a literal interpretation of the Bible. To prevent corruption by the traditional faiths, such groups began to withdraw from the community.

Of these sects, one of the most significant was the Mormons. Millennialism (the belief that the second advent was coming) and utopianism were important strands in the birth of the faith that became the Church of Jesus Christ of Latter Day Saints. A Vermont farm boy named Joseph Smith founded the religion during the Great Awakening of the 1820s. Smith claimed to have seen two personages who announced that they were the Savior and God the Father. Later, he was directed by a divining-stone to the discovery of a book made of golden tablets that contained the creed of a new faith. Smith translated this ancient text, *The Book of Mormon* (1830), and discovered that it described the history of Israelites who had emigrated from Jerusalem to America in biblical times. He established the Mormon Church to continue the beliefs and practices of these purer Christians.

Determined to create a new Zion in the West, Smith and a small band of followers founded a community in Ohio in 1831. But the Mormons' religious unorthodoxy caused hostility, and they were forced to move to Independence, Missouri. Again the community encountered resentment, persecution, and violence. In 1839 the governor of Missouri expelled them. They next settled at Nauvoo, Illinois, and within a few years the town grew to be the richest and most populous in the state. But once more local sentiment turned against the Mormons.

Tensions climaxed when the Mormons organized the Military Nauvoo Legion, and Smith announced his candidacy for the presidency of the United States. Believing rumors that the Mormons wanted to take over the Northwest, local authorities arrested him on a charge of treason. He and his brother were then murdered by an angry mob.

Under their new leader, Brigham Young, the sect moved into the far West and settled at what is now Salt Lake City. Here in the desert, like the Israelites departed from Egypt, members built shelters and used irrigation to plant their first crops. After years of incredible hardship, they saw the desert bloom, and the eleven thousand Mormons enjoyed prosperity when the area became incorporated into the Utah Territory in 1850.

Secular Communities. The factors that account for the rise of experiments in secular communism were equally numerous. The 1820s and 1830s witnessed the birth in Europe of theories of "utopian socialism." These theories were carried across the Atlantic by immigrants who came over after the devastation of the Napoleonic Wars and the revolutions of 1820, 1830, and 1848. Those that had the greatest impact on Americans were the theories of Robert Owen and Charles Fourier.

A British utopian socialist, Owen believed that the perfect society could be built if well-intentioned capitalists devoted their wealth to creating socialistic communities based on a balanced economy of farm and factory. In such communities wealth would be shared equally. After experimenting with benevolent capitalism in his cotton mills in New Lanark, Scotland, Owen came to America to try a more radical experiment. Along the Wabash River in Indiana, he built a "perfect community" called New Harmony. It consisted of model dwellings, surrounding vineyards, orchards, wheatfields, cotton and flour mills. Intellectuals, mechanics, and farmers shared tasks and profits. Discussions, concerts, and balls made up the social life of the community. Although New Harmony collapsed because of internal mismanagement and dissension brought about by Owen's advocacy of free love and "enlightened atheism," something of the pattern of capitalist paternalism remained as a residue in American economic thought.

The American followers of the French utopian socialist Charles Fourier were more successful in their worldly ventures. One reason for the lack of hostility they provoked among outsiders was that, unlike the Mormons and the Owenites at New Harmony, American Fouricrists conformed to contemporary religious and sexual practices. For example, in Brook Farm, the most famous Fourierist community, couples were monogamous.

Fourier proposed to transform society by means of anarchistic "phalanxes." A phalanx could be formed if any 1,620 people agreed to farm in common 5,000 acres of land and engage in the handicrafts necessary to maintain the community's existence. Each member in the phalanx was free to find his or her own vocation and in this way add to the community's wealth. Profits were not to be divided equally, as in New Harmony. Instead, individuals could keep whatever was left over after contributing to a common community fund.

Brook Farm. The most spectacular experiment in Fourierism was made at Brook Farm, originally established by "transcendentalists" (see p. 115 for a discussion of this philosophy) as a model community based on Unitarian and transcendental principles. In 1844 the founder of Brook Farm, George Ripley, converted to Fourierism and the community then became a phalanx. After a ruinous fire in 1847, the Brook Farm experiment ended.

At its height, Brook Farm served as a training school for transcendentalist and Fourierist missionaries. As such, it attracted some of the finest minds of its day: Ralph Waldo Emerson, Nathaniel Hawthorne, Margaret Fuller, Timothy Dwight, Horace Greeley, and Samuel Peabody, among others. Its greatest success was education. The Brook Farm School, based on the ideal of complete freedom between students and teachers who lived, worked, and studied together, gained national recognition.

Abolitionism. The South's rabid defense of slavery did not arise until the sections had become more distinct and until abolitionism was born in the North and West. Abolitionism was the work of a very small minority, but their agitation was enormously effective. The spiritual father of the nineteenth century movement was William Lloyd Garrison who, in 1831, founded the abolitionist journal *The Liberator*. Having seen the evils of slavery firsthand, Garrison hated the institution. He broke with his employer, Benjamin Lundy, on the issue of gradual versus immediate emancipation. Garrison condemned gradualism as timid, unjust, and immoral and called for the "immediate enfranchisement of our slave population." His call to arms was certainly not timid. In *The Liberator* he proclaimed: "I am aware that many object to the severity of my language; but is there not cause for severity? I will be harsh as truth and uncompromising as justice. On this subject I do not wish to think, or speak, or write with moderation. No! No! . . . I am in earnest—I will not equivocate—I will not excuse—I will not retreat a single inch—and I will be heard."

He was heard. In the West James G. Birney and Elijah Lovejoy began printing abolitionist journals. Birney was mobbed and Lovejoy killed. Virginia's Nat Turner was inspired to launch his insurrection. In 1833 the American Anti-Slavery Society was founded to spread the knowledge that "Slaveholding is a heinous crime in the sight of God, and that duty, safety and best interests of all concerned require its immediate abandonment without expatriation." Theodore Dwight Weld, head of the Society, preached across the land and converted many to the cause. He subsequently trained his followers in missionary work. Wendell Phillips, a well-born Bostonian, joined the movement after witnessing a near-lynching of Garrison by a Boston mob. Quakers led the organizing of an "Underground Railroad" to encourage runaways and to help them steal by night from the South to the North and then to Canada. Each year witnessed heavier traffic on the "road."

Finally, the abolitionists turned to political action. Lobbyists were successful in securing a congressional antislavery bloc that legislated at every favorable opportunity against the institution. In 1840 and 1844, they ran James G. Birney for president. Garrison was heard, indeed. His voice echoed throughout the nation and forced Americans to consult their consciences.

Black Abolitionists. Many free blacks became abolitionists. White abolitionists eagerly solicited them as speakers, especially those who were runaway slaves. One of these speakers, the runaway Frederick Douglass, was an extraordinary man. In 1845 he became famous in Europe and America with the publication of his autobiography, *Narrative of the Life of Frederick Douglass.* An eloquent speaker, he convinced many who heard or read him that the Southern argument that all blacks were inferior and resigned to slavery was a delusion.

The Accomplishments of the Abolitionists. The abolitionist movement failed to convert most Americans to the antislavery cause. In the South it inspired a counterattack, a more rigid defense of the institution. In other segments of society it produced intense hatred. In the North and West violence erupted against members. Working-class whites who feared economic and social competition from freed blacks made up one element of the opposition. Many of the mob participants were "gentlemen of property and standing" aroused, perhaps, by an intense anxiety that the social order would be overthrown.

The abolitionists did, however, succeed in making many other Americans more aware not only of the realities of slavery but also of its immorality.

Women's Rights. The women's rights movement grew out of abolitionism. Attracted to the antislavery cause, women joined the abolitionist movement. Yet when they tried to participate equally, they ran into a wall of male opposition. This experience radicalized a number of female abolitionists, who began to believe that, like blacks, women were entitled to emancipation. If slavery meant a caste system that assigned members to restricted social and economic roles, preventing their full development, then women were certainly slaves. The issue was joined when delegates to the World Anti-Slavery Convention held in London in 1840 refused to allow women to participate. Outraged by this rejection, Lucretia Mott and Elizabeth Cady Stanton organized a meeting at Seneca Falls, New York, in 1848. Delegates to the convention issued a "Declaration of Sentiments" condemning the treatment of women, demanding female suffrage and the right to control their own property, person, and children.

During the 1850s this first wave of feminists attracted more supporters, the most influential of whom was Susan B. Anthony. Nevertheless, throughout this period, feminists achieved little in the way of reform.

Literature's "Golden Day"

An American Literature. The ferment in American life was reflected in its literature. The mix of nationalism, sectionalism, democracy, and reform combined with the influence of the romantic movement produced a truly American literature. Enduring literary works were written by Ralph Waldo Emerson, Edgar Allan Poe, Henry David Thoreau, Nathaniel Hawthorne, Herman Melville, Oliver Wendell Holmes, Louisa May Alcott, and Walt Whitman; classic histories were written by George Bancroft, William Prescott, Francis Parkman, and John Lothrop Motley; a basic feminist text was written by Margaret Fuller; songs and ballads, many still sung today, originated among anonymous, ordinary people along the frontier and in the slave belts. Why one period in the history of a people will produce a sudden flowering of genius is an unresolved question, but between 1820 and 1860 American literature enjoyed a "Golden Day," expressing the spirit of the time.

Individualism. The doctrine of individualism was introduced into American thought by the spread of the Enlightenment. Individualism consisted of an unbounded faith in the goodness of human beings and in their ability to shape the good society; it was linked with the Enlightenment doctrine of the perfectibility of human beings. Individuals were encouraged to become self-reliant and to realize the universe within themselves. According to these views, nothing was sacred but the integrity of the individual's own mind. Larger-than-life heroes became symbolic of human potentiality. Poe's conquering Tamerlane, Melville's demonic Captain Ahab in pursuit of the huge white whale Moby Dick, the frontiersmen Mike Fink and Davy Crockett, are literary examples of the exaggerated individualism and expanded egotism that permeated the literature of the era.

Democracy. Individualism brought new democratic dignity to the common man, as shown politically in the ascendancy of Andrew Jackson. Farmers, lumbermen, shoemakers, village blacksmiths, tenement dwellers—in brief, the people—course through the works of Emerson, Thoreau, and Whitman. Whitman especially gave literary stature to the common man. He tried to create an epic for all Americans in *Leaves of Grass* (1855). These twelve poems, written in a language many readers found shockingly coarse, are virtual inventories of American types and American surroundings. Whitman's "barbaric yawps," his egoistic absorption of all humanity into himself, along with his efforts to enshrine spontaneity and sensuousness, his choice of ordinary subject matter, and his experiments in free verse—all combined to make a complete break with the aristocratic European past and to produce an American statement.

Sectionalism. Sectionalism, too, was a literary force during the Golden Day. Indeed, much of it reflected the "flowering of New England." John Greenleaf Whittier and Henry Wadsworth Longfellow recorded its local legends; James Russell Lowell, its dialect; Holmes, its Brahmin caste system; Melville, its whaling past; and Hawthorne, the divided soul of Puritanism. Southerners produced their own literary voices in Augustus Baldwin Longstreet, John Pendleton Kennedy, and William Gilmore Simms. Popular songs and folktales were western in theme, dialect, and essence.

Nationalism. Some writers, needing wider spaces, made the nation their theme. Historians took the lead. Bancroft saw God's hand in America's history; Prescott retraced the roots of America's colonization during the Spanish Period; Parkman chronicled the French and Indian wars and the northwest trek along the Oregon Trail; Motley read the march of American democracy into the struggles of the sixteenth-century Dutch against their Spanish overlords. And, in his 1837 address at Harvard, "The American Scholar," the philosopher Ralph Waldo Emerson announced the intellectual and literary independence of America.

Romanticism and Transcendentalism. There is probably no mid-nineteenth century writer who was untouched by the romantic movement, which sprung up in reaction to the Enlightenment's glorification of pure reason. Thus romantics valued emotion and intuition over thought, and the individual over society. Of the American writers, perhaps the most remarkable romantic was Edgar Allan Poe, whose wildly imaginative short stories and poems reveal a preoccupation with mystery and supernatural horror. Romanticism as a way of thought also deeply influenced the transcendental movement in America.

Transcendentalism was a religious and humanistic philosophy developed in New England that sought to transcend or pass beyond all usual methods—church, clergy, and Scriptures—of communicating with God. Transcendentalists attempted to establish direct and unmediated contact with God. They believed this was possible because God possessed a "universal mind" of which each individual was an incarnation. By inward reflection an individual could transcend the self and reach God. The means for this direct passage was intuition. All human beings, therefore, are spiritually equal and divine because they are part of nature. Intuitive knowledge transcends rational knowledge if restrictions on it are removed. These restrictions are the dead weight of the past as it is incorporated in science, tradition, history, conventional morality, and organized churches. Human beings must cast these restraints aside and discover new knowledge and invent new institutions better adapted to their present purposes. In their applications of this theory, transcendentalists substituted for natural science a nature-mysticism; they held individual conscience to be superior to conventional morality.

The major transcendentalist thinker was Emerson, who emphasized self-reliance. According to him, "The less government we have the better." Henry David Thoreau, Emerson's friend, also disliked the restrictions society placed on the individual. In 1845, to prove that a person does not have to depend on society, he built a cabin at Walden Pond in Massachusetts and lived there by himself—some have said in a utopian society of one—for two years. In 1854 he wrote *Walden*, an account of his life there and a stinging indictment of social conformity. *Walden* remains one of the great achievements of American literature.

Fantasia. Not everyone could escape the workaday world via transcendentalism. Writers like Poe escaped into carefully created realms of the grotesque, the terrifying, and supernatural; others, like Longfellow, into a sentimental past or, like Melville, to the South Seas. Some Southerners created a never-never land out of the old plantation South. The "heroic Indian" tradition founded by James Fenimore Cooper continued to flourish.

In sum, these writers, whatever their literary path, were artists, interested in word, form, and aesthetic effect. Hawthorne and Melville made the American novel into a great literary art form. Poe and Hawthorne developed the short story as we know it. Emerson taught all writers to love language. Thoreau created a great prose style. Poe and Lowell founded modern American literary criticism. Through these efforts and achievements American writers cut their umbilical cord to Europe. No one would ever again ask, "Who reads an American book?"

CHAPTER ELEVEN

Toward Southern Secession

In her diary entry for April 12, 1861, Mary Boykin Chesnut, the wife of the ex-senator from South Carolina, recorded the Southern attack on Fort Sumter. "At half past four, the heavy booming of a cannon. I sprang out of bed, and on my knees prostrate I prayed as I never before. . . . The regular roar of the cannon, there it was. And who could tell what each volley accomplished of death and destruction?" In the period preceding the attack against Fort Sumter, the nation struggled desperately to find a way out of the problems that would lead to the southern secession and ultimately to civil war.

Tyler's Triumph

The Tariff and the Bank. With Tyler's assumption of the presidency following Harrison's death (1841), the South in effect returned to power. Soft-spoken but stubborn, Tyler was no Whig; or rather, he was a Whig only in his opposition to Jackson. A more accurate description of Tyler would be a states'-rights Southerner. In his message to a special session of Congress, the new President stressed respect for states' rights, supported lowering the compromise tariff of 1832, and called for elimination of the hard-money subtreasury system. These positions put him in opposition to Clay, who considered himself the leader of the Whigs. Clay favored the tariff, more federally financed internal improvements, and distribution of the government's cash surplus from land sales to the states.

As one part of a comprehensive plan, he now asked Congress to set up a new Bank of the United States, but Tyler vetoed the Bank bill as unconstitutional. Overnight he became a hero to Southerners and Jacksonians. The Whigs, however, repudiated his leadership and those in the Cabinet resigned—except for Secretary of State Daniel Webster, who stayed on to try to settle the boundary dispute between Maine and New Brunswick. As a result of his efforts, the Senate ratified in 1842 the Webster Ashburton Treaty establishing a definite Northeast boundary between the United States and Canada.

Tyler replaced the departed Whigs with states' rightists and set up a "kitchen" cabinet of pro-slavery propagandists. When Congress then passed a new protective tariff and a distribution-of-the-surplus bill, Tyler vetoed them, too.

Expansion.   Having won over the issues of the Bank and the tariff, Southerners now pressed for the annexation of Texas. Texas was independent and, with Sam Houston as President, eager to enter the Union. To southern eyes, it was also in trouble: Mexico had renewed its threats, the economy was being buffeted by a paper inflation, and, even more disturbing, England was offering a defensive alliance with the republic if it agreed to remain independent and abolish slavery. Southerners felt they must have Texas at all costs. If the republic entered the Union, it could be divided into at least five states—a gain of ten "slave Senators" and a large number of "slave Representatives."

From his retirement Jackson also kept up continuous pressure for annexation. As a Southerner, Tyler made no secret of his desire to annex, but restrained himself until Webster—violently opposed to annexation—concluded the Ashburton Treaty and resigned.

After his new Secretary of State was accidentally killed, Tyler appointed Calhoun to the office. Despite Mexico's threat that annexation would mean war, and in the face of mounting antislavery propaganda caused partly by his association with the pro-slavery South, Calhoun drew up a treaty. In April 1844, it went to the Senate for ratification. Southerners supported their case for annexation by appeals to nationalism (the national domain would be increased), widespread hatred of En-gland, sectionalism, and pro-slavery sentiments. Their efforts failed because, with a national election coming up, northern and western senators joined to reject the treaty in June by a vote of thirty-five to sixteen.

The Referendum of 1844.   The Texas Question was one of the issues that dominated the political scene of 1844. Jackson's influence in the Democratic Convention was still strong. His original choice as the party's presidential candidate, Van Buren, had made the mistake of publishing a letter opposing Texas's annexation. Jackson and the Democrats promptly repudiated him and the party chose a "dark horse," James K. Polk of Tennessee.

The Democratic Party platform made its position on annexation clear: it called the "reannexation of Texas at the earliest practicable period" one of the "great American measures which this Convention recommends to the cordial support of the Democracy of the Union."

Meanwhile, the Whigs renominated Clay. The party platform ignored the Texas issue. In the election the balance was tipped to Polk by an antislavery group, the Liberty Party, with James Birney as its nominee. If Clay had won New York, he would have held a majority in the national electoral count. But the Liberty Party, which had strong support in the state, drew 15,800 votes from Clay, and he lost New York by 5,000 votes. Tyler interpreted Polk's victory as a popular mandate to proceed with annexation. Since there was still no two-thirds approval in the Senate, Polk recommended a parliamentary device to evade possible defeat. This device, known as a joint resolution, required a simple majority in both houses plus the president's signature. A few days before Tyler left office, Congress finally annexed Texas by joint resolution.

The resolution provided that Texas could be divided into four states, but only if she agreed. The new state would also retain her public lands but pay the debts incurred when she was a republic. Polk accepted this agreement, and Texas became a state at the end of 1845. The South was clearly victorious.

Northern Attitudes toward Slavery. Northern hostility to slavery intensified during Tyler's administration. Remaining Black Codes in northern states were repealed; abolitionists won control of some local offices and increased their influence in state governments; a number of northern states passed laws to hinder the return of fugitive slaves by according them full due process under the law.

Slavery and the Churches. The churches especially felt the escalating tension over slavery. The Presbyterian, Baptist, and Methodist churches were nationwide organizations. Because of northern antislavery pressure, they now split into sectional wings. Southern Methodists seceded to form the Southern Methodist Church. Presbyterians divided into the "Old School," with fourteen slaveholding synods, and the "New School," with twenty free synods. In 1843 the American Baptist Free Mission Society was founded. The society admitted no slaveholding members and abolished racial discrimination and segregation within the church. The national Baptist organization remained shakily intact, although badly hampered by the existence of two noncooperating groups. These schisms not only reflected the divisions in the hearts of the membership, they also deepened them.

Foreign Relations. England's abolition of slavery in the British West Indies (1833) further complicated Anglo-American relationships. Instituting a naval watch over efforts to reopen the African slave trade, the English began to search and seize vessels flying the American flag. To reduce the growing friction over this practice, the British government suggested a cooperative policy of search and seizure by the two countries of vessels from either country to identify those engaged in the slave trade. Secretary of State Webster was willing to cooperate if England agreed to formally surrender the practice of impressment. When she refused, each country continued to maintain independent squadrons searching for slave ships.

In 1841 the *"Creole* Affair" increased tensions between the two countries. The *Creole* was an American brig hauling a cargo of slaves from Virginia to New Orleans. En route, the slaves revolted, overpowered the ship's crew, and sailed the vessel to British-ruled Nassau, where they claimed asylum. The English set the white crew free, arrested the mutiny's leaders, and held the remaining slaves in custody as free men. The United States protested, but after much negotiation reluctantly accepted a monetary settlement for the lost slave property.

Polk's Progress

The Tariff and the Bank. The South had a reliable friend in the efficient, hardworking Polk. Southerners were heavily represented in his cabinet, with the posts of State, Treasury, Postmaster General, and Attorney General in their hands. Just as the South wished, Secretary of the Treasury Robert J. Walker persuaded Congress to lower the tariff of 1842 and to revive the Independent Treasury system established by Van Buren for handling federal funds. The Independent Treasury Act (1840) stipulated that federal funds be removed from state banks and placed in newly created government depositories.

Expansion: Oregon.   As the annexation of Texas preoccupied Tyler, so the annexation of Oregon was the first order of business for Polk. The English still made claims to that territory. During the national campaign of 1844 tensions between England and America over Oregon had escalated. Democrats rallied behind the campaign slogan "fifty-four forty or fight." Although in his inaugural address, Polk claimed the entire Oregon territory, privately he was willing to accept a boundary along the forty-ninth parallel to the Pacific Ocean.

In July 1845 Secretary of State James Buchanan relayed Polk's real intentions to the British ambassador in Washington. When the American offer was rejected, the angry Polk asked Congress to terminate the 1818 treaty providing for joint occupation. Congress complied in April 1846. Fearing the possibility of war and her inability to defend the Oregon country, Great Britain finally decided to compromise and accepted the forty-ninth parallel boundary. In return the English requested Vancouver and navigation rights on the Columbia River. Having achieved his goal, Polk willingly agreed, and the Senate passed the treaty (June 1846) by a large

majority, with one change, permitting England only temporary rights to navigate the Columbia. The ease of its passage reflected the general belief that the treaty was in the national interest.

The Mexican War.   The Oregon compromise meant that the United States didn't have to worry about war with Great Britain. This was a relief, since she was already at war with Mexico. In dispute was the southern boundary of Texas, which Mexico claimed was the Nueces River, farther to the north. The United States insisted that it was the Rio Grande, farther to the south. After the United States annexed Texas and claimed the disputed area, Mexico broke off diplomatic relations. In January 1846 Polk sent General Zachary Taylor with about 1,500 troops to occupy this region. In response, Mexico ordered 1,600 soldiers into the same area with orders to fight if necessary.

On April 24, 1846, the first blood was shed when the Mexicans attacked an American mounted patrol. Polk welcomed the news of the attack; it gave him the ideal pretext to go to war with Mexico. A brief and successful conflict would, he hoped, force Mexico to give up California and New Mexico to the United States. Responding to the President's request, Congress declared war on May 13 and authorized him to send 50,000 more soldiers against the Mexicans.

In less than a year Mexico was decisively beaten. Pushing down from Texas, Taylor won battles first at Monterey and then at Buena Vista. The land north of Mexico City was opened wide. For political reasons, however, Taylor was kept idle at Buena Vista. A westerly thrust by a cavalry squadron led by Colonel Stephen

Watts Kearny subdued New Mexico and then linked up with the forces of Captain John C. Frémont, which had moved into action two weeks before the war to create an independent California. Their combined forces destroyed the Mexican garrison near Los Angeles. Finally, General Winfield Scott sailed to Vera Cruz to strike from the south. After eighteen days the city surrendered. Next, in the most significant battle of the war, Scott outflanked the Mexicans at Cerro Gordo and annexed the road to Mexico City. By August the Americans were outside the Mexican capital. On September 14 Scott captured the city.

Peace. On February 2, 1848, Mexico signed the Treaty of Guadalupe Hidalgo, ceding New Mexico and California to the United States. She also accepted the Rio Grande as the southern boundary of Texas. In return the United States paid Mexico $15,000,000 and assumed the claims of American citizens against Mexico totaling $3,250,000. Although Polk felt his negotiator, Nicholas P. Trist, had given away too much, he submitted the treaty to the Senate. The President knew that the war had become increasingly unpopular and that he must end it.

Who opposed it? Congressman Abraham Lincoln launched a stinging attack on Polk and the war; the abolitionist press called it a "war for slavery"; a majority of the Whig party openly sympathized with the Mexicans; and some leading writers and intellectuals—among them Thoreau, Whitman, Lowell—openly voiced their dismay. Responding to these pressures, the Senate approved the treaty on March 10 by a vote of thirty-eight to fourteen.

The Wilmot Proviso. The northern reaction failed to dampen southern joy, but Congressman David Wilmot of Pennsylvania did. On August 8, 1846, he offered an amendment to a military appropriations bill proposing that "neither slavery nor involuntary servitude (should) ever exist in any part of the territory acquired from Mexico." This amendment, now called the Wilmot Proviso, became a storm center. It passed the House but was defeated in the Senate by a combination of Southerners and loyal Democrats.

Two compromises were then proposed to settle the territorial problem. The first extended the Missouri Compromise line to the Pacific. Although this plan was backed by President Polk, it was unacceptable to Northerners, because the major portion of the Mexican cession was to the south of this line and would therefore become slave territory. The second possibility left the decision regarding slavery in new territories to local legislatures. This approach, pushed by Senator Lewis Cass of Michigan, became known as "popular sovereignty" or "squatter sovereignty." The advantage of this second possibility was that it got Congress off the hook; the settlers themselves would have to choose. By the time of the election of 1848, the future of slavery in the Mexican cession was still unresolved.

The Election of 1848. Both parties carefully selected candidates who would not drive the extremes even further apart. The Democrats chose Lewis Cass, "a northern man with southern principles," and the Whigs nominated "Old Rough and Ready," Zachary Taylor, better known for his military than political abilities.

Despite Cass's identification with popular sovereignty, the Democratic Party platform was completely noncommittal on the future of slavery in the Mexican cession, while the Whigs did not even present a party platform. Vigorous antislavery men, members of the Van Buren wing of the Democratic Party and of the antislavery Liberty Party, organized the Free Soil Party. The new party nominated Van Buren under the slogan "Free soil, free speech, free labor, free men."

Taylor defeated Cass by 36 electoral votes, while the South retained control of the Senate. But in the House, the Free Soilers, with only 13 representatives, held the balance of power between the Democrats, with 112 votes, and the Whigs, with 105. The emergence of the Free Soilers suggested the potential strength of a sectional party based on the slavery issue.

Taylor, Fillmore, and the Last of the Whigs

The Dispute Over California. Slavery was the dominant issue when Congress returned to debate the Mexican cession. Outside events that occurred while the election campaign of 1848 was being fought made compromise even less likely.

California had, by virtue of the gold rush, quickly become eligible for statehood. The region's population growth was so rapid that Congress had not even organized it as a territory. Realizing that California needed a government, President Taylor proposed that Congress immediately admit it into the Union and let the Californians themselves decide what they wanted to do about slavery. He suggested that the rest of the Mexican cession be admitted as a separate state.

Enthusiastic about Polk's proposal, California applied for admission to the Union as a free state. Southerners reacted to Taylor's initiative with dismay. They had assumed that, as a plantation owner himself, Taylor would favor new states entering as slave states. Fearful that both California and New Mexico would choose to be free, Southerners turned their wrath against Taylor and talked secession. The situation was grave. If all the new lands became free, Southerners reasoned, the institution of slavery might be threatened in the South itself.

Clay's Proposals. Aware that the issue might destroy the Union, Clay offered a compromise plan. On January 29, 1850, he introduced a series of resolutions proposing that California be admitted as a free state and that Utah and New Mexico be organized as territories with no reference to slavery. He proposed further that Texas surrender her claim to New Mexico and disputed land along its border. In return the federal government would assume $10,000,000 of Texas's pre-annexation debts. Further, the slave trade was to be abolished in the District of Columbia. Finally, Clay proposed that Congress enact a more effective Fugitive Slave Law.

These proposals sparked a great debate in the Senate. One obstacle was the President, who steadfastly opposed them and stubbornly stuck to his own plan of bringing California and New Mexico directly into the Union. Taylor's death on July 9 broke the impasse, as his successor, Millard Fillmore, favored the compromise. The decision to divide the omnibus bill into parts, each to be voted on separately, also moved the compromise forward.

The Compromise of 1850. The bitterness of extremists on both sides only momentarily overshadowed the fact that more moderate men were not yet ready for a test of secession. In the end compromise prevailed. Congress adopted the Clay proposals with little modification. California entered free. The rest of the Mexican cession was to be divided into the territories of Utah and New Mexico, which were to be admitted to the Union when they qualified, each having decided after popular sovereignty whether to be a free or a slave state. Texas surrendered to New Mexico her claims to the disputed land and was indemnified. The slave trade was abolished in the District of Columbia, and the Fugitive Slave Act of 1793 was amended to provide for federal commissioners to enforce the law. Runaway slaves could now be seized without a warrant, interference with such seizure was a criminal offense, the evidence of slaves was inadmissible in court, and they were to be returned to the South without jury trial.

The Reaction to the Compromise. The compromise passed because its proposals were broad and conciliatory enough to win the support of northern and southern moderates in Congress. Afterward there were doubts whether the compromise was feasible. Moderates outside Congress, however, recognized that the nation had gained some measure of peace. The question was whether it was permanent or temporary.

Uncle Tom's Cabin. Northern antislavery extremists focused their anger on Dan-

iel Webster. His support of the compromise made him a pariah. He was the "Benedict Arnold," the "Fallen Star," the "Judas." Some northern states engaged in a form of nullification by enacting new personal liberty laws that encouraged citizens to interfere with the arrest of fugitive slaves. Antislavery newspaper circulation boomed, and in 1851 one paper, the *National Era*, published the first installment of Harriet Beecher Stowe's *Uncle Tom's Cabin* (which appeared in book form in 1852). The novel, by a woman who was not even an abolitionist, was written as a protest against the Fugitive Slave Act. Mrs. Stowe's black prototypes were noble, pious, even majestic, and they suffered terrible fates at the hands of the brutal Simon Legree, a symbol of southern cruelty. The gripping story of Uncle Tom, Little Eva, Cassy, and Topsy shocked readers and left a deposit of hatred toward the institution of slavery that had a deep and lasting effect. Not since Tom Paine's *Common Sense* had there been such a bestseller; three hundred thousand copies were sold in 1852 alone. Perhaps as much as any single factor, *Uncle Tom's Cabin* disposed the North to espouse abolition.

Foreign Relations. By 1846 both Southerners and Northerners regarded the Pacific Coast as a potential trading area. The domestic market was large and everything pointed to the likelihood that an active Far Eastern trade would soon center there. Considerable discussion arose concerning the possibility of an Isthmian canal to shorten the east-west route. President Polk succeeded in securing from New Grenada the rights to such a canal, and a group of American financiers undertook construction of an Isthmian railroad. England was also interested in such a project and moved to take over the Nicaraguan route. This resulted in the "Polk Doctrine," the first in a number of extensions of the Monroe Doctrine. In it, Polk notified England that the Monroe Doctrine prevented the extension of foreign influence into the Western Hemisphere, even at the invitation of a native country.

Tension between England and the United States escalated to the point where there was talk of war. To settle the matter, President Taylor encouraged the negotiation of the Clayton-Bulwer Treaty (1850). Both nations agreed that neither would obtain or exercise exclusive control over an interoceanic canal. The approving Senate vote, 42–10, indicated that both North and South favored expansion, although their reasons differed.

The Election of 1852. The disruption caused by the Compromise of 1850 showed clearly in the nominating conventions of 1852: the split between northern and southern Whigs was now complete. It took fifty-three ballots to nominate General Winfield Scott for the presidency. Similar confusion reigned at the Democratic convention. A complete deadlock continued for thirty-five ballots and was broken only by the nomination of a "dark horse," Franklin Pierce of New Hampshire, whose only qualification appeared to be his extreme opposition to abolitionism.

During the campaign Scott allied himself with the antislavery wing of his party. His betrayal cost him the Deep South, and Pierce also outdistanced him in the free states. Scott's defeat may have revealed the weakness of the Whig party, but even the victorious Democrats had reason

for concern. The voters had been apathetic, and the slavery question remained unsettled.

Pierce's Pro-Southern Politics

Expansion. Although Pierce surrounded himself with men from every faction, some of his closest advisers were Southerners like Jefferson Davis, Caleb Cushing, James Buchanan, and James Gadsden. Supporting aggressive expansion in the interests of cotton and slavery, they encouraged expeditions designed to overthrow existing governments in Mexico, Nicaragua, and Cuba. They also forced through the Gadsden Purchase (1853) from Mexico of thirty thousand square miles to make room for a southern railroad from Santa Fe to the coast.

The Ostend Manifesto. In 1854 Pierce instructed his minister to Spain, Pierre Soulé, to offer that country $130 million for Cuba. Soulé was first sent to Ostend, Belgium, to confer with the ministers to France and England. The three ambassadors issued a confidential dispatch, the Ostend Manifesto, suggesting that if Spain refused to sell, the United States should seize Cuba. When word of the existence of the Ostend Manifesto leaked out, the administration had to release its contents. Seeing a "slaveholder's plot," Northerners opposed the plan so vehemently that the administration dropped any ideas of obtaining Cuba.

Nebraska and Slavery. By 1854 Americans who favored compromise on the slavery issue had cause for self-congratulation.

There was political peace in the land. Every inch of American soil was covered by some measure regulating the practice of slavery. In some areas the Northwest Ordinance applied; in others, the Missouri Compromise line; and in still others, popular sovereignty. But slavery was too broad and deep an issue to be easily resolved; it affected elements of American life that seemed at first glance to be entirely separate from it—such as railroads.

The Louisiana Territory contained a large area of unorganized land west of Missouri and Iowa, which, according to the Missouri Compromise, was to be nonslave territory. Settlers in this area pressed Congress for territorial organization. A group of railroad promoters simultaneously demanded federal assistance for a transcontinental branch to extend from Nebraska southward and westward to the coast. Their demand placed Southerners in a dilemma: they needed the railroad, but its construction meant the rapid population of Nebraska, which would hasten the territory's entry into the Union as a free state.

The Kansas-Nebraska Act. A way out of the dilemma was offered by Senator Stephen A. Douglas in 1854. He introduced a bill to organize the land west of Missouri and Ohio into two territories, Nebraska and Kansas. To win southern support, he also proposed that the Missouri Compromise line that excluded slavery north of latitude 36°30′ be repealed and that the issue of slavery be settled by popular sovereignty in the territory covered by the compromise.

The South, of course, strongly supported the measure—under the Missouri Compromise it was impossible that new territories would become slave states. The North responded with fury to Douglas's concession to the South. Not only did the proposed bill contain no concession to the North, it applied popular sovereignty to a region that was free soil. Even moderate Northerners were appalled and became radicalized.

The furor had little demonstrable effect in the legislature and, backed by the South and the President, the bill passed. Whatever Douglas's motives may have been for proposing the Kansas-Nebraska Act, there is no doubt that the measure helped bring the slavery conflict to a climax.

The "Know-Nothings." The Kansas-Nebraska Act changed the political complexion of the country. The Whig party collapsed, while the Democrats lost many supporters in the North. A new party, the American, or "Know-Nothing" party, emerged, attracting some of the dissidents. The "Know-Nothings" (in response to questions about their organization, members replied, "I don't know") appealed to voters' nativist sentiments by idealizing "native" Protestants while denigrating Catholics and new immigrants. Thus, the party attracted not only ex-Democrats and Whigs but native-born workers afraid of competition from immigrants, mainly Irish, who had flooded the country after 1845. The party program included proposals to exclude Catholics from public office, raise naturalization requirements to twenty-one years, and require members to swear to vote only for American-born Protestants. For a brief period the new party's ideas caught on. In 1854 and 1855 members won control of a number of state legislatures. Then, in 1856, the party suddenly collapsed. Probably the lack of experienced leaders and organization contributed to its rapid demise.

The Republican Party. In 1854 another new party was born. It sprang from a meeting in Ripon, Wisconsin, of a group of citizens, mostly Free Soilers, Conscience Whigs, and "Anti-Nebraska" Democrats gathered to protest the pending Kansas-Nebraska Bill. They drew up resolutions protesting the opening of the Louisiana Territory to slavery and called for a new party dedicated to the Wilmot Proviso; that is, to no further extension of slavery into the territories. Five months later in another meeting at Jackson, Michigan, participants created a formal party organization to advocate repeal of the Kansas-Nebraska Act and the Fugitive Slave Law and the abolition of slavery in the District of Columbia. They next issued a call to all states for conventions to adopt this program. The response was overwhelming. The Wisconsin and Vermont conventions popularized the name "Republican Party," and it stuck. By 1856 the new party had firmly established itself in all the free states and was preparing to run a presidential candidate.

The Republican Party appealed to people primarily because of its opposition to slavery in the territories. This region, Republicans argued, was a land of opportunity, but only if slaves were kept out. Otherwise, the rights of free white laborers would be denied; that is, if permitted to enter, slaves would be unfair competition. The Republican Party's appeal was potentially broad. Both voters who opposed slavery and voters who wanted to keep their states white could easily embrace the new party.

John Brown and "Bleeding Kansas." In newly organized Kansas the slavery issue moved from ballots to bullets. Since squatter sovereignty meant that the majority decided whether a state was slave or free, Northerners organized an Emigrant Aid Society to send settlers into the territory to join with neighboring free farmers to build a large antislave vote. Only a few New Englanders actually left for Kansas, but they caused Southerners to organize "border ruffians" from Missouri primed to pour into the territory on election days to establish a pro-slave majority in the territorial legislature. (After these elections, they returned home.) When the ballots were stuffed in this manner, antislave settlers refused to recognize the newly elected legislature and set up their own in Topeka. The ultimate result in Kansas was that two governments and two constitutions were submitted to Congress. Then violence broke out between the two regimes.

In May pro-slavery settlers attacked the free-state town of Lawrence. In retaliation the implacable abolitionist John Brown and six followers murdered five pro-slavery settlers at Pottawatomic Creek. In the next months, free-staters and pro-slavery men fought each other in a kind of guerrilla war. By the end of 1856, the violence had caused the deaths of two hundred people in Kansas. The northern press heightened tensions through exaggerated accounts of "Bleeding Kansas." These reports were accurate in one respect—the Pierce administration's partisanship. Instead of condemning the illegal elections in Kansas, the government looked the other way.

Violence even spread to the United States Senate. Senator Charles Sumner of Massachusetts made a fierce speech on "the crime against Kansas." The speech contained a personal attack on his colleague, Andrew P. Butler of South Carolina. Two days afterwards on the floor of the Senate, Butler's nephew Preston S. Brooks beat Sumner unconscious with a cane. Northerners saw Sumner as a hero, while Southerners applauded Brooks, re-electing him to the office he had resigned after the House censured him for his action.

The Election of 1856. For the election of 1856, the Republican party nominated one of the heroes of the Mexican War, John C. Frémont. (Abraham Lincoln was passed over for the vice presidency.) The Republicans, who were primarily from the northern states, advocated restricting slavery to areas where it already existed. The party platform demanded immediate admission of Kansas under the Topeka constitution, condemned the Ostend Manifesto, and advocated federal aid to transcontinental railroads. The Democrats wisely chose James Buchanan, who had the virtue of having been, as minister to England, remote from the tense national scene. The Democratic platform denounced sectional groupings and called for frugality, low tariffs, and states' rights. A remnant of the Know-Nothing Party nominated ex-President Millard Fillmore.

Buchanan received 174 electoral votes to Frémont's 114. But he won only a minority in the popular vote, with just 500,000 votes more than Frémont. The possibility that a future Republican candidate could win loomed on the horizon.

Buchanan: The Breakup of the Democrats

Dred Scott. On March 6, 1857, two days after Buchanan's inauguration, the Supreme Court handed down a decision in the case of Dred Scott that divided North and South even further. An earlier decision had already caused northern hostility to the Supreme Court to mount, as the Court threw its great weight behind the enforcement of the new Fugitive Slave Law. Republicans charged that the justices were deserting the judicial chambers for the political arena.

Dred Scott had been a slave belonging to Dr. John Emerson, an army surgeon, who took him into the territory of Wisconsin and later to Missouri. After Emerson's death, Scott sued Emerson's widow for his freedom, contending that his residence in a free territory (Wisconsin) and a free state (Missouri) made him a free man. Following years in the lower courts, the case *Dred Scott v. Sanford* finally reached the Supreme Court. By a decision of six to three, the Court, headed by Chief Justice Roger B. Taney, ruled that Scott could not sue in federal courts because slaves were not citizens (1857). Moreover, Scott's residence in Wisconsin territory did not make him free because the Missouri Compromise was unconstitutional. The judges based their decision on the Fifth Amendment. According to it, the federal government can not deprive any individual of life, liberty, or property without due process of the law. Thus, the Court stated, "an Act of Congress which deprives a person . . . of his liberty or property merely because he came himself or brought his property into a particular Territory . . .

could hardly be dignified with the name of due process of law."

Besides declaring the Missouri Compromise illegal, the decision implied that popular sovereignty was also illegal. If Congress could not prohibit slavery in a territory, how could the territorial legislatures do it?

The North viewed the Court's decision as part of the pro-slavery conspiracy. Five of the six judges who voted in the majority were Southerners. Northerners also suspected that the President had caved in to southern pressure and encouraged the justices in their verdict. The decision rendered the Republicans' entire program unconstitutional, yet it also garnered more support for the party. The previously unconvinced came to believe that the Republicans were right in claiming that the South was engaged in an aggressive attempt to use the Constitution to extend slavery.

The Lecompton Constitution. While the Supreme Court was deciding the Dred Scott case, a constitutional convention was being convened at Lecompton, Kansas. Because Free Soilers outnumbered them, the pro-slavery faction wanted to set up a fraudulent election for convention delegates. On learning of this plan, the Free Soilers vowed not to participate in the election. When the "convention" then proceeded to draw up a pro-slavery constitution and subsequently refused to permit all settlers to vote on it, the governor of the territory criticized the constitution and reported the situation to the President.

Buchanan responded by requesting that Congress admit Kansas as a slave state. His action brought him into direct opposi-

tion with Senator Stephen A. Douglas, the originator of the idea of popular sovereignty. Their confrontation split the Democratic party in two. Douglas, who hoped to be nominated for President, now was considered to be a traitor by southern Democrats. On the other side, the Lecompton controversy strengthened the Republicans' belief that the Democratic Party was the party of the South.

Lincoln Emerges. Before he tried for the presidency, Douglas needed to win reelection to the Senate from Illinois in 1858. Seeking a strong candidate to go against Douglas, the Republicans chose the moderate Abraham Lincoln. In his speech accepting the candidacy, Lincoln attracted national attention with such statements as, "A house divided against itself cannot stand. I believe this government cannot endure permanently half *slave* and half *free*. I do not expect the Union to be dissolved—I do not expect the house to fall—but I do expect it to cease to be divided. It will become all one thing or all the other."

The Lincoln-Douglas Debates. Douglas attacked Lincoln as an abolitionist and warmonger. He himself, Douglas said, stood for popular sovereignty and the rule of the white man, since the black is inferior. Lincoln then challenged him to a series of public debates, and Douglas accepted. Thousands flocked to these confrontations, which were widely reported in the press. Douglas's strategy remained the same: to cast Lincoln as an abolitionist. Lincoln denied the charge, although he opposed the extension of slavery. Lincoln tried to paint Douglas as a pro-slavery defender of the Dred Scott decision. In Freeport, Illinois, Lincoln laid a trap for his opponent, asking him to choose between the Dred Scott decision and his doctrine of popular sovereignty. Douglas responded with his "Freeport Doctrine." He accepted the Dred Scott decision but added that if a territory did not want slavery, it could exclude it by failing to pass the local police ordinances needed to support the institution. This answer satisfied Illinois, and Douglas beat Lincoln; but it did not satisfy Southerners. How could they back a man who suggested a way to get around the Dred Scott decision? In the long run the debates helped Lincoln more than his opponent. The challenger not only proved himself Douglas's equal in argument, he became nationally known and respected.

"John Brown's Body Lies . . ."   In July 1859, five miles from the arsenal at Harpers Ferry, Virginia, a small band of men led by the abolitionist John Brown gathered, posing as farmers and cattlemen. Their aim was to capture the federal arsenal and launch a military maneuver to arm and free all the slaves in the surrounding area. In October the group began their attack and seized the arsenal. A marine detachment dispatched from Washington captured Brown and killed or wounded ten of his men. On December 2, 1859, Brown was hanged.

Although Republican politicians denounced the raid, a wave of admiration and pity for Brown swept the North. Emerson hailed him as the "New Saint." To Southerners, the northern sympathy showed that the section was entirely abolitionist. The incident marked the further deterioration of North-South relations.

The Election of 1860.   In anticipation of the election of 1860, the Democrats met at Charleston, South Carolina. Douglas commanded the solid support of the conservative (majority) wing, which sought some compromise on the slavery issue. He managed to get the convention to endorse popular sovereignty in its platform; but in the process, the Southern delegates walked out. The split in the Democratic Party was complete. Two Democratic candidates were nominated—Douglas, chosen by the northern wing, and John Breckenridge of Kentucky, by the southern.

With no internal dissent, the Republicans selected Abraham Lincoln primarily because of his moderate views on slavery. A fourth group, made up of Whigs and Know-Nothings and known as the Constitutional Union Party, selected John Bell of Tennessee as their candidate.

What were the choices confronting the American electorate in this momentous election? Southern Democrats declared that they stood for the right of all people to bring their property into the territories, the responsibility of the federal government to protect such property, the admission of slave states into the Union, the acquisition of Cuba, the enforcement of the Fugitive Slave Law, and the construction of transcontinental railroads.

The northern Democrats adopted basically the same platform but avoided the slavery issue, merely stating support for the decisions of the Supreme Court.

The Constitutional Union Party stood for generalities: union and the Constitution.

The Republican platform was more comprehensive and was targeted to broaden the party's appeal. It called for a high tariff (favored by manufacturers), free land for settlers (favored by farmers), and federal appropriations for internal improvements and support for a transcontinental railroad (favored by every section). The platform came out clearly against extension of slavery into the territories.

Since the North and the West held the majority of the electoral vote, the race of four really narrowed to two: Lincoln and Douglas. Although Lincoln got only 40 percent of the popular vote, he received a clear majority in the electoral college, mainly because he swept the North and the West. Even if his opponents had been unified behind a single candidate, Lincoln would have become president.

Secession.   After the election, events began to move with a terrible momentum. In December 1860 South Carolina, by previous agreement with other Southern states, seceded by unanimous vote. By February 1, 1861, six other states—Mississippi, Florida, Alabama, Georgia, Louisiana, and Texas—had followed suit. Buchanan evaded the crisis by proclaiming himself helpless. In contrast, President-elect Lincoln thought the South was bluffing and that if he refused to make concessions, moderates in that region would support him.

A congressional effort to save the situation put forward by Senator John Crittenden from Kentucky, the Crittenden Compromise, failed to be adopted. On February 4, 1861, the Confederacy was established. Its constitution duplicated that of the United States except for provisions guaranteeing states' rights and slavery. (To win French and British support for the Confederate cause, a provision prohibited the importation of slaves.) The Confederacy chose Jefferson Davis as its provisional President.

Fort Sumter.   The Confederacy began to seize federal property within its boundaries. Buchanan made a feeble effort to supply one of them—Fort Sumter, on an island in Charleston Harbor—with supplies and reinforcements, but when Southern shore batteries repulsed the United States vessel *The Star of the West*, he offered no resistance. On February 11 Abraham Lincoln began his journey from Springfield to Washington. He arrived in Washington twelve days later and on March 4 was inaugurated.

Lincoln decided to send a provision ship to supply the garrison at Fort Sumter with food and notified South Carolina of his intention. In response, on April 11, South Carolina demanded its immediate surrender. Major Robert Anderson refused, and on April 12, at 4:30 A.M., Confederate General Pierre G. T. Beauregard opened fire on Fort Sumter before the arrival of the supply ships. After thirty-six hours Major Anderson surrendered. The Civil War had begun.

CHAPTER TWELVE

Consolidation of the Union

In the Battle of Shiloh, a young Confederate soldier saw firsthand the devastation of war.

> I felt curious as to who the fallen Greys were, and moved to one stretched straight out. . . . Close by him was a young Lieutenant, who, judging by the new gloss on his uniform, must have been some father's darling. A clean bullet hole through the centre of his forehead had instantly ended his career. . . . It was the first Field of Glory I had seen in my May of life, and the first time that Glory sickened me with its repulsive aspect, and made me suspect it was all a glittering lie.

Like all wars, the Civil War was fought by young men; at its end over six hundred thousand lay dead, and the Confederacy was in ruins. Yet out of this destruction, a new South was to emerge, as the wounds of war began gradually to heal.

The Civil War Itself

Lineup. The Confederacy could not expect to win the war; it could only hope not to lose. To defeat the North, the South needed to overwhelm a region with 23 million people, when it had a population of only about 9 million, of which 3.5 million were slaves. The North also had about six times as much manufacturing capacity, and a far more extensive railroad system. Most of the federal arsenals lay in Union territory. The merchant marine and the navy were also under northern control, making possible a blockade of the southern states. Moreover, the Confederacy was composed of only eleven of the slave states. The border slave states of Kentucky, Missouri, Delaware, and Maryland stayed in the Union.

Despite these material disadvantages, the South might possibly not lose if it could effect a prolonged military stalemate or stave off decisive defeat. The Union forces faced a more difficult task: they had to invade and conquer the South. If it entered Confederate territory, the North would have a serious supply problem, face unfamiliar terrain and an unfriendly civilian population, and be less able to choose the time and place of combat.

The South was well equipped for its limited military objective. Confederate troops could fight defensively along interior lines of communication and on familiar terrain, enabling them to retreat with deadly advantage. Such a strategy would require brilliant tactics, but the Confederacy was proud of its military traditions. A large number of high-ranking U.S. Army officers were southern and had quit their posts to join the cause. Southerners thus assumed that rebel armies would have the advantage of being better led. Moreover, their ranks would be composed of young men who were more experienced than northern troops in riding and shooting. The Confederacy also believed that England and France would be sympathetic to its cause. They would, Southerners dubiously reasoned, support a people who were defending their homes and families.

The Eastern Front.   The early eastern campaign showed how accurate Southern estimates were. The northern press exhorted the army "On to Richmond," the capital of the Confederacy. General Winfield Scott reluctantly took up the challenge and sent an untrained army under General Irvin McDowell to take that city. The southern army under Beauregard, Joseph E. Johnston, and Thomas "Stonewall" Jackson assumed defensive positions and smashed the northern assault at Bull Run Creek (July 1861), turning it into a rout. Fortunately for the Union, the Confederates seemed unable to take advantage of their victory. The humiliating defeat at Bull Run nevertheless caused a shakeup in the northern command.

Lincoln made General George Brinton McClellan the commander of all Union forces. His first job was to whip an assault army into shape, which he did admirably, for he was meticulous, disciplined, and thorough. Moving slowly he brought his troops to within twenty-five miles of Richmond in what has been called the Peninsular Campaign. But his deliberation cost him, as the Confederates attacked part of his force at Seven Pines (May 1862). Although the outcome of this battle was indecisive, the Confederate commander, Johnston, was badly wounded, and General Robert E. Lee replaced him. Thus, the South now possessed a superb commander, while the North had to wait to find leadership equal in quality.

Earlier, to relieve the pressure on Richmond, Stonewall Jackson had been sent to the Shenandoah Valley. But after Seven Pines, Lee ordered Jackson to head his troops secretly back to Richmond to hit the right flank of the army of the Potomac. Jackson's troops gave Lee a numerical advantage and he made a surprise attack on June 24. The battle for Richmond lasted seven days (June 25–July 1, 1862), ending with McClellan's retreat. The North had lost 15,800 men and the South almost 20,000. Exasperated with McClellan and his indecisiveness, which had probably cost the battle, Lincoln replaced him with General Henry W. Halleck.

Halleck ordered McClellan to move his army to the Potomac, and join it between Washington and Richmond with a new army led by General John Pope. Lee marched swiftly against Pope's troops near Bull Run (August 1862), forcing them to retreat to Washington. The distressed Lincoln stripped Pope of his command, replacing him with McClellan.

Lee next began a sensational offensive northward through Maryland. McClellan followed the Confederates laterally and caught up with them at Antietam. Here one of the bloodiest battles of the war to date (September 1862) occurred—in one day twenty-two thousand were killed or wounded. Although the two sides fought to a draw, Lee was in a dangerous position and crossed the Potomac into Virginia. Instead of following for the kill, McClellan paused to lick his own wounds.

Once again Lincoln removed him from his command. Soon after, McClellan's successor, General Ambrose Burnside, was ignominiously defeated at the Battle of Fredericksburg (December 1862). Shortly afterward Lincoln replaced him with General Joseph Hooker, whose army of 125,000 was then routed by a Confederate army half its size led by Lee at Chancellorsville (May 1863) near Fredericksburg.

The Confederate triumph was a costly one, for during the battle Stonewall Jackson was accidentally killed by his own men. In securing victory the Southerners also lost twelve thousand men, or 22 percent of their forces. Although the North suffered seventeen thousand casualties, these made up only 15 percent of their troops. Moreover, the victory made Lee overconfident, causing him to advance into southern Pennsylvania.

The Western Front. The Civil War began in the East, but it was won in the West. The Union strategy in the West was to divide the Confederacy along the Mississippi and then cut through Georgia to the Atlantic Ocean. Missouri, a pivot point on the western flank of the Union, had not seceded. Now everything was up to Major-General Ulysses S. Grant.

Grant set out to release Tennessee from the southern grip. In a joint army-navy attack commanded by Grant, Union troops captured forts Henry and Donelson (February 1862) and rolled the Confederates back from Kentucky and Tennessee to Mississippi and Alabama. In these early campaigns in the West, Grant revealed that, given numerical superiority, he would not hesitate to sacrifice men to win, and that nothing less than "unconditional surrender" satisfied him.

He now pursued the retreating Confederate army toward Corinth, a Mississippi railroad junction. To reach it, Grant smashed the Confederate forces at Shiloh, Tennessee (April 1862), twenty miles north of Corinth. The numbers of dead or wounded at Shiloh were enormous; the Union suffered 13,000 casualties and the Confederates, 10,699, including General Johnston. Grant was so upset by the number of men lost that he failed to pursue the fleeing Confederates.

After New Orleans fell to Admiral David Farragut (April 1862), the Union army was in a position to advance on the Mississippi River from both north and south. Vicksburg, the last barrier to Union control of the Mississippi, became the goal of northern maneuvering. On the way there, Grant captured Jackson, Mississippi (May 1863), and cut off the army defending Vicksburg from other Confederate forces. After nearly six weeks of siege by the Union troops, Vicksburg fell (July 1863). Grant's great victory focused attention on this laconic but fiercely tenacious man. Lincoln was also watching. As a result of Vicksburg, he made Grant commander of all federal armies west of the Appalachians.

Gettysburg. July 4, 1863, was the turning point in the war. Not only did Vicksburg fall on that day, but on the same day an invasion of the North by General Lee was crushed at Gettysburg, Pennsylvania. Late in June an overconfident Lee, flushed with his victory at Chancellorsville, had begun an advance into southern Pennsylvania. He hoped that a victory in northern territory would show that the South was far from finished. Heading the Army of the Potomac, General George Gordon Meade retreated along the path of Lee's advance until the two armies met at Gettysburg. Here one hundred thousand Union troops faced seventy-five thousand Confederates—with this difference from earlier battles, that the Rebels were now on the offensive. The Battle at Gettysburg lasted three days. Union forces dug in deeply on Lee's flanks, leaving him two choices—to retreat or to make a frontal assault against the Union center situated on Cemetery Ridge a mile away across an open field. With his customary boldness, Lee chose a direct attack.

It was the unfortunate assignment of General George Pickett to attempt the assault. After an intensive artillery barrage, Pickett began his charge with fifteen thousand men. Sheer slaughter resulted; three quarters of his men were killed or wounded. Lee then beat a hasty retreat. Instead of pursuing the defeated Confederates, Meade allowed them to slip across the Potomac into Virginia. When Lincoln learned of the Confederate escape, his joy at victory turned to anger. In the President's mind, Meade had missed an opportunity to bring the war to a quick end.

Completion in the West. Bitter battles characterized Union victories at Stones River (January 1863), Chickamauga (September 1863) and Chattanooga (November 1863), as well as the near-routs at Lookout Mountain and Missionary Ridge—all in Tennessee. Out of these battles emerged two outstanding Union generals, George H. Thomas (who never lost a battle) and William T. Sherman ("War is Hell!"). After Lincoln appointed Grant as general in chief of all Union armies early in 1864, Sherman replaced him as commander in the West.

Grant quickly devised a strategy for winning the war. His plan was for the Army of the Potomac to keep Lee's army so busy that it could not link up with other southern forces and in the process bleed it daily. Simultaneously, Sherman was to thrust eastward from Tennessee into Georgia and capture Atlanta, the heart of the Confederacy.

In November 1864 Sherman began his "march to the sea" virtually unopposed, the South having outmaneuvered itself by advancing northward to Nashville, expecting that Sherman would follow. Instead, Thomas was to follow the southern force to Nashville and crushed it in December 1864. Meanwhile, Sherman was marching through Georgia in a war against things, not men. Union soldiers devastated the countrysides, destroyed or seized roads, bridges, factories, rails, gins, and livestock. This was "total war"—the destruction and seizure of everything that could possibly enable the South to continue fighting.

Sherman was well aware of the psychological effect of his campaign. "If the North can march an army right through the South," he wrote to Grant, the Confederacy will believe "that the North can prevail." In September 1864 Sherman burned Atlanta and then moved toward Savannah, which fell in December 1864. He next turned his forces north to the Carolinas

(February–March 1865), where he repeated the tactics of war by devastation. The Carolinas fell; Virginia was outflanked.

Completion in the East. Grant was not satisfied with simply outmaneuvering the South. He wanted to crush the Confederates and concluded that only a frontal assault on Richmond could achieve this goal. Union forces tested the strength of the South's defenses in Virginia during the Wilderness Campaign and at Spotsylvania (May 1864). The North's losses were large in these experimental thrusts, but Grant could better afford them than Lee.

General Philip Sheridan now took the Shenandoah Valley and Grant crept forward to Petersburg, southeast of Richmond. A noose had been wound about Lee's army. It was tightened by a Union victory at Five Forks (April 1865) and the Southern abandonment of Petersburg (April 1865) and retreat to Appomattox. There, with 115,000 fresh Union troops facing his 30,000 starved Confederates, Lee surrendered to Grant on April 9, 1865.

During the meeting at Appomattox courthouse, Grant agreed to Lee's request that his men retain possession of their horses, because the defeated Rebels would need them "to put in a crop to carry themselves and their families through the next winter." Lee thanked Grant for his generosity. The surrender completed, the two generals saluted and parted. The Civil War was over.

Blacks in the Civil War. It is estimated that about 85,000 blacks from the eight states of the upper South fought in the Union armies. These men were enrolled in segregated units led by white commanders. During the final two years of the war, they performed heroically in battles such as Petersburg. Other freedmen were conscripted to work on cotton plantations in the occupied regions of the Deep South. The loyalty and bravery of blacks during the war helped convince Lincoln to push for a constitutional amendment banning slavery, and in 1865 the Thirteenth Amendment was ratified.

Reasons for the Defeat of the South. There were many reasons for the Confederate defeat. First, the Union forces outnumbered them by two to one during most of the war. From the start the North commanded greater economic resources and logistical capacities. The South had no sea power, and control of the ocean lanes gave the Union limitless access to goods and credits abroad and a free path to sell its wheat in payment for foreign purchases. Moreover, its navy strangled southern overseas trade by establishing an effective blockade from Maryland to Texas and split the South along its Mississippi spine. Under Farragut's command ("Damn the torpedoes! Full speed ahead!"), the navy captured Norfolk, Roanoke Island, Wilmington, and New Orleans.

Southerners tried desperately to avoid oceanic strangulation. They ran the perilous blockade and experimented with submarines unsuccessfully. Then they successfully launched the ironclad *C.S.S. Merrimac* and built up—with England's aid—a fleet of sea raiders, the most notable being the *Shenandoah* and the *Alabama*. Yet blockade-running was ultimately ineffective; the submarines all sank; and the threat of the *Merrimac* was eliminated by the construction by the North of the *U.S.S.*

Monitor (John Ericsson's "cheesebox on a raft"). Built of iron and possessing a revolving turret, the *Monitor* fought the *Merrimac* to a draw. A draw, however, was a Northern victory; after this one battle the *Merrimac* made no further appearance. Southern sea raiders were much more effective and accounted for the destruction of 250 Union vessels. The *C.S.S. Alabama* in particular was a terror until the *U.S.S. Kearsage* sank her.

The Home Front.   The home front of the Southern Confederacy was unequal to the task of a four-year war. War demanded unity, but throughout the South Davis's efforts at centralization were fought and stymied. Some governors engaged in a continuous states' rights conflict with the Richmond government; non–slave owners disliked what they saw as a rich man's war and a poor man's fight; slaves defected to the North whenever possible; and increasing doubts among slave owners about the morality of their cause contributed to the loss of southern will.

For these reasons, conscription (April 1862) was ineffective; desertions rose to over one hundred thousand; state governors retained a strong control over the movements of their own militia; taxes on tobacco, liquor, and salt went unpaid; (the South's wealth was tied up in land and slaves) absence of specie caused bond drives to fail; prices soared; hoarding and speculation became commonplace; food shortages were widespread, and paper money depreciated rapidly and by 1865 was valueless. All efforts at price control turned out to be similarly useless. The South was consumed by its own philosophy of decentralization.

The North was also often divided by dissent. Elements there, too, strongly opposed conscription (March 1863) and taxation. There, too, certain governors acted independently of Union efforts. And at various points during the war, northerners lost confidence in their cause and government. The difference was that in the North the Republican Party supported the war effort and effectively blocked the opposition, while in the South, no well-organized and powerful group existed to overcome internal dissent and resistance. Also, after 1862, the North entered a boom economy based on the production of food and materials for the war. Even with the inflation that accompanied this prosperity, most Northerners escaped the economic distress endemic in the South. But despite its prosperity, the North also had some difficulty financing the war, partly because it had counted on a shorter one. In 1862 the treasury began printing paper money unbacked by coinage called greenbacks. In mid-1864 the Union armies were still experiencing difficulties, and the value of greenbacks dropped precipitously; but afterward, as victory seemed increasingly possible, it rose steadily.

Foreign Relations During the Civil War. Before the war England bought three quarters of its cotton from the South. During 1861–62 the Confederacy tried to turn this dependency to its advantage by enlisting Great Britain's help in breaking the Union blockade. The South also wanted England to recognize its independence. Confederate delegates sent to Great Britain in May 1861 gained permission for Confederate privateers to be built and armed in English shipyards. Later the same year, England almost declared war on the Union when one of its warships stopped a British steamer and arrested two Confederate envoys to Great Britain, James M. Mason and John Slidell (the Union later released them).

But the English pulled back and decided not to recognize the South as an independent nation for fear it might lead to war with the Union. Northern military victories reinforced this position. Even a great shortage of cotton in late 1862, which caused widespread unemployment in their textile industry, did not cause the English to align themselves with the Confederates. Britain's overall economy in fact did well under the policy of neutrality. The shipping industry benefitted from less American competition, and wool and linen manufacturers profited by the short-lived depression in the cotton industry. In 1863, recognizing that its attempts to woo England had failed, the Confederacy broke off relations.

The South also approached France. During late 1862 Napoleon III was tempted to recognize the Confederacy but finally decided that he could not go it alone. Since Britain refused to join him, Napoleon did not acknowledge the South's independence.

Abraham Lincoln

A Man of Faith. Throughout the war the North possessed one huge advantage over the South. Although the Confederacy's Jefferson Davis was an intelligent and honorable man, Lincoln's extraordinary abilities gave the Union a big edge. The South possessed an able leader, but the North had a great one.

Why has Lincoln achieved such legendary dimensions? He was an example of an American who by his own superb endowments could rise from complete obscurity to world renown. In the course of his meteoric ascent, he retained the most admirable characteristics of his origins—extreme simplicity, infinite patience, honesty, moderation, humility, plainness of approach, and deep religiosity. To advance the Union efforts he willingly endured insults. With a few notable exceptions he often seemed a better military strategist than his own generals. His mode of expression was simple but profound, clear but flavored with western wit and Biblical rhythms, enlivened by illuminating anecdotes or "tall tales."

He was no philosopher, as Hamilton and Jefferson were, but he had a philosophy. It flowed from his unbounded faith in the equality of human beings and in human rights above property rights. Institutions that deform or suppress this basic equality, Lincoln believed, are doomed to extinction, and he placed himself philosophically on the side of dooming them. But to doom them did not signify violently uprooting established ways and constitutional sanction. It implied reform by free consent of the majority of the governed. Lincoln's faith was democratic to the core. He believed in "government of the people, by the people, for the people" as he phrased it in his celebrated Gettysburg Address. And such government had to allow for the struggle of the economically lowly to rise in the social scale. Like Jackson he became the spokesman for the average citizen—the farmer, mechanic, laborer—and it was the average citizen who enshrined him.

Lincoln and the Union. The way Lincoln handled the first crisis of his presidency—whether to yield Fort Sumter to the Confederates—shows his dedication to the idea of Union as well as his moderation, realism, fortitude, and political acumen or genius.

Lincoln became president after several southern states had seceded and the question about what to do about Fort Sumter was in everyone's mind. Despite the rage prevalent in both the North and South, neither side wanted war. On March 6 Lincoln learned that the fort would run out of supplies in six weeks. The new President had to come up with a solution. Several possibilities presented themselves. He could give Sumter over to the Confederacy, and by this perhaps keep the upper South in the Union and preserve the peace at least temporarily. But surrender would demoralize the North and the Republican party. Also, by implicitly recognizing the Southern secession, he might encourage European countries like England and France to do the same. Or he could order his warships to supply the fort by force, which would probably divide the North, unite the South—and ignite a war, with the North appearing the aggressor. Or he could do nothing, playing for time, and see if some solution would evolve from the developing situation that would allow him to retain Fort Sumter without provoking war.

Finally, Lincoln came up with a compromise. He would send an unarmed task force to transport supplies to the fort and notify South Carolina's governor of this action in advance. If the Confederates fired on unarmed boats carrying food, they would be guilty in the eyes of the world of starting the war. Such an aggressive act would unite the North and perhaps prevent the upper South from seceding. If, on the other hand, the South did not fire, peace would be prolonged, and the Union would have shown firmness. Although Lincoln never told anyone how he expected the South to react, many historians think that he believed the rebels would fire on the supply boats. Whatever was in his mind, Lincoln's behavior reveals the traits that he demonstrated repeatedly throughout the war.

Lincoln and Slavery. Lincoln's ideal was union and peace; the terrible reality of war made him a man of war. In his view, the goal of the war was preservative, not revolutionary. The South was to be brought back into the Union in the same state it left. Lincoln emphatically asserted that the North was not fighting to abolish slavery but to preserve the Union. Whatever his personal feelings about slavery, he was convinced that if it were abolished during the war the border states of Maryland, Kentucky, Missouri, and Delaware and the antiblack elements in the North, encouraged by the Democrats, would desert the Union.

But these views were not fixed. As the war dragged on, Lincoln gauged carefully the pressures for emancipation—the increased abolitionist attacks against him for remaining quiet, the refusal of English workers to mill southern cotton, the military's need to recruit black regiments in the North following the draft riots of 1863 and the arguments of some of his generals that rebel resistance would be weakened if the Union "took" their property from them.

"This government," Lincoln said, "can not much longer play a game in which it stakes all, and its enemies stake nothing. These enemies must understand that they can not experiment for ten years to destroy the government, and if they fail still come back into the Union unhurt." In sum, when military and political necessity compelled it, Lincoln acted on emancipation. Victory at Antietam (1862) gave him the final push. The timing seemed perfect to warn the Confederates that unless they returned to the Union by January 1, 1864, their slaves would be "forever free."

The Emancipation Proclamation. Lincoln's proclamation of January 1, 1863, did not directly free any slaves. A war measure, it expressly omitted the border slave states that had remained in the Union and the occupied territories from its terms; it freed the slaves in rebel states or where the Union government was seemingly unable to put emancipation into effect. The reaction of Southerners was predictable. They saw it as an instrument to encourage slaves to rebel. In contrast, abolitionists applauded Lincoln's move, although a minority thought it did not go far enough in liberating only slaves outside the Union's control. Free blacks were generally enthusiastic: "We shout for joy," wrote Frederick Douglass. In England conservatives treated the Proclamation with contempt, while liberals approved of it. The reaction of the newly freed slaves was even more dramatic. When the Union troops approached, many fled the plantations, to the horrified surprise of their owners.

Lincoln and the Draft. A war for freedom must sometimes be fought with limited freedom. To recruit armies Lincoln initially relied on volunteers and men willing to fight for "bounties," or monetary rewards. After a year even this pool started drying up. Volunteers quit the moment their time of duty was over—no matter what the military situation—and payment of bounties caused "bounty jumping," or desertion from one paying regiment to another.

To remedy the situation, Lincoln attempted in 1863 to institute a form of federal conscription. The draft went into effect when a state failed to meet its voluntary quota; physical and occupational exemptions were permitted. Unfortunately a draftee could buy his way out of service if he could hire a substitute or pay a commutation fee of $300. This loophole caused objectors to raise the cry, "Rich man's war, poor man's fight." (Confederates had previously raised the same objection to their conscription law passed in 1862.) In New York City tensions over the draft rose to such a pitch that on July 12 rioters initiated four days of violent protest that terrorized the entire city. Mobs sacked draft offices, looted private homes, attacked blacks, and burned a Colored Orphan Asylum before federal troops restored order.

Lincoln and Executive Power. That a national emergency should result in an increase in executive power is a commonplace today, but it wasn't in the 1860s, when any departure from strict adherence to the separation of powers represented a radical innovation. It is ironic that Lincoln, with his staunch belief in consent of the governed, greatly increased the power of the executive by assuming new powers.

Early in the war he delayed calling Congress into special session until the three-month enlistment of the state militia under arms was up. This maneuver forced Congress to act without time for deliberation in securing new forces. Lincoln also took the constitutionally dubious, but necessary, steps of declaring a blockade of the Confederacy and expanding the regular army without congressional authorization. In April 1861, he declared martial law, which permitted the military to arrest and detain possible enemy agents in the North, and suspended habeas corpus between Philadelphia and Washington because of mob attacks on Union soldiers passing through Baltimore, a move that opened the way for arbitrary arrests and wholesale suspension of due process of law. (Habeas corpus is the right to have the government show cause before a judge why a prisoner is being detained without trial.) In September 1862 Lincoln extended this measure to all parts of the country where "disloyal" elements existed. In *Ex parte Merryman* (1863), Chief Justice Taney ruled that the President had no right to suspend habeas corpus since that right belonged to Congress alone, nor could he violate due process, which is protected by the Sixth Amendment. Lincoln's answer was, in effect, that in this emergency he would interpret the Constitution in a manner fit to preserve the laws of the United States.

Arrests of those suspected of antigovernment activity, and debate over this, continued until March 1863, when Congress granted Lincoln the right he was already exercising. He next drew up a list of actions to be judged as criminal. Those apprehended were given military, not civil, trials. Congress authorized neither the actions nor the trial procedures. And, in *Ex parte Milligan* (1866), the Supreme Court ruled that military trials of civilians were unconstitutional if the civil courts were to function normally. But in taking these measures, Lincoln went no further than was necessary to wage war, and he showed considerable restraint in other areas. For example, he did not muzzle opposition newspapers or congressional critics.

The Opposition to Lincoln.   The President's most formidable opposition came from two sources: the "Copperheads" and the "Radical Republicans." The Copperheads, the antiwar faction of the Democratic Party, were recruited from disaffected Northerners loyal to the Confederate cause. It was they who were behind peace efforts in 1863; they bombarded Lincoln in the columns of the Chicago *Times* and the New York City *Daily News* and intrigued with rebel agents in Canada in 1864.

The Radical Republicans, on the other hand, considered Lincoln's prosecution of the war and of the antislavery crusade as weak and vacillating. After a struggle between radicals and his supporters, the Republican National Union Party renominated Lincoln for president in 1864. The popular vote was close, but he won overwhelmingly in the electoral college over the Democratic candidate, General George McClellan. One month after his inauguration, on April 14, 1865, Lincoln was assassinated. This violent act—the first assassination of an American president—destroyed any middle ground between the victorious Northerners and defeated Southerners.

The bullet fired from behind a curtain in the President's box at Ford's Theater by John Wilkes Booth—an insane, fanatical secessionist—started Lincoln on the road to legend. That either radical Republicans or Confederate leaders were involved with Booth in a conspiracy to kill the President is implausible. What is plausible is that with Lincoln's death the South lost a wise and tolerant friend.

The Human Consequences of the War

During the four years of the Civil War, about 360,000 Yankees and 260,000 Rebels died. Their deaths temporarily raised the proportion of single women in the nation. Besides the human destruction, the war caused huge physical devastation, particularly in the South, where large sections lay in ruins. The human and physical loss left a legacy of bitterness and hatred that was to last for generations. At this great cost, about 3.5 million slaves became free, and the Union was preserved. Other signs of hope appeared as the nation began to heal itself. For example, since so many blacks had served bravely and honorably in the Union army, many Americans hoped that postwar society would be more tolerant. Yet even in most northern states blacks did not receive equal treatment under the law and were denied the right to vote.

The Economic Consequences of the War

The United States after the war was not the same nation that had split into two halves in 1861.

Agriculture. The Homestead Act of 1862 stimulated an agricultural revival. The act granted 160 acres of public land to any settler who resided on the land for five years and improved it. America's long history of cheap land thus evolved into a policy of free land. Immigrants and neighboring farmers rushed westward to stake their claim, and the railroads pushed west as well. Also, now that the availability of large tracts of land made extensive farming possible, and many men had been called off to war, the sales of laborsaving machinery—mowers, horse-rakes, grain drills, threshers, and so forth—rapidly increased. Agriculture prices rose as farmers supplied the military and the new industries. A series of bad harvests in Europe also kept prices high by increasing the demand from abroad.

Manufacturing. The Morrill Tariff of 1861 instituted a policy of government protection of infant industries from foreign competitors. Duties in 1861 averaged only 10 percent; but by 1864 the act had been amended and average rates rose to 47 percent. Extensive profiteering occurred behind these protective walls—manufacturers sold inferior goods at high prices, wild speculation paid off because of the Union's pressing need for goods, and lobbyists secured a wide range of favorable legislation. With demand rising steadily, production in all manufacturing lines increased.

Labor. Workers were the hardest hit by the war. Wages did not keep pace with rising prices, and at the end of the war laborers were worse off than before. Yet labor was optimistic. One cause for optimism was that, because so many immigrant workers had fought on the Union side, nativist feelings had diminished.

Capital. The war greatly helped the expansion of capital, as armed confrontation created scores of millionaires. War taxes favored the growth of industries. Business started to consolidate to secure the advantages of large-scale organizations able to operate across state lines. Military needs, for example, forced the centralization of separate railroad lines into trunk systems. Business not only consolidated, it expanded tremendously, helped by the government. The Pacific Railway Act (1862) authorized the loan of government bonds to the Central Pacific and the Union Pacific companies to enable them to complete a transcontinental line. Congress lavishly granted each railroad five square miles of public land for every mile of track; the total land grant to these two companies alone amounted to 33,000,000 acres. Finally, men who had served in the army and people of both sexes on the home front who had worked became accustomed to large bureaucracies, which had rarely existed before the war.

Finance. Civil War financing in the North had lasting effects. High tariffs proved an excellent source of revenue. For the first time, the government imposed an income tax. Borrowing became the chief method of obtaining revenue to pursue the war; private agents floated bond loans. To widen the market for government bonds and fulfill a campaign pledge to restore a national banking system, Congress passed the National Banking Act of 1863, creating a national banking system. The need for such a law was clear; in 1862 treasury notes were circulating beside several hundred species of bank notes of varying soundness.

The National Banking Act (1863) finally established a uniform and stable currency. A bank could be federally chartered by investing one third of paid-in capital in United States bonds. Banks could then issue currency up to 90 percent of the value of those bonds. In 1865 Congress protected this currency by imposing a 10 percent tax on state banking notes. This tax drove state banking notes out of circulation. To supervise the system, Congress created a comptroller of the currency, and to safeguard depositors, a system of cash reserves.

Philanthropy. The accumulation of sudden wealth produced a splurge of expenditure on luxury items, gambling, and conspicuous consumption. But philanthropic enterprise also expanded. Fifteen colleges were founded during the 1860s; private endowments to education mounted to more than $5 million. And in the Morrill Land-Grant Act of 1862, the government granted public lands to each territory and state, even the southern States if and when they returned to the Union, to support colleges of agricultural science and mechanical arts.

Sanitary and welfare work among soldiers also became more effective through the efforts of Clara Barton (who later founded the American Red Cross), the U.S. Sanitary Commission, and the U.S. Christian Commission. About $25 million worth of clothing, bandages, medicine, food, and tobacco were distributed; soldiers' homes were maintained; advice agencies for soldiers (on back pay and pensions) were set up; and hospitals were built. Newspapers, sanitary fairs, theaters and schools—all instituted campaigns to ensure the collection of the funds for these projects. Generosity and self-sacrifice more than matched the self-indulgence of the war years.

The Political Consequences of the War

A Stronger Federal Government.   The major political consequence of the war was that it established finally the supremacy of the federal government over that of the states. After 1865 no state or states attempted secession from the United States.

Lincoln's Plan for Reconstruction.   As early as 1863 Lincoln proposed a plan for the readmission of the Southern states. When the holocaust was over he sought to restore the secessionists quickly, proclaiming the duty of reconstruction to be his alone. The southern states, he argued, had never left the Union, since they could not. Rather, they had been in rebellion. If 10 percent of those who had voted in the election of 1860 in an occupied state now pledged by oath to support the Constitution of the United States and the acts on slavery passed during the war, that state might reenter the Union. By 1864 Louisiana and Arkansas had taken the oath.

Only those who had resigned federal military and civil posts to join the Confederacy or who had served in important positions in the Confederate government and army were ineligible to participate in the reconstructed governments.

Lincoln's plan stirred immediate rebellion within Republican ranks. For different reasons Radicals and moderates in Congress opposed it. The Radicals wanted a state to be readmitted only if blacks in it were fully enfranchised and had equal rights. Moderates distrusted the Confederates who might be in power after the South's defeat. Both groups also worried that Lincoln was usurping their authority to help determine the course of Reconstruction. They backed instead the Wade-Davis Bill, which Congress passed in July 1864. It provided that no southern state be readmitted until 50 percent of its voters took a loyalty oath. Lincoln exercised his right of pocket veto, refusing to sign the bill before Congress adjourned. This deadlock continued until Lincoln's assassination.

Johnson's Plan.   Vice President Andrew Johnson of Tennessee, who succeeded Lincoln, was a moderate Democrat, loyal to the Union, but nonetheless a border Southerner. Although he attacked the southern aristocracy, he shared his non–slave owning constituents' prejudice against blacks. "I wish," he said, that "every head of family in the United States had one slave to take the drudgery and menial service off his family." Radical Republicans treated his plan for Reconstruction, which he announced on May 29, 1865, as nothing less than the continuation of the southern conspiracy. Yet Johnson's was essentially a variation of Lincoln's original proposal: a general amnesty for all Southerners except those who, owning $20,000 worth of property or more, were to receive individual pardons; immediate admission of Virginia, Tennessee, Arkansas, and Louisiana into the Union; the election of constitutional conventions in the other southern states by eligible voters (including qualified blacks) who agreed to take an oath to support the Constitution; repeal of every act of secession; repudiation of all debts incurred in the Confederate cause; and ratification of the Thirteenth Amendment abolishing slavery. Southerners responded readily to this moderate program, and by December 1865 every state but Texas had complied with it and elected senators and representatives.

Congress's Plan. Congress refused to seat the Southerners. Republicans worried that blacks would be exploited and wanted to protect their rights. Some Radicals even sought absolute racial equality. What essentially alarmed Republicans were the so-called Black Codes that the new southern governments had put into effect. Under them, blacks could only be employed in farming and domestic service, were not allowed to bear arms, receive back pay if they left their jobs, testify in court, or intermarry with whites. Southerners justified these Codes as the only way of putting millions of uprooted blacks back to work and destroying their supposed delusion that Congress had given them "40 acres and a mule." Republicans also opposed Johnson's plan because if they seated the Southerners, the balance of congressional power might swing to the Democrats.

Congress proceeded to write its own program for reconstruction in a series of enactments. First, it expanded the Freedman's Bureau created during the war to care for the socioeconomic needs of the freed slaves. Next, Congress passed a Civil Rights Act, which effectively nullified the Black Codes by declaring blacks to be citizens and prohibiting the states from restricting their rights to hold property or testify in court. When Johnson vetoed these measures, Congress overrode him. The President and the Congress were now at war.

In June 1866 Congress sent the Fourteenth Amendment to the states for ratification. The amendment made blacks citizens by defining a citizen as a person born or naturalized in the United States. It then gave them constitutional protection against discriminatory measures like the Black Codes: "No State shall make or enforce any law which shall abridge the privileges or immunities of citizens of the United States, nor shall any state deprive any person of life, liberty or property without due process of law; nor deny to any person . . . equal protection of the laws. The next section declared that any state denying voting rights to any class of adult male citizens (the amendment did not address the denial of female suffrage) would suffer a proportionate loss in representation. Another clause barred prominent ex-Rebels from office unless Congress pardoned them. Finally, the amendment repudiated the southern war debt and any claim to compensation for loss of slave property.

The Congressional Elections of 1866. The 1866 congressional elections turned into a referendum on the Fourteenth Amendment, with Johnson and the South opposing it. The results showed overwhelmingly that Northerners did not support Johnson's views. Radical Republicans increased their majority to more than two thirds in both the House and the Senate. The Radicals had won the day.

Radical Reconstruction. Empowered by the elections, the Radicals pushed through the First Reconstruction Act on March 2, 1867. It illegalized all Reconstruction governments except that of Tennessee (which had ratified the Fourteenth Amendment); split the South into five military districts, each governed by a military commander empowered to enforce equal rights; and made restoration of civil government dependent on adoption of a state constitution guaranteeing black suffrage and ratification of the Fourteenth Amendment, which finally occurred in 1868.

In their first presidential election, that of 1868, blacks showed that the Radical Republicans had acted none too soon in granting them voting rights. Voters had to choose between the Republican candidate, Ulysses S. Grant, and his Democratic opponent, Horatio Seymour of New York. Grant won easily in the electoral college but only by 300,000 in the popular vote. He owed his victory to the 450,000 newly enfranchised southern blacks who voted for him.

The Fifteenth Amendment. The 1868 election bolstered the Radicals' desire to guarantee the right of blacks to vote. Congress quickly passed the Fifteenth Amendment and sent it to the states for ratification in February 1869. The amendment prohibited the denial of franchise to anyone because of race, color, or past servitude. A majority of the southern states (still effectively under federal control) speedily approved it, but there was considerable opposition in the North and the West by voters who opposed blacks voting in their own states. The amendment was finally ratified in March 1870.

Congress subsequently passed a second act that required military commanders to register voters and oversee elections of delegates to constitutional conventions. A third act clarified the processes involved in the second act.

The Impeachment of Johnson. To silence President Johnson's violent opposition to their plans for reconstruction, Congress removed his right to issue commands to the troops occupying the South, and in the Tenure of Office Act (1867) prohibited him from dismissing, without senatorial approval, officials who had been appointed with its consent. Johnson then tried to discharge Secretary of War Edwin Stanton, a Radical sympathizer. The House immediately impeached him.

The charges against Johnson were patently political. Some Radicals wanted to take advantage of the Presidential Succession Act of 1792 to establish Benjamin Wade, president pro tempore of the Senate, as President of the United States, and Wade himself went so far as to create his cabinet. The Senate, however, acquitted Johnson by one vote. Although vindicated, he was effectively silenced. The failed impeachment had some positive effects. It reaffirmed the independence of the executive and guaranteed the continuation of

Reconstruction, for during his trial Johnson pledged to enforce the Reconstruction Acts, a promise he kept.

Reconstruction Governments. The governments established under military protection were dominated by the southern Republican Party, organized in 1867. The party was composed of blacks and their white allies—northern whites (derisively called "Carpetbaggers") who either drifted south to aid the blacks or sought to settle and find economic improvement, and southern whites (contemptuously called "Scalawags") who were antislavery and antisecessionist. The whites dominated the coalition.

During Reconstruction state debts and taxes rose alarmingly. Waste, corruption, and confusion were common. This corruption should, however, be seen in perspective. In the North, political crime occurred on an even larger scale. New York City's notorious Boss Tweed and his "Ring" probably stole more than all the embezzlers in the South combined. The southern Republican regimes could also boast of some real achievements: they established equal rights; created free public schools which, although segregated, aided the entire population; repaired and expanded roads, bridges, and railroads; abolished dueling and imprisonment for debt; and expanded women's rights.

The Failure of Radical Reconstruction. These were real successes, but in the long run Congress failed in its overall policy of Reconstruction. Poor white farmers feared that blacks would surpass them economically. Unable to prevent blacks from voting legally, they formed secret societies like the Ku Klux Klan, the Knights of the White Camellia, and the Pale Faces. These groups resorted to terror and murder to keep blacks from the polls.

The most frightening of the groups was the Klan. Organized originally in 1866 as a social club, it was taken over two years later by vigilante elements. Soon Klansmen in white sheets were riding across the South intimidating Republicans, and if this failed, beating and killing them. In Arkansas over two hundred people were assassinated.

By such means organizations like the Klan won control of the legislatures and promptly disenfranchised blacks. Congress finally had to send troops in, and by 1872 the Klan's power was diminished; but the damage was done. The success of the Klan inspired other terrorist groups to form. In Mississippi Red Shirts publicly whipped and frequently killed black militants.

The spread of such groups was aided by a failure in northern will. The idea of imposing a forcible solution to the problems of the South was fading as the war receded. In 1872 the Radicals themselves granted general amnesty to all ex-Confederates. Finally, in 1877 the new Republican President, Rutherford B. Hayes, withdrew the last federal troops from the South. Freed from bayonet coercion, the region settled down to new forms of segregation and a "solid South" vote for Democrats in the ensuing presidential elections by an almost all-white electorate. Blacks had learned a bitter lesson. If they valued their lives, they had better not vote.

President Grant. Although he served two full consecutive terms (1864–77), Grant failed as president. He was honest, but the people around him often were not. The result was an administration rife with scandal. Among those who used their positions and influence to enrich themselves during Grant's first term were his Secretary of War, his private secretary, and officials in the Treasury and Navy departments. A dislike of the responsibilities of executive office added to Grant's troubles; after learning of the scandals, he refused to take measures to punish unscrupulous friends or to prevent any further corruption.

One of the biggest scandals involved the Union Pacific Railroad built by a construction company, Crédit Mobilier of America, owned mainly by Union Pacific promoters. In their capacity as directors of the railroad, these men awarded Crédit Mobilier large sums of money for its construction work on the railroad, thus enriching themselves and depriving the railroad's stockholders of their rightful profits. When Congress threatened an inquiry into these affairs in 1868, they used Massachusetts Congressman Oakes Ames (a stockholder in both companies) to distribute stock to key members of Congress and to government officials to block any investigation. The ensuing scandal, which broke during the 1872 campaign, reached the highest echelons of government, ruining the political career of Vice President Schuyler Colfax.

Grant's second administration was marked by more revelations of official wrongdoing. The unmasking of the Whiskey Ring of St. Louis, which had defrauded the government of millions in internal revenue charges, implicated the president's secretary, Orville Babcock, who, through Grant's intervention narrowly escaped prison. In another scandal, involving brib-

ery, Secretary of War William W. Belknap saved himself from impeachment by resigning.

In sum, Grant's inexperience, honesty, trust, and innocence made him the prey of dishonest individuals. Once their corrupt practices had been discovered, his sense of loyalty prevented him from dealing with them with the proper authority. Thus he allowed the people around him to compromise his presidency.

Rehabilitation

Wasteland. After the Civil War, the South was an economic wasteland, completely at the mercy of northern financiers for its economic survival. Over $2 billion of property in the form of slaves had been wiped out. Everywhere lay denuded fields and forests, slaughtered livestock, destroyed or decayed homes, blasted cities, ripped-up railroads and bridges. Banks and insurance companies were shut, currency and bonds were worthless. Farmers had no seed to begin planting. About 3.5 million freed blacks waited patiently for some program of land redistribution to enable them to begin lives anew as small, independent farmers.

The "New South." With money borrowed at outrageous rates from northern bankers, the South started the slow process of rehabilitation. Oversized plantations were reduced in size. Land redistribution doubled the number of farms. The chief beneficiaries were poor whites and small farmers. Sharecropping and tenant farming also appeared, as freedmen received small shares of land to work in exchange for either a fixed portion of the crop produced or for cash; housing, fuel, pastureland, and gardening areas were usually included. Most blacks failed to gain title to their land and thus had little possibility of ever owning the acres they worked. (Many even returned to work on plantations.) So meager were the returns to blacks and poor whites that most soon sank into "perpetual debt."

Smaller-scale farming nevertheless resulted in crop diversification, and by 1880, the value of other crops exceeded that of cotton. But due to improved and intensive farming (that is, producing more per acre), by 1870 the cotton crop was greater than in 1860.

The situation of blacks worsened after Reconstruction. They were virtually disfranchised because of white violence in the 1890s; they had to endure a string of Jim Crow laws, which ensured strict segregation in the South during the same period. Not only their rights, but their lives, too, were constantly threatened: approximately 200 blacks who supposedly defied white laws or customs were lynched annually between 1889 and 1899.

Investment capital from the North had by this time ventured into southern cotton manufacturing. In 1880 there were 15,000 looms and 714,000 spindles consuming 102,000,000 pounds of cotton a year. Southerners also began to tap their coal and iron resources. In 1880, 400 coal and 200 iron companies dotted the landscape.

In sum, the northern conquest was complete, with one important exception. The price for the healing of the wounds of war and of Reconstruction was that the North now gave the South a free hand in its treatment of blacks. The results were tragic, as once again blacks found themselves in positions of servitude and degradation.

With this turn to industrialism, the New South rose, and the old South receded into the imagination of novelists, poets, and playwrights.

CHAPTER THIRTEEN

Industrialization: Causes and Results

On a Friday in March 1876, Alexander Graham Bell—who had immigrated from Scotland to Ontario to Boston—shouted into a speaking-tube mouthpiece to his assistant Thomas A. Watson, two rooms away. "Mr. Watson," Bell exclaimed at the top of his lungs, "Come here—I want to see you." A few moments later Watson raced excitedly into the room. Bell wanted to be absolutely certain. "Repeat my words," he ordered his assistant.

"You said, 'Mr. Watson—come here—I want to see you.' "

These words convinced Bell that the device he had invented transmitted the sound of the human voice through an electrical current. In the decades after the Civil War, he was only one of many who, through their practical inventiveness, helped transform America into an industrial giant.

The Advance of Industry

At the beginning of the Civil War, America's industrial output lagged behind that of the major European countries. But by 1900 the United States had become the most fully industrialized nation in the world. The effects of this change on the government's domestic and foreign policies as well as on American life and thought were incalculable.

Inventive Genius. During the latter half of the nineteenth century, an unusually large number of inventive geniuses appeared who responded to increasing demands for machines by people with the capital to finance them. This surge in American inventiveness is illustrated by the proliferation of patents: from 1865 to 1900 about 640,000 were issued. Many were gadgets aimed at lightening labor in the kitchen and on the workbench. A good number, such as Ottmar Mergenthaler's linotype machine (1896) and Christopher Shole's typewriter (1868), increased the speed and efficiency of processes previously done by hand. Others, such as Henry Bessemer's open-hearth steel process (late 1850s), made possible the creation of vast new industries. Still others changed the quality of American life. Among these were Alexander Graham Bell's telephone (1876), Thomas Alva Edison's incandescent lamp (1879) and phonograph (1878), and George Eastman's camera (1888). Travel would be revolutionized by Wilbur and Orville Wright's airplane (1903).

Financial Genius. Inventive genius needs to be supported financially. Successful exploitation of an invention often required large outlays of capital to secure a profitable production. This is particularly essential in the heavy industries— the production of steel, oil, machines, and machine parts. In the steel industry Andrew Carnegie was the financial genius. Born in Scotland, Carnegie came to America in 1848 when he was twelve. His talents enabled him to rise rapidly from bobbin boy to Western Union messenger to telegrapher to private secretary to divisional railway superintendent. Shrewd investments soon made him rich. Having decided to specialize in steel, he built the huge J. Edger Thompson Steel Works in 1872.

Carnegie was able to amass a huge supply of capital by collecting wealthy patrons as partners rather than by selling stocks. This gave him both a commanding position and liquid capital. From such a vantage point he began to unify steel production by buying out competitors in bad times, acquiring sources of raw materials, and building his own transport. Between 1889 and 1900 Carnegie boosted his steel production from three hundred and twenty-two thousand to three million tons; he simultaneously invested huge sums in a drive to lower costs—chiefly by encouraging experiments in new fuels, mechanical processes, and the like.

Carnegie surrounded himself with able steel men and gave them a personal stake in his success; he is said to have created forty millionaires in his lifetime. By 1890 Carnegie Steel dominated the industry. Profits soared from $2 million in 1888 to $40 million in 1901.

When it was to his advantage, Carnegie was a ruthless competitor—forcing railroads to give him rebates, entering monopoly pools for limited periods, playing politics to gain special tariff protection, and keeping down labor costs by paying low wages and breaking any efforts to unionize the steel industry. These tactics were not, however, the secret of his success. This he owed to the fact that, rather than dissipating his profits, he constantly plowed them back into his business, building more furnaces, mills, mines, tracks, and ships and bringing greater modernization. In 1901 he sold Carnegie Steel to J. P. Morgan for $492 million (of which $250 million went to Carnegie himself) and devoted the rest of his life to philanthropic activities. Morgan then (1901) combined Carnegie Steel with other companies to form United States Steel, the first billion-dollar corporation.

Administrative Genius. The rationalization of factory production—the arrangement of processes for the achievement of maximum production at lowest cost—also helped transform American industry. Rationalization required the application of scientific methods of management to industrial enterprise. Carnegie was a pioneer in such methods.

But the real innovator was Frederick W. Taylor, an inventive mechanical engineer whose name is synonymous with scientific management. Taylor was the first to conduct time-and-motion studies to measure "wasted" motion and then re-train workers to enable them to achieve maximum production in minimum time. Taylor's method included training workers for highly specialized tasks and rewarding the fastest workers with higher pay.

The effects of Taylorism, or scientific management, were profound: cost accounting was developed; special, psychologically trained personnel managers were introduced; a new approach to wages was formulated—the system of payment by "piece-rates," in which workers were paid by how much they produced. Although the unions bitterly opposed Taylor's "speed-up" processes, the movement caught on. Henry Ford, for example, applied it to produce a popularly priced car, the Model T Ford, which he designed in 1908. In one year the Ford Motor Company sold eleven thousand Model T's. Ford combined the Whitney process of producing standardized parts with a "conveyor-belt system" long used in meat-packing plants, thereby setting up moving assembly lines. He also added his own idea of breaking the labor process down to thousands of small operations, requiring little or no skill. These mass-production methods dramatically lowered the production time and cost of each car. By 1925 Ford workers produced a new car every ten seconds. The low price of a Model T, below $300, meant that the automobile could be available for the vast middle-income market.

Raw Materials. The appetite of these new industries for raw materials became insatiable. They tapped virtually every inch of the continent for new sources. In the 1870s and 1880s the Minnesota-Michigan belt, an apparently inexhausti-ble store of iron ore, began to be mined—the Mesabi Range in Minnesota by itself eventually produced one third of the nation's supply of iron ore. Coal was discovered in abundance in Pennsylvania; surrounded by coal deposits, Pittsburgh became the center of the country's iron and coal industries. Oil made an early dribbling appearance in Pennsylvania and then a gushing one in the Southwest; in the early 1880s, over twenty million barrels of oil were produced in America. Lumber was found throughout the north and southwest regions; from Colorado and Nevada came silver; from California and South Dakota, gold; from Montana and Arizona, copper. And, as the electrical industries were created and expanded, a call for lead, aluminum, and zinc went forth, and they, too, appeared in relative abundance. Each year, as well, the amount of corn, cattle, cotton, and wheat produced in the United States steadily rose. The natural resources of America were equal to industrial demands.

Capital. Expansive market and labor conditions raised the confidence of European and American investors who provided the capital needed to fuel industrial growth. Although this growth was mostly domestically financed, foreign capital played a significant role. Between 1860 and 1900 financiers from England, Germany, and Holland invested almost 3.5 billion dollars in American industrial progress.

Labor. A large supply of labor was required to support industrial expansion. From 1860 to 1890 the numbers of industrial workers rose from 885,000 to over 3.2 million. Many came from the farms, for the increased use of farm machinery was creating a pool of rural unemployed. It is estimated that in the twenty years from 1870 to 1890 almost 4.5 million persons were released from farm labor; they became an important source of factory recruitment. Immigration provided a second major source. Between 1866 and 1915 the well-advertised opportunities in the United States, declining economic opportunities at home, religious or political persecution, and the desire to avoid the military draft, encouraged about 25 million foreigners to leave their countries for America.

Until 1885 the old patterns of immigration persisted. Most immigrants came from Scandinavia, Germany, and Ireland, although during this period some seventy thousand Chinese were imported to work on the transcontinental railroads. Then, after 1885, the "new immigrants" appeared. Coming from Russia, Poland, Austria-Hungary, the Balkans, and Italy, they usually concentrated within the large cities. These new immigrants constituted a reserve of unskilled labor for the nation's steel mills, mines, automobile plants, and railroads. They were not popular with many Americans: because necessity compelled them to work for low wages, the new wave of immigrants were seen as taking away jobs from American workers. Employers, however, hired the immigrants eagerly. In effect, these foreigners bore the brunt of the brutalizing work of the new industrialization.

The Market. The incredible industrial expansion would have been less marked if domestically manufactured goods had to find their market abroad. Competition from England and Germany might have been too much for America's infant industries. Fortunately American goods found an expanding home market that resulted from a tremendous expansion in the population. From 1860 to 1900 the number of Americans grew from 31,443,000 to 75,994,000. This increased population needed food, shelter, clothing, and transport, providing a growing market for the country's growing industries.

Transportation. Railroad transportation kept pace with the expanding industrial economy and in many ways stimulated it. Railroads were America's first big business, requiring an organizational scale and a level of decision-making previously unheard of. As in other industries, invention, administrative genius, increased raw materials and capital, steadily rising demand, plentiful labor, skilled engineers, and munificent government subsidies helped expansion. Steel rails replaced iron; locomotives became larger and heavier, with more tractive power; dining cars, heated cars, and Pullman sleeping cars (1864) added comfort; refrigeration cars helped in transporting food; block signal systems, Westinghouse automatic couplers (1868) and air brakes (1869) aided safety; mechanical devices for handling bulk freight were introduced; engineers like John Augustus Roebling built bridges big and strong enough to handle the heavier loads; and a standard gauge of 4 feet, 8 ½ inches was established (1886). Also, our present system of time zones was begun to be applied in 1883 by the railway.

Railroads began to reach into every community. Before the Civil War, there had been no integrated systems of railways. Companies had different schedules and separate stations. The tracks of one often differed in width from those of another. After 1865 railroad owners and managers focused on building up integrated systems. Larger companies acquired the smaller. For example, in 1861 the New York Central ran from Albany to Buffalo. By 1877 the Central, controlled since 1867 by "Commodore" Cornelius Vanderbilt, operated a rail network of over 4,500 miles of track between New York City and the major cities of the Midwest, having absorbed such railroads as the Lake Shore and Michigan and the Michigan Central.

During this period the first transcontinental railroad was built. Construction was divided between two companies, the Union Pacific (which was to build westward from Nebraska) and the Central Pacific (which was to build eastward from the Pacific Coast). In 1869 the two lines met at Promontory, Utah. The transcontinental railroad not only showed that builders understood the need for direct connections to eastern markets and the complete integration of feeder lines, it also symbolized the nation's unity and progress. During the next twenty years, four more transcontinental rail lines were completed.

In 1865 less than 35,000 miles of track had been laid. By 1900 there were over 190,000 miles of track. Besides Vanderbilt, the railroad magnates who accomplished this transportation miracle included Leland Stanford, Collis P. Huntington, Charles Crocker, and Mark Hopkins, builders of the Central Pacific; Jay Gould of the Erie; and James J. Hill, who built the Great Northern without any government subsidy.

Such subsidies to the railroads were enormous; the Union Pacific received over $27 million in grants and loans; the Northern Pacific secured 42 million acres of land without charge. Subsidies were frequently gained through corrupt means, and shameful profiteering occurred at the expense of customers and stockholders. Despite these dubious practices, the railway transportation system that was built in this era irrevocably transformed American commerce and life. It reduced the cost of transporting manufactured goods and raw materials and opened up more distant rural and urban markets. The railroads also linked widely separated cities and towns, helping to end their relative isolation and self-sufficiency. By bringing in outside products, they tied Americans together. Because of the railroads, a national market became possible. The railroads were also America's first big business, employing thousands of people. And by their consumption of iron, steel, lumber, and coal, they encouraged growth in other industries.

Government and Industrial Growth. From 1865 to about 1890—the period of industrial expansion—the federal government pursued a policy of laissez-faire. During this period, it enacted no laws restricting business practices, nor did any federal commission issue regulations or investigate how corporations did business. Paying low wages, charging what the traffic would bear, combining to establish monopolies, discriminating in rates against certain persons and places, collecting rebates or "kickbacks," and refusing to let workers bargain collectively—none of these were illegal activities.

Laissez-faire did not, however, mean a policy of "hands off." From the time when

Alexander Hamilton was the nation's first Secretary of the Treasury, state aid to business was part of the government's nonregulatory policy. This aid assumed many forms: tariff and banking laws; the distribution of public domain to farmers, lumbermen, and railroaders; direct subsidies to the merchant marine and the railroads, and judicial decisions protecting private property against inroads by state legislation.

Monopolies.   Of great significance in the transformation of America into an industrial giant was the growth of monopolized industry. As the century drew to a close, fewer and larger companies controlled a greater share of business. If any company refused to follow the lead of the monopolists, it was usually crushed in a ruthless price war. The Standard Oil Company illustrates how monopolies were formed and the effects they could have on an industry.

The first drillings for oil were made in 1859 at Titusville, Pennsylvania, by Edwin Drake, who had been sent on his quest by a shrewd promoter. Drake's success started an oil rush, and by 1872 production was in the millions of barrels. Crude petroleum must be refined before it can be used, and about 1862 twenty-four-year-old John D. Rockefeller entered the refinery business, allying himself with Samuel Andrews, the inventor of an improved refining process. Centering his activities in Cleveland, Rockefeller, who believed competition to be wasteful, took over five companies. This gave him both capital and skilled managers. By 1870 Rockefeller's Standard Oil Company was refining about 4 percent of the nation's oil.

By operating out of Cleveland, Rockefeller had located near competing railroad lines. These roads now began to vie for his oil by offering him a 10 percent rebate. Favorable rates gave Rockefeller a competitive edge, and he instituted a relentless war against all other refiners. Rockefeller sent spies into the competitors' firms and bribed politicians to force the competition out of business. He also undercut their prices until, on the verge of ruin, they were forced to capitulate and sell out to him. By 1879 Rockefeller controlled 90 percent of the country's oil-refining capacity.

About forty companies were involved with Rockefeller in this monopoly. To tighten Rockefeller's control, Samuel T. C. Dodd, Standard Oil's attorney, created the first modern trust. The forty companies turned over their stock to nine trustees (selected by Rockefeller), who were "to hold, control, and manage" them. In the exchange stockholders received trust certificates on which dividends were paid. Consequently competition within the petroleum industry virtually disappeared and profits soared sky-high. From Rockefeller's viewpoint, he had set up the trust, not to create a monopoly (he already had achieved this), but to manage it. In 1890, when this trust arrangement was successfully prosecuted as illegal under the new Sherman Antitrust Act—the first attempt at federal control and the result of rising public anger over artificially raised prices and other abuses of the trusts—he substituted the holding company. Under this form of business organization, one oil company—Standard of New Jersey—owned controlling shares of stock in each of the forty subsidiaries. In 1911 the Supreme Court dissolved this holding company, causing separate companies to be reestablished, but not for long. A new form of monopoly now appeared, known as the "community of interest." Under it, chosen individuals received controlling interests in the companies and then met together privately to make decisions about production and pricing. Thus, every effort to dissolve the oil monopoly failed.

Monopolistic Devices. In the making of corporate combines, the means were many. The earliest was the pool, which appeared after the Panic of 1873, and rails led the way. Competition was eliminated by careful division of the territory, rate-fixing, profit-sharing, and pools. Essentially secret "gentlemen's agreements" among competitors to reduce production, maintain prices, and divide up markets, pools remained together only as long as it was profitable. Even more effective was the stock exchange maneuver that produced the trust. Standard Oil pioneered here; but before long there was a Whiskey Trust, a Sugar Trust, a Lead Trust, and many more. After this device was declared illegal, the holding company appeared. An early exploiter of this device was the American Bell Telephone Company, and soon many other companies followed in its path. Since the holding company was also open to possible legal attack, business employed many other devices: interlocking directorates, or strategic placement of officers of the parent company on the boards of directors of subsidiaries; mergers, or outright purchases of one company by another; community of interest, or individual ownerships informally united; dummy directorships; monopoly through deposits in a common bank; and numerous variations.

The Mining Frontier

"Strike" and "Rush." Industry needed minerals—metals, for raw material and alloy; gold and silver, for an expanding currency vital to large-scale industrial operations. The task of uncovering the boundless (or so it seemed) wealth that lay buried in the land between the Mississippi River and the Rockies fell to the prospecting pioneers. The individual strike, or discovery, followed by a mad "rush" characterized the period from 1848 to 1890. When the California gold rush of 1849 petered out, prospectors fanned out eastward into Nevada, Colorado, and Montana in search of new strikes. Individual strikes, however, could not provide for the enormous metal needs of an industrial economy.

Large-Scale Mining. Much of the ore lay imbedded in quartz veins. Extracting it required lode mining (ore extraction), rather than placer mining (collection of pure ores on the surface). Lode mining demanded heavy machinery, and the capital investments needed were far beyond the resources of individual prospectors. Therefore, the great wealth of the Colorado fields went untapped until the massive Guggenheim Corporation took them over. Similarly, only the considerable capital of the Anaconda Copper Mining Company permitted the full realization of Montana's mineral wealth.

Individual prospectors faced other liabilities in their pursuit of ores. They struck for the richest metals, ignoring the less spectacular ones, such as antimony, arsenic, and manganese. Their community patterns were inadequate to the conduct of organized business: wealth was wasted extravagantly; gambling and thievery were rampant; murder à la Billy the Kid was common; housing was inadequate and sanitation nonexistent.

These features of the first mining communities ended with the appearance of the large-scale mining enterprise. The need for organized community life asserted itself, and those who had a stake in a law-abiding existence—such as retailers, mining-company officials, lawyers, and newspaper editors—formed elected groups or vigilante committees to enforce law and order. (Vigilante committees were volunteer police forces who applied somewhat summary justice to law violators.) They also pressed for more formal territorial organization and, eventually, for their areas' admission to statehood. Through these influences the mining community changed: attractive homes appeared, stagecoaches like the Butterfield Overland Express gave way to railroads, and the Pony Express mail delivery surrendered to the railroad and the telegraph pole. By 1900 the mining frontier had faded into the romantic past.

The Mining Frontier's "Romantic" Heritage. The era of the mining frontier left a rich deposit of tradition. There are many familiar images: The lone prospector facing the elements and hostile Native Americans; the deadly feuds over claims; the wars of miners and homesteaders, and of miners and cattleowners; the lawlessness of temporary mining towns with their gamblers, gunmen, prostitutes, and confidence men; the gun battles for law, order, and morality; the dance hall, saloon, barroom, and gambling joint; the attacks by outlaws on railroads and Wells, Fargo and Company stagecoaches. All of these elements comprise a wealth of material for retelling the story of the miner's frontier.

The Indian Frontier

The "Vanishing American." Native Americans were the primary victims of the United States' march across the frontier. In 1865 nearly 250,000 Native Americans lived in the western part of the country. While America was primarily agricultural, they fought a rearguard battle, slowly retreating against the settlers moving west. This kind of warfare became impossible, however, when the enemy was advancing industrialism. Till the mid-1860s, the Plains Indians—including the Sioux, Cheyenne, Apache, and Nez Percé—had lived off the thirteen to fifteen million buffalo that roamed the region. Then the slaughter of these buffalo began, in order to provide food for railway construction crews and trophies for sportsmen. In 1891 the development of a method making possible the commercial use of hides led to the slaughter of approximately nine million buffalo during the next three years. The nomadic Plains Indians, doomed to starvation, now waged bitter battle against every advance in settlement—railroads, highways, stagecoaches, homesteading, and mining.

The federal government had tried to persuade the Indians to clear the western lands and leave them for the white settlers. In 1851 the government persuaded each tribe to accept definite boundaries to its hunting ground. This policy, known as concentration, was short-lived; many Indians soon ignored the boundaries. Meanwhile, during the 1850s, white settlers surged into Kansas and Nebraska, pushing the Indians out. In 1859 a gold rush into Colorado drove the Cheyenne and the Arapaho from the land designated for them in 1851, and touched off five years of warfare. In 1864 the Colorado militia led by Colonel John M. Chivington attacked sleeping Cheyennes at Sand Creek in southeastern Colorado, killing about 450 men, women, and children. Although the massacre was met by a storm of protest in Colorado and the East, the Indians still had to give up their Sand Creek reservation in exchange for other lands. The following year the influx of gold prospectors in Montana ignited the Sioux War. Under their chief, Red Cloud, the Sioux scored their greatest triumph, the 1866 ambush of eighty-two soldiers led by Captain William J. Fetterman. In 1867 a peace commission suggested that all Plains Indians be confined to two reservations, one in Oklahoma and the other in the Dakota Territory, and the tribal chiefs reluctantly agreed.

Many young warriors, refusing to submit to the agreements, waged guerrilla warfare against the army. In the Southwest the Comanche and the Kiowa caused havoc, until they were decisively defeated in 1875. Other fighting began in the Northern Plains after the discovery of gold there in 1874 precipitated a gold rush in which thousands of prospectors trampled across the land reserved for the Indians. Under the leadership of Rain-in-the-Face, Crazy Horse, and Sitting Bull, the Sioux warriors focused on the area around the Little Bighorn River in Montana. In 1876, 265 men, led by Colonel George A. Custer—who mistakenly believed that he had surrounded a small number of Sioux on the banks of the Little Bighorn—found themselves encircled by 2,500 warriors. Although the soldiers fought bravely, none of them survived. "Custer's Last Stand" turned out to be a short-lived triumph for the Indians. By autumn insufficient food and their great numerical inferiority caused the Sioux to surrender and return to their reservation.

After the Sioux War, the plains fighting slackened into occasional outbreaks such as the unsuccessful Nez Percé rebellion in Oregon in 1877. The defeated Nez Percé tribe was moved to the harsh lands of the Oklahoma reservation, where most died of disease. And, in 1890, about two hundred Sioux men, women, and children were massacred by troops at Wounded Knee, South Dakota. The massacre at Wounded Knee was the deathblow to the attempts of the Plains Indians to defend their traditional way of life. Their bravery, horsemanship, and military cunning were in the end unable to win against the United States Army's superior firepower and technology.

Indian Policy. A new Indian policy was also being formulated throughout the 1870s and 1880s, that of trying to persuade Native Americans to abandon their tribal culture and assimilate into white society. Thus, in 1887 the Dawes Severalty Act was passed. It directed its main effort against tribalism. Out of about 48 million acres, each head of a family was to receive 160 acres, with 40 additional acres for each dependent. Indians who accepted such land allotments, lived away from the tribe, and "adopted the habits of civilized life," were granted American citizenship. To protect them against speculators, the land had to be kept for twenty-five years. Any unsold reservation land was to be placed on the market, with the proceeds from its sale to be used for educating and training Indians.

Failure of the Policy.   The policy of destroying Indian tribalism and substituting compulsory assimilation failed. White settlers in Oklahoma squatted on reservation territory despite the weak efforts of the United States Army to restrain them. And much of the 90 million acres in reservation land was eventually sold to white settlers. Moreover, since most Indians knew nothing about farming, those who received allotments proved unable to farm successfully and their landholding often deteriorated. The situation was made worse by unscrupulous politicians, cattlemen, liquor salesmen, and land speculators, who defrauded Indians without any governmental check. For example, to get around the twenty-five-year limit on sale of allotments, settlers leased farmland from Indians usually paying virtually nothing.

This disastrous policy deprived the Indians of their tribal culture without helping them adjust to new ways. Thus, in 1900 most of the nation's two hundred thousand Indians lived a life of poverty, alcoholism, and unemployment on reservations. In 1906 "remedial" legislation was finally enacted, deferring Indian citizenship until the end of the twenty-five-year period. But this legislation produced no noticeable improvement. In 1934, from the 138 million acres disposed of under the Dawes Act, only 52 million, mostly infertile, remained in Native American hands.

The Cattle Frontier

Obstacles to Expansion.   The treeless, semi-arid Great Plains eastward from the Rockies were ideal for cattle grazing. Between 1830 and 1860 a "cattle kingdom" was informally established, centered in Texas and extending into neighboring states. The first cattle kings were hampered by many obstacles in expanding their production. Because meat spoiled, they had to rely on local markets supplying settlers, miners, and transients; they were unable to tap the potentially enormous eastern seaboard market because of poor transportation. The Ozark Trail to Missouri was overlong, and the cattle herded on it were unmanageable and lost weight. The farmers along the route showed extreme hostility to the movement of Texas longhorn herds across their land. There was ruinous competition for the open ranges; cattlemen fought over limited water supplies; sheepherders warred with cattlemen over grazing ground; homesteaders, or "nesters," fenced in their land, thus cutting off more grazing land; miners contaminated rangeland with slag.

Moreover, disorder was apparent throughout the industry; herds grazed in common (this was called open-range ranching) and the individual rancher's cow brand proved an ineffective identification; wide-ranging cattle proved easy prey for marauding rustlers like Billy the Kid and Scarface Ike; and cattlemen had no way of isolating diseased cattle.

The Rise and Fall of the Cattle Kingdom.   The invention of the refrigerated railway car (ca. 1870) revolutionized the transportation of meat. Every city in the nation now became a potential market. The extension of the Kansas-Pacific Railroad to Abilene also eliminated the problem of transporting the cattle to shipping points. Dozens of "cowtowns" (e.g., Abilene, Dodge City) were founded at railroad terminals. (For example, Abilene was on the Kansas-Pacific line, and connected Abilene with Chicago, where the cattle were slaughtered and then shipped East.) These towns had every facility for the delivery, sale, and shipment of cattle. Everywhere new trails, such as the Chisholm Trail and the Pecos or Goodnight Trail, were carved for the "long drive" to market. This drive, moving two to three thousand cattle over a thousand miles, was usually directed by only a handful of a new breed of men—cowboys.

The homesteaders won the battle for the ranges primarily because they secured legal title to the land, because the ideal fence material—barbed wire—was invented by Joseph F. Glidden in 1874, and because they were willing to "shoot it out" with cattlemen.

Severe overproduction of cattle caused beef prices to collapse in the 1880s, and the blizzards of 1886–87 (which submerged 80 to 90 percent of the cattle in snowdrifts) forced many cattlemen into bankruptcy. Those who survived financially began to fence their own land in, dig for water, grow hay for food, and reduce the size of their herds. Fencing in also allowed a cattleman to engage in intensive breeding (bringing in pedigree bulls to improve the stock). Smaller ranges were also made possible by expansion of the cattle kingdom to the far north, when it was found that the herds (ranchers by now had bred Texas longhorns with heavier Hereford and Angus bulls) could survive the severe winters there.

Before the downfall of the cattle kingdom, cattlemen had taken the first steps to organizing their industry by forming stock-growers corporations, employing detectives, blacklisting cowboys with bad records, supervising roundups, inspecting brands, and so forth. Vigilantes waged open war on the badmen, most of whom were killed with the help of federal authorities. Finally, rough beginnings were made in state and federal legislation to protect animals from contagious disease.

The Cowboy Heritage. Today's stereotype of the gun-toting, lean, laconic, fast-shooting cowhand living romantically and dangerously in the small spaces between a hail of bullets is far from the truth. The work of the "cowboy" was hard, unrewarding, and monotonous. Its real character is reflected in the melancholy songs and ballads that survive from this period; their keynotes are loneliness and obsession with death. The stereotype of the cowtown is more accurate with its dance halls, saloons, gambling dens, and brothels. Here all the frustration and loneliness of the cowboys, accumulated during the dull work season, could be released in acts of violence that were more sordid than romantic, and also less frequent than the legend would have us believe. One reason for this was that police forces were generally well organized and effective.

The Farmer and the Worker

Mechanization on the Farm. Industrialization antiquated horse-drawn plows, hand-sown seeds, handpicked cotton, hand-sickled-and-flailed grain, hand-milked cows, and hand-churned butter. After 1860 mechanical methods for performing every agricultural operation appeared. To aid in soil preparation, factories produced steel plows, gang plows, spring-tooth and disc harrows, and seed-drills. The result was that soil preparation was reduced from about thirty-three minutes per bushel of wheat to little more than two minutes. To harvest crops there were harvesters, reapers, wire-binders, combines, threshers, feeders, weighers, straw-stackers, corn husker-shellers, and binders, as well as ensilage and silo-filling machines.

At the turn of the century, the chief unsolved problem for American farmers was what to use as a source of power for light and traction; the gasoline tractor and the electrified farm only appeared after World War I. Even without these advances, the amount of time in human labor required to produce a bushel of wheat fell from 183 minutes in 1830 to 10 minutes in 1900.

Significant consequences flowed from the spread of industrialization to the farm. The Department of Agriculture joined the ranks of experimenters and, through land-grant colleges and its own laboratories, increased the farmers' knowledge of fertilizers, dry-farming techniques, and irrigation methods. Scientific farming led to crop diversification; farmers started to set aside specific areas on their farms for cotton, corn, wheat, and fruits. Crop diversification meant production of a cash crop and commercialization of farm enterprises. Farmers became primarily businesspeople who had to sell what they produced and buy what they consumed.

Market factors became the arbiters of farmers' continued existence. Although the bulk of the market was domestic, they began to depend increasingly on exporting their surpluses; foreign markets often constituted their margin of profit. As the size of farms increased, farmers became large employers of labor in the form of share-croppers, tenant farmers, and migratory workers. As the nation moved into the twentieth century, farming itself was on the point of becoming a large-scale business.

Industrialization and the Worker. In 1860 there were 885,000 industrial workers in America. By 1890 the number had risen to 3.2 million. Although machines displaced some workers, in general they increased the number of jobs. The nature of the work created differed enormously from what had been displaced. Formerly workers were craftspeople who owned their own tools, possessed a scarce skill and thus commanded a good bargaining position, had pride in their craft, and were free to pursue a schedule of combined laboring and farming.

Now workers were machine-tenders, mostly semiskilled, their contribution to the end product unrecognizable. Consequently, they were defenseless against discharge, and, divorced from farming as a substitute, they became slaves to factory routine. At the mercy of the law of supply and demand, workers took whatever wages, hours, and conditions of work they could find, mainly because job competition increased with each' influx of immigrants, blacks, displaced farmhands, women, and children into the labor market. Between 1870 and 1900 the number of working women rose from 15 to 20 percent, while the number of children who worked increased by almost 130 percent. Both women and children received less pay than adult male workers.

The majority of working women were young and single; after working approximately six years, many married and then quit their jobs to raise a family. Women also entered new fields of work. As business grew, so did the need for employees. Women now moved into formerly male-held positions, such as that of secretary, bookkeeper, and typist. They became sales clerks and cashiers in the new department stores. But men still retained the management positions. The professional woman was also a rarity—few women became doctors or lawyers. The few professions more open to women included nursing and teaching.

Although they earned less than men, women made more than child laborers. Similarly Native Americans were paid better than foreigners, whites more than blacks or Asians, and Protestants more than Catholics or Jews. Generally holding manual jobs, blacks were the most poorly paid of all workers, although the Chinese—congregated mainly on the West Coast—suffered much economic and social discrimination.

Thus, while industrialization of America resulted in better living standards through the mass production of affordable goods, a rise in real wages, and improved working conditions, for many workers the social, health, and even eventually the economic, costs were high. Industrial workers were helpless whenever economic panic or depression ensued or some new technological invention displaced them. Inside the factory work was monotonous, and the number of industrial accidents was high. Moreover, many workers suffered from illnesses they acquired at the workplace from chemicals, dust, and other pollutants. Additionally, relations between employer and employee became more impersonal, and the machine, more than the worker, controlled the pace of work.

Before 1900 most laborers worked a ten-hour day, six days a week. Skilled workers earned twenty cents an hour, while unskilled workers made about ten cents. Most companies did not permit employee vacations. Thus, work was often an endless, grueling task for a growing class of laborers.

CHAPTER FOURTEEN

Industrialization: Political and Social Consequences

It was "a stink enough to knock you down," noted one observer. He was referring to the stench from open privies, stagnant water, and garbage-filled streets that characterized the country's densely crowded urban area, where masses of newcomers crammed into tenements. During the last forty years of the nineteenth century, the huge wave of immigrants, many coming to work in industries, changed not only the physical face of the American city—its sights, sounds, smells—but urban political life as well.

Political Results

Post-Reconstruction Equilibrium. From the administration of Ulysses S. Grant to that of William McKinley (1897–1901) the American political system remained in equilibrium, with minimal differences between the two major parties. Both parties supported a laissez-faire policy toward businesses, subsidies for private enterprise, protective tariffs, a deflationary "hard-money" policy (withdrawal of

greenbacks from circulation and a return to a standard in which money was redeemable in and backed by gold), and easing the Radical Reconstruction of the South. Opposition was largely within rather than between parties. The Republicans and the Democrats each enjoyed the solid support of relatively stable voting blocs.

Geographically, New England was the Republican stronghold, but the party could also usually count on most of the states west of the Mississippi. The Republican Party was generally composed of businessmen—who associated it with favorable banking, tariff, and monetary legislation—grain growers reaping some of the rewards of the Homestead Act, blacks, and northern Civil War veterans. Since these groups comprised a majority of the voters, the Republicans controlled the executive and judicial branches of the government. Between 1861 and 1913 the only Democratic president was Grover Cleveland.

The Democratic strongholds were the "Solid South" and, in the northeast, the urban areas controlled by machine politicians. Ohio, Indiana, and Illinois were usually in the Democratic camp, too. Businessmen opposed to high tariffs also supported the party, and, probably in reaction, most minority groups—with the exception of blacks—voted Democratic.

The American electorate was primarily composed of white males. In 1875 (*Minor v. Happersett*) the Supreme Court had upheld the right of states to deny women the vote. Moreover, southern states found various ways to keep blacks from voting. In 1877 Georgia passed a poll tax, which, by making voters pay an annual tax before they could vote, virtually excluded poverty-stricken blacks from the voting booth. By the end of the century, literacy tests closed the door completely on black voters. Blacks who were brave enough to take these white-administered tests universally "failed" them. The results were devastating. Because of the literacy test, registered black voters in Louisiana declined from one hundred and thirty thousand in 1896 to five thousand in 1900.

Machine Politics. The nation's presidents during this period, which Mark Twain ironically called the Gilded Age, were remarkable for their mediocrity and colorlessness. They refused to head any reform movements and seemed to agree that the chief executive should be honest but passive, with no real responsibility in shaping national policy. The presidency of Rutherford B. Hayes (1877–81) was especially notable for its passivity. When southern whites began to mistreat blacks after the withdrawal of federal troops from that region, Hayes deplored the situation but did not use his power to protect blacks. Congress stepped in to fill this power vacuum, but often had to share power with an "invisible government"

centered in the private kingdoms of party bosses. Of these probably the most notorious was New York City's Boss William Tweed. Between 1869 and 1871 the Tweed "Ring" defrauded the city of at least ten million dollars. In Twain's novel, *The Gilded Age* (1873), coauthored by Charles Dudley Warner, the era's vitality and corruption are scathingly described.

Corruption and Reform. Indeed, business and politics during this period became mutually corrupting forces: politicians blackmailed businessmen, businessmen bribed politicians, and the civil service was a patronage tool in the hands of the politicians. One of the chief entertainments of the Gilded Age was afforded by political elections, and huge turnouts showed the public's fascination with them. About 80 percent of eligible voters cast ballots in the six presidential elections between 1876 and 1896.

Without real issues, however, national and local elections became campaigns of personal vilification characterized by bribery and lying. The private lives of candidates were exposed mercilessly; the lowest instincts of the electorate were appealed to; and racial, religious, and national prejudices were inflamed. Intraparty strife became as scurrilous as interparty conflict. In 1880 the Republicans were divided into opposing groups, the Stalwarts and the Half-Breeds. The Stalwarts believed in seeking the spoils of office openly, whereas the Half-Breeds had the same goals but thought they should be pursued more discreetly. Meanwhile Half-Breeds fought Mugwumps, those Republicans who wanted to cleanse the party of corruption and increase government efficiency. The Mugwumps were honest, but they were not reformers on social and economic issues.

Nevertheless, reform movements stirred continuously within the two parties, showing the American social conscience to be merely dormant, not dead. Issues abounded to stir up legitimate reformers: farmers complained about monopolies, workers about employers, debtors about creditors. But the editors, preachers, novelists, and feminists who raised their voices on behalf of reform were drowned out by the great silence generated by the political equilibrium of the Gilded Age.

The Presidents

Rutherford B. Hayes (1877–81). In 1876 the Republicans nominated Rutherford B. Hayes to oppose the Democratic governor of New York, Samuel Tilden, for the presidency. Hayes, the governor of Ohio, advocated reform of the civil service, which had been corrupted by political patronage. Tilden had established a national reputation for his part in breaking up the notorious Tweed Ring. In the election Tilden secured a majority of 242,292 popular votes and an electoral vote of 184. But Republican strategists suddenly realized that returns from three states (Florida, Louisiana, and South Carolina) still controlled by Republicans, and with a combined electoral vote of 19 (the exact number Hayes needed to win) had not come in. When two sets of votes came in from these states, both parties claimed victory. It was left to Congress to decide whether to accept the Republican or the Democratic count for these states.

To resolve the impasse Congress created an Electoral Count Commission, composed of eight Republicans, eight Democrats, and one "independent," Supreme Court Justice David Davis. Unfortunately for the Democrats, Davis quit and was replaced by a Republican. Voting strictly according to party affiliation, the Commission went on to give all disputed electoral votes to Hayes. Both houses of Congress still had to ratify the decision. To ensure ratification, the Republican leadership secretly met with conservative southern Democrats. In return for Hayes's promise to end Reconstruction, the Southerners withdrew their opposition to the commission's recommendation. This informal bargain, in which the South swung the election to Hayes, was called the Compromise of 1877.

Hayes had been a notable governor, personally honest and politically moderate. Yet as President he believed that Congress, not himself, was mainly responsible for governing. In his cabinet choices he defied the Stalwarts, particularly their leader, Senator Roscoe Conkling of New York, and sought to give his administration a reformist tinge by naming reformers such as Carl Schurz to high positions. Hayes also ended Reconstruction by recalling federal troops from the South. Following a precedent set by Andrew Jackson, he crushed the Railroad Strike of 1877 with federal troops. Supported by Half-Breeds and Democrats, Hayes cleaned up corruption in the New York Customshouse; this act won him the bitter hatred of Conkling, Chester Arthur, and other Stalwarts. Yet he did not succeed in all his endeavors. Although he vetoed an 1878 act that would inflate the currency by calling for limited coinage (unlimited would have meant that silver had replaced gold as the nation's legal tender), Congress overruled his veto. He also failed to achieve a complete reform of the civil service, which he had promised. Viewed by his party and the people as a mediocre president, Hayes was not renominated for a second term.

James A. Garfield (1881).   For the election of 1880, the Republicans offered the voters a ticket consisting of Congressman James A. Garfield for President and Chester A. Arthur—who had been collector for the Port of New York until Hayes removed him for engaging in party politics (in other words, abusing his office)—for Vice President. Garfield was a Half-Breed and Arthur a Stalwart. Upon election, Garfield was greeted with a patronage fight, this one involving bosses Conkling and Thomas C. Platt of New York. The newly elected President resisted, but his support of an investigation of a post office scandal and his appointment of a Half-Breed collector of the Port of New York indirectly cost him his life after only four months in office. In July 1881 a Stalwart office seeker, Charles Guiteau, shot him. The President died from his wounds on September 19.

Chester A. Arthur (1881–85).   The Stalwarts enthusiastically greeted Arthur's presidency. But Garfield's death had produced a transformation in him. Throughout his administration, Arthur steered a moderate course in patronage matters, even supporting the investigation of post office scandals despite Republican involvement in them. Still, the highlight of his administration was civil service reform.

The idea of civil service reform was fathered by Thomas Jenckes in a report to Congress in 1868. Grant appointed a commission to investigate the possibility of such legislation, but Congress refused to appropriate funds for the commission. Hayes, devoted to civil service reform, was unable to revive the idea. But following Garfield's assassination, a National Civil Service Reform League, headed by George William Curtis of the *Nation* magazine, was formed. In 1883 it succeeded in persuading Congressman George Pendleton to introduce a bill for reform. With Arthur's support, the Pendleton Act was passed in the same year after considerable debate. The law created a bipartisan Civil Service Commission to administer open competitive examinations for "classified" posts (constituting 10 percent of all government jobs) and to appoint officeholders in order of placement on the exam. Additionally, the Act prohibited officeholders from making political contributions and permitted the President to increase the list of classified positions.

Arthur also worked to lower the tariff and modernized the American Navy. Although he was a good administrator and a better president than many expected, the Stalwarts refused to forgive him for his defection, and he was not renominated.

Grover Cleveland (1885–89).   In the election of 1884 the choice was between a corrupt candidate and an immoral one—or so it seemed, according to the campaign literature. The charges against Republican James G. Blaine were contained in the widely circulated "Mulligan letters," which accused the highly popular candidate of corrupting Congress on behalf of the Little Rock and Fort Smith Railroad. The charge against the Democrat Cleveland, a bachelor, was that he had fathered an illegitimate child. When the accusations against him were made public, Cleveland acknowledged their truth. The race was close, with Blaine in the lead until an earnest supporter referred to the Democrats as the party of "Rum, Romanism and Rebellion." The remark, skillfully exploited by the Democrats, provoked enough offended Catholics in New York to vote against Blaine to cost him the state. Cleveland won by a slim majority of twenty-five thousand in a total vote of ten million. If he had not lost in New York, Blaine would have been president.

Cleveland made a dignified, honest, and hardworking president. His guiding principle was, "A public office is a public trust." Cleveland's first administration (1885–89) was plagued by a treasury surplus, which Congress attempted to dispose of by enacting pork-barrel (projects that produce benefits in legislators' districts) and veterans' pension legislation. Cleveland responded by issuing a record number of vetoes. He himself hoped to reduce the surplus by lowering the tariff, one of the chief sources of treasury income. Congress refused to submit to such heresy, and the surplus remained. But Cleveland and Congress did agree on certain important measures that became law: an Electoral Count Act to prevent duplicate sets of electoral returns; the Dawes Severality Act to aid Indians on reservations; the Presidential Succession Act, providing for succession through Cabinet positions in chronological order of creation; and the Interstate Commerce Act, the first effective blow against the policy of federal laissez-faire.

The Interstate Commerce Act (1887).
The Granger laws of the 1870s offered the first intimation of government interventionism. State laws, framed by the legislatures captured by the Grangers (an agrarian cooperative and political movement), defined railroads and grain warehouses as private businesses "affected with public interest." In other words, the public had the right through its government to regulate or draw up the rules for proper practice of private business to protect itself.

This interventionist philosophy was initially upheld by the Supreme Court. But, in *Wabash, St. Louis and Pacific Railroad v. Illinois,* (1886) the Court ruled that state intervention was incompatible with the constitutional mandate giving the control of interstate commerce to Congress. Railroads ran interstate; therefore, it was up to Congress to intervene—if it would. After this decision federal action appeared more necessary than ever. Moreover, several congressmen had previously recommended government regulation. Thus, in 1887, the Interstate Commerce Act was passed and signed by Grover Cleveland. The act had bipartisan support, for members of Congress felt that such regulation would benefit the railroads' owners as well as their customers.

Terms. The act made illegal special rates or secret rebates, pools (which divided territories among railroads, thereby eliminating interroad competition), traffic-sharing agreements, and other practices considered unfair. Railroads also were now required to publish schedules and rates. To enforce these regulations, the law established the Interstate Commerce Commission (ICC), the first federal regulatory board. Such boards were to become the chief means by which American

Government policy was transformed from laissez-faire to interventionist. The ICC was empowered to supervise the railways' accounting systems, rate schedules, and business methods and, if necessary, to issue "cease and desist" orders when companies broke the law.

Weaknesses of the Act. Attempted enforcement revealed basic weaknesses. The ICC could not fix rates; it had to ask the courts to decide if they were too high. It also did not have the power to compel the testimony of relevant witnesses; the railroads could continue their malpractices until the courts ruled otherwise; railroad attorneys were able to tie up cases in the courts for years; and the courts were hostile to abandonment of the philosophy of laissez-faire and ruled against the ICC in rate violation cases (e.g., the Maximum Freight Rate Case of 1897) and long-haul (shipments over the road's entire length)–short-haul (shipments along a small part of the road) violation cases (e.g., the Alabama Midlands Case of 1897). Congressional clarification of the Act and a reversal of attitude on the bench were required before this first venture in government intervention into business could succeed. With its built-in weaknesses, however, the ICC became deadwood by 1900. But a crucial precedent had been established.

The Sherman Antitrust Act. Monopolies increased in strength and number in the two generations following the Civil War. Well protected by tariffs against foreign competition, American industries such as oil, tobacco, steel, and sugar engaged in financial and business practices that crushed marginal producers and forced those more powerful to combine or fight it out to the death. Legal devices such as pools, trusts, holding companies, interlocking directorates, and mergers were invented to form combinations. And, while some southern and western states attempted to regulate monopolies, other states deliberately avoided regulatory practices to encourage incorporation for tax benefits within their jurisdiction.

But protests against monopolies, mostly from small businesspeople and consumers, would not be stilled. In 1884 some of the more vocal of these elements formed the Anti-Monopoly Party, which won considerable attention but few votes. A group of indignant publicists joined the crusade. Henry George published *Progress and Poverty* (1879), attacking the unequal distribution of wealth in the United States. Edward Bellamy's utopian novel *Looking Backward, 2000–1887* (1888), depicting a noncompetitive society of the future, sold over a million copies in the first years of its printing. Another influential critic of monopolies, Henry Demarest Lloyd, attacked the Standard Oil Company in *Wealth Against Commonwealth* (1894). Farmer and labor organizations also joined the attack against monopolies. By 1890 neither President Harrison nor Congress could ignore the many-sided protest.

Terms. The result was the Sherman Antitrust Act of 1890. It declared that "every contract, combination in the form of trust or otherwise, or conspiracy, in restraint of trade or commerce among the several states, or with foreign nations" was illegal. Violators were subject to a fine of $5,000 and one year's imprisonment. Federal district attorneys could take action, and those injured by trade restraints could sue for damages.

Weaknesses of the Antitrust Act. Yet the Act had its weaknesses. Its language was vague; it did not provide specific legal prohibitions. The act also left enforcement to federal prosecutors, private citizens, and the United States circuit courts rather than putting it in the hands of one agency or commission.

Benjamin Harrison (1889–93). Cleveland's opposition to high tariffs gave the Republicans an issue in the 1888 election. Despite winning the popular vote after a vicious campaign, Cleveland was defeated in the electoral college by the Republican candidate Benjamin Harrison, a staunch defender of the tariff.

Under Harrison, Congress, not the President, dominated the national scene. "Czar" Thomas B. Reed of Maine, the Speaker of the House, assumed extraordinary powers for that office. For example, the Democrats had adopted the "disappearing quorum" rule to block Republican-sponsored acts. This rule permitted members of the House to debate a measure but then refuse to answer the roll call to determine if enough Congressmen were present for a vote to be taken. After two months of being held hostage by such tactics, Reed recognized as present any member seated in the Congress whether or not he answered the roll call. In mid-February the Republicans adopted Reed's rules and pushed through their program. The Republican-dominated Congress then enacted the McKinley Tariff, the highest ever.

In 1890 it passed the Sherman Antitrust Act. Another piece of legislation passed by Congress was the Sherman Silver Purchase Act (1890), which directed the treasury department to buy 4.5 million ounces of silver every month and to pay for it with treasury notes. The act was ardently backed by mining companies and supporters of inflationary policies. The House also pushed through a federal elections bill to protect the voting rights of southern blacks, but in the Senate the legislation was defeated by the Democrats, who denounced it as a "force bill," because troops were stationed in the South to enforce these rights.

Grover Cleveland (1893–97). Grover Cleveland easily defeated Benjamin Harrison in the election of 1892, becoming the only American President to be elected to two nonsuccessive terms. Yet at the end of his term, Cleveland was one of the most unpopular presidents in American history. He entered his second term just as the economy collapsed in the Panic of 1893, a depression brought on by the declining economic condition of many farmers, the overexpansion of railroads, a gold drainage caused by the failure of the English banking concern of Baring Brothers, and the collapse of important industries in America.

During 1893 fifteen thousand companies failed, as did over six hundred banks. A year later three million Americans had joined the ranks of the unemployed. Faced with this national calamity, Cleveland's main concern was to stop the drainage of gold, which he believed had caused the panic. In October 1893, with congressional support, he pushed through the repeal of the Silver Purchase Act. Bond sales were also launched, and the treasury borrowed $62 million in gold from a syndicate of private bankers led by J. P. Morgan. Critics bitterly assailed Cleveland for having "sold out" the government to the private bankers. Congress ignored his appeals for a lower tariff and in 1894 passed the Wilson-Gorman Tariff Act, which averaged just a trifle below the McKinley rates. Cleveland refused to sign the bill; but, curiously, he permitted it to become law without his signature—for which he was roundly condemned. Moreover, although the repeal of the Silver Act ultimately did what Cleveland had hoped it would—that is, restore business confidence—it did not immediately revive the economy.

Big business was clearly in the ascendancy. It scored heavily in two decisions of the Supreme Court. In *Pollock v. Farmer's Loan and Trust Company (1895)*, the Court invalidated the Populist supported income tax provision of the Wilson-Gorman Tariff, imposing a 2 percent tax on incomes above $4,000. In *United States v. E. C. Knight Company* (1895), it held the Sherman Act to be inoperative against the Sugar Trust.

Cleveland's passivity in relation to big business sharply contrasted with his efforts against unionized labor. Resisting pay cuts, the workers for the Pullman Company struck in the spring of 1895. In July they were joined by the American Railway Union (ARU), led by Eugene V. Debs. Over the protests of Governor John Peter Altgeld of Illinois, Cleveland sent in federal troops "to protect the mails." By late July the huge strike had been smashed, and Debs was sent to jail for violating a court injunction against the ARU. In 1895 the Supreme Court upheld Debs's sentence *In re Debs*, supporting the use of injunctions in strikes. Because of this decision, government and business

gained a weapon to use against unions throughout the 1890s. For working people, Debs became a hero, and Cleveland a villain.

The Changing Society

Feminism. During the period between 1850 and 1900, a growing number of women rejected their role of passive obedience and second-class citizenship, stepping up their fight for political equality. In 1869 Elizabeth Cady Stanton and Susan B. Anthony organized the National Women's Suffrage Association (NWSA) to secure equal political rights through a constitutional amendment. Preferring to work through the states and to focus solely on the issue of voting, Henry Ward Beecher and Lucy Stone organized the American Women's Suffrage Association (AWSA). In 1890 the two organizations merged, becoming the National American Women's Suffrage Association (NAWSA). With winning the vote as its goal, the NAWSA focused on a state-by-state approach. By 1896 four western states had granted women's suffrage: Utah, Colorado, Wyoming, and Idaho. Part of the NAWSA's success can be attributed to new leaders such as Carrie Chapman Catt, whose exceptional organizing and political skills led her to the presidency of the organization in 1900.

New Americans and the Cities. By 1890 approximately 15 percent of the American population were foreign-born. The impact of the "New American" immigrant on American codes and customs was profound, especially in the big cities that became the settling ground for these newcomers. For example, in 1890 four fifths of New York City's population either was foreign-born or had parents who were. Ten years later, three out of every four residents of Chicago were foreign-born or of foreign-born parentage. Gathered in ethnic enclaves or ghettos—areas where others of their nation or region lived—the immigrants spoke in languages strange to American ears, ate exotic foods, practiced odd customs, supported "national" churches, schools, and newspapers, crowded into English-for-foreigners classes, and went through the agonies of simultaneously trying to preserve old customs and adapt to the New World, all the while watching their children adjust more easily than themselves.

The sudden multiplication of residents in overcrowded, unhealthy, and crime-ridden slums forced city governments to cope with building codes, sewage disposal, water distribution, fire prevention, and gang warfare. Substandard living conditions—many immigrants were jammed together in tenements—caused or contributed to other problems, such as the disintegration of family life and high rates of infant mortality. For example, in 1900, three of five babies in one poor Chicago district died before the age of one. In response to some of these problems, such as the rising crime rates, many rich city residents moved to other sections of the city or to the suburbs, abdicating any responsibility to help improve the plight of the immigrant poor.

City Government. As naturalization rolls swelled, big-city political bosses were left to deal with these problems and with a new political constituency. Most neighborhoods were headed by a ward boss, who performed numerous useful functions for the newcomers such as finding them jobs, distributing food, and offering assistance with the law in exchange for votes. Above the ward bosses were the city bosses. Corrupt and powerful, they acquired immense sums of money mainly through kickbacks. For example, a city boss granted a contract to build a municipal building if the contractor agreed to pad his bills, turning the excess over to the boss. Or the boss received money through outright bribes. For example, gas and electric companies routinely paid enormous sums to gain favorable franchises. But one good legacy of the big-city bosses and their political machines was that they introduced immigrants into the complexities of life in the New World. Before long these new citizens became a determining factor in urban politics, demanding their fair share of the leadership.

Meanwhile, more established elements of the population watched the "invasion" of immigrants with increasing concern. Their anxiety is reflected in the ethnic epithets introduced during this period into popular speech, such as "wop" for Italians, and "kike" for Jews. Anti-Semitism and anti-Catholicism were on the rise. And by the 1890s a number of organizations, such as the Immigration Restriction League, began to agitate to restrict or even end immigration.

The Modernization of the City. As the cities expanded and became more crowded, and the public began to understand the connection between polluted water and the spread of disease, improvements began to be made in the water and sewage systems. Other improvements in urban life were also implemented, spurred on by the realization among all classes of city dwellers that something had to be done about noise, dirt, and ugliness. Streets were paved, gaslights and—after Edison's invention of the incandescent lamp—electric lights enabled the city to be lighted after dark. The new brightness helped the police fight crime, encouraged nightlife, and allowed factories to close later. In the 1880s urban transportation also dramatically improved with the substitution of the electric trolley for the horse-drawn car. Cheaper and faster than horse-cars, streetcars also made it easier for city dwellers to move from area to area and for the radius of the city itself to expand.

Other technological advances enhanced the quality of city life. By radically improving the design of the steel-suspension bridge, John A. Roebling also permitted city dwellers to move freely between sections. Roebling's masterpiece, the Brooklyn Bridge, linking Brooklyn and Manhattan, was completed in 1883, and more than thirty-three million people crossed over it yearly.

The small, crowded buildings that constituted the urban landscape motivated architects to look upward, as did the invention of steel frames and girders that freed walls from bearing their own weight. Accordingly, in 1886, the Chicago architect Louis H. Sullivan conceived of the skyscraper, and as the 1890s began, cities competed with each other in their rush to build to the skies.

Education.   The demand for schools rose steadily between 1860 and 1900. From 1870 to 1900 the number of pupils in the public schools increased from 6.8 million to 15.5 million. Per capita expenditure on students rose from $1.65 to $4.64. The number of high schools increased from five hundred in 1870 to six thousand at the end of the century. Except for the southern states, education became compulsory. The quality of education also improved as new educational methods and tools gradually replaced older ones. Corporal punishment yielded to child guidance, the *McGuffey Readers* to the objective picture-text, the three R's and rote learning to activity-oriented methods. Vocational subjects such as sewing, machine- and woodshop, drawing, and typewriting were introduced into the curriculum.

These changes were influenced by the ideas of two early nineteenth century German educational innovators, Friedrich Wilhelm Froebel in kindergarten work and Johann Friedrich Herbart in the areas of student interest and motivation. The American John Dewey also had a great impact on the new direction of education. Dewey believed in learning by doing and in the integration of the classroom with society, so that the country's youth would be prepared to perform in the modern world. These new theories received increased attention in the teacher-training colleges, for educators realized that the rapid pace of social change was rendering the old methods useless. Those who worked with poor urban children, for example, saw that hygiene and good citizenship were of equal significance with reading and writing. Thus, the graduates of the teacher-training institutions were sent out as pedagogic missionaries into the schools of the nation. Moreover, educational opportunity for the untrained adult grew apace with formal child education.

Higher education also advanced significantly. In 1869 President Charles W. Eliot of Harvard revolutionized the college curriculum by introducing the elective system, permitting students to pick and choose their courses. To accommodate popular demand, physics, international law, political economy, fine arts, music, and modern languages received equal status with Latin, Greek, and theology. Eliot raised the standards of the medical school by lengthening terms and introducing written exams. In the law school, the case method was introduced. Across the country other specialized schools began to appear in architecture, education, business, and finance. All-women colleges were established, such as Vassar (1865), Smith (1875), and Bryn Mawr (1885). After 1887 northern philanthropists supported black schools, among them the Hampton Institute (1868), and Booker T. Washington's Tuskegee Institute (1881). Also of especial importance for the future of American scholarship was the founding of Johns Hopkins University in 1876. Under the brilliant leadership of its first president, Daniel Coit Gilman, the university specialized in graduate education. Hopkins sought out the best scholars to teach there and emphasized rigorous research and a free intellectual environment. Its impact was tremendous. Among the university's graduates were Woodrow Wilson, who was to become the nation's twenty-eighth President, the historian Frederick Jackson Turner, and John Dewey.

Science. American science was an early beneficiary of the new scholarship. In chemistry Americans made key advances in the study of colloidal suspensions; in improved techniques of metrical analysis; and in the formulation of chemical law. Josiah Willard Gibbs, for example, created the science of physical chemistry, extended the method of thermodynamics, and introduced the "phase rule," which partially paved the way for the theory of relativity. (Unfortunately American appreciation of Gibbs lagged behind that of Europeans, and his fame in the United States was posthumous.)

In geology vital information was discovered about historical geologic strata, glacial formations, and fossils. Foundations for a theory of glaciation were laid by Thomas C. Chamberlin. In astronomy Harvard's Edward Pickering catalogued forty thousand stars. Other astronomers worked on methods of photographing nebulae, measuring stellar temperatures, and so forth. In mathematics Gibbs also created the theory of vector analysis. In physics Albert Michelson of the University of Chicago invented the interferometer, by means of which he determined accurately the speed of light. Then, with Edward Morley, he established that it was constant. As it turned out, this work also paved the way for Einstein's theory of relativity (1905). In 1907 Michelson became the first American scientist to win the Nobel Prize.

In psychology pioneering scientific studies were made by Edward Thorndike, who investigated the laws of learning, G. Stanley Hall, who studied the phases of adolescence, and William James, whose *Principles of Psychology* (1890) virtually established the discipline itself.

Social Sciences. In history Americans emulated the massive research of the nineteenth-century German historians such as Johann Herder, Theodore Mommsen, and Leopold von Ranke. Henry Adams wrote imposing volumes on the history of the United States. Some American historians began to work boldly in the area of speculative history, searching for universal laws to explain the American past. Henry Adams, for example, thought he found the key to all history in the laws of thermodynamics, whereas Frederick Jackson Turner pronounced it to be in the experience of the American frontier. In sociology Yale's William Graham Sumner studied "folkways" in the light of Darwinian laws. In economics Thorstein Veblen, Wesley Mitchell, and John R. Commons carefully analyzed the psychological forces underlying the dynamic structure of economic systems. In *The Theory of the Leisure Class* (1899), Veblen dissected the "conspicuous consumption" and "predatory wealth" of the business class.

Philosophy. By the 1870s Darwinism began to influence American thought, especially philosophy. Previously Americans had championed the philosophy of idealism. This philosophy taught that the human mind was unique and unlike anything in nature; that every human being was composed of a mortal body and an immortal spirit; that this spirit corresponded with the real, or spiritual, nature of the universe; that God, having created both human beings and the universe, was Himself the ultimate substance of everything. In contrast, Darwinism suggested that human beings are animals, the latest in a long line of evolutionary species; the human mind is merely a material adaptation to the struggle for existence; there is no evidence of divine creation; and everything that exists is the product of environment and accident. Taking up these beliefs, social Darwinists argued that indi-

viduals who were the fittest survived best in society. In other words, those at the top belonged there, and those at the bottom also belonged *there*.

Darwinian thinking instigated a bitter warfare between science and technology—expressed philosophically as materialism (explaining things by natural causes)—and theology—expressed philosophically as idealism (explaining things by spiritual causes). Unhappy with this ideological war, a number of philosophers sought some middle ground.

In the 1870s, out of this effort at reconciliation, came the American philosophy of Pragmatism, which attempted to answer the question, what is truth. According to the pragmatists, there is no universal, eternal, or absolute truth. What is true depends upon experimental results and practical effects. With each new discovery, the truth is modified; therefore, it is relative. It is also a means to a useful end; whatever works is true. Ideas and theories are only of value when applied to specifics.

These ideas were first worked out by Charles S. Pierce (who coined the term "pragmatism") and then popularized by William James (who was not only a psychologist, but a philosopher) and John Dewey. Americans took readily to pragmatism: it represented what the average person felt; it was experimental and fitted, therefore, with modern science; and it endorsed religious beliefs if they worked—that is, if these beliefs made the world a happier place to live in. Finally, pragmatism was easily adaptable to any movement for social reform. In fact, it motivated much of the late nineteenth century reform movement. Settlement-house workers, reform economists such as Richard T. Ely, and educational innovators like Dewey were greatly impressed by it.

Religion. Darwinism was not the only enemy that churchmen had to contend with in the last decades of the nineteenth century. When scholarship was applied to the Bible in a movement called the "Higher Criticism," ministers had to contend with assertions that their sacred text contained factual errors, evidence of primitive religious practices, gross contradictions, and varying styles suggesting many authors. Based on comparative studies, folklorists argued that the stories in the Bible resembled those in the mythologies of other peoples. The implications of these assertions were clear. Many churches responded by undergoing a ferment of revivalism. Theologians attempted strenuously to reconcile evolution and religion. Some argued that science and religion were two unrelated, independent spheres, others that they complemented each other. Still others, like Henry Ward Beecher, viewed God as the First Cause and evolution as an elaboration of His handiwork. There were even theologians who began to treat the Bible, not as a divine book that was invariably true, but as a moral guide and literary masterpiece.

Not all of the clergy sought reconciliation. Some escaped into religious emotionalism, and such sects multiplied. Madame Blavatsky founded Theosophy and preached occult mysteries and human brotherhood; Mary Baker Eddy started the Church of Christ Scientist and taught that evil, sickness, sin, and death were products of a diseased soul and could be healed only by direct appeal through prayer to God, the Eternal Mind; revivalists spread the evangelical message. In the 1870s evangelists like Dwight L. Moody brought back the techniques of the old frontier circuit riders and won thousands of public converts to repentance and faith. While most did not concern themselves with the urban poor, some evangelists established mission schools in the slums and helped found the Young Men's Christian Association (1851) and the Salvation Army (1880).

In fact, all the churches made efforts to keep the poor from drifting from their parishes, developing what became known as the "social Gospel." Thus, Josiah Strong and Washington Gladden found sanction in the teachings of Jesus for advocating such social reforms as labor's right to organize and strike, factory protection laws, restrictions on child labor, regulation of monopolies, and civic reforms to prevent political corruption.

Most conspicuously successful in aiding the poor was the Salvation Army, distinguished by its uniform and brass band. In 1910 it supported workingmen's hotels, women's hotels, food depots, industrial homes, farm colonies, employment bureaus, secondhand shops, children's homes, day nurseries, slum settlements. Less conspicuous, perhaps, but equally widespread was the work of the Roman Catholic Church, whose membership had grown between 1880 and 1910 from six to sixteen million. Caring for the needs of the urban poor was not new to this church, for the great bulk of its parishioners were immigrants. The efforts of James Cardinal Gibbons of Baltimore was typical: to Americanize his flock, he advocated rapid assimilation, openly supported labor against management, and fought valiantly for the separation of church and state.

Journalism. The invention of both the web press, which printed simultaneously on both sides of paper (1871), and the linotype machine (1886), which cast rows of type directly from molten metal as needed made printing enormously cheaper and faster. Telegraph and transoceanic cables increased the potential sources of news. Press associations like the New York Associated Press expanded greatly, and the first newspaper chains began to develop. Publishers could now also reach a mass audience. The first truly mass publisher, Joseph Pulitzer, bought the New York *World* in 1883; by the end of the century the *World* sold over one million copies. Another successful mass publisher, William Randolph Hearst, purchased the New York *Journal* in 1895, quickly transforming it into a sensationalistic paper.

Gaining readers was the primary goal of these publishers and editors in the presentation of news and features. Catering to the public taste for the lurid and intimate, they began to exploit the society story and to report scandals and murders. Reporters were encouraged to compete for scoops. Sensational headlines, color, pictures, and cartoons became attention-getting features of the newspapers.

News articles were also geared toward mass consumption. Editors launched crusades—sometimes sincerely, more often with an eye to sales. But newspapers also inaugurated muckraking campaigns—exposés of corruption and misconduct—against political bosses, trusts, bankers, and so forth. War was good press, and the threat of it was even better, so news stories became jingoistic, and papers made sabre-rattling daily fare.

Features, too, were exploited to the full, and new items began to appear, such as comic strips and columnists, household hints for wives, advice for the lovelorn, sentimental verse, and simple short stories. Advertisements spreading over two columns broke the monotony of the page and provided revenue for an increasing number of pages. Publishers also used big names to gain readers, using the promise of fabulous salaries to attract writers of the caliber of Stephen Crane, Richard Harding Davis, and Mark Twain to work for them.

Magazines. The gentleman-scholarly magazine—*Harper's*, the *Atlantic*, *Scribner's*, and the *Nation*—continued to publish. These were essentially literary journals. But now a number of new magazines appeared, competing with each other for the mass-circulation market. Edward W. Bok's *Ladies' Home Journal*, *Munsey's Weekly*, and *McClure's* muckraked, crusaded, advised the lovelorn, and offered recipes. They emphasized the visual with photoengravings and published respected novelists. Circulation for such magazines began to approach the millions. By 1900 the *Saturday Evening Post*—staid, conservative, moral, and very middle-class—had two million readers.

Popular Books. Popular taste ran to love stories with happy endings, historical romances, escape adventures—each chapter except the last ending on the note of an approaching death—or "by gosh" fiction about "real clever" hayseeds from the back region.

Literature. During the 1870s serious American literature was in a transitional phase, moving from a sentimentalized romanticism toward realism. By the 1880s the transition was complete. Many novelists became regionalists, trying to reveal life in a particular section of the country. Sarah Orne Jewett surveyed New England and, without moralizing, described the social problems they found—decay, stagnating seaports, loneliness, and crabbed lives. Similarly George Washington Cable examined the "old Creole days" in Louisiana; Twain and Edward Eggleston laid bare the Midwest; Thomas Nelson Page and Joel Chandler Harris depicted life in the South, and Bret Harte that of the Far West. Twain (born Samuel L. Clemens), the greatest writer of his age, cannot be categorized. There was a bumptious nationalism in his first major work, *The Innocents Abroad* (1869), that became biting, social satire in *The Gilded Age* (1873); there was romantic nostalgia in *The Adventures of Tom Sawyer* (1876) and much more realism in his masterpiece, *The Adventures of Huckleberry Finn* (1884); and, in his last works, such as *A Connecticut Yankee in King Arthur's Court* (1889), there was deep pessimism.

Another important American realist was William Dean Howells. *The Rise of Silas Lapham* (1885) critically observed the industrialist on the decline. A later novel, *A Hazard of New Fortunes* (1890), contrasted wealth and poverty in New York City. Other authors working in the realistic vein ventured beyond it to naturalism, writing novels in which the character's fate was environmentally determined. Thus, in *Maggie: A Girl of the Streets* (1893), Stephen Crane unsentimentally described the sordid life and suicide of a young woman, and in his classic *The Red Badge of Courage* (1895) showed the grim realities of war. In *McTeague* (1899), Frank Norris chronicled the descent of a man of limited intelligence who murders his greedy wife. Another tragic naturalist was Theodore Dreiser, whose first novel, *Sister Carrie* (1900), followed the seduction of a young midwestern country woman after she moves to Chicago and her subsequent liaison with a married man. The novel's realistic style and subject matter so offended the publisher's wife that it was not widely circulated.

In a class by himself stood Henry James, the younger brother of William James. Having become acquainted with European cosmopolitan society, he felt acutely America's cultural inferiority. In his early works, such as *The Americans* (1877) and *Daisy Miller* (1879), James makes these feelings clear. In 1876 he settled abroad, eventually becoming a British citizen. From the distant perspective of an expatriate, and with considerable sympathy, he viewed Americans as innocents baffled by the sophistication of Old World culture. Although inclined by temperament to European values, James was aware of the considerable amount of decay that underlay them. As his writing matured, his aim became less to imitate naive realism or naturalism. He increasingly concerned himself with examining the consequences of the pursuit of art as a way of life and with probing into the consciousness that underlay human behavior. This required intensive experimentation with a new style and a sharper, more exact use of words. His later novels, such as *The Wings of the Dove* (1902) and *The Golden Bowl* (1904), represent the intricate, complex, and delicately woven fruits of this experimentation. Henry James was the first American to make an art of being an artist. He could not accomplish this task in a land where big business, big moguls, and big money consumed the minds of even the literate.

Painting. During the Gilded Age, American taste was tasteless. While the nouveau riche engaged in an orgy of collection that gave to their gaudy homes the appearance of salesrooms, popular taste insisted on art as moral-bearing or storytelling illustration. Whatever the reasons for their initial acquisition, many of the large collections of the rich found their way into newly built museums, where they helped raise the level of public taste. And some illustrators, such as Frederic Remington (famous for his descriptions of the West), became brilliant craftsmen.

Most American painters of the Gilded Age were primarily romantic. The earliest form of insurgency was in the realistic mode. Thomas Eakins and Winslow Homer worked on American subjects and landscapes in a startlingly realistic mode. Although these two painters showed that artists remaining on American soil could produce great art, other painters became European expatriates. Of these, three achieved international stature: the impressionist Mary Cassatt, the society portraitist John Singer Sargent, and James McNeill Whistler, who painted both in the realist and the romantic vein. A leader in the war on the Philistines, Whistler was an articulate advocate of art for art's sake. The artist's portrait of his mother made him famous in his own country.

Sculpture. Those who could afford it surrounded their homes with plastered sculptures of mournful females and noble males in classic Greek robes or with iron deer. In 1876 from Paris came new ideas emphasizing naturalism, broken surfaces, and originality. A group of American sculptors responded with a series of carvings of great vitality and depth of feeling, mingling realism, symbolism, and earnest nationalism. Augustus St. Gaudens, George E. Barnard, and Daniel Chester French sculptured the great American men (such as Lincoln, Washington, Grant) in a new heroic mode that inspired nationalist faith. Sculpture approached a high-water mark in this period.

Architecture. So did architecture. It fought its way up from the depths of vulgarity and materialism, represented by ostentatious scrolls, brackets, gables, and turrets on banks, homes, museums, and college buildings, while freeing itself from incessant duplication of alien styles. According to one of its leaders, Louis Sullivan, the new style emphasized the notion that form follows function. He and other like-minded architects began to build upward as cities grew more crowded and space more difficult to find. Previously this had been difficult as enormously thick masonry walls were required to support sides and interiors. But the introduction of iron supports on buildings now freed the walls from supporting the great weight of a tall building. This technological innovation was introduced by a group of Chicago architects in the Jennings Home Insurance Building (1885). It was followed by Sullivan's Prudential Building in Buffalo and his Wainwright Building in the early 1890s, both architectural masterpieces of design and function. Soon other architects were rushing to build skyscrapers in cities across the country.

Music. Americans took slowly to symphonic music, and it was not until the end of the century that the New York, Boston, and Philadelphia symphony orchestras were well established. Opera fared better. In 1883 New York's Metropolitan Opera House was completed. Popular taste ran to band music by John Philip Sousa and songs like "After the Ball," and "Sidewalks of New York."

CHAPTER FIFTEEN

The Struggle Against Laissez-Faire

In 1894 a farmer's wife wrote a letter to the governor of Kansas. "I take my pen in hand," she explained, "to let you know that we are starving to death. It is pretty hard to do without anything to eat here in this god forsaken country. We would of had plenty to eat if the hail hadn't cut our rye down and ruined our corn and potatoes. . . ."

As Susan Orcutt indicates, American farmers were indeed restive and unhappy during much of the last quarter of the nineteenth century, and, feeling that government was not doing enough, tried to take control of their own destiny.

The Farmer-Labor Protest

The Grangers.   Causes for unrest among the farmers were numerous. Between 1870 and 1895 there was a steady and severe decline in farm prices while those for manufactured goods rose. Severe droughts in 1887 and 1889 cut harvests. Angry farmers complained about monopolistic controls over manufactured goods, strong protec-tive tariffs, the "hard money" policy of bankers, high industrial prices, rising rail-road rates, and heavy mortgages.

To win back some of the power and pres-tige farmers believed they had lost, Oliver H. Kelley organized the National Grange of the Patrons of Husbandry in 1867. The Grange provided social and cultural activ-ities for members living in isolated rural communities. It also tried to secure state laws regulating the rates of railroads and storage plants; reduce farm costs by en-couraging farm cooperatives for the pur-chase of manufactured goods; pool pro-duction and sell it in one lot in order to have a favorable bargaining position; and build cooperative grain elevators, ware-houses, farm machinery factories, insur-ance companies, flour mills, and banks.

The Grangers hoped to achieve their agenda by influencing the state legisla-tures. By 1875 eight hundred thousand farmers belonged to the organization, and Grangers won majorities in the legisla-tures of Illinois, Wisconsin, Iowa, and Minnesota. They put their programs of railroad regulation and grain-elevator regulation into effect in these states. In

Munn v. Illinois (1877), the Supreme Court ruled that government regulation of private property is constitutional when that property, such as a railroad or a grain elevator, "is affected with a public interest" and that the states were free to regulate interstate commerce where Congress has not acted.

Nine years later the Supreme Court reversed itself. In *Wabash, St. Louis and Pacific Railway v. Illinois* (1886), it denied the right of states to fix rates in interstate commerce; this was a power reserved to Congress alone. In the face of this decision, Granger legislation collapsed, and all that remained of Kelley's dream was some success in effecting a social life for farmers and their families.

Inflation.   The collapse of regulation of railroads and grain elevators caused discontented farmers to advocate inflation as a cure-all. The inflationist logic was simple. For example, between 1865 and 1890 currency in circulation was relatively fixed at about two billion; in the same period business tripled. In other words, one dollar in 1890 was doing the work that three dollars had done in 1865. Thus, the dollar rose in value, and this meant decreasing prices. During the same time, farmers' debt remained fairly fixed in dollar value; but when prices declined, the "real debt" mounted.

With wheat at one dollar a bushel, one bushel paid one dollar of debt. With wheat at fifty cents a bushel, two bushels paid one dollar of debt. Therefore, the rise in the debt would be one bushel. The obvious answer to this dilemma, many farmers felt, was to triple the amount of currency in circulation. This would lower the value of the dollar, force prices up, and enable them to pay off a debt of one dollar with one bushel of wheat.

Greenbackism.   Greenbacks were unbacked money issued during the Civil War. By 1870 they had already fallen considerably in value. Following the Panic of 1873, the farmers organized the Greenback Party to push the government to increase the number of these unbacked dollars in circulation. This was contrary to the wishes of eastern bankers and industrialists, who wanted to place the outstanding greenbacks on a gold standard and make them worth one hundred cents on the dollar. Since eastern financial interests led Congress, they were able to push through the Specie Resumption Act (1875), which ordered the Secretary of the Treasury to accumulate sufficient gold to redeem all greenbacks by 1879. Interpreting the act as deflationary, farmers responded with dismay. With their support, the Greenback Party had polled almost a million votes in 1878. But after 1879, the Greenback Party collapsed.

"Free Silver."   Prior to 1873 the United States was on a bimetallic standard: paper money was backed by gold and silver in a ratio of 16 to 1. The discovery of gold out West, however, had cheapened its value while increasing that of silver. Those who used silver for industry were willing to give 1 ounce of gold for only 15 ½ ounces of silver. Since the United States mint required 16 ounces of silver for 1 of gold, no silver was presented for coinage. Therefore, in the Coinage Act of 1873, Congress failed to provide for coinage of the silver dollar; in other words, it demonetized silver. In the same year, silver was struck at the Comstock Lode in Nevada and began to flood the market. Silver then cheapened considerably until it took many more than 16 ounces to buy 1 ounce of gold. Farmers now realized that if the treasury would print "silver" dollar bills at the ratio of 16 to 1, the country would soon be flooded with dollar bills and a monetary inflation would follow. They raised a hue and cry about the "crime of '73"—referring to the act of Congress that had demonetized silver.

Farmers joined with silver miners and other inflationists in demanding a return to bimetallism. In 1878 the inflationists were able to pass, over President Hayes's veto, the Bland-Allison Act, which required the Secretary of the Treasury to buy between $2 to $4 million of silver a month for coinage. Yet prices failed to rise because the government consistently bought the minimum amount. Inflationists then demanded increased purchases of silver. In 1890, as previously indicated, the Sherman Silver Purchase Act was passed, requiring the Secretary of the Treasury to buy a minimum of 4.5 million ounces of silver a month payable in Treasury notes (dollar bills). But because of increasing supplies, prices continued to fall.

Populism. During the 1880s and 1890s farmers continued to suffer acute distress. Meanwhile, the "Billion Dollar Congress" splurged its bounties on tariffs, pensions, and pork barrels. In reaction, by the end of the 1880s Farmers' Alliances had been formed in the Northwest and in the South; their aim was to capture the national government in a presidential election. By 1890 the membership of the Alliances was about five million, and they were expertly led by, among others, Ignatius Donnelly

of Minnesota, Mary Ellen Lease ("raise less corn and more hell!"), "Sockless" Jeremiah Simpson of Kansas, James B. Weaver of Iowa, Tom Watson of Georgia, "Pitchfork" Ben Tillman of South Carolina and William Jennings Bryan of Nebraska. Agreement on common principles was worked out slowly as the Alliances began to attract workingmen and socialist elements as well as farmers. In St. Louis in 1892, farm leaders joined with representatives of the Knights of Labor and various reformers to organize the Populist Party, calling for a national convention in Omaha in July. The convention nominated Weaver for president and drew up a platform that became a landmark in American history.

Principles of Populism. Populism was a revival of the Jacksonian protest in the context of the growth of big business. Its core, like that of Jacksonian democracy, consisted of a protest against monopolization of economic opportunity that limited the possibilities of advance. Thus much of Populist rhetoric was radical, but the movement was not radical at all. It was primarily interested in restoring individual freeholders to their land. The Populists regarded themselves, not as outsiders, but as the majority, victimized by powerful and selfish special interest groups. The farmer's alliance in the Populist Party with labor was largely tactical. Although the Populists did make a few thrusts in the direction of socialist ownership of public utilities, their basic demand was that government intervene to curb those who tended to restrict private enterprise. In this demand for intervention, the Populist reform movement differed from the Jacksonian revolt, which had sought to institute laissez-faire as a defense against special privilege. By 1890 the farmers had decided that laissez-faire resulted in monopolization, and that the cure was government control.

The Populist Platform. The Populist platform called for direct election of senators as well as government ownership of railroads, and telephone and telegraph companies. Its financial program was extensive: a safe, sound, flexible currency issued by the government and not by banks; a subtreasury plan permitting farmers to keep crops off the market when prices were low; further distribution of public money through a program of public improvements; free, unlimited coinage of silver at 16 to 1; increase in the circulating medium until it reached $50 per capita; a graduated income tax; and strict state and national economies to prevent accumulation of a treasury surplus. To win worker support, the platform condemned the use of Pinkerton agents in strikebreaking and backed a shorter workday and the restriction of immigration.

In the election of 1892, Weaver won over one million popular votes and twenty-two electoral votes. Populists won the governorships of Kansas and North Dakota as well as ten seats in the House and five in the Senate. Yet Weaver failed to attract the southern, midwestern, and urban votes; and although Populist candidates ran for president in the next three elections, the movement's popularity waned.

Labor Unrest. Between 1865 and 1890 workers complained that they were underpaid, had no job security, and were denied the right to organize into unions. During this period wages rose but very slowly.

In 1890 unskilled labor earned an average of $10 weekly and skilled labor, $20. As a result wives and children had to work for supplementary income. Hours of work had dropped from twelve to eleven hours per day, six days a week. The flood of new immigrants kept wages depressed and hours long. Conditions in factories, mills, and mines lagged far behind recognized health and safety standards. Rapid industrial and railroad advances often resulted in overexpansion followed by depression and mass unemployment. At such times, out-of-work laborers' meager savings were drained, and they had to subsist on charity. Increased use of mechanical equipment also caused temporary layoffs. Workers had no protection against injuries, ill health or old age; nor were families safeguarded against the death of the breadwinner.

These conditions posed serious difficulties, but workers felt that their legal inferiority presented an even greater problem. Since employers were not compelled to bargain collectively with unions, the strike became the workers' only weapon. But strikers feared that police, state militia, and federal troops would be sent in against them or that hostile judges would employ an effective new weapon, the injunctions against picketing. Moreover, employers often hired large forces of armed Pinkerton agents to act as strikebreakers. Discontented workers also had no redress against the employees' use of the blacklist, the lockout, and the "yellow dog contract"—each designed to cripple incipient union organization.

The Knights of Labor. In 1869 a group of Philadelphia garment workers under the leadership of Uriah S. Stephens, established the Knights of Labor, a secret fraternal organization. Stephens was an heir to the Jacksonians, believing in currency reform and fighting against special interest groups. To him "labor" meant all labor, regardless of craft or skill. As the unit of organization he chose the residential area. Within a specific land area all workers, whether they were mill hands or independent farmers, miners or artisan-shop owners, skilled or unskilled, black or white (so long as they were not gamblers, saloon keepers, bankers, lawyers, or stockbrokers) were to belong to one big union organized as a local assembly. Centralized control over local and district assemblies was vested in a National General Assembly. The Knights hoped to destroy the system of laissez-faire by securing government intervention in legislating an eight-hour day; compelling employers to recognize unions and to arbitrate industrial disputes; setting up minimum health and safety standards; establishing equal wages for equal work among men and women; abolishing child labor, contract labor, and national banks; and instituting a graduated income tax and government ownership of railroads and communications. These goals were, however, to be accomplished by education and agitation—not strikes.

In 1878 Terence V. Powderly succeeded Stephens and ended the organization's secrecy. The Knights also now modified their antistrike policy. In 1884, after a massive strike led by a local assembly of Knights against the Missouri Pacific Railroad was successful in restoring a wage cut, membership mounted. By 1888, 5,892 locals reported 702,924 members. But this represented the pinnacle of the Knights' success; the organization's subsequent decline was as rapid as its rise. The national group squabbled with the locals, cooperatives went bankrupt, and a major strike against the Texas and Pacific Railroad failed after draining funds from the organization. In the public's mind, the Knights also became unfavorably identified with the radical anarchistic wing of the labor movement through its participation in the Haymarket Affair in 1886.

The Haymarket Riot. On May 1, 1886, the Knights sponsored a nationwide strike in support of the eight-hour day. In Chicago a small group of anarchists joined the workers in a meeting. In attempting to break up the meeting, the local police shot and killed several workers. The next evening the anarchists called a protest in Haymarket Square. While it was breaking up, the police moved in. Someone threw a bomb, killing seven policemen and wounding sixty. Eight anarchists were seized, and so great was the public hysteria that they were sentenced to death, although no evidence showed that they had thrown the bomb or had been in any way connected with it. Four men were eventually executed, and the fifth, who was sentenced to die, committed suicide. When the hysteria subsided somewhat, making possible a more impartial review of the evidence, the innocence of the executed anarchists was clearly established and Governor John Altgeld pardoned the other three.

But in the immediate aftermath of the Haymarket incident, the public viewed the Knights of Labor as breeders of violent subversion. Employers across the country blacklisted anyone who was a member of the organization, causing skilled workers to leave the organization in droves. Those

Knights who remained loyal merged with the Populists, only to disappear from the scene along with them. The Knights had, however, fulfilled a historic function—their ideas regarding government intervention on behalf of labor were to bear fruit half a century after the organization's demise.

The American Federation of Labor (AFL). In 1886 Adolph Strasser and Samuel Gompers, of the Cigarmakers Union, founded the American Federation of Labor. In contrast to the Knights, who sought to organize all workers into one huge union, membership consisted only of skilled workers organized into national craft unions. The central body was a federation of all the separate crafts, and care was taken to divide the powers to permit each local considerable autonomy. Intergroup organization on a statewide or citywide basis allowed locals to deal with political problems that arose in their areas. Thus, the AFL achieved a division of function the Knights had not.

Unlike the Knights, the AFL concentrated on wages, hours, and working conditions for skilled workers in a specific shop. The union's leadership developed new collective bargaining techniques that often involved cooperation with the employer—even to the extent of helping the company out of financial difficulty. But the ultimate weapon of the federation was the strike, and funds from the dues-paying members were accumulated for this purpose. Each strike was to be a major effort; there were to be no "wildcat" or unauthorized strikes. Successes were registered on a shop-to-shop, mine-to-mine basis. The AFL's strategy consisted of trying to win public support for a boycott of the struck plant. Union traditions were nurtured: people were urged not to buy products without a union label, and not to cross a picket line. Gompers and Strasser fostered loyalty by creating welfare services and recreational activities for members. The AFL leadership also avoided supporting political parties but backed individual friends of labor, whatever their political loyalty.

Success came slowly to the AFL. In 1890 it had 190,000 members; in 1901, membership exceeded 1 million, and by 1914, 2 million. But what the AFL got, it kept; the union secured for its members closed-shop agreements (only union workers were to be hired); improvements in hours, wages, and working conditions; and, most importantly, public acceptance. (Not everyone could join the AFL, however. Before 1900 only two AFL locals accepted women as members; and, while not directly excluding blacks, the union used a number of devices such as high initiation fees to discourage them from joining.)

Radical Unionism. The history of the labor movement in this country reveals that American workers are basically conservative. They strike against the level of wages, not the wage system itself, and they use violence only as a last resort. However, when a wage dispute broke out in the Pennsylvania coalfields in 1876, the "Molly Maguires," an outgrowth of an Irish antilandlord movement and the fraternal Ancient Order of Hibernians, committed a number of crimes, including murder, against coal operators. Then, in 1877, after management cut wages on three railroads—the Baltimore and Ohio, the New York Central, and the Pennsylvania—railway and other workers instituted a "general strike." The strikers set fire to hundreds of freight cars, seized depots and junctions, and engaged in rioting. Federal troops crushed the strike in Pittsburgh and Martinsburg, West Virginia. In the aftermath, ten Molly Maguires were found guilty of murder and hanged. But they failed to become martyrs to the American labor movement because it refused to countenance "Molly" tactics.

At the end of the Gilded Age, socialists made a strenuous effort to capture the labor movement. Daniel De Leon organized the Socialist Labor Party in 1895, and in 1901 Victor Berger and Eugene Debs established the Socialist Party. Both of these political groups worked within the AFL in an effort to destroy "Gomperism"; that is, the conservative craft policies practiced by the AFL president. They did not succeed; so, in 1905 they met with the Western Federation of Miners (a group not averse to the use of violence) to create a new organization, the Industrial Workers of the World, better known as the IWW, or "Wobblies." The new union's goal was to unite all workers of all skills, races, and ethnic groups and to use labor's full arsenal—boycotts, strikes, even sabotage—in the creation of a socialist, egalitarian, and classless society.

By 1908 factionalism had driven all three of the organizing groups from the IWW. The remaining faction was led by "Big Bill" Haywood of the Western Federation of Miners (WFM) into a series of rough-and-tumble industrial battles. Wobblies violated city ordinances to get themselves arrested and fill the jails until taxpayers would be forced to take their side. During strikes they used mass demonstrations, sabotage, and strong-arm tactics to resist strikebreakers and the police.

The full fury of public opinion was turned against them when they employed the same tactics to protest the First World War, which they considered imperialist. By the mid-1920s the IWW—after leading several big strikes—was smashed, and its leadership scattered.

Employer Weapons. The managers of America's vast new industries watched these successive waves of unionization with indignation and fear. Post–Civil War industry encouraged the illusion that any interference with business decisions was illegal and that private property was inviolate. Most business managers acted to crush unionism with every means at their command. In their determined opposition to labor militancy, they found government, at least initially, an eager partner.

Employers relied on federal troops, state militia, and municipal police to enforce the open shop in their industries. In the Railroad Strike of 1877, President Hayes sent in federal troops after violence had broken out and rail yards were burned. The strike was broken. The violent Coeur d'Alene mining strikes of the 1890s were again crushed by federal troops after martial law was imposed on strikers. In the Homestead Strike of 1892 against the Carnegie Steel Company, state militiamen took over, and not only was the strike suppressed, but the union itself destroyed. The defeat was a tremendous setback for organized labor, not only in the steel industry, but throughout the nation.

In 1894, over the bitter protest of the pro-labor governor of Illinois, John Altgeld, President Cleveland sent federal troops to put down the strike of Eugene Debs's American Railway Union against the Pullman Palace Car Company. The strike had caused chaos by tying up trunk lines running in and out of Chicago. Cleveland's excuse for ignoring Altgeld's demand for noninterference was that he had to protect the mails.

In the courts the strikers were restrained by judicial application of the common law that regarded unions of workers as conspiracies in restraint of trade. Under such an interpretation, the Coeur d'Alene strikers were sent to jail. The courts also freely granted injunctions to employers to prevent destruction of property by the union. Such injunctive proceedings were employed to imprison Eugene V. Debs during the Pullman strike. After Debs was jailed for defying the federal injunction, the strike was effectively broken.

Employers also made use of the press, the pulpit, and the public, three constituencies that were almost always on their side. Their opposition prevented strikers from obtaining financial support to sustain long strikes. In some areas, employers succeeded in organizing "citizen's committees"—in reality, vigilante committees—to oppose the strikers. For example, during the Railroad Strike of 1877, businessmen organized local militias to restore order to Chicago streets. Over the years employers showed that they would not easily surrender their control over wages, hours, and working conditions.

The Election of 1896: The Populist-Democrat Merger. Controlled by an Ohio businessman, Marcus Alonzo Hanna, the Republican Convention nominated William McKinley, author of the country's highest tariff and a deserter from the cause of silver. Hailing "the full dinner pail" as its goal, the Republican platform condemned free coinage of silver, hailed the protective tariff, pledged an enlarged navy, and supported the annexation of Hawaii. The platform courted the labor vote by calling for compulsory arbitration of labor disputes in industries involved in interstate commerce.

Early in the Democratic Convention the anti-Cleveland forces, or Silverites, mostly Southerners and Westerners, took control. In their platform the Democrats called for enlarged powers for the Interstate Commerce Commission; free, unlimited coinage of both silver and gold at the ratio of 16 to 1; and tariffs for revenue only. Former Populist William Jennings Bryan was nominated for the presidency, primarily because no Populist of his prestige wanted to risk opposing someone so charismatically attractive. The "Boy Orator of the Platte" was only thirty-six; but he spoke at the convention with what seemed to the delegates to be the voice of the ages. He thrilled listeners with his "Cross of Gold Speech." Bryan championed wage earners, small merchants, miners, farmers, and businesspeople who worked for their money. He invoked the spirit of Andrew Jackson in a strong plea against the moneyed interests. "We beg no longer; we entreat no more. . . . We defy them." He ended with the famous line: "You shall not press down upon the brow of labor this crown of thorns, you shall not crucify mankind upon a cross of gold!"

After naming their own vice-presidential candidate—Tom Watson—the Populists accepted Bryan for president. The decision had not been easy. On the one hand, the Populists realized that by supporting the youthful orator they ran the risk of losing their party identity; but on the other hand, nominating someone else would throw the election to McKinley.

Bryan crossed the country in an eighteen-thousand-mile campaign; in six hundred speeches he addressed about five million people. Ably directed by Hanna, McKinley stayed on his front porch and politely welcomed delegations. Meanwhile Hanna, having scared a war chest of millions of dollars out of already-frightened corporation heads, rallied professors, editors, orators, and authors to attack "free silver" and to castigate the Populists as vicious, subversive radicals. The "people's crusade" marched to defeat. McKinley won by nearly half a million popular votes and by 271 to 176 in the electoral college. The Populists as an effective political force expired. But Populism as an idea had come to stay.

CHAPTER SIXTEEN

The Progressive Movement

After President Theodore Roosevelt ordered Attorney General Philander C. Knox to try J. Pierpont Morgan's Northern Securities Company for conspiracy in restraint of trade, the financier went to the White House and spoke with the president. During their conversation Morgan reportedly asked, "Are you going to attack my other interests, the Steel Trust and the others?" "Certainly not," Roosevelt said, "unless we find out that in any case they have done something that we regard as wrong."

This conversation symbolized the change in government's attitude toward big business. The Progressive era had begun.

The Roots of Progressivism

The Intellectual Background. Social Darwinism, which had earlier gained popularity, now became the general target of American intellectuals. As postulated by the influential English philosopher Herbert Spencer, it stated that Darwin's theory of survival of the fittest in an unavoidable struggle for existence applied to individuals in society. Critics now began to claim that such ideas were wrong, cruel, and inhumane. Equally erroneous, they felt, was the related thesis that the state must remain neutral while people struggled—a powerful few to victory and the great mass to certain defeat.

In 1883 Lester Ward launched the first attack against social Darwinism in America, with his *Dynamic Sociology*. In it, he challenged Spencer's contention that human beings were the helpless victims of senseless evolution. Instead, Ward argued that the human species survived because its members combined to control their environment.

In 1885 a number of American economists, such as Richard Ely of Johns Hopkins, challenged the belief of classical economists that inalterable laws regulated economic life. Together they formed the American Economic Association to propagate the doctrine that the state must intervene to ensure human progress.

In 1889 the social critic Thorstein Veblen analyzed the concept that American capitalists had contributed to the nation's progress in *The Theory of the Leisure Class*. He credited American economic greatness to the engineers and managers of industry rather than to those who supplied the capital. Veblen portrayed capitalists as wasteful consumers, not producers of wealth, interested only in acquisition and prestige, in having more than the next person, and only to show it off.

The Pragmatists William James and John Dewey also convinced many Americans that there are no fixed truths, that whatever works is right—particularly if it works for the majority of people—and that ideas are useful only when they help to transform society.

In his book *An Economic Interpretation of the Constitution* (1913), historian Charles A. Beard led a major assault upon one of the holiest and most cherished American ideas: that the American Constitution was a sacred document, the almost divine product of our sainted forefathers. Beard produced evidence to show that the constitutional fathers were "a small group of men immediately interested through their personal possessions in the outcome of their labors." Careful readers of the book concluded that the Constitution was a class-oriented document designed to protect the interests of propertied Americans. This conclusion led to another: the Constitution could be amended to serve the interests of the many as well as of the few.

Finally, three widely read books—Herbert Croly's *The Promise of American Life* (1909), Walter Weyl's *The New Democracy* (1912), and Walter Lippmann's *A Preface to Politics* (1913) argued that laissez-faire had served its purpose and was now the source of all national evil and that, if permitted to continue, it would lead to the violent overthrow of American democracy by the dispossessed. The only alternative was a "planned society," using the best brains of the country to produce objective, scientific legislation that would preserve democracy while eliminating the abuses of laissez-faire.

The "Muckrakers." Between 1900 and 1914, publicists translated these doctrines into popular terms. The inexpensive magazines developed by S. S. McClure (*McClure's, Cosmopolitan, Munsey's*) proved ideal mediums for the public exposure of the evils of monopolies. "Muckrakers" (the term was coined by Theodore Roosevelt), were writers and reporters who made a profession of exposing political evil and corruption and of espousing the cause of the unfortunate and oppressed. Henry Demarest Lloyd fathered the movement in his two exposés of the Standard Oil Company. Building on this early study, Ida Tarbell wrote a series of articles in 1892 for *McClure's* on the Standard Oil Company, carefully documenting the vast array of unscrupulous business tactics used by Rockefeller to crush his competitors. In a second series that same year, Lincoln Steffens exposed municipal corruption and corrupt alliances between politicians and businessmen. The two series unleashed a flood of muckrakers who investigated political corruption, labor unions, child labor, the food industry, prostitution, and many other elements of American life. Even muckraking novels appeared. One of the most celebrated, Upton Sinclair's *The Jungle* (1906), exposed the horrible conditions of Chicago's slaughterhouses.

Until about 1910 the muckrakers generally wrote careful studies intended to force reform; as such, they were read eagerly by the public. Thereafter exposure turned into sensation-mongering. But by then muckraking had served its purpose: it had revealed the squalid relations of business and politics, and this exposure led to demand for reform. Most of all, the muckrakers forced businessmen to realize that they could not avoid their social responsibility.

The Crusade for Social Justice

Pioneers.   In 1890 Jacob Riis wrote *How the Other Half Lives* about the conditions in urban slums to convince Americans that there were evils that had to be wiped out; the social conscience of America was still dormant.

The work of transforming that conscience begun during the Jacksonian Era and, resumed by muckrakers, was taken up by a number of American ministers, priests, rabbis, and social workers whose flocks and charges lived in the turn-of-the-century slums. These men and women were able to convince philanthropists to support surveys of existing conditions in order to accumulate data to use in urging remedial legislation. When collected these data revealed that more than 8,000,000 women were at work, mostly in dismal sweatshops; 1,700,000 children under sixteen labored in cotton mills and on farms; and the death rate in slum areas was four times that of other urban areas. They also collected facts about juvenile gangs, organized crime, prostitution, and police corruption. When publicized, these facts shocked Americans to action.

Charity.   Private philanthropies and agencies acted before the government intervened. Private clinics, orphanages, children's aid societies, and settlement houses were established, usually by social workers and ministers. Located in poor sections, settlement houses were essentially community centers offering guidance, education, and needed services to the community. Two of the most famous were Chicago's Hull House, founded in 1889 by Jane Addams, and the Henry Street Settlement, established by Lillian Wald in 1893. Settlement house workers focused on social problems such as health care, school dropouts, and hunger. Most of the settlement house workers were young, middle-class women, usually college educated. Seeing that American society permitted them little opportunity to exploit their talent, they seized the chance to work with the poor, applying their energy, ability, and idealism to the practical problems facing the urban poor. Settlement house workers sought reform of tenement house laws, regulation of child and women's labor, and improved schools. They established libraries, playgrounds, social clubs, and day nurseries. But, supported by private donations, settlement houses offered—despite their real accomplishments—only a partial solution to the problems of the urban poor.

During this period visiting Nurses' Associations, YMCAs, and the Boy Scouts flourished, too. Reforms also began to be seen in the treatment of criminals. Inspired by experiments at the State Reformatory at Elmira and by the penal philosophy of Thomas Mott Osborne, prisons now separated first offenders from habitual criminals. The legal system also experimented with indeterminate sentences, early release under parole, special institutions for female offenders, industrial training programs, special juvenile courts, and other techniques to help in the rehabilitation and fair treatment of convicted criminals.

Remedial Legislation. Bowing to continuous pressure from the National Child Labor Committee, every state had established a minimum labor-age limit by 1914; usually the cutoff age was fourteen. A number of states prohibited children between the ages of fourteen and sixteen from working at night or at dangerous occupations. In 1916 the Congress passed the Keating-Owen Child Labor Act, prohibiting the shipment across state lines of goods manufactured in whole or in part by children under sixteen. This law was subsequently declared unconstitutional, but other legislation followed: Illinois pioneered an eight-hour-a-day law for women (1893); between 1909 and 1917 thirty-nine states enacted legislation limiting work hours, with nearly every state limiting the hours of women workers. Agitation for minimum-wage legislation also began, with Massachusetts leading the way in reform. By 1917 about ten states had enacted minimum-wage laws for women. By 1916 thirty states and territories had passed accident insurance plans or workmen's compensation laws, making accident awards to injured employees automatic; formerly, a worker had to bring a suit against the employer to establish negligence. Moreover, tragedies like the 1911 Triangle Fire, in which 150 women workers died because the New York City shirtwaist factory had no fire escapes, forced cities to pass stricter building codes and states to legislate factory inspection acts. In many of the struggles over social and economic reform, women were at the forefront. Women's continued support for the right to vote was often expressed in their support of reform in general.

The Reactionary Supreme Court. The courts proved to be the most formidable barrier to social reform. To conservative lawyers and jurists who revered property rights (viewing them as synonymous with liberty) legislation for social rights seemed anarchistic, an unwarranted extension of governmental power. This attitude was clearly revealed in the Supreme Court's decision in 1905 in the case of *Lochner v. New York*. The question before the Court was the legality of a New York statute limiting the working hours of bakers to ten a day and sixty a week. By a five to four decision the Court held that the statute constituted meddlesome interference with the rights of the individual worker to make a labor contract. In his dissent Justice Oliver Wendell Holmes, Jr., pointed out that the Fourteenth Amendment did not contain any particular economic theory and defended the right of the government to intervene and limit liberty if it seemed necessary to correct a current evil.

In *Muller v. Oregon* (1908), however, the Court did respond to the arguments of attorney Louis D. Brandeis. The case involved a challenge to an Oregon law limiting to ten the number of hours for women laundry workers. Brandeis, who had been persuaded to take the case by the Consumers' League, the most effective women's organization of the era, depended chiefly on sociological and economic data that he had compiled on the harmful consequences to women of overlong hours of work. In other words, Brandeis based his case on the "logic of facts," as he labeled it, rather than legal precedent. The Court's acceptance of Brandeis's argument marked its first support of social legislation and sociological jurisprudence. Eight years later President Woodrow Wilson appointed Brandeis to the Supreme Court, making him the first Jewish American to sit on the Court.

Municipal Reform. City government was the disgrace of democratic politics. Machine government had replaced representative government. In most large cities, an all-powerful political boss ruled over an army of precinct captains and ward heelers. The boss decided on the election of aldermen to office, distribution of patronage, and contract awards. Loyalty to the machine was fostered among the people by careful distribution of small favors and by giving slum-dwelling immigrants a sense of belonging to the community. Behind this benevolent front, bribery and graft were rife in protecting criminals, prostitutes, and saloon keepers, or in awarding franchises and contracts for railways, sewage systems, gas and electric lines, garbage disposal, and other public services.

Corruption caused the rise of civic leagues, reform movements, non-partisan groups, and municipal voters' leagues. Under these umbrellas, reformers cleaned up Chicago's political machine; defeated Tammany Hall in New York City (1913) by electing a reform mayor, John P. Mitchell; and imprisoned the mayor of Minneapolis. A new municipal leadership arose in such figures as Samuel M. "Golden Rule" Jones of Toledo and Tom Johnson of Cleveland who readjusted tax burdens, reduced tramcar rates, fostered city-owned public utilities to correct franchise evils, and expanded city social services.

Reformers also stepped up the war on the political machines by introducing the direct primary for nominating candidates, securing increased powers of "home rule" to break the hold of state politicians over the city, and experimenting with citizen initiatives in legislation. For example, citizens now could introduce bills into the municipal legislature by petition (this was known as an initiative); compel the legislature to submit issues to the people for decision by referendum; and, using the referendum, force an incompetent official to run again for office before his term expired (recall).

Frontal assaults were launched on the mayor-council structure of city government. In 1903 Galveston, Texas, began to experiment with municipal rule by commission. Voters elected five commissioners, experts in city management, to run Galveston, which had been devastated by a hurricane. When it was discovered that the commission government failed to centralize responsibility sufficiently, cities tried a new plan, the city-manager plan, first adopted in Dayton, Ohio. This plan retained the commissioners but had them choose a professional manager to administer the city.

By 1916 municipal reform had succeeded in large measure. Although corruption persisted, it was driven underground. City administration had become professionalized and efficient.

State Reform. Conditions in the state governments between 1900 and 1914 seemed no better than in the cities. Political power remained concentrated in two interlocked agencies, the state lobby and the state party committee. The lobby was maintained by the big business interests, while the state committee operated through the party caucus in the legislature. By bribing a majority of the caucus through the state party committee, the lobby could write or kill legislation at will or have its own agents appointed to cabinet posts, state boards, and judgeships.

The wave of progressive reform produced many state crusaders devoted to honest government: Robert LaFollette in Wisconsin, Albert Cummins in Iowa, Albert J. Beveridge in Indiana, Charles Evans Hughes in New York, Woodrow Wilson in New Jersey, and Hiram Johnson in California, to cite a few. These reformers faced a difficult task. They had to battle vested railroad and public utility interests, and push through reforms such as direct primaries on a compulsory, statewide basis; the short ballot; the direct election of senators; the initiative and the referendum (first in South Dakota, 1898); the recall (first in Oregon, 1908); and a variety of corrupt-practices laws to limit and control campaign expenditures. Once the governmental structure was overhauled, the more progressive states began to regulate public utilities and railroads to secure reasonable rates and prompt service for the public.

By 1914, then, the idea of laissez-faire government was on the wane at the municipal and the state levels.

The "Presidency of Theodore Roosevelt (1901–9)

The "Square Deal." When an anarchist assassinated President McKinley in Sep-tember 1901, Vice President Theodore Roosevelt assumed the office. In his inaugural address the forty-two-year-old New Yorker made a passionate plea for federal intervention to eliminate evils and abuses in the nation. Congress was then dominated by the Old Guard Republican dictator Uncle Joe Cannon who, as Speaker of the House and chairman of the all-powerful Rules Committee, determined the composition of committees, the measures to come before the House, and those representatives who might speak on the floor. The Senate was similarly dominated by the Old Guard, with Mark Hanna as their leader. These legislators viewed the Republican Roosevelt's program for government intervention (and the young President himself) with unease bordering on hostility. The energetic and outspoken Roosevelt, therefore, took his case to the people during an extensive speaking tour. Committed to the ideals of public service, he called for a "square deal" for the harassed small businessmen and the oppressed workers and farmers.

Congress might still have ignored him, but the anthracite coal strike of 1902 played into his hands. Led by John Mitchell, the United Mine Workers struck for union recognition, higher wages, and shorter hours. The mine operators refused either to negotiate or arbitrate, and the country was faced with a winter without coal. When Roosevelt offered to mediate, the miners accepted, but the operators refused. The furious President threatened to call out the troops, not to break the strike, but to operate the mines. This threat of intervention caused the operators to submit to arbitration.

Roosevelt was acclaimed as a fearless champion of the people and his triumph led to his overwhelming reelection in 1904, despite bitter Old Guard opposition. When his two terms were completed, he had firmly fixed the pattern of federal intervention as part of the constitutional processes of the United States.

Regulation of Trusts.   Although Roosevelt was known as a "trustbuster," in fact he moved cautiously in this area, and usually only after consultation with congressional leaders. In 1903 he persuaded Congress to create a Department of Labor and Commerce and within it a Bureau of Corporations to investigate business and warn those engaged in harmful operations. In the same year Congress, under his skillful prodding, also passed the Expedition Act, which speeded up the handling of antitrust suits in the courts.

Roosevelt's fame as a trustbuster originated when he ordered the Justice Department, under the Sherman Antitrust Act, to prosecute the Northern Securities Company, which controlled the Northern Pacific; the Great Northern; and the Chicago, Quincy, and Burlington railways. The company had been created in 1901 during the battle between James J. Hill and Edward Harriman for control of the Burlington Railroad. Backed by J. P. Morgan, Hill controlled the Great Northern and the Northern Pacific railroads, while Harriman, associated with Rockefeller, dominated the Union Pacific; both wanted the Burlington as a Chicago link. Through aggressive stock purchases (which pushed the price from $110 a share to $1,000), Hill and Morgan won a majority of the stock and turned the Northern Securities Company into a stock-holding company. The company virtually controlled the western railroads. In 1904, by a five to four decision, the Supreme Court upheld the government and ordered Northern Securities dissolved.

Having asserted the power of the Sherman Act and the government's willingness to vigorously prosecute violators, Roosevelt wielded the antitrust club during the remainder of his administration. The Justice Department brought suits against the Beef Trust, Standard Oil, the American Tobacco Company, and the Du Pont Corporation. Yet the President continued to seek the advice of big business and to ask for its support during his reelection campaign. Moreover, he did not seek to break every trust. For example, in 1907 he allowed Morgan's U.S. Steel to take over an important competitor. The "malefactors of great wealth" learned that Roosevelt's bark was often worse than his bite. They were, nevertheless, forced to tread more cautiously.

Regulation of Railroads.   Roosevelt led Congress to strengthen the Interstate Commerce Commission in its dealings with the railroads. The Elkins Railroad Act (1903) increased the ICC's power by making rebates illegal and by providing for the punishment of both grantors and recipients. In 1907 Standard Oil was fined $29,000,000 for violation of this law. (A higher court later set aside this fine.) The Hepburn Act (1906) enlarged the Commission from five to seven members; extended its jurisdiction over express companies, pipelines, ferries, and terminals; gave it power to fix rates; forced the burden of a judicial contest on the carriers (that is, the Commission's rates went into effect immediately until a court reversed them); made it illegal for a railroad to carry goods it had produced; set up a uniform system of accounting as an aid to determining uniform rates; and forbade the issuance of free passes to any but railroad employees.

Regulation of Resources. The first warnings that America's resources were being depleted by reckless railroad, lumber, and cattle magnates had been sounded during Cleveland's first administration. Not only did private owners illegally possess more than eighty million acres of public domain, but they made no effort to protect existing resources against natural destruction or to replace what was being destroyed. Public conscience was unaffected by revelations of these matters.

In 1891 the first halting move toward conservation was effected with the passage of the Forest Reserve Act. It was followed in 1894 by the Carey Act, permitting the government to aid private contractors who constructed irrigation projects to reclaim poor land. But not until the nature-loving Roosevelt dramatized the destruction of natural resources and blasted the "predatory" private interests did Congress enact meaningful conservation legislation.

By the end of his administration Roosevelt had effected a revolution in public protection of natural resources. In the Newlands Act of 1902 the government used funds from the sale of public lands to reclaim large amounts of land via dam construction and irrigation. Farmers paid for water they received from these projects, thus creating a revolving fund for new projects. By 1907 twenty-eight projects were underway in fourteen states. To protect the forests, the government revived the Forest Reserve Act of 1891 and

set aside 148 million acres of timberland. Roosevelt made this land into national parks, placing them under the supervision of Gifford Pinchot who, in turn, founded the National Forest Service.

By devoting his annual message of 1907 to conservation, Roosevelt brought the problem to national attention. He called a Conservation Conference in 1908 that was attended by state governors, legislators, scientific experts, and prominent citizens. The conference laid down some basic principles of conservation: extension of forest fire-fighting forces; protection of navigable waterways; control over timber-cutting; and retention of government rights to coal, oil, and natural gas. Pinchot became the head of the National Conservation Commission. Although this commission soon expired for lack of congressional financial support, progress was made toward its goals. By 1909 forty-one state conservation commissions had been created.

Roosevelt also formed an inland waterways commission to determine the best use of the nation's waterways for transportation, irrigation, and water power. Historians are virtually unanimous that his achievements in conservation are Roosevelt's most enduring contribution to American life.

Regulation of Foods and Drugs. Muckrakers Mark Sullivan and Samuel Hopkins Adams analyzed the manufacture of patent medicines and showed that in hundreds of instances the public was being defrauded or harmed through worthless potions claiming to be panaceas or those containing harmful elements such as unadvertised alcohol, opium, or corrosives. After the chief chemist of the Department of Agriculture confirmed these revelations, Roosevelt pressured Congress to pass the Pure Food and Drug Act (1906), forbidding the use of certain narcotics in patent medicines, restricting the use of preservatives and adulterants in foods, and forcing manufacturers to list all ingredients on labels. (Since there were no regulations covering false advertising, the size of print on the label, or the intelligibility of the language on it, manufacturers easily evaded the act.)

Meat manufacturers had already been denounced for "embalmed beef" sold to the armed forces during the Spanish-American War. After Upton Sinclair's *The Jungle* (1906) appeared, Roosevelt ordered an official survey of the meat-packing industry. It revealed that Sinclair had been conservative in his revelations. Congress responded with passage of the Meat Inspection Act of 1906, which established rules for sanitary meat packing provided for by examination and approval of meat by federal inspectors. The meat packers had no choice but to clean up their establishments.

The Presidency of William Howard Taft (1909–13)

His progressive work done, Theodore Roosevelt named his Secretary of War, William Howard Taft, as his successor and went to Africa to hunt lions. Taft won the election of 1908 handily against the Democratic candidate, William Jennings Bryan, a third-time contender. The experienced and able Taft was hardly a militant progressive, but the achievements of his one term added considerably to the accretion of progressive legislation and governmental action.

Trusts. Loyal to Roosevelt's "Square Deal," Taft continued a number of his policies. The Mann-Elkins Act of 1910 corrected some of the faults of the Hepburn Act: ICC jurisdiction was extended to telephone and telegraph lines, no automatic rate increases were permitted without ICC consent, and a special court was created to expedite appeals of ICC decisions. Taft's antitrust division instituted twice as many suits as Roosevelt's had. The administration won significant victories over Standard Oil and American Tobacco. In these cases the Court ruled that the Sherman Act made manufacturing monopolies illegal. The Court also limited prosecution of "restraint of trade" to unreasonable restraint, the so-called "rule of reason." (This often-criticized ruling actually made the Sherman Act workable. Many illegal business contracts have the effect of restraining trade without primarily intending to; the Court held only such contracts illegal where the primary intent was to restrain trade and effect a monopoly.) In the field of conservation, Taft removed important oil lands from sale and created the Bureau of Mines to guard over other mineral resources.

Reforms. Taft not only continued Roosevelt's policies but added some of his own reforms. He divided the Department of Commerce and Labor into two departments for more efficient administration; signed into law an act limiting campaign expenditures and forcing them to be made public; encouraged the Sixteenth Amendment to the Constitution legalizing the income tax; created a postal savings bank and a parcel post system; and extended the eight-hour day to workers involved with government contracts. These policies clearly show that Taft was in the progressive tradition.

Criticism. Taft was not, however, always in the progressive camp. He supported the highly protective tariffs of the Payne-Aldrich Act (1909) which most progressives—who now called themselves "insurgents"—opposed. And when Pinchot accused Richard A. Ballinger of the Department of the Interior of leasing public waterpower sites and coal lands to private syndicates like the Guggenheim-Morgan combine, Taft removed Pinchot. The evidence never sustained Pinchot's charge, but conservationists subsequently regarded Taft with hostility.

In 1910 a full-fledged revolution to oust the dictatorial Old Guard Uncle Joe Cannon of Illinois from his privileges as Speaker met with Taft's silence. Progressives saw this as siding with Cannon, although the President had tried but failed to curb the congressman's powers previously. The progressives now succeeded in stripping Cannon of his power to appoint the standing committees and to serve on the Rules Committee. Next Taft alienated farmers by agreeing to a reciprocity treaty with Canada under which that country lowered the tariff on American manufactured goods and the United States lowered its tariff on Canadian wheat. (The Canadian Parliament rejected this treaty, however, after the United States Senate approved it, costing Taft a loss in stature.)

The Election of 1912. The upshot of Taft's inconsistencies was a serious split in Republican ranks during the election of 1912. The "Standpatters" took over the Republican Convention and nominated Taft. The Insurgents, led by Senator Robert LaFollette of Wisconsin, left the party and regrouped as the Progressive Party, with the Bull Moose as their symbol and Theodore Roosevelt as their standard-bearer. Incorporating his doctrine of government intervention under the slogan "The New Nationalism," Roosevelt marched to battle on two fronts, against the Old Guard Republicans and against the liberal governor of New Jersey, Woodrow Wilson, the Democratic nominee.

Roosevelt's nationalism called for a national approach and a strong president to deal with the country's problems. It favored reforms to protect women, children, and workers and distinguished between "good" and "bad" trusts. The Progressive Party gained the backing of many women, some of whom actually worked in the campaign, the first time a political party had enlisted women in its organization.

The "Great Commoner" William Jennings Bryan himself had nominated Wilson at the Democratic Convention. To meet Roosevelt's "New Nationalism," Wilson put forward his own "New Freedom." Although he received only 40 percent of the popular vote, Wilson won overwhelmingly in the electoral college. Taft garnered the hard-core Republican vote, Roosevelt got that of the party's progressive wing, while Wilson gained the support of both conservative and liberal Democrats. Together, Wilson, as the progressive Democrat, Roosevelt, as the insurgent Republican, and Eugene V. Debs, who was the Socialist candidate, polled 75 percent of the vote. The election of 1912 was a requiem for laissez-faire. The modern world had simply become too complex for such an approach.

Woodrow Wilson and the New Freedom

Politics and Morality. The progressive movement reached a climax during the first administration of Woodrow Wilson. The idealistic Wilson saw politics as a moral war, with righteousness on the side of reform. Unrighteousness, he felt, stemmed from the extremes of plutocracy and mobocracy. Government must steer a middle course between the greed of big business and popular excess, either of which could destroy free, competitive enterprise. The "New Freedom" was for the "man who is on the make rather than the man who is already made." Since those who are on the make were in the majority, the machinery of government had to be put in their hands. With government in the hands of the people (i.e., in Wilson's hands, for like Roosevelt, he believed in a strong chief executive) each institution in America, whether derived from capital or labor, was to be called to the bar of judgment. There it would have to state "by what principle of national advantage, as contrasted with selfish privilege" it drew on the resources of the government. In this spirit, Wilson called the "money" interests to be judged and found them guilty.

Regulating the "Money Trust." In 1907 the country was economically sound, yet a "Banker's Panic" occurred that brought about a collapse of business followed by severe unemployment. Overspeculation by private banks in stocks and bonds was one cause of the panic. But a basic flaw in the National Banking Act of 1863 also contributed. This law provided that an expansion of currency could occur only by sale of government bonds. In good times the government paid off its debts; hence, it sold no bonds. Yet it was precisely during good times that more currency was needed. Therefore, when America entered into a period of prosperity, it lacked sufficient currency to sustain it. (The situation reversed itself in bad times. In other words, the currency was "inversely elastic," that is, there was too little of it in good times and too much in bad times.)

Passage in 1908 of the Aldrich-Vreeland Act permitted national banks to make emergency issues of currency in good times. This was a patchwork solution, however. Somehow the currency had to be made directly elastic so that it would expand with prosperity and contract with recession. The problem of inverse elasticity was only one of seventeen defects in the banking structure uncovered by a congressional investigation in 1912. Even more sensational was the revelation by the Pujo Committee a year earlier that a few financiers controlled the banking system and, through interlocking directorates, almost all of big business as well. These investigations produced major legislation to correct tendencies toward plutocracy permanently.

The Federal Reserve System. Banking was placed under federal regulation and forced to assume national responsibility in the Federal Reserve Act of 1913. This act made currency elastic, centralized bank deposits so that stronger banks could help the weaker, and compelled private bankers to share their control over money with the government. The measure divided the country into twelve districts, each supervised by a central bank. In every district national banks had to deposit 6 percent of their capital and surplus with the Federal Reserve Bank. These deposits created an immense pool of money for emergencies.

Banks in trouble could also request help from the Federal Reserve Bank. To secure an elastic currency, the Federal Reserve Bank was permitted to issue Federal Reserve Notes backed up by gold and commercial paper (such as promissory notes, drafts). When a business needed cash, the private banks could take commercial paper to the Federal Reserve Bank, pay a rediscount rate, and get Federal Reserve Notes (cash) in exchange. If private banks had too much cash, the process was reversed. To prevent overspeculation with depositors' money by banks, the act created required ratios between loans and cash. Finally, to manage and supervise this system, a Federal Reserve Board of Governors was established. The nation finally had a true central banking system and a flexible but safe currency.

Regulating Tariffs.   On the day after his inauguration, Wilson called a special session of the House and the Senate. The significance of this action was underscored by the fact that Wilson appeared personally before Congress. (The last president to have done so was John Adams in 1801.) Wilson asked Congress to reduce tariffs so that American industry might become truly competitive with European industry. Congress responded to the President's plea and skillful maneuvering with the Underwood Tariff Act of 1913. This measure permitted products manufactured abroad that competed with those produced by the "trusts" (iron, steel, etc.) free entry into the United States or to enter after payment of a nominal sum. The overall average of duties was lowered from the Payne-Aldrich rates of 40 percent to about 25 percent. And, to make up for the loss of revenue, the act levied a graduated tax based on income, authorized by the Sixteenth Amendment, which had been ratified in February 1913.

Regulation of the Trusts.   Wilson felt that the failure of the Sherman Act lay in its inability to define "combination" and "restraint of trade." He sought a law that would contain precise definitions of these concepts, making it easier to prosecute unlawful combines. The Clayton Antitrust Act (1914) undertook this task. It forbade stock-holding where the intent was to lessen competition; prohibited interlocking directorates in competing concerns with assets exceeding $1,000,000 or banks with assets exceeding $5,000,000; outlawed numerous practices that encouraged unfair competition, including price discrimination and tie-in agreements; made officers of corporations liable for illegal acts committed by corporations; spelled out methods for securing relief for victims of these malpractices; and exempted labor unions and farm associations from antitrust prosecution, while restricting the use of injunctions in labor disputes.

In 1914 Congress created the Federal Trade Commission. This nonpartisan board could investigate complaints about unfair practices or institute its own investigation wherever monopoly was suspected. If it found monopolistic practices, the FTC could issue "cease and desist" orders to the offender and then, if necessary, secure judicial injunction to enforce its orders.

Regulating Labor Practices.   Throughout his presidency, Wilson showed sympathy for labor. In 1914, after state militia and mine guards killed twenty-six men, women, and children in a tent colony of strikers in Ludlow, Colorado, he sent in federal troops to end the violence. A year later the President signed the LaFollette Seaman's Act establishing a minimum wage and improved working conditions for seamen sailing under American registry. The Keating-Owen Child Labor Act of 1915 prohibited interstate commerce in goods made by child labor (the Supreme Court declared this act unconstitutional in *Hammer v. Dagenhart*, 1918). And the Adamson Act (1916) established an eight-hour day for workers in interstate transport.

Regulating Farmers.   During this period, what farmers needed most were long-term loans at low rates of interest, which were difficult to secure from private banks. In 1916 Congress passed a Federal Farm Loan Act creating Federal Loan Banks empowered to make long-term loans on mortgages at reasonable rates to farm cooperatives. Farmers rapidly organized such cooperatives to take advantage of the law.

The Limits of Wilson's Progressivism. Wilson had entered office with relatively little political experience, but he proved himself a vigorous, effective, and inspiring leader. Nevertheless, there were limits to his progressivism. For example, he did not campaign for the prohibition of child labor and refused to support a constitutional amendment granting women the vote. His record on racism was especially poor. During his administration southern segregation hardened and white opposition to black voting became widespread. Lynchings continued, and the educational situation for southern blacks was abysmal. These problems even reached the federal government. Government employees were segregated and Congress was controlled by white Southerners.

Wilson failed to confront these issues. He refused even to appoint a commission to study the problems blacks were experiencing. In his disregard for their rights, he was a typical progressive, since most progressives were strongly prejudiced against nonwhites. In their struggle to gain the vote many progressive suffragettes denigrated the intelligence of black voters. The attitude of progressives—who constituted one of the most liberal elements of white society—dismayed black leaders and encouraged the development of black militancy.

Black Militants.   The foremost militant was William E. B. Du Bois, the first black to receive a Ph.D. from Harvard. Believing that many blacks were willing to settle for second-class citizenship, Du Bois sought to make them proud of their blackness ("beauty is black") and to organize themselves to run their own businesses, newspapers, and colleges. He encouraged the growth of a black literature. In pursuing the preservation of black identity, Du Bois rejected the assimilative and accommodating response of leaders like Booker T. Washington who advocated that blacks not waste their energy in fighting segregation but accept it in return for economic opportunity and advancement. In 1905 Du Bois and other black militants met at Niagara Falls and issued a list of demands including an end to segregation, the right to vote freely, equal justice, equal economic opportunity, and an end to union discrimination. Stirred by the Niagara meeting, a group of white liberals founded the National Association for the Advancement of Colored People (NAACP) to end racial discrimination. Although the NAACP's leaders were initially mostly white, Du Bois became a national officer and the editor of its journal.

The Niagara meeting and the establishment of the NAACP spelled the end of the accommodation preached by Washington, as blacks began to study their own history to stimulate pride in their heritage and identity. In 1915 Carter G. Woodson established the Association for the Study of Negro Life and History and a year later created *The Journal of Negro History,* the first major scholarly publication devoted to black studies. The new black militancy, however, had little effect on Wilson. He remained convinced that segregation was good for both blacks and whites.

CHAPTER SEVENTEEN

American Expansion Overseas

The man in the white suit strode in the rain through the streets of Panama City, climbed aboard a steam shovel to do some digging, and afterward inspected the canal's locks. "This is one of the greatest works of the world," he told the workers clustered around him. "It is a greater work than you, yourselves, at the moment realize."

The man in the white suit was President Theodore Roosevelt, and the place was the site of the Panama Canal. Its construction symbolized the change in American foreign policy from isolationism to expansionism in the latter part of the nineteenth century.

The Challenge to Isolation

Civil War Legacies. By 1898 America had turned from isolation to overseas expansionism. What brought about this transformation? The Civil War raised a number of issues that forced America to concern itself with the activities of foreign powers. During the war France had cre-

ated a protectorate in Mexico and installed Archduke Maximilian of Austria as its titular head. Secretary of State Seward pressured the French to withdraw and in 1867 they did.

Next, the United States had to deal with the damages done by the British-built Confederate cruiser the *Alabama*. Convinced that England had violated its own neutrality laws, America sought either $220 million in payment of direct and indirect damages or, as Senator Sumner preferred, the cession of Canada to the United States. In 1871 both countries signed the Treaty of Washington, providing for arbitration of the *Alabama* claims. A year later an arbitration tribunal, meeting in Geneva awarded the United States $15.5 million in direct damages.

In 1867, prodded by Seward, the government purchased Alaska from Russia for $7.2 million, partly to "sandwich" in western Canada—which it hoped to annex—between United States' territories and partly to remove another foreign power from the continent. (To gain congressional approval for what opponents quickly dubbed "Seward's Folly," the Secretary of

State orchestrated a massive campaign to win over the public by educating them about Alaska's great potential.)

Hawaii. The end of the Civil War brought an expansion in foreign trade and overseas investments. Some of the nation's surplus capital went into Hawaiian sugar and pineapple plantations. (New England missionaries had paved the way for American interests in Hawaii as early as 1819.) Since the 1840s Americans had considered Hawaii as within the Western Hemisphere and thus subject to the restrictions of the Monroe Doctrine; that is, there was to be no further colonization of the Islands by European powers. To ensure this America signed a reciprocity treaty with Hawaii in 1875, permitting Hawaiian sugar to enter the United States duty-free. It also forbade Hawaii to make a similar arrangement with any foreign power or to grant or lease to another power a port, harbor, territory, or special privileges. When the treaty was renewed in 1887, it gave the United States the right to have a naval base at Pearl Harbor. American sugar growers in Hawaii were struck hard, however, after the McKinley Tariff of 1890 removed sugar from the free list.

When the ruling monarch, Queen Liliuokalani, acted to strip them of their political power, the resident Americans organized a native "revolution" in 1893 and deposed the Queen with the unofficial aid of the United States Navy. A delegation sent to Washington successfully negotiated an annexation treaty with the Harrison administration, but the new president, Grover Cleveland, withdrew it. When McKinley became President, the treaty was resubmitted, and the Senate failed to muster the necessary two-thirds majority to pass it. Supporters offered several arguments: Hawaii was a strategic necessity for the American Navy; it would provide the United States with a tremendous outlet for surplus capital; the American people had a moral obligation to the Hawaiians to protect and nurture them; America must fulfill its "manifest destiny" overseas; and if the United States did not annex the Islands, some other country would. These arguments finally prevailed, and on July 7, 1898, Hawaii was admitted to the United States by a joint resolution of Congress. (Such resolutions required only a majority vote.)

Samoa. Arguments for American imperialism had actually appeared earlier. The Navy, such as it was in the 1870s, regarded the harbor of Pago Pago on the Samoan island of Tuitula as an ideal South Pacific naval base. In 1878, by a formal treaty, the United States acquired Pago Pago. But this act of securing a remote naval base proved incompatible with isolationism when England and Germany challenged America for possession of Samoa. In 1889 a war was shaping up among the naval squadrons of the three powers in a Samoan harbor when a typhoon wrecked all their ships. This disaster had a sobering effect, and a month later the three nations negotiated a settlement, dividing Samoa between the United States and Germany, with Britain receiving other land in the Pacific as compensation.

Latin America. With the Pan-American Conference of 1889, Secretary of State James G. Blaine sought to correct an unfavorable balance of trade. The bulk of Latin America's exports went to the United

States, and 87 percent of them entered duty-free; most of the nation's imports came from European countries. This situation had been desirable when the United States had no exportable surplus. Now that it did have one, the government insisted that this imbalance be adjusted by a policy of reciprocity. The Latin Americans responded unsympathetically to this demand, and the conference broke up with the issue unresolved.

But Latin Americans had taken note of the new aggressive attitude emanating from the United States State Department. In 1891 an unpleasant incident, in which two American sailors were killed in a barroom brawl in Valparaiso, Chile, confirmed this impression. Instead of ignoring the event, President Harrison blew it up into an international incident, and the two countries came close to war. Only the coming to power of a new government in Chile averted conflict. But Latin Americans noted with alarm the new look of American foreign policy.

Conflict with England. If the Chilean episode disturbed Latin America, the Anglo-Venezuelan boundary dispute (1895) doubled its anxiety. Gold had been discovered in a disputed border region between Venezuela and British Guiana. Each party to the dispute intensified its land claims. Venezuela then appealed to the United States to arbitrate the matter, but England refused arbitration. Taking advantage of anti-British feeling in the country, President Cleveland, who was seeking an election issue, and Secretary of State Richard Olney composed a tough note charging that England was violating the Monroe Doctrine and insisting she submit to arbitration of the disputed areas. American

interest, according to the note, stemmed from the fact that the United States "is practically sovereign on this continent and its fiat is law upon the subjects to which it confines its interposition."

Although the note threatened war, the British Prime Minister, Lord Salisbury, was unmoved. But Latin America was outraged—here was an unforeseen extension of the Monroe Doctrine. When Salisbury dismissed Olney's note, the furious Cleveland, in undiplomatically blunt language, asked Congress to ignore the British rejection and to set up a compulsory arbitration commission. The United States, he said, was prepared to take the consequences—the Navy was in readiness. The situation was saved when England backed down because of trouble with the Boers in South Africa and with Germany. In 1899 the commission awarded most of the disputed area to England.

The Rise of Imperial-Mindedness. By 1898 America obviously had a split policy: on the one hand it was officially isolationist; on the other, it was unofficially involved in economic expansion, political assertion, and "entangling" alliances. What had caused this situation?

Imperialism is the conscious creation of an empire, a deliberate expansion of a country's domain and dominion. Many factors lead to imperialism, including the need for resources and markets. A rapidly growing domestic industry may require cheap sources of raw materials from foreign lands. That this factor was already operating in the American economy is attested to by the growth of American imports from $363 million in 1860 to $850 million in 1900. A nation may produce an exportable surplus which, although not large when compared with its domestic market, could be the margin between profit and "break-even." Thus, United States exports rose from $333 million in 1860 to $1.4 billion in 1900.

Another reason for imperialism is that accumulated capital may be searching for more profitable areas of investment. American surplus investment capital mounted from almost nothing in 1860 to $500 million in 1900. Finally, the military may see in such a policy an opportunity to increase its power. Thus, distressed by the poor condition of the navy, Captain Alfred Thayer Mahan impressed upon the public the need for sea power through two books, *The Influence of Sea Power upon History* (1890) and *The Influence of Sea Power upon the French Revolution and Empire* (1892). If the United States wanted to win the race for power, Mahan persuasively argued, a strong oceangoing navy was necessary as were overseas bases to maintain it. Mahan's ideas greatly affected Benjamin Tracy, who became Secretary of the Navy in 1889. Mainly because of Tracy's vigorous sponsorship, the American Navy, which ranked twelfth in the world in 1893, rose to third in 1900.

The Spanish-American War

Cuba. In 1898 Spain owned Cuba. To many Americans and most Cubans this seemed outlandish. Spain's ownership profited neither herself nor the Cubans. Furthermore, all of the sixteenth and seventeenth century conquering powers had been driven from the Western Hemisphere except Spain. (Canada had become virtually independent. There were, of course,

British Honduras and British, French, and Dutch Guiana; but Americans felt that such small ownership did not materially alter the argument.) Cuba looked more to the United States than Spain anyway: American investments in Cuba surpassed $50 million by 1898 and Cuban trade with the United States was at least $100 million annually. Yet Spain was in a position to choke off this economic investment at will.

Cubans, for their part, were in almost constant revolt against the corrupt and economically exploitative Spanish authority. It became inevitable that the Americans and the Cubans should forge a strong bond, and they did, as evidenced by the establishment of a revolutionary Cuban junta on American shores, popular American support for filibustering expeditions to overthrow Spanish rule, and congressional efforts to grant the rebels the rights of belligerents, which virtually constituted formal recognition. When a rebel vessel, the *Virginius*, was seized in 1878 and eight Americans executed, the United States and Spain almost went to war. Spain apologized, however, and paid indemnities.

In 1894 the United States decided that Spain had an undeservedly privileged position in Cuba's economy since all Cuba's exports went to the United States, but all her imports were forced to come from Spain. The Wilson-Gorman Tariff of that year removed Cuban sugar from the free list. Cubans now had to pay a 40-percent impost. Since Cuba's economy was based on this one crop, the tariff meant economic ruin for the island, and rebellion ensued in February 1895. Spain sent General Valeriano Weyler y Nicolau to put down the rebellion. As part of his campaign, the brutal general built prison camps for captured rebels. In one province fifty thousand of the incarcerated died.

The American "jingo," or yellow, press (as the sensationalist papers were called) reported lurid stories of Spanish atrocities. But fearful of disturbing Spanish-American relations, President McKinley initially preferred to mediate through normal diplomatic channels.

"Remember the Maine." On February 15, 1898, however, the American battleship *Maine*—which McKinley had sent to Cuba to protect American citizens—exploded and sank in Havana's harbor and 260 crewmen died. Theodore Roosevelt expressed the popular view that the "Maine was sunk by an act of dirty treachery on the part of the Spaniards," though investigation could not determine guilt for the explosion. (To this day it is unresolved.) The case was tried in the yellow press; during this period the circulation of Hearst's New York *Journal* increased from 416,885 to 1,025,624. War fever rose even higher.

The Small Voice of Peace. American business leaders opposed American intervention. The financial press waged an anti-war crusade in its editorials; the stock market slumped with every war scare. It seemed to the business community that, having finally emerged from the depression of 1893, the nation should not jeopardize its prosperity over the pittance represented in Cuban investments. Moreover, the President himself was personally opposed to war.

Yet McKinley knew that if he didn't declare war, Congress would, and he would look weak. Therefore, he sent a message to Congress asking for the right to use military and naval forces to end the Cuban hostilities and to establish a stable government there. On April 20, 1898, Congress declared war. Simultaneously it adopted the Teller Resolution, renouncing any American claim to the territory of Cuba and promising to turn the island over to the Cubans as soon as Spain was defeated. Four days later Spain declared war on the United States.

The Course of the War. Active operations did not begin until May; by August 12, the war was over. The all-steel American Navy was organized into an Atlantic Fleet under Rear Admiral William Sampson, a Flying Squadron under Commodore Winfield Scott Schley, and an Asiatic Squadron under Commodore George Dewey. Over one hundred auxiliary craft were also battle ready. The two hundred thousand army volunteers were not; nor was the War Department, which, under unaccustomed pressure, broke down. More casualties resulted from poor food, improper clothing, inadequate medical equipment, and deficient arms than from battle.

Commodore Dewey secured victory in the Pacific by destroying the Spanish fleet in Manila Bay on May 1 without a single American casualty. When army reinforcements arrived, they allied themselves with Filipino guerrillas (who had engaged in their own rebellion against Spanish dominion) led by Emilio Aguinaldo and captured Manila on August 13. In the Atlantic Spanish Admiral Pascual Cervera took shelter in Cuban waters under protection of powerful shore batteries. Sampson and Schley therefore could do no more than hold the Spanish fleet captive by instituting a blockade on May 29. With the Spanish navy pinned down, the American army (and Colonel Theodore Roosevelt's "Rough Riders") broke through Spanish defenses and stormed San Juan Hill; General Nelson Miles occupied the flank at Puerto Rico. His protective covering of shore batteries lost, Admiral Cervera could only capitulate or attempt to escape the blockade. He chose to fight his way out and in the ensuing battle the entire Spanish force was destroyed. Only one American sailor died during the encounter. Santiago surrendered on July 17, and on August 12, Spain agreed to exit Cuba and to cede Puerto Rico and the island of Guam to the United States. A peace conference was set for October 1 that would decide the fate of the Philippines.

The War Against Disease. The greatest battle in the war occurred after it was over. The enemy was malaria, or yellow fever, and the hero of that battle was Dr. Walter Reed. Following up a brilliant deduction of the Cuban Dr. Carlos Finley, the American army surgeon proved that mosquitos transmitted yellow fever. The attack on malaria now focused on eliminating mosquito-breeding swamps. Reed's discovery opened vast areas of tropical lands to human exploitation and habitation.

The Treaty of Paris (1898). In the peace treaty signed at Paris, Spain ceded to the United States the Philippine Islands for the sum of $20 million. Pending the establishment of a Cuban government and independent state, the United States was to occupy Cuba. The cession of the Far Eastern Philippines unpleasantly surprised many Americans and Filipinos. In response Emilio Aguinaldo turned his guer-

rillas on the American occupation forces, initiating a bitter, three-year war for independence that required the use of seventy thousand American troops before the island was "pacified." A war of liberation had turned into a war of conquest.

Many anti-imperialist voices cried out, including Grover Cleveland, William Jennings Bryan, Carl Schurz, Mark Twain, William Dean Howells, and William James. They insisted that conquest of the Philippines made a mockery of democracy and established the United States as a nation of hypocrites. McKinley denied this, and the campaign of 1900 was waged on the issue of imperialism, the "paramount issue" according to Bryan, the Democratic candidate. McKinley won. The American people had clearly endorsed imperialism.

The American Empire. Americans were confronted with the problem of reconciling democracy and imperialism in the overseas areas ceded to them by force, treaty, or purchase. The United States could free or subjugate these territories as it pleased. How should they be ruled? One possibility was that old and tested precedents could be followed in the territories of Alaska, the Philippines, Puerto Rico, Guam, Hawaii, Samoa, or Midway. In other words, they could be placed under the terms of the Northwest Ordinance, and population would determine the degree of local autonomy, with statehood as the ultimate goal.

But objections arose almost immediately to applying the Northwest Ordinance to these areas. A vocal minority argued that these territories were noncontiguous with the continental United States; they were unlikely to be settled by an overflow of Americans; they were composed of peoples of the most diverse races, religions, languages, social customs, and stages of civilization. In opposing these arguments, expansionists pointed out that these territories were important to America; if kept and made subject to the Northwest Ordinance, then their populations would become American; as Americans they would be entitled to the rights and privileges of citizenship under the Constitution of the United States and to be admitted as states. It was not long before these opposing ideas were contending in the Supreme Court.

"Does the Constitution Follow the Flag?" A number of legal cases gave the Supreme Court an opportunity to take a decisive stand on the issue of the United States' relationship to its territories. The Court resorted, instead, to ambiguities, establishing two kinds of territorial status. An incorporated territory was entitled to full citizenship for its residents and was eligible for membership in the Union—Alaska and Hawaii became incorporated territories. An unincorporated territory had limited citizenship rights and, while privileged with certain rights such as life, liberty, and property, did not enjoy common-law privileges such as trial by jury and freedom of the press unless the Congress voted to confer them. As "appurtenances of the United States," unincorporated territories could look forward to independence, not statehood—if Congress willed it. Congress became the arbiter of the fate of these dependencies.

Still another irritating problem arose. Did exports from Puerto Rico and the Philippines enter the United States free of duty? The Constitution provided that duties must be uniform throughout the country. In *DeLima v. Bidwell* (1901) the Court held that Puerto Rico did not have to pay a duty. Then, later in the same year (*Downs v. Bidwell*), it reversed itself and held that tariff equality was not a "fundamental" right and that Congress could discriminate against the products of Puerto Rico and the Philippines. After these decisions, the extent to which the Constitution followed the flag was left entirely to Congress.

The Panama Canal

The Need for a Canal. The Spanish-American War revealed the need for a canal across the Isthmus of Panama. The *U.S.S. Oregon* was in Puget Sound when the war broke out, and it was ordered to Cuban waters. The trip was fourteen thousand miles around Cape Horn to the battle area. This distance appeared unthinkable from the point of view of an adequate defense. Either an Isthmian canal or a two-ocean navy would have to be built; the canal seemed the cheaper option. But three major obstacles stood in the way of its construction: England, Colombia, and nature.

England. In 1850 the United States had placed a barrier in the way of England's construction of a canal by getting her to sign the Clayton-Bulwer Treaty, which provided that any canal across Central America should be built jointly and left unfortified. In 1898 this treaty became a millstone around America's neck. To win a friend in her time of trouble (she was fighting the Boer War in South Africa), England informed the United States that the Clayton-Bulwer Treaty might be renegotiated. Thereupon Secretary of State John Hay and Ambassador Sir Julian Pauncefote negotiated a new agreement. The Hay-Pauncefote Treaty (1901) provided that the United States could construct, own, and fortify a canal, and that all nations should have equal access to it.

Colombia. Ferdinand de Lesseps, renowned builder of the Suez Canal, had decided in the 1880s to construct a canal at Panama. He organized a company, secured a franchise from Colombia, who owned the Isthmus, and began building. His effort in the midst of rugged and malaria-infested terrain proved an utter fiasco; millions of francs and thousands of lives were lost. A new company, formed in 1890, had but one hope—that the United States would purchase the franchise. After the Spanish-American War, the French asking price was $109 million. Because of this the Walker Commission, set up by Congress to investigate alternatives, recommended a Nicaraguan route instead. A most unusual public relations man, Philippe Bunau-Varilla of Panama (a member of the successor of de Lesseps's defunct company), now entered the negotiations. His assignment was to sell the Panama project to Congress. He won Roosevelt's support and then had the asking price lowered to $40 million. Effective lobbying did the rest. The Spooner Bill, passed by Congress, authorized the Panama route if the franchise could be bought and authority to build secured from Colombia.

It was now 1903 and the French contract was due to expire in 1904. Bunau-Varilla realized—as did President Roosevelt—that Colombia had to act immediately.

Thereupon Hay negotiated a treaty with a Colombian diplomat, Tomas Herrán, which provided the United States with a six-mile-wide zone through the Isthmus for $10 million and an annual rental of $250 thousand. But when submitted to the Colombian Senate for ratification, the treaty was rejected. The Colombian Senate preferred to wait until 1904, when the French contract had expired, and thus to get for Colombia the extra $40 million. Roosevelt was furious and did not balk when Bunau-Varilla suggested that the Panamanians were ripe for revolution from the tyrannical rule of Colombia.

Bunau-Varilla himself composed a declaration of independence and a constitution and designed a flag for the as-yet-unborn Republic of Panama. Meanwhile Roosevelt dispatched the *U.S.S. Nashville* to Panama. The revolution took place as scheduled on November 3, 1903. The American navy prevented Colombian troops from landing on the Isthmus to suppress the rebellion, and on November 4 the new republic was proclaimed. On November 6 the United States recognized the independence of Panama and a week later accepted Bunau-Varilla as the Panamanian envoy to America. On November 18 Roosevelt signed the Hay–Bunau-Varilla Treaty, giving the United States a ten-mile-wide zone for $10 million and an annual rental of $250 thousand. The French Company received its $40 million.

Roosevelt denied any part in preparing, inciting, or encouraging the Panamanian Revolution. However, some years later, after he had left office, he said, "I took the Canal Zone and let Congress debate." In 1921 the United States paid Colombia $21 million for damage to her rights and interests in the Canal; some historians see in this move the pangs of a bad conscience. Latin Americans, too, reacted with fear and resentment to the aggressive behavior of an American president who, in their eyes, showed contempt for the nations south of the border.

Nature. The formidable obstacle represented by nature is evidenced in some construction figures. The Canal took seven years to build (1907–14); the total cost was $336.6 million; 240 million cubic yards of earth were removed; a set of three locks on the Atlantic side had to be constructed to achieve an elevation of 85 feet above sea-level, and another three were required on the Pacific side. This colossal undertaking was planned and executed by Colonel George Washington Goethals and his Army engineers and it remains their enduring monument. It would also have been impossible to build the Canal, as French experience had shown, without the elimination of malaria, a feat accomplished by Dr. William Gorgas.

Constructing and Defending the Canal. Construction of a canal and the defense of it seemed related problems. The first requirement for both was to remove all foreign economic and political influence, direct and indirect, from the Caribbean. This led to an aggressive Caribbean policy. The second requirement was to fortify the approaches to the Canal. For this reason the United States purchased the Virgin Islands from Denmark in 1917 for $25 million. A third requirement was to ensure that alternative routes, such as the proposed sea-level canal through Nicaragua, would be built solely by the United States. For this purpose the Bryan-Chamorro

Treaty of 1916 was forced on Nicaragua. Under this treaty Nicaragua ceded the right-of-way for a canal and the United States received a lease on the Corn Island in the Atlantic Ocean and a naval base in the Gulf of Fonseca. In exchange the United States paid Nicaragua $8 million.

Cuba and the Platt Amendment. The Teller Resolution had promised Cuba freedom when she was "ready" for it. Under General Leonard Wood, who became military governor of Cuba in December 1899, American occupation forces rehabilitated the war-torn island and restored normal conditions. Wood overhauled Cuba's administrative machinery and its financial system; constructed roads, bridges, schools, and hospitals; and provided the means to eradicate yellow fever.

In 1900 a Cuban constitutional convention met to draw up a constitution without much interference from the United States. The document did not mention future relations with America; if Cuba was a free country, there was no need to do so. Congress, however, took offense and added a rider to an Army appropriations bill consisting of a resolution defining United States–Cuban relationships. Supported even by opponents of imperalism, the Platt Amendment (1901) prohibited Cuba from borrowing beyond her income and from making any treaty with a foreign power that might impair her independence; nor was she to permit any foreign power to alienate any of her territory. The United States could intervene militarily to preserve Cuba's independence; protect life, liberty, and property; and enforce the provisions of the Treaty of Paris. Finally, the United States could lease or buy naval and coaling stations on the island. The Cubans were forced to add the "Platt Amendment" to their constitution.

Secretary of State Elihu Root assured Cuba in 1901 that the Platt Amendment was a normal extension of the Monroe Doctrine. But it obviously restricted Cuba's freedom severely. Invoking the amendment, the President sent marines into Cuba in 1906 to supervise orderly elections; the troops remained until 1909. Three years later the marines landed again to put down race riots, and once again in 1917 to suppress election disorders. Cuba remained under virtually permanent American occupation.

This occupation proved exceptionally profitable for American business interests in Cuba. Capital investments expanded from $50 million in 1898 to $1 billion in 1924. While the bulk of this investment was in sugar plantations, it also penetrated into railroads, tobacco, public utilities, government bonds, mines, mills, and so forth. In 1924 83 percent of Cuba's exports went to the United States, while 75 percent of her imports came from there. American economic investments did not in any way help Cuban peasants, who lived in dire poverty and were virtual slaves on sugar plantations. Yet the source of Cuban hostility to the United States did not lie solely in these capital and commercial investments. The limitations imposed on her freedom by the Platt Amendment were equally, if not more, critical.

Stretching the Monroe Doctrine

European Intervention. Economic expansion was not the sole force disrupting America's isolationist policy in this period. Ownership of the Panama Canal pushed America to become concerned with the stability of the Caribbean region—that is, with keeping war, revolution, and foreign intervention out of the Western Hemisphere.

Latin American countries did not share this concern and engaged in practices that openly invited European intervention. Most of the region's economies were based on a single crop, which had to be sold abroad. All other economic ventures in industrialization had to be financed through the sale of government bonds abroad. Thus, Latin American countries were continuously in debt to foreign financiers (who systematically cheated them), and when Caribbean governments did not repay their debts—as often enough they did not—international law permitted European countries to collect them by force. (In 1907, however, the Hague Conference adopted the Drago Doctrine, sponsored by the United States, providing that default of debt constituted insufficient reason for military intervention.)

Why were Latin American governments so frequently unable to pay off their obligations? In these countries property was concentrated in the hands of a tiny minority of native aristocrats and foreign investors. From the ranks of the aristocracy came the caudillo, the dictator, whose support rested on army bayonets. Caudillos treated their countries as private possessions, disposed of the land's wealth irresponsibly, and punished native protest with incredible cruelty. The caudillos maintained close connections with foreign investors, knowing that the latter could easily organize a "revolution" and put in place another caudillo who would shut his eyes to the most ruthless exploitation if handsomely bribed. Exploited wealth did not remain in the Latin American countries but was removed to the foreign banks of the foreign investors. The result was the pervasive and continuous bankruptcy of Latin America.

Out of this miserable state of affairs came war, revolution, and foreign intervention. Thus, in 1902, the Venezuelan caudillo refused to meet his obligations to Great Britain, Germany, and Italy. Ignoring the Monroe Doctrine, these three powers sent warships into the Caribbean, blockaded the Venezuelan coast, and fired on some fishing villages. Theodore Roosevelt initially consented to the collection; but strong public reaction against the bombardment of the fishing villages forced him to intervene.

American Intervention. Roosevelt—whose motto was "speak softly but carry the big stick"—assigned Admiral Dewey to command the Atlantic Fleet and then demanded that the three powers arbitrate the debt dispute in the Hague Tribunal, a recently established court of arbitration. By accepting this demand, England, Germany, and Italy also accepted American supremacy in the Caribbean.

With the United States now protecting them from foreign intervention, unscrupulous caudillos realized that they could easily default on all their obligations. In 1903 Santo Domingo (now the Dominican Republic) defaulted on a debt of $40 million owed to Europeans, a default preceded by prolonged civil war. The American State Department negotiated an agreement with Santo Domingo, which provided that customs receipts be placed in receiver-

ship, with the United States as receiver and responsible for the prompt liquidation of the debt. The American Receiver General, having been able to get the debt reduced from $32 million to $17 million, then refunded it into a fifty-year loan held by a United States bank at a sharply lower rate of interest than the original. The great winners in this intervention were the people (more accurately, those in power) of Santo Domingo.

The Roosevelt Corollary. Liberty, peace, and security, then, did not exist in this part of the world where American economic and political stakes were so great. When Roosevelt was forced to abandon the policy of nonintervention, so vital to America's isolationist policy, he was seeking a democratic way out of the dilemma. Intervention, he claimed, flowed from an extension of the Monroe Doctrine.

While negotiations with Santo Domingo were pending, Roosevelt took the occasion of his annual message on December 2, 1904, to announce this corollary to the Monroe Doctrine:

> If a nation shows that it knows how to act with reasonable efficiency and decency in social and political matters, if it keeps order and pays its obligations, it need fear no interference from the United States. Chronic wrongdoing, or an impotence which results in a general loosening of the ties of civilized society may in America, as elsewhere, ultimately require intervention by some civilized nation, and in the Western Hemisphere, the adherence of the United States to the Monroe Doctrine may force the United States, however reluctantly, in flagrant cases of such wrongdoing or impotence, to the exercise of an international police power.

Secretary of State Elihu Root invoked this "police power" sparingly; interventions in Cuba, Panama, and Santo Domingo were limited to specific purposes; where possible the United States carefully invited other Latin American countries to collaborate in intervention.

Protest.   Latin American reaction to the Corollary was intensely bitter. Poets, publicists, and historians led the protest, whipping their countries up into a frenzy against American culture; that is, against a business and machine culture. They painted America as a crude, materialistic power forcing her will upon the refined and spiritual Latins. Propagandists revived the Spanish past of Latin America and fostered Pan-Hispanic and Pan-Latinist movements. The United States, they said, was dominated by "Yanqui" imperialists; it had become the "Colossus of the North."

Dollar Diplomacy.   Latin American bitterness was more justly leveled against President William Howard Taft and his Secretary of State Philander C. Knox than against Theodore Roosevelt and Elihu Root. Taft and Knox realized that Roosevelt's Corollary was a perfectly designed instrument for gaining absolute political and economic control of the Caribbean. On behalf of American business interests, Knox attempted to oust all European concessionaires and creditors from the region. The State Department organized American banking groups to assume Latin American obligations; it placed political and military pressure on Latin American governments to refund existing obligations into American bonds that were then turned over to the American bankers. Sim-

ilarly, it secured mines, banana plantations, and railroad-construction privileges for American investors. The marines were sent in to install puppet caudillos and to war against rebels who objected to United States selection of Latin American heads of state. Haiti, one of these "banana republics," as they became known, and Nicaragua felt the full brunt of Taft's policy of "dollar diplomacy," the use of foreign policy to foster the private interests of Americans. The United Fruit Company, for example, not only owned banana plantations, but railways and other properties in the region. Latin American fears concerning the Roosevelt Corollary were certainly justified.

Woodrow Wilson and Latin America. In an encouraging address at Mobile, Alabama, in 1913, President Wilson proclaimed a "new freedom" for the oppressed Latin American countries. Human rights were to be set above material interests, and American conquest was repudiated forever. To hammer home these two principles, Wilson chose William Jennings Bryan, the country's outstanding anti-imperialist, as his Secretary of State.

How did Wilson and Bryan carry out the "new freedom"? During the 1915 Haitian revolution, they sent in the marines to establish order and to take over the country's economy. American occupation lasted ten years as Haitian rebels waged relentless guerrilla war against the United States. Then, in 1916, American marines occupied Santo Domingo and Nicaragua.

In each of these countries the occupation produced an efficient constabulary, law and order, better roads, and honest customs collections, but at a large price for the occupied countries—American-supervised elections and the suspension of basic freedoms. Latin Americans, with some justice, denounced Wilson; but he was caught in the same dilemma as his predecessors, as illustrated by his Mexican policy.

The Mexican Revolution

Causes of the Revolution. Wilson's Mexican difficulties began when the Mexicans overthrew the caudillo, Porfirio Diaz. Diaz had been particularly brutal, deliberately fostering serfdom and industrial slavery while allocating the nation's resources to himself and foreign investors. Americans were among his beneficiaries, receiving about one billion dollars' worth, largely in oil resources. But when Diaz, pursuing a divide-and-rule policy, began to favor the English, American investors openly supported the revolution (1911) that led to his downfall.

At first the revolution was in the hands of the idealistic Francisco Madero, but he was murdered, less than a month before Wilson's inauguration, by the supporters of a new "Diaz," Victoriano Huerta. Condemning Huerta as "unspeakable," Wilson refused to recognize the new regime, calling it "a government of butchers." This reversed a policy begun by Thomas Jefferson of recognizing de facto governments, that is, any government that is actually, though not legally, in control.

Wilson was, in effect, perpetuating the Mexican Revolution and thus resorting to indirect intervention. He blockaded the Mexican coast and openly supported Huerta's opponents, Venustiano Carranza and Francisco "Pancho" Villa. Wilson called this policy of indirect intervention "watchful waiting." It was temporarily suspended and a more active policy adopted when, to avenge the arrest of some American sailors and to secure a public apology from Huerta for an insult to the American flag (and to stop a shipment of German arms to Huerta), Wilson sent the marines in to occupy Veracruz. Four hundred Mexicans died resisting the American forces. Although the Mexicans retreated, Huerta remained in power. Only the intercession of the "ABC powers" (Argentina, Brazil, and Chile), who suggested mediation, prevented war. Wilson accepted their intervention, but before any solution was reached, Huerta resigned and Carranza took over.

Pancho Villa. Now it was Pancho Villa who incited intervention. Rising up against Carranza, he took control of Mexico City. To force the American government to undermine Carranza by intervening, Villa killed sixteen Americans on a train in Mexico and then crossed over the Rio Grande to murder nineteen more on American soil. Pressured by public opinion, Wilson ordered General John Pershing to capture Villa, and the American army crossed the border, committing one aggression after another against Carranza's troops. The American troops were still looking for Villa in 1917 (and war with Mexico was narrowly averted) when America's entry into World War I forced Wilson to recall them. With the country at war, Wilson reversed his policy and extended to Carranza de jure (legal) recognition.

Now free to pursue an independent existence in the community of nations, Mexico adopted a new constitution. This document confiscated the property of foreign corporations and distributed it in small parcels to serfs and tenant farmers. It also gave to the Mexican nation title to subsoil properties such as oil, jeopardizing foreign holdings in Mexico.

Wilson's initial intervention in Mexico's internal affairs provoked anti-Americanism in that country, but in the end his more restrained handling of the situation, signified by his recognition of Carranza, who stood for representative government, aided its establishment in Mexico.

CHAPTER EIGHTEEN

The Origins of American Collective Security

For many Americans, including President Woodrow Wilson, World War I came "like lightning out of a clear sky." As Wilson wrote to a friend, "The more I read about the conflict across the seas, the more open it seems to me to utter condemnation." Clearly the President hated the idea of war, and during the years before the United States' entry, he worked feverishly to keep her out of the European conflagration.

Far Eastern Policy

Imperialism. The Sino-Japanese War of 1895 revealed that China, under the Manchu Empress Dowager, Tz'u-hsi, was a corrupt and backward nation. Japan easily defeated the Chinese armies, thereby securing the independence of Korea and the cession of the Liaotung Peninsula and Formosa (now Taiwan). Their own imperialist hopes threatened by this aggression, the great European powers set aside Japan's conquests and partitioned China into spheres of influence for themselves.

Within its sphere, each power collected customs duties and harbor fees, while distributing to its own nationals desirable mining, railroad, and other concessions.

Enter the United States. The United States was on the periphery of these events. During the nineteenth century, it had lacked any formal Far Eastern policy. With the acquisition of the Philippines and Guam, however, the nation entered the Far Eastern arena, only to find that the European spheres of influence had closed all the doors to opportunities in trade there. The European powers were rattling sabres at each other, and a new, expansionist, warlike Japan was being driven to satisfy her enormous need for raw materials and population outlets.

What policy did the situation require? Logically it should be one that reduced foreign threats to the safety of the Philippines and simultaneously encouraged commercial opportunities. The McKinley administration was sensitive to the strong anti-imperialist sentiment in the country, and so, to protect its own trade interests with China without risking war or encouraging future partition, the United States resorted to diplomacy. Secretary of State John Hay drew up a series of "Open Door Notes" advocating equal access to trade (1899). The first note, sent to all the powers with interests in China, asked that there be no interference with the twenty-two ports already opened by treaty within the spheres of influence. It further requested that Chinese tariffs be applied equally and collected by China, and that no nation discriminate on behalf of its own citizens in harbor dues and railroad charges.

The responses to Hay's note were cold, evasive, indifferent, and qualified; Russia did not even answer. But with remarkable diplomatic bravado, Hay announced in March 1900 that all the powers had accepted the Open Door Policy.

The "Boxer" Rebellion. In its original formulation, the Open Door Policy seemed to accept the division of China into spheres of influence, provided equal commercial opportunity was preserved. This interpretation was tested in the spring of 1900, when reactionary Chinese anti-imperialists, led by a society called the "Boxers"—formally the "Patriotic Order of Harmonious Fists"—revolted against the "foreign devils." The uprising led to the destruction of all properties, such as railroads, designed to westernize China. The Boxers occupied Peking and besieged all foreign legations there. Hay insisted that an international relief force be organized to save the legations, and about twenty thousand troops representing all the western powers were sent and broke through to free the foreigners inside the legations.

An outrageous indemnity of $330 million was levied by the united interventionists against China for damages done by the Boxers, of which $24.5 million went to America. This was scaled down to $12 million, and then, in 1924, the unpaid balance was remitted. China used the returned American share to fund scholarships for Chinese students to American universities.

Hay now began to fear that this force would become a Frankenstein's monster and that the other powers, now united, would partition China politically. He therefore quickly circulated another note (July 3, 1900), stating that the United States had joined the expedition "to seek a solution which may bring about permanent safety and peace to China, preserve Chinese territorial and administrative integrity, protect all rights guaranteed to friendly powers by treaty and international law, and safeguard for the world the principle of equal and impartial trade with all parts of the Chinese empire." The Open Door, Hay asserted, could rest only on China's "integrity"—that is, independence. In these remarks, Hay extended the Open Door Policy geographically beyond the spheres of influence to include all of China.

In taking a firm stand against the dismemberment of China, the United States maintained its traditional determination to make no foreign alliances. But the Open Door Policy did form the basis for increased United States' influence in the Far East.

The Threat to China's Integrity. In 1895 Russia had loomed as the chief threat to China's integrity. Russian troops had penetrated into Manchuria, seizing the Liaotung Peninsula with its valuable Port Arthur. When the Japanese took this same territory following the Sino-Japanese War of 1895, relations between Russia and Japan deteriorated rapidly. In 1904 a Japanese torpedo squadron moved without warning against the Russian fleet at Port Arthur and sank it. This was followed by a declaration of war on February 10, 1904. Rapid maneuvers on land and sea gave Japan an advantage but brought her to the point of economic exhaustion.

Theodore Roosevelt was aware that both Russia and Japan menaced the Open Door. But as long as they served to balance one another, the military destruction of either was not to the interest of the United States. Accordingly, Roosevelt offered to mediate. In the 1905 Treaty of Portsmouth he consented to a modification of the Open Door Policy. Japan received dominant rights in Korea, a leasehold on the Liaotung Peninsula, and the southern half of Sakhalin Island. The President rejected Japan's additional demand for an indemnity. For his work as mediator, Roosevelt won the Nobel Peace Prize (1906), but, unfortunately for China, he had shown that a little pressure could modify the Open Door Policy.

The Threat to the Open Door. Roosevelt was anxious to keep Japan friendly, but not too strong. Toward that end, the Taft-Katsura Agreement was signed in 1905 stating America's acquiescence in Japan's proposed seizure of Korea in exchange for Japanese recognition of American control of the Philippines.

Japan, too, felt friendly to America—for a while. But her hostility bristled when America's jingoistic press found a new issue with which to increase circulation— the "yellow peril." On the West Coast the press was in a frenzy over Japanese immigration into the United States. Spurred on by opposition to the influx of cheap labor from Asia, the San Francisco school board segregated ninety-three Japanese children in 1906; West Coast labor unions organized a Japanese and Korean Exclusion League, and hoodlums sacked all Japanese-owned stores. Roosevelt had to promise some form of international restrictive action on Japanese immigration to persuade the school board to rescind its policy of segregation.

Such a restriction was finally secured in the Gentleman's Agreement of 1907. Japan promised to withhold passports from laborers intending to enter the United States; the United States agreed not to bar the Japanese completely. With this face-saving maneuver, Japan's ruffled temper subsided somewhat, and the Root-Takahira Agreement was passed in 1908. By this agreement both powers proclaimed the Open Door Policy in effect while they simultaneously pledged to recognize Japan's priority in Manchuria and to keep the status quo in the Pacific. Japan was clearly willing to accept an Open Door that sanctioned its engaging in the piecemeal partition of China—first Korea and now Manchuria.

The Twenty-One Demands. Taft's efforts to extend his "dollar diplomacy" from Latin America to the Far East failed miserably when American bankers refused to enter into competition with their European and Japanese counterparts for Chinese railroad securities. Later, Wilson openly repudiated "dollar diplomacy" in both Latin America and China. With the outbreak of World War I, American attention was distracted to Europe; thereupon, Japan declared war on Germany and seized all German holdings in China as well as the German islands in the Pacific north of the equator. Then, in 1915, Japan made her brutal twenty-one demands on China, which would, in effect, convert that nation into a Japanese protectorate.

The United States protested strongly against this wholesale violation of the Open Door Policy and forced Japan to hesitate before implementing the twenty-one demands. But by 1917 America had entered the European war. Japan exploited this event to force the United States into the Lansing-Ishii Agreement of 1917, in which both powers solemnly reaffirmed China's territorial integrity and the Open Door, and then with equal solemnity recognized that Japan had "special interests" in China because of her territorial "propinquity." Here was a strange doctrine indeed—conquest justified by geographical closeness. In the Lansing-Ishii Agreement, Americans agreed to the closing of the Open Door. World War I permitted them no other choice.

The United States and the First World War

"He Kept Us Out of War."   World War I began on July 28, 1914. On August 4 President Wilson, who hated war and was stunned by the outbreak, issued a proclamation of neutrality; on the 19th he demanded that Americans be "impartial in thought as well as in action." Thereafter, every violation by the belligerents of the "rights of neutrals" was formally protested. Protest notes were sent to England when she made arbitrary extensions in the contraband list or invoked the doctrine of "continuous voyage"—which permitted

her to seize neutral ships going to Germany or its neighbors—or blockaded German ports or rifled American mails. The American government sent even stronger protests to Germany when it proclaimed the waters around England a war zone within which enemy ships would be sunk at sight without regard for the safety of the passengers or the crew. After a German submarine, or U-boat, sank the British steamship *Lusitania* (May 7, 1915) with 128 Americans aboard, one of Wilson's protests was so strong that Secretary of State Bryan, fearing war, decided to resign rather than sign it.

Wilson attempted to bring the warring powers to their senses. In 1915 he sent his friend Colonel Edward M. House on a secret mission to Europe to seek a negotiated peace; in 1916 he asked all the powers to state their war aims as a basis for possible mediation. He called upon them again in January 1917 for a "peace without victory" to be maintained by a proposed international organization that the United States was prepared to join. That Americans wanted to stay at peace in the warring world was evident in the reelection of Wilson over Charles Evans Hughes in 1916, for the President made the cry "He kept us out of war!" his platform. Yet six months after the election, despite neutrality laws and peace resolutions, the United States was at war. Why?

Unneutral in Thought.   The reason for America's entry into World War I remains one of the most complex issues in American history. Many hypotheses have been advanced. One is that Americans, even in the early years of the war, were unneutral in thought. The majority of the people felt much closer to the Anglo-French cause than to the German, so the argument goes, for many reasons: because English was a common tongue; Great Britain was the "mother country"; American and Anglo-French institutions were democratic; and Germany and Austria-Hungary appeared to be the aggressors when they refused to negotiate the Serbian crisis.

One problem with this argument is that the eight million Americans of German and Austrian descent and the four million from Ireland (who hated the British) tended to be sympathetic to Germany. Furthermore, despite whatever affirmities they may have felt for one side or the other, Americans were not ready to desert their nonbelligerent status because none of the powers had sought actively to avoid the conflict—the Tsar was hardly a democrat, and the British and French were imperialistic. In addition, the Germans were such a highly cultured people that to war against them seemed incredible.

Whatever doubts the United States may have had, however, dwindled once the British cut the Atlantic cable. War news now began to pour into America solely from censored British sources, and slowly the complexities of the war were reduced to simple black-and-white patterns. The Germans became mad, ruthless "Huns" who murdered Belgian babies, trampled on neutral countries, and slaughtered nurses like the Englishwoman Edith Cavell; and the British became the defenders of democracy, the French a nation of Lafayettes, and the Russian aristocrats the people who had befriended the States (i.e., the Union) during the Civil War. When a British blockade led a desperate Germany to begin unrestricted submarine warfare against Allied shipping, many Americans were convinced of the truth of Allied propaganda and were ready to enter the war.

Unneutral in Action.   Another argument for why the United States entered the war is that Americans were unneutral not only in thought but in action, specifically, economic action. Wilson attempted to persuade England to accept the Declaration of London of 1909 which guaranteed neutral trading rights with respect to contraband goods. This would have permitted shipment of food and raw materials intended for civilian use to Germany and her allies. England refused and seized all goods en route to the Central Powers. Wilson repeatedly protested these violations of America's neutrality, but Britain managed to retain its policy without seriously disrupting relations between the two nations. In 1914 American trade with the Central Powers amounted to about $169 million; by 1916 it had fallen to virtually nothing. American trade with the Allied Powers rose from $825 million in 1914 to over $3.214 billion in 1916. There was no doubt where American sympathies lay economically.

Similarly, when the war broke out in Europe, the administration discouraged loans to the belligerents in order to preserve neutrality and restrict the flow of gold out of the country. As Allied purchases mounted, pressure for extension of credit to them increased. In 1915 the government removed the bar on loans. Within a year and a half American bankers had extended more than $2 billion in credit to the Allies, while their loans to Germany did not exceed $27 million.

These factors, according to the financial argument, tied the American economy to an Allied victory. With production, employment, and profits at record heights, any German move to cripple production and the flow of war goods could have serious consequences.

The German Reaction. Still another argument has it that Germany herself was responsible for America's entry into the war against her. Germany's answer to America's unneutral trade was the U-boat, which it used against all ships supplying its enemies. Early in 1915 Wilson warned the Germans that he would hold them strictly accountable for illegal destruction of American ships and lives. The sinking of the *Lusitania* put this doctrine to the test. In a series of notes, Wilson demanded that German submarine commanders warn their potential victims and provide safety for passengers and crew; any other type of sinking would be regarded by the United States as "deliberately unfriendly." When U-boats sank the passenger liner *Arabic*, in August 1915, Germany sought to avoid an American declaration of war by agreeing not to sink any more unresisting liners without warning. But when, in March 1916, without warning, a U-boat torpedoed the French liner *Sussex*, injuring several Americans, Wilson sent an ultimatum to Berlin threatening the severance of diplomatic relations unless Germany stopped such attacks. Once again Germany (the *Sussex* pledge) promised to halt unrestricted submarine warfare—if the United States forced England to abide by international law.

Despite sympathy to the Allied cause and provocation by the Germans, many Americans did not want to go to war. Indeed, prominent pacifists like Jane Addams and Lillian Wald fought to keep the United States out of the conflict. For two years Wilson resisted the pressure by the National Security League of industrialists and munitions manufacturers, the Navy League, the Army League, Theodore Roosevelt, and General Leonard Wood to begin a preparedness program.

The submarine menace and the approaching election of 1916 now forced Wilson to abandon his resistance. In 1915 Wilson quietly told congressional leaders that he advocated an increase in the size of the army and navy. Later that year, after a furious legislative struggle, Congress passed a National Defense Act, which increased the size of the army, placed the state militia under national control, and inaugurated a program of military training in the schools and colleges. Congress also pushed through a Naval Appropriations Bill for construction of dreadnoughts and auxiliary vessels to accommodate the flood of goods being sent overseas.

These apparently warlike moves were accompanied by Wilson's most intensive peace efforts. In his memorable "peace without victory" address to Congress (January 1917), he called for abandonment of secret treaties and balance-of-power politics, recognition of the rights of self-determination and the equality of all nations, limitations on arms, guarantees of freedom of the seas and, finally, for a league of nations to enforce the peace. Although the speech greatly impressed Europeans, the President's idealistic proposals were drowned in a new clash of arms as the Germans, who had decided to try to end the war quickly, launched large-scale torpedo attacks from their submarines.

America Enters the War. On April 6, 1917, Congress declared war on Germany, joining the Allied cause. What had happened between January and April to cause this radical shift from peace to war? Was it the resumption of unrestricted submarine warfare begun by the Germans on February 1? U-boats sank the *S.S. Housatonic* on February 3 after warning the vessel. Wilson broke off diplomatic relations with Germany and armed all merchantmen by executive order after Senator La-Follette's filibuster prevented Congress from taking such action. Other sinkings followed immediately.

The Zimmermann Telegram.   This was a code dispatch by the German Foreign Secretary Arthur Zimmermann to the German Minister to Mexico proposing a Mexican-German alliance and promising in exchange the restoration of New Mexico, Arizona, and Texas to Mexico. British intelligence intercepted and decoded the message (February 1917) and then passed it on to the American government. Its publication on March 1 caused a great public outcry.

Mounting German Sabotage and Espionage.   Documents planning sabotage had been discovered in the possession of Austrian and German diplomatic personnel; a munitions dump exploded on Black Tom Island, New Jersey, and another at Kingsland in the same state. Both these explosions, with damages running to $75 million, were attributed to German agents.

The Russian Revolution.   The revolution of March 1917 had put into power a liberal-democratic government and made the Allied cause truly democratic and therefore, perhaps, irresistible to America.

In sum, whatever the causes, by 1917 the majority of Americans had decided that booted and helmeted Kaiserism menaced the world. This explains the highly idealistic note, the crusader's cry, the burst of patriotism with which the United States entered into battle. For the American people, this was truly a struggle for a freer, safer world for all mankind.

The Home Front

Mobilization for War.   Having made the agonizing decision to enter the war, Wilson moved swiftly and effectively to organize the war effort. In May 1917 Congress passed the Selective Service Act. It provided for universal registration and conscription of all men between the ages of twenty-one and thirty. Eventually 2,810,296 men were inducted; combined with the regular army and units of the National Guard, the total number of men under arms amounted to 4,800,000, of whom 2,000,000 were sent overseas. The government established thirty-two training camps fairly well equipped with small arms but woefully deficient in artillery and such new weapons as tanks and airplane bombers. Fortunately the British and French made up the deficiency. By the time American factories converted to the production of heavy artillery, the war had ended.

Of the five thousand new federal agencies established to win the conflict, the War Industries Board (WIB) under Wall Street speculator Bernard M. Baruch, was one of the most effective. The WIB allocated scarce materials, fixed prices, standardized production, and determined industrial priorities. Wilson also appointed Herbert Hoover, a mining engineer who had been in charge of the wartime Belgium Relief Commission, as the head of the new Food Administration. Hoover fixed the price of wheat to raise production, convinced Americans to plant "victory gardens," and encouraged them to save food with "meatless" and "wheatless" days. Food exports increased from 12.3 million tons to 18.6 million tons.

Other agencies regulated shipping, railroads, fuel, and foreign trade. After workers threatened to strike the telephone and telegraph industries, the government took them over. Americans had never witnessed such widespread government intervention. On the other hand, as a result of government cooperation, industries like steel and aluminum flourished. Thus the war engendered a close partnership between business and government.

Labor and the War Effort.   The war also brought about a partnership between labor and the government. The National War Labor Board (NWLB) under Frank P. Walsh and William H. Taft was established to settle labor disputes. A War Labor Policies Board (WLPB), headed by Felix Frankfurter, standardized wages and hours and helped to create a United States Employment Service, which placed over 3.7 million workers in vital industries. The WLPB also protected the right of unions to organize and bargain collectively. Consequently, more than 2.3 million workers joined unions during the war.

The government raised the money to finance the war by enacting enormous increases in the percentages and varieties of taxes and the sale of vast numbers of Liberty Bonds. Government appropria-

tions amounted to about $33.5 billion, of which $10.5 billion was raised by taxation—higher rates, surtaxes, excess profit taxes, luxury taxes, and sales taxes; five Liberty Loan drives netted $21.4 billion. Each drive was oversubscribed.

Propaganda and Civil Liberties. In 1917 Wilson formed the Committee on Public Information (CPI), headed by the progressive journalist George Creel, which imposed a "voluntary" press censorship. The CPI recruited seventy-five thousand actors, artists, writers, and scholars to participate in a propaganda campaign to expose the Germans as the enemies of democracy and civilization. Their efforts proved too successful. Anti-German feeling reached hysterical proportions; many schools suspended the teaching of the German language; German music disappeared from the concert halls; statues of German heroes vanished from public view; sauerkraut became "liberty cabbage" and German measles "liberty measles." Even more ominously, German-Americans, Irish-Americans, and pacifists were ridiculed, abused, and sometimes assaulted and even killed.

With Wilson's support, voluntary organizations put the country on a vigilante footing. The Espionage Act of 1917 imposed heavy fines and long prison terms for any person who aided the enemy, incited rebellion in the armed forces, or obstructed recruitment. It also allowed the Postmaster General to deny the use of the mails to anyone suspected of violating the Act; Socialist and anti-British publications were thus effectively banned. The Sabotage Act (1918), also backed by Wilson, made willful sabotage of war materials, utilities, or transport a federal crime.

(This Act was used to break the IWW.) The Sedition Act was also passed in 1918. Under the Espionage Act of 1917, the state had to prove that injurious effects resulted from seditious utterances; now, under the Sedition Act, the mere utterance or printing of any disloyal, profane, scurrilous, or abusive statement about the American form of government, flag, or uniform, or any words intended to obstruct the war effort were punishable—whatever the effects. In 1918 Eugene V. Debs received a ten-year prison sentence for an antiwar speech. Finally, the Alien Act (1918) provided for deportation without jury trial of any alien advocating the overthrow of government. These laws clearly went beyond protecting the national interest. Conservatives used them to crush the Socialists. So effective were these efforts that the Socialists never regained their political equilibrium.

Women and Minorities. The war effort brought new opportunities for women and other minorities. The WIB mandated that women receive equal wages for equal work in war industries. Moreover, the draft caused a labor shortage, and blacks, women, (including Mexican women), and Mexican-Americans filled the gap. A million women held jobs in the war industries. Northern labor agents traveled down South, promising blacks jobs and transportation. In response, nearly a half-million blacks left the South to work in northern factories, railroads, coal mines, steel mills, department stores, and restaurants. Also, seventy-five thousand blacks eventually served in the army, although in segregated units.

Meanwhile, farmers and ranchers in the Southwest needed cheap labor, and pressured the government to relax immigration rules. Between 1917 and 1920, over one hundred thousand Mexicans migrated to the Southwest, and thousands more flooded midwestern cities like Chicago, where they found jobs and lived in barrios.

The war climate also encouraged a variety of reform. The women's suffrage movement succeeded at last with the ratification of the Nineteenth Amendment in 1920. Other reformers began to raise the issues of health insurance for workers and workmen's compensation.

Racial Tensions. The competition for jobs and housing caused racial tensions in northern cities to rise. In 1917 nine whites and approximately forty blacks died during clashes in East St. Louis, Illinois. Two years later race riots erupted in New York, Chicago, and Omaha. Lynchings also mounted. In 1917 forty-eight blacks were lynched; in 1919 the number increased to seventy-eight. When Wilson finally took a strong public stand against lynching, W.E.B. Du Bois applauded him. Du Bois raised no objection to the segregated training of the 1,200 black officers in the army. His accommodating stance was unpopular among blacks, but he believed that the war (and black cooperation with the war effort) would improve the condition of blacks in America. Indeed, after the war was over, Du Bois resumed his old militancy.

American Contributions

America's Military Contributions. Before the American fighting forces moved into action, Allied prospects were bleak indeed. Great Britain and France were scraping the bottom of their manpower barrels; French soldiers were mutinying; the British were stalled in the mud of Flanders, the Russians were in the throes of revolution; German submarines were sinking Allied vessels ten times faster than Allied ships were being built. By the time the first American military operations had begun, the Italians had been routed at Caporetto; the Bolsheviks had seized power in Russia, which soon (1918) signed a separate peace treaty with Germany (the Treaty of Brest-Litovsk); and the Germans had shattered the quiet on the western front with a tremendous offensive that brought them within fifty miles of Paris.

The American navy came to the rescue. It enabled protective convoying (of the 2 million American soldiers sent abroad, only one transport with 210 men was lost) as antisubmarine mines, the renowned "ash-cans," took a heavy toll of German submarines. The German navy no longer dared to engage in direct combat; when ordered to do so, the men mutinied against what they considered to be a suicidal order. The American army also contributed in a limited way to the Allied victory. In June 1917 the first American soldiers reached France. General John J. Pershing and his American Expeditionary Force (AEF) engaged in military action in 1918 at Château Thierry on the Marne (just fifty miles from Paris), where they bolstered the French against a heavy German attack. The Americans then participated more fully in the counteroffensive that followed the weakening of the last German drive. The first independent American action was in the St. Mihiel sector on September 12, 1918, and then two weeks later in an extremely costly operation through the Ar-gonne Forest along the Meuse River. This operation broke the southern flank of the German salient and paved the way for the successful French and British offensives in the North that ended the war.

The Bolsheviks. After Russia's withdrawal from the war, in an effort to spread discontent among the Allied soldiers, the Bolsheviks began to publish a number of inter-Allied secret treaties to which Tsarist Russia had been a party. These treaties had arranged for a redivision of colonial holdings at the expense of Germany, Austria-Hungary, and Turkey, if the Allies were victorious. Wilson felt impelled, therefore, to make America's war aims and peace goals clear and unmistakable.

The Fourteen Points. On January 22, 1918, hoping to secure a nonpunitive peace, he set forth his visionary Fourteen Points at the peace conference in Paris. No settlement was possible, Wilson said, until the troops of the Central Powers had been evacuated from Belgium, France, Rumania, Serbia, Montenegro, and Russia. Once they had been removed, a peace would be made by eliminating the causes of future wars. Open covenants would replace secretly negotiated balances of power; the seas would be made free in peace and war; the removal of trade barriers would end economic warfare; the arms race would cease, and all nations would disarm; imperialism would be eliminated by some "absolutely impartial adjustment of all colonial claims"; restoration of Alsace-Lorraine and the creation of an independent Poland with access to the sea would remove two threats to the peace of Europe; the principles of nationality would be applied to Austria-Hungary and

Turkey to end nationalistic conflict within those empires; no decision would be made without the self-determination of the peoples concerned. As a crowning glory, a League of Nations would be created to preserve forever the political independence and territorial integrity of every nation, large and small. Thus, Wilson shaped a vision of a wonderful new world. His message swept like a beacon of light over the world's exhausted armies, even those of the Central Powers. The Fourteen Points became the basis on which the Germans finally, on November 11, 1918, accepted Allied terms for an armistice.

The Versailles Treaty. At the peace conference, which began in January 1919 and ended in May, Wilson confronted a triumvirate of bitter men—France's George Clemenceau, England's Lloyd George, and Italy's Vittorio Orlando—each determined to exact a terrible vengeance on Germany and to secure for his own country the territories promised in the secret treaties. (This would, of course, make a mockery of the Fourteen Points.) How did America's peace fare at Versailles in the face of such determined opposition?

The provisions in the treaty restored Alsace-Lorraine to France and disarmed and demilitarized Germany, mandated for the eventual elimination of imperialist control of backward areas, constructed Poland with a corridor to the sea, and created a League of Nations based on the sovereign equality of all states. These terms all seemed to accord with the Fourteen Points.

But to achieve his goals, Wilson had to relinquish the idea of peace without victory. The treaty ignored the issues of freedom of the seas, disarmament, and tariff reductions. It also savagely punished Germany by forcing her to accept the entire responsibility for the war and making her pay astronomical reparations.

The League of Nations. Wilson believed (and said) that what he had surrendered were sacrifices to secure a League of Nations, which became Article 1 of the Treaty of Versailles. The League, he felt, was worth each of his concessions on the treaty. The aims of this covenant of nations were to protect its members in their political independence and territorial integrity (that is, to preserve the results achieved at Versailles); to force the submission of all disputes to the League for settlement, thus preventing war; to reduce armaments, eliminate imperialism gradually by means of mandates, and to improve social and economic conditions, thus eliminating the causes of war; and to provide for political, economic, and (as a last resort) military sanctions against any aggressor that disturbed the peace. The agencies by which these purposes would be realized were an Assembly of all the member nations, a Council of five powerful permanent members and four elected nonpermanent members, a Permanent Court for International Justice, a Secretariat, and an International Labor Organization. After it began operating, the League would, Wilson believed, permit the solution of those problems, such as disarmament, that the treaty left unsettled.

The Return to Isolation. When Wilson returned home with the treaty, most Americans supported the League. But a number of powerful figures in Congress remained opposed. On March 19, 1920, the Treaty of Versailles and the League of Nations went down to defeat in the Senate; the vote of forty-nine for and thirty-five against left it short of the two-thirds majority needed for ratification. The battle for ratification had been dramatic and bitter, but the isolationist forces of Hiram Johnson, William Borah, Henry Cabot Lodge, and other "irreconcilables" and "reservationists"—that is, those who refused categorically to support the League of Nations and those who supported it with decisive qualifications—proved stronger than Wilson and the many pro-League forces.

Ratification failed for numerous reasons, including Wilson's refusal to compromise with Lodge; isolationist fears for the future of the Monroe Doctrine and the power of Congress to declare war; hatred on the part of German- and Irish-Americans for any association with England; revulsion toward the punitive Treaty of Versailles; and postwar disillusionment. Wilson's health may have also been a factor. In Paris he apparently suffered a minor stroke, which left his judgment impaired while increasing his stubbornness. At a crucial point in the debate, this stubbornness prevented him from accepting Lodge's proposals, which would have broken the impasse without a presidential loss of face. Later in 1919 Wilson suffered a stroke that partially paralyzed him on one side and left the supporters of the League without their leader.

Wilson made the election of 1920 a popular referendum on the issue of joining the League, although his poor health made it impossible for him to run. Seeking a return to normalcy, Republican isolationists and their candidate, Senator Warren G. Harding of Ohio, won overwhelmingly over their Democratic rival, James M. Cox of Ohio. The League of Nations was permanently shelved, and by joint resolution Congress concluded a separate peace treaty with Germany and Austria-Hungary in July 1921.

CHAPTER NINETEEN

The Twenties

In his novel *Main Street* (1920), Sinclair Lewis describes Midwesterners during the 1920s. They are, he writes, a "savorless people, gulping tasteless food and sitting afterward, coatless and thoughtless, in rocking-chairs . . . listening to mechanical music, saying mechanical things about the excellence of Ford automobiles, and viewing themselves as the greatest race in the world." During the twenties, the prevailing mood—loss of idealism and return to materialism combined with religious, racial, and ethnic bigotry—was deeply disturbing to some. Yet other Americans, tired of war, saw it as a period of social experimentation and vitality.

The Aftermath of Progressivism

Contradictory Moods. The Progressive era and the war left the American people in a contradictory mood. On the one hand, the move to extend democracy and government intervention was now brought to completion. In 1919 the Eighteenth Amendment, outlawing the manufacture, sale, and transportation of intoxicating liquor, was ratified. Prohibition was almost universally considered one of the crowning achievements of progressive reform, a measure that would improve the health, safety, and morals of the American people. A year later (1920) the Nineteenth (or "Susan B. Anthony") Amendment guaranteed women the vote. The Amendment doubled the size of the electorate, but, as it turned out, it did not help any party or cause. Also, in the Esch-Cummins Transportation Act of 1920, Congress made the ICC the virtual czar of the railroad industry. The measure gave the ICC complete control over rates, as well as the rights to supervise the sale of railroad securities, recapture profits over 6 percent, approve or reject proposed expenditures, and consolidate systems to achieve economy and efficiency. Finally, in the General Leasing and Water Power Act of 1920, the government extended its control over oil and mineral reserves, placing them in the public interest and removed from private exploitation. The act also extended government control to waters that might be used for conversion to electric power.

Such measures could have easily fitted into either the "Square Deal" or the "New Freedom."

Yet, many Americans appeared ready to reject the idealism, morality, and responsibility characteristic of the Progressive era.

Political Parties

The Republicans. No serious opposition to Republican domination of the presidency emerged during the twenties. In 1920 Ohio Senator Warren G. Harding won easily over the Democrat James M. Cox. When Harding died in 1923, his vice president, Calvin Coolidge, succeeded him. In 1924 Coolidge handily defeated Democrat John W. Davis; in 1928 Herbert Hoover swamped the Democratic governor of New York State, Alfred E. Smith.

Harding and Coolidge were exceptionally mediocre men committed to a do-nothing policy. Harding's amiable passivity and his almost helpless reliance upon subordinates encouraged a wave of corruption in high office equalled only by that of Grant's administration. Although some of his cabinet members, such as Secretary of State Charles Evan Hughes, Secretary of Commerce Herbert Hoover, and Secretary of the Treasury Andrew Mellon, were efficient and honest, others were thoroughly corrupt. The involvement of Harding's Ohio crony, Attorney General Henry M. Daugherty, in a series of questionable deals finally forced the President to sack him. One of Daugherty's friends, Thomas W. Miller, the Alien Property Custodian, went to jail for fraud.

The notorious "Teapot Dome Scandal" capped the corruption of Harding's administration. Secretary of the Interior Albert B. Fall persuaded Harding to transfer naval oil reserves at Elks Hill, California, and Teapot Dome, Wyoming, from the Navy Department to the Interior. Fall then leased these reserves to his oil friends Edward L. Doheny and Harry F. Sinclair, in exchange for bribes. After Harding's death from a heart attack in 1923, Fall's sudden wealth (he was known to be in financial straits) provoked a senatorial investigation which exposed the scheme. Both Fall and Secretary of the Navy Edwin Denby then resigned. Fall was prosecuted, convicted, fined, and sentenced to jail for one year, while Sinclair and Doheny were acquitted of conspiracy. Following the scandals, sadness at Harding's death turned to indignation and scorn.

Populist-Progressivism. The only real challenge to Republican standpattism came from within the party itself. A solid phalanx of Populist-Progressive supporters remained, in particular Wisconsin's Robert LaFollette, Montana's Burton K. Wheeler, George W. Norris, and Idaho's William E. Borah. In 1924 they organized the Conference for Progressive Political Action, receiving the solid backing of farmers, the powerful Railway Brotherhoods, the AFL, the Socialist Party, and many intellectuals. The Progressives chose LaFollette to oppose Coolidge and the conservative Democratic candidate John W. Davis in the election. The neo-populist platform on which LaFollette ran—government ownership of water-power, railroads, and financial credit; legalization of labor's right to organize and bargain collectively; and the direct election of the President—was too radical to win popular support. The laconic, conservative, and honest Coolidge won by a wide margin.

The Democrats. Although the Democrats provided little opposition to Republican ascendancy, they did supply spectacular political drama within their own ranks, as various intraparty rifts occurred. Prohibition offers an excellent example. The traditional wing of the Democratic Party, centered in the South, pushed through the Eighteenth Amendment. (In the Volstead Act of 1920, which implemented the Amendment, an intoxicating beverage was defined as any substance with more than 2.5 percent alcohol.) But another powerful wing of the party, centered in the larger cities of the North and the Midwest, opposed Prohibition. These "new" Democrats, either immigrants or descendants of immigrants, were mainly Catholic or Jewish, and were scared of the values of rural Democrats. The Democrats now split into Northern "wets" and Southern "drys," and the two factions fought bitterly throughout the decade.

A second schism occurred in Democratic ranks over the revival in the South of the KKK, with its violently antiblack, anti-Catholic, and anti-Semitic program, a program that many Northern Democrats saw as a violation of their entire system of values.

An additional split occurred over party emphasis: Southerners were profarmer and antilabor, Northerners were the opposite. During the nominating convention of 1924, for example, Southerners supported William G. McAdoo (who was Doheny's lawyer during the Teapot Dome Scandal), while Northerners supported the Irish-Catholic governor of New York,

Alfred E. Smith. When the Smith forces sponsored an anti-KKK resolution for the platform, it was defeated by 543 to 542; nor could the two factions agree on Prohibition or on whether the United States should join the League of Nations, among other issues. After 95 ballots they had still failed to decide on the party's nominee. Finally, on the 103rd ballot, the Democrats chose a "dark horse," John W. Davis.

In 1928, however, Smith was named on the first ballot. The campaign pitted Smith against the Republican nominee, Herbert Hoover. The differences seemed clear; whereas the Quaker Hoover was "dry," the Catholic Smith was "wet," and as governor of New York State the Democrat had compiled an excellent liberal record, whereas his opponent showed no special concern for the underprivileged. Yet the two candidates were both self-made men and both conservative. Religious bigotry marred the campaign; the Protestant clergy made Smith's defeat the object of virtually a religious crusade. Republicans hammered at his "wetness," his ties with the Tammany machine, and his Irish-Catholicism. Hoover won easily, 444 to 87 in the electoral college, and 21.4 million to 15 million in the popular vote. For the first time since the Civil War, the South went Republican. Yet, although his Catholicism and his machine connections hurt Smith badly, the main reason for his defeat was the nation's prosperity. The majority of voters saw no reason to vote out of power the party they believed responsible for their economic well-being.

Political Issues

The Veterans' Problem. Established in 1919, the American Legion almost immediately became a powerful pressure group to secure special benefits for veterans. In 1917 provision had been made for the permanent care of totally disabled veterans and for the sale, on easy terms, of life insurance to all servicemen. In 1918 and 1919 Congress liberalized veterans' compensation terms, and in 1921 a Veterans' Bureau was organized. But the American Legion sought additional benefits, particularly for non-disabled ex-soldiers. Contending that they had received low pay during the war compared with war workers, the veterans demanded grants equal to a dollar a day for each day they had served. Agitation for a "bonus bill" ended successfully in 1924 when Congress passed, over Coolidge's veto, the Adjusted Compensation Act, providing for adjusted service certificates in the form of twenty-year life-insurance policies. Veterans could borrow against these policies at 6 percent interest.

Prohibition. The noisiest political issue of the twenties was the enforcement of the Eighteenth Amendment. The "noble amendment" did accomplish some of what supporters had hoped. The national consumption of alcohol fell, mainly in rural areas and among the lower classes. Arrests for drunkenness were also sharply reduced. But in the cities, especially among the well-to-do, the insistence on total abstinence—beer and wine were prohibited in addition to hard liquor—encouraged resentment and disobedience, even among moderates. In place of barrooms, there now arose "speakeasies," "beerflats," and "blind pigs." These establishments sold liquor with impunity, unimpeded by the mostly corrupt or inefficient local police and federal agents. In the privacy of their own homes, many

Americans also defied the law by manufacturing "bathtub gin." The spread of murderous gangs engaged in "bootlegging" and racketeering (and led by such men as Chicago's Al Capone) also undermined public morality.

Moreover, the split between urban Democratic immigrants who detested the law and southern Democrats who loved it led to the near-dissolution of the Democratic Party. The "wet-dry" factions clashed bitterly in local and national political elections. Finally, in 1931 President Hoover's Wickersham Commission reported that the "noble experiment" had failed and, with the election of the Democrats in 1932, the era of Prohibition came to an end. In December 1933 the Twenty-first Amendment was ratified, repealing the Eighteenth. From then on, the states assumed the legal control of liquor, and the problem of alcoholism moved essentially from the province of morals to medicine.

Economic Development

The Technological Revolution. The twenties were characterized by greater mechanization in the basic industries, improvements in existing machines, wider application of electric power, and radical innovations in standardization of parts and assembly belts, especially in the manufacture of durable consumers' goods, such as automobiles. These improvements in efficiency resulted in an astonishing 75-percent increase in productivity per manhour during the decade. The economy flourished, and until 1929, Americans had the highest standard of living of any nation in the world.

But the technological revolution created problems. Work on the assembly line was monotonous, and many skilled jobs were eliminated, causing unemployment and great distress. Also worrisome was the increasing size of industrial combines and the gradual disappearance of the small, independent producer.

The Rise of New Industries: The Automobile.   Automobile production was easily the most prominent industry of the twenties. In 1920 there were ten million cars on the highway; by 1929 there were twenty-three million. The three major producers—Ford, General Motors, and Chrysler—were giant corporations organized both vertically (moving from raw material to finished product) and horizontally (producing different models within one corporation). The auto's effect on steel, glass, oil, rubber, asphalt, and cement production was immense. Many new jobs opened up in filling stations, tourist lodges, drive-in movie theaters, and roadside stands. The tourist industry expanded as a result of the easy mobility autos offered, and the movement from the cities to the suburbs accelerated as commutation by car became possible. The auto's ubiquity also led to problems of highway construction and traffic management, and new patterns of indebtedness (chiefly installment buying) developed.

The Airplane.   The use of airplanes in World War I advanced flight technology, and they became a source of mass entertainment. Aerial "daredevils" would travel from town to town, displaying their feats of derring-do at county fairs and other public gatherings. Then, in 1927, the American aviator Charles A. Lindbergh captured the world's attention by flying nonstop from New York to Paris in less than thirty-three hours in the single-engine *Spirit of St. Louis*. Lindbergh's achievement whetted public interest in flying and signalled the coming of routine passenger flights. Later the same year, William E. Boeing's Air Transport (the ancestor of United Airlines) began passenger and mail flights between Chicago and San Francisco. In 1930 Boeing manufactured the first all-metal, low-wing plane and three years later, the twin-engine 247.

Other New Industries.   Inventions and technological breakthroughs created a wealth of new or improved products from electric appliances such as vacuum cleaners and refrigerators, which made life easier, to gadgets like cigarette lighters. New entertainment media such as radios (the first radio station, Pittsburgh's KDKA, started broadcasting in 1920) and movies (the first sound motion picture, *The Jazz Singer*, appeared in 1927) made life more pleasant for many Americans. Their impact on ways of thought and values was, of course, vast and incalculable.

Chemicals.   Production of chemicals mounted rapidly when German goods were cut off by World War I. After the war American producers bought up German patents. Once the industry was launched, the Fordney-McCumber Tariff Act (1922) granted it total protection. By means of heavy subsidies to colleges, the chemical industry turned thousands of "chem labs" to its own use and profit.

The Increased Concentration of Wealth. By 1929, 594 corporations owned 52.2 percent of all corporate assets. This amazing concentration of ownership had been achieved in various ways. Automobile production was characterized by the horizontal and vertical combination and consequent control of the auto market and suppliers; cross-licensing enabled the Radio Corporation of America to control over two thousand patents; holding companies predominated in the public utilities (the ownership of twenty-three thousand shares of the voting common stock in a parent holding company enabled the Standard Gas and Electric Company to control $1.2 billion in corporate assets); mergers proliferated in the chemical and banking industries; the "chain" (the so-called "circular merger") appeared in movie theaters, groceries, drugstores, shoe stores, and so forth. Industries united to protect their assets by forming "trade association" organizations that advised members on antiunionism, industrial practices, market controls, research, standardization, credit information, fair trade practices, and the like.

This pyramiding of business created an enormous chasm between the millions of small stockholders at the bottom and the few managers at the top who owned large blocs of voting shares. Virtually unchecked, the managers were able to vote excessive bonuses for themselves, inequitable division of dividends, fat contracts for services to their subsidiaries, and other measures in their own interest.

Patterns of Finance. The philosophy of Harding's Secretary of the Treasury Andrew Mellon dominated government finance. Mellon, a multimillionaire banker, believed that it was the duty of the government to create funds for investment by reducing the tax load on big business. If, simultaneously, the government were to economize by cutting expenses, increasing its efficiency, and pursuing a strict laissez-faire policy, the budget could be balanced.

Agriculture. Mellon's tax and tariff proposals met with strong congressional opposition from the Farm Bloc, a coalition of Midwestern Republicans and Southern Democrats. Despite general prosperity, a deepening depression afflicted agriculture throughout the decade. During World War I the introduction of the all-purpose tractor, the increased use of machinery, and the application of scientific methods of farming had boosted output. Then, after the war, the revival of European agriculture eroded the farmer's market at home and overseas. Surpluses piled high, prices plummeted, and market shifts created havoc (e.g., the population growth slowed, and high-calorie foods were rejected as slender figures became fashionable). Once again the familiar farm cycle was enacted: debt, foreclosure, and tenancy.

After defeating Mellon's more radical measures, Congress passed the Revenue Act of 1921, which raised taxes on corporate profits, abolished the excess-profits tax, reduced taxes on high incomes from 73 to 50 percent (Mellon had proposed a two-thirds reduction), and left inheritance taxes as they were. (Mellon had suggested eliminating them.)

Despite these setbacks, Mellon managed to balance the budget and greatly reduce the national debt. The Coolidge administration enthusiastically continued the pro-business policies of Harding and Mellon, thereby earning its strong support.

Labor

Immigration. Labor attained one of its primary goals during the twenties—the elimination of competition from immigrant workers. The economic argument against immigration was only one objection. Others stemmed from prejudice against the "new immigrant" of recent decades. After 1880 the number of immigrants from the north of Europe dwindled to a trickle, while immigrants from southern and eastern Europe flooded the country.

In response to this huge influx of foreigners, irrational racist stereotypes prevailed in the early twenties: the new immigrants were "racially inferior" to the "superior Nordic" types; they created slums; they were "radical." Members of Congress were not immune to these prejudices (some warned about "barbarian hordes"), and in 1921 the legislature imposed quota restrictions. It limited immigration from a particular country to 3 percent of the number of immigrants from that country who were in America in 1910, thereby ensuring that very few of the new arrivals would come from southern and eastern Europe; the act banned Asians completely. (Natives of the Western Hemisphere, on the other hand, were free from quota restrictions.) In 1929 Congress restricted immigration to 150 thousand a year and based national quotas on origins of the total white population in 1920, a system greatly weighted in favor of new arrivals from England.

Cheaper Labor. Employers were somewhat hard-pressed by this legislation, for it tended to make labor more expensive. Other factors were also increasing the cost of labor. The eight-hour day became standard in most industries; mechanization nearly eliminated the cheap, unskilled worker (semiskilled workers at the machine received higher pay); welfare legislation forced employers to provide for health and sanitation needs of employees; and unions had grown powerful enough in some areas to compel steady wage increases. To counteract rising labor costs, employers began the widespread practice of hiring Canadians, southern whites, Mexicans, women, and southern blacks, who then migrated north. These workers could be hired at considerably lower wages.

The Labor Movement. The failure of great strikes in the coal, steel, meat-packing, and railroad industries from 1919 to 1922 broke the back of organized labor. To prevent a revival of the trade-union movement, employers experimented with welfare plans such as group insurance, pension schemes, and stock ownership (so-called "welfare capitalism") while using traditional antilabor methods such as company unions, blacklists, and lockouts. Established unions became conservative in their goals during the twenties, concentrating on developing union welfare programs. This relative inactivity allowed Communists to penetrate successfully into the leadership of the textile, coal, food, fur, and furniture unions.

Foreign Policy

Disarmament in the Far East. Shocked by the senseless destruction of war, Americans retreated into isolationism. The

United States wanted to scrap its arms and also to avoid new production of weapons so that the national debt might be paid off and taxes reduced. How could this be accomplished without leaving the nation open to attack? The aggressor the United States feared most was Japan, which was a destabilizing element in the Far East. How could the Japanese be curbed and isolation maintained? To resolve this dilemma, in the summer of 1921, America invited Great Britain, France, Italy, Japan, Belgium, the Netherlands, Portugal, and China to Washington to consider stabilizing the Far East and limiting arms. After prolonged negotiation, the Washington Armament Conference drew up three treaties.

The Five-Power Treaty. In this 1922 treaty, the United States, France, England, Italy, and Japan, agreed to impose a ten-year moratorium on the construction of battleships and to reduce their fleets to a fixed ratio, with the United States and Great Britain limited to 525 thousand tons apiece; Japan to 315 thousand tons; and France and Italy to 175 thousand each. For the United States this meant junking thirty existing warships and nine in construction; England had to scrap only four in construction; and Japan destroyed one twenty-year-old battleship. Since the 525 thousand American tons had to be divided into a two-ocean navy, Japan secured a clear edge in the Pacific. Yet the treaty also maintained the dominance of the United States and Great Britain.

The Four-Power Treaty. In the same year, Japan, China, England, and the United States agreed to maintain the status quo in fortifying Pacific island posses-sions; respect each others' interests in the Pacific; and consult each other if a conflict broke out among the signatories. As a result of this treaty, the American string of defense from Samoa to the Aleutians remained unfortified—the United States kept its pledge—in the face of Japanese fortification of its mandate islands in violation of the treaty. Furthermore, since the United States was not a member of the League of Nations, it had no right to check on the fulfillment of Japanese mandatory obligations.

The Nine-Power Treaty. All the powers agreed in 1922 to respect China's independence and to retain the Open Door—the sole obstacle to Japanese domination of China. A separate agreement allowed the Chinese to raise import tariffs. The excellent sentiments behind the Open Door, however, would prove only as strong as the enforcement supporting them. By retreating into isolation, the United States withdrew from enforcement and, in effect, abandoned China to Japan.

Further Conferences. Further conferences were called to correct the deficiencies of the Washington Armament Conference. One at Rome in 1924 and another at Geneva in 1927 proved fruitless. A third was held in London in 1930. Once again the United States favored disarmament. It granted Japan new ratios—10 to 6 for big-gun cruisers, 10 to 7 for small-gun cruisers, and parity (10 to 10) in submarines; agreed to six more years of a naval holiday (no further construction beyond treaty limits); renewed the pledge of non-fortification of its island possessions in the Pacific; limited heavy cruiser construction; and allowed the inclusion of an "escalator clause" in the treaty, permitting England to have a navy equal in size to that of any two great powers.

Postwar Debts. The United States was committed to collecting its war debts of over $10 billion from the Allied powers. But the Allies made debt payment contingent on the receipt of German reparations payments, which they said amounted to $33 billion. When Germany defaulted, the Allies did, too. To collect its debts, the United States resentfully undertook to finance Germany's reparations payments. The Dawes Plan (1924) and the Young Plan (1929) reduced reparations and awarded Germany a $200-million loan, which she used partly to pay her reparations bill and partly to rebuild her army in defiance of the Treaty of Versailles. The depression that overwhelmed Germany in 1931 forced the United States—itself in the midst of the Great Depression—to declare a one-year moratorium on the payment of Allied debts and German reparations. This moratorium proved to be permanent.

In 1933 at Lausanne, Switzerland, Adolf Hitler repudiated all reparations payments; and since the Allies had hitched debt payments to reparations, they also repudiated their already considerably scaled-down debts. This, then, was the ironic situation in which the United States found itself: a victor in World War I, it footed the bills for both German reparations and Allied debts—except for Finland, which completely paid its debt.

The League of Nations. Isolationism had prevented American participation in the League of Nations. But the United States could not ignore so vast a body of nations. In 1923 unofficial American observers began to sit in on League committees considering nonpolitical matters. A year later, official American delegates were sent to League conferences. The United States signed nine international draft conventions on such matters as narcotics control, control of slavery, and forced labor.

But while it sought benefits from League activities, the United States was unwilling to assume the responsibilities of membership. Harding, Coolidge, and Hoover were keenly aware of the awkwardness of America's position and urged that the nation enter, at the very least, the World Court. Party platforms echoed this sentiment. Moreover, the American statesman Elihu Root had helped to frame the Court's charter; four Americans—John Bassett Moore, Charles Evans Hughes, Frank B. Kellogg, and Manley O. Hudson—had sat as jurists on the Court. But the Senate rejected every proposal to join, despite the inclusion of remarkable reservations that the League of Nations was prepared to accept. For example, under the "Root Formula," if the United States joined the World Court, it would be informed of any opinion by the Court affecting the United States and then be permitted to state its case against the Court's opinion to the League Assembly or to the Council. If the opinion, nonetheless, went against the United States, it could leave the Court so that the opinion would have no effect. Even such concessions failed to persuade the Senate to support the Root Formula.

The Kellogg-Briand Pact. America did enter into a commitment for peace. In the Kellogg-Briand Pact (1928) the United States and France condemned any recourse to war, renounced it as an instrument of national policy, and pledged themselves to peaceful settlement of all disputes. Since the pact included no provision enforcing these noble sentiments, nearly every nation in the world signed the agreement, which even gained overwhelming approval (the vote was eighty-five to one) from the formidably isolationist Senate. This meaningless treaty, relying on world opinion to enforce peace, symbolized postwar American foreign policy.

Latin America.   Isolation did not mean a withdrawal from Latin America, although the government retreated from the use of force, seeking instead to expand trade and investment. American marines withdrew from Haiti, the Dominican Republic, and Cuba, but the government placed restrictions on the economic activities of these regions. In Nicaragua, however, renewal of unrest resulted in American occupation, which lasted until 1928. Relations with Mexico, in contrast, improved considerably. In 1928 Mexico protected its interests with a Petroleum Law that vested ownership rights of subsoil resources in the government, demanded that foreigners abide by the law or forfeit their properties, granted fifty-year leases only to properties acquired before 1917, limited the amount of grazing and agricultural land foreigners might own, and forbade them to request protection from their own government. The law aroused violent protest in America from the Secretary of State, Frank B. Kellogg, and from the Hearst press. But Coolidge's ambassador to Mexico, Dwight Morrow, met with Mexican President Plutarco Calles and by skillful diplomacy secured two concessions: the legalization of oil titles acquired before 1917, and the modification of Mexico's anticlerical program to permit public religious services. Hard feelings between the neighbors then subsided.

In 1930 came a harbinger of the future in Inter-American relations—the Clark Memorandum, written by Under Secretary of State J. Reuben Clark. Repudiating the Roosevelt Corollary, it reaffirmed America's right to be the sole interpreter of the Monroe Doctrine but denied that the doctrine sanctioned intervention in Latin American affairs. The United States could intervene to protect the lives and property of its citizens only under international law. Later, Hoover's successor, Franklin Roosevelt, continued this "Good Neighbor Policy."

Society and Culture

Intolerance.   No generalizations about social and cultural trends during the twenties can be made easily. It was an era of contradictions, of continuous ferment, reevaluation of values, and trial and error. This experimentation and turmoil left a profound mark on American institutions and thought.

One of the striking characteristics of the decade was its spirit of undemocratic intolerance. Perhaps needing outlets for the aggression unleashed by war, Americans searched for other targets after the Germans were defeated. Although the number of American Communists was small, they became the new targets of this aggressive nationalism. In such a climate, the "Red Scare" that began in 1919 got out of hand. Under the leadership of state legislatures and via the notorious "Palmer raids" (named after Wilson's Attorney General A. Mitchell Palmer), thousands of alien "radicals" were rounded up. Often denied the most elementary civil liberties, they were "third-degreed," and, if foreign-born, they were to be deported. (In actuality, out of the 6,000 apprehended in the raids, only 556 were eventually deported.) Initially these raids were supported by a public persuaded of the menace of Communism. But then various government officials and established public figures began to object. Attempting to keep up the momentum, Palmer went too far. Warning that a huge terrorist demonstration was scheduled to take place on May Day 1920, he was left looking ridiculous when nothing happened.

Yet the Red Scare did not completely subside. After their arrest in 1920, two Italian aliens, Nicola Sacco and Bartolomeo Vanzetti, were tried and executed (1927) in Massachusetts for a payroll robbery–killing they did not commit; what was really on trial were their anarchist and pacifist sentiments. The Sacco and Vanzetti affair not only symbolized the decade's political intolerance, but its religious and ethnic bigotry as well.

Indeed, religious intolerance matched the era's political intolerance. Henry Ford sponsored the publication and distribution of a vicious and fraudulent anti-Semitic tract called "Protocols of the Elders of Zion," which purported to prove that Jews were planning to conquer the world. Ford later withdrew his support in the publication and apologized for his mistaken judgment, but his recantation had little effect on the unpublished "quotas" that Jews encountered when seeking jobs or admission to colleges and professional schools. Anti-Catholicism, also rife during the twenties, was revealed in all its ugliness in the election of 1928, in which the Catholic Alfred E. Smith lost to Herbert Hoover after a campaign marred by attacks against the Democrat based on his religion.

Even more disturbing was the treatment of those blacks who had begun a mass migration to the northern cities. Not only were they greeted in St. Louis, Omaha, Detroit, and Chicago by race riots, but after these subsided, restrictive covenants forced them into ghettos or segregated parts of the city. In the North as well as in the South, blacks had to endure Jim Crow restrictions on their use of public places, educational facilities, and employment opportunities. In the South the revived KKK embarked on an orgy of lynchings, floggings, and terrorist actions unparalleled in American history. The Klan also found followers in small towns and cities throughout the Midwest and West. In addition to blacks, it targeted Jews, Catholics, foreigners, prostitutes, and other nonconformists. One explanation of the Klan's revival is that it offered a sense of security to people made anxious first by the war and then by a rapidly changing postwar society. By the mid-1920s nearly five million Americans belonged to the organization. But its violent behavior and its leadership's misuse of funds not only roused liberals and conservatives but even repelled many Klan supporters, and by 1930 membership had shrunk to about nine thousand.

Religious intolerance also was manifested in the revival of fundamentalism. The fundamentalists, who came mostly from rural America, rejected Darwin's theory of evolution, and with it, implicitly, urban or modern, culture. The trial of John Scopes (1925) showed how deeply embedded the fundamentalist doctrine was in southern religious life. In that year Tennessee outlawed the teaching of the theory of evolution. John T. Scopes, a high school biology teacher, was arrested for challenging the law. He retained the famous lawyer Clarence Darrow as chief defense counsel; the prosecutor was William Jennings Bryan. The match between these two giants, one representing the skeptical spirit of Science and the other the dogmatic spirit of Religion, attracted international attention. In the end Scopes was convicted and fined a token $10. Although the conflict of science and theology remained unresolved, the trial exposed the fundamentalist position more fully than before to public scrutiny. Nevertheless, rural Americans held on to their strong religious beliefs, even when they moved to the cities. The evangelist Aimee Semple McPherson drew thousands to revival meetings in Los Angeles.

The New Sexual Freedom. The twenties, known as the "Jazz Age," was marked by a self-conscious revolt against Puritan restraints. Young women adopted freer styles in appearance and behavior: wearing the new "flapper" mode of dress and gaudy cosmetics; participating in "wild" parties where they danced the "Charleston" and "Big Apple"; devouring "confession" magazines, the new urban tabloids, and novels on such daring subjects as adultery. They imitated the movie "vamp" and "It girl." Young men were not far behind, flaunting raccoon coats, bell-bottom trousers, hip flasks, and outlandishly decorated "tin lizzies."

Moral standards relating to courtship and marriage changed radically within a generation. For example, most states had by now liberalized their divorce laws, and under the leadership of Margaret Sanger, the birth control movement was attracting attention. Much of this change can be attributed to the popularization of the psychology of Sigmund Freud, with its emphasis on the role of sexual drives in personality. No longer taboo, sex began to be talked about openly, especially by young men and women, eager to prove themselves "emancipated."

Black Life and Culture. The atrocities of the Klan was only one of many problems facing blacks after the war. The surge of southern blacks into large cities created urban ghettos, such as New York's Harlem, which, until 1910, had been a white, middle-class area. Ghetto life turned out to be as degrading in its own way as life in the rural South. In these crowded areas, disease, and crime flourished. Living conditions were no better in smaller, northern cities, where blacks soon discovered the prevalence of de facto segregation. These disappointments caused many blacks to become militant. For example, W. E. B. Du Bois, who waivered throughout his life between advocating migration and black separatism, now attempted to create an international black movement by organizing Pan African conferences. Marcus Garvey, who was antagonistic toward light-skinned blacks like Du Bois, went even further, advocating that blacks go "back to Africa." Founded to promote black pride, his Universal Improvement Association attracted hundreds of thousands of members in the early part of the decade. Garvey put his message of black self-reliance into action, establishing a variety of black-owned businesses. Their differing ideas about what blacks should do brought Du Bois and Garvey into conflict, each sharply criticizing the other. In 1923 Garvey's steamship company for transporting blacks to Africa filed for bankruptcy. He was subsequently imprisoned for defrauding its investors. His message, however, helped make blacks proud of themselves and to resist the cruelties inflicted by white society.

But while life in the northern ghettos was often one of despair, there was also a thriving cultural development taking place there. Harlem became the cultural center of black life in America, fostering black newspapers, magazines, theater companies, and libraries. And although it originated with black musicians in New Orleans at the beginning of the century, jazz found much of its audience in ghettos before spreading beyond their boundaries.

Women. Although women were permitted greater sexual freedom and could smoke and drink in public without being labeled prostitutes, the twenties promised them greater progress than was actually achieved. The double standard still existed. While the number of women working rose to 10.6 million at the end of the decade, most of them held menial positions or those men had rejected, and were paid far less than men. Nor did the Nineteenth Amendment give women independent power—it soon became apparent that women generally voted for the same candidates as their husbands. The disillusionment with suffrage caused some radical women, led by Alice Paul, to fight for an equal rights amendment. A greater number joined the moderate League of Women Voters, an organization that supported a wide range of reforms, not all of them feminist. During the twenties, then, the women's movement lost a focused and united sense of direction.

Ballyhoo. Riding on the wave of prosperity, the advertising and public relations promoters were the kings of the twenties. It was they who built the businessman into a myth, created the idea of the American "standard of living"—consisting of everything from a second car in a double garage to a mink coat—built up the "million-dollar" gate for a prize fight, baseball or football game, or six-day bike race; made Babe Ruth, Jack Dempsey, Red Grange, and Shirley Temple into national idols; created the "sheik" and "flapper" styles; and promoted every kind of zany, from flagpole sitters to Brooklyn Bridge jumpers to marathon dancers.

Lawlessness. Almost immediately after the Eighteenth Amendment was ratified in 1919, systematic violation of it began. Enforcement proved nearly nonexistent; home brews multiplied; bootlegging became a major industry; and gangsters flourished. The king of gangsterdom, Chicago's Al Capone, commanded a private army of thugs; his business embraced not only bootleg whiskey, but "collections" from businesses and politicians for "protection," sale of narcotics, extortion, and prostitution. Enemies of gangsters were "rubbed out" or "taken for a ride."

The American public remained either apathetic toward gangsters, fearful of them, or secretly sympathetic. Many gangsters fostered this attitude by presenting themselves as latter-day Robin Hoods. In this veiled form, the gangster became a kind of popular hero.

Social Advances.   If it was the seamy side of the twenties that captured attention, still the decade quietly recorded some rather dull but solid gains. Businessmen's associations like the Kiwanis, Elks, and Rotary instituted extensive service programs; living standards rose, encouraging greater leisure; hundreds of new vocations became available to enterprising women; the Model T and Model A Fords opened up the entire country to travel and recreation; colleges expanded their physical facilities to accommodate a tremendous upsurge in enrollment.

Popular Reading.   The most sensational development in popular literature was the appearance of the tabloid, an illustrated and heavily featured paper specializing in lurid and sensational news stories and racing tips. Daily circulation of these newspapers soared to the millions. The popular magazines, such as the *Ladies' Home Journal*, kept pace, but they were being pressed by lurid "confession" magazines, western pulps, and magazine tabloids called "digests."

Popular Music.   Music entered the jazz age, and composers began to exploit its possibilities, with George Gershwin, Irving Berlin, Cole Porter, Hoagy Carmichael, and William C. Handy producing songs that have endured as jazz classics. In his "Rhapsody in Blue," Gershwin tried to extend the American jazz idiom into quasi-symphonic form.

Scientific and Artistic Developments

Medicine.   By the end of the twenties, diphtheria and typhoid had succumbed to vaccines. Life expectancy continued to rise. Harvey Cushing advanced the frontiers of neurological surgery. Vitamin E was isolated. American medicine had clearly come of age.

Physics.   So, too, had the pure science of physics. Robert A. Millikan and Arthur Compton made basic discoveries, which earned them the Nobel Prize. Millikan measured the charge of an electron and found it constant. Elaborating his findings, he proved an Einstein equation and evaluated fellow physicist Max Planck's constant. Compton showed that X rays had a corpuscular structure (the "Compton effect").

Biology.   Thomas Hunt Morgan made basic contributions to the science of heredity. Although he completed most of his studies on genes, chromosomes, and sex-characteristics before the 1920s, his students continued to expand his findings in these fields. Of particular importance was the discovery by the geneticist Hermann Muller that X rays increase the rate of mutation among fruit flies.

Psychology.   John B. Watson elaborated the Russian Ivan Pavlov's "conditioned reflex" into the science of behaviorism. According to Watson human behavior was reduced to mechanical-neural activity, a reduction that eliminated consciousness, and free will, as motives in people's actions. While Watson's work received much publicity and encouraged laboratory experiments in psychology, American psychiatrists were turning instead to the epoch-making studies of Sigmund Freud and beginning to apply his theories in psychotherapy.

The Fine Arts. The turning point in American painting and sculpture was the controversial 1913 Armory Show in New York City, America's first view of the European revolution in the fine arts. Exhibited were works by Renoir, Rouault, Picabia, Picasso, and Brancusi—works whose strangeness shook the world of art. Following this showing, many American artists became impressionists, expressionists, cubists, futurists, abstractionists—in short, "modern" artists. Their works reduced forms to abstracted planes and curves; distorted perspective to achieve aesthetic tension; made color and line independent of theme.

A Growing American Literature

Fiction. With the war's end, American novelists entered a period of self-conscious revolt, depicting a "lost generation" of sad young men and women. For these writers the war was not a crusade, as Wilson had contended, but a mass slaughter rife with pain and agony, destructive of artistic values, humane ideals, and the free mind. In the war tales of John Dos Passos, e. e. cummings, and Ernest Hemingway, American protagonists are detached, disillusioned, sensitive observers of life.

Generalizing from this bitter experience, American novelists believed that all ideals are shams and that the only free person is one who is permanently detached. They received considerable support for these beliefs from the rapid spread in America of Freudianism in its most imprecise and popularized forms. A misreading of Freud led many writers to conclude that absolute freedom of the individual and unlicensed self-expression represented the sole path to stability and balance, the only way out of the quagmire of pessimism and nihilism. In their works they preached the right to sexual license, damning any protest against it as "puritanical inhibition." As one expression of their freedom, a number of young writers, including Ernest Hemingway, became expatriates, many fleeing to Paris. Others, like F. Scott Fitzgerald, remained at home but shared a similar disdain for contemporary American society.

Sherwood Anderson remained in America but left his job, wife, and family to become a novelist and short-story writer. In such works as *Winesburg, Ohio* (1919) and *The Triumph of the Egg* (1921), he produced a gallery of fumbling small-town adolescents, eccentrics, and embittered old failures. Most of these rejected and frustrated individuals pursued mangled dreams and private obsessions, grasping for something beyond their reach, their search ending in confusion. Because his types were so extreme, Anderson's vision did not unduly disturb Americans.

Sinclair Lewis, the most popular novelist of the decade, did unsettle his readers. In *Main Street* (1920) he attacked the complacency of small-town American life. His next novel, *Babbitt* (1922), assaulted the "boobus americanis" named by H. L. Mencken (perhaps the most influential social critic of the decade) in the form of the typical twenties businessman, George Babbitt: backslapper, go-getter, booster, joiner, a man lacking insight into his own hypocrisies. In *Arrowsmith* (1925) Lewis exposed the corruption of medicine and in *Elmer Gantry* (1927) that of religion.

In 1930 he became the first American to win the Nobel Prize for literature. Despite his biting satire, Lewis was essentially a reformer rather than a critic, using his novels to improve the community, the people, and the faiths he identified with.

Ernest Hemingway's first novel, *The Sun Also Rises* (1926), depicted the rootless lives of expatriates who were casualties—physical and spiritual—of the war. In *A Farewell to Arms* (1929) he described the horror of war itself. His laconic characters followed a rigid personal code, drank to excess, engaged in violent sports, distrusted intelligence, resisted sentiment, and believed in nothing. Hemingway's much-imitated, bare, reportorial style matched his credo. Probably for these reasons the early Hemingway became the prototype of the "lost generation," a pessimistic, nihilistic, generation that had come to expect nothing but sudden death.

Hemingway's heroes were young men grown old too soon. F. Scott Fitzgerald's simply refused to grow old. In such novels as *This Side of Paradise* (1920) and *The Great Gatsby* (1925), Fitzgerald molded his characters in his own image—young, handsome, clever—and then projected his own conflicts and desires onto them. His protagonists were romantics with an inordinate longing to be eternally young and rich beyond all care and responsibility. Yet, like Hemingway's, Fitzgerald's characters evoked the confusions and despair of the lost generation.

Finally, John Dos Passos (*Three Soldiers*, 1921; *Manhattan Transfer*, 1925), William Faulkner (*Soldier's Pay*, 1926; *The Sound and the Fury*, 1929), and Thomas Wolfe (*Look Homeward, Angel*, 1929) began publishing their novels. Dos Passos wrote of the artist struggling to free himself from a machine-oriented society; Faulkner dissected southern violence and decadence; and Wolfe wrote about his own youth.

Poetry, Criticism, and the Return to the Past. During the twenties American poets continued the experiment in verse forms created in the previous generation by Ezra Pound. Among the most experimental works were those of e. e. cummings, who showed his contempt for received ideas by a singular assault upon the English language. In his poems he assailed mediocrity and celebrated the individual's right to love, sometimes employing eccentric typographical devices to represent and extend meaning.

Extending into the twenties was the influence of Ezra Pound and T. S. Eliot. Pound combined in his poetry an extreme modernism with a profound sense of the past. He employed obscure allusions to and quotations from ancient and medieval writers (often in their original language), coupling them with English colloquialisms.

Eliot, who spent most of his adult life in England, was profoundly influenced by Pound; he also sought to fuse past and present. In *The Waste Land* (1922) he described the fragmentation and sterility of the modern world.

Strongly influenced by the French symbolists and by Eliot, Hart Crane achieved fame with his long poem *The Bridge* (1930), written partly in response to the despair of *The Waste Land.* In Crane's poem the Brooklyn Bridge becomes the symbol of America's "constructive future."

Aside from the spiritual ravages of war, advances in science and mechanics had deeply disrupted a sense of stability. A resulting "traditionalism" during the twenties was partly an effort by some intellectuals to find values in the American heritage by which to live. The essayist Joseph Wood Krutch listed the "illusions"—God, love, tragedy, and aesthetics—that would have to be dismissed now that science and mechanics ruled the universe of the mind.

There arose a group of writers who indignantly rejected a gloomy appraisal of the present. They, too, looked to the past for solutions. Calling themselves the "New Humanists," Stuart Sherman, Irving Babbitt, and Paul Elmer More urged Americans to return to Emerson, Thoreau, and Melville; they promoted religion and philosophy, and a more abiding faith in democracy and the values of Puritanism. Such a return to the past, they argued, would provide Americans with an "inner check" on their undisciplined emotions.

Using similar reasoning, poet/critics Allan Tate, John Crowe Ransom, and Robert Penn Warren evoked in their writings the southern agrarian past when people had, they argued, a sense of propriety, rules of conduct, and codes of manners. In such novels as *My Antonia* (1918), Willa Cather focused on the difficult lives of women in the South and the Midwest. Ellen Glasgow wrote sadly, ironically, but lovingly of the vanishing southern aristocracy, while Edith Wharton examined the snobbery of old New York society.

Theater. The greatest American playwright of the twenties was Eugene O'Neill (*The Emperor Jones*, 1920; *Strange Interlude*, 1928). In the inner life of his characters, O'Neill thought he had discovered the essential sickness of his time: "the death of the old God and the failure of science and materialism to give any satisfactory new one for the surviving primitive, religious instinct to find a meaning for life in and to comfort its fears of death." Thus O'Neill, too, belonged to the disillusioned, the lost, and the disinherited generation of the First World War.

The Harlem Renaissance. During the twenties, sociologist, poet, novelist, and editor W. E. B. Du Bois and poet James Weldon Johnson became the leaders of the black literary community that was developing in Harlem. The movement, also called the "Black Renaissance," or the "Golden Age," emphasized the African heritage of black Americans and the writers' pride in their blackness, culture, and folk traditions. Other leaders in this creative flowering were the poets Claude McKay, Countee Cullen, Jean Toomer, and Langston Hughes—who wrote eloquently about racial injustice—as well as the novelist and short-story writer Zora Neale Hurston.

CHAPTER TWENTY

The New Deal

After her husband Franklin's inauguration on March 4, 1933, Eleanor Roosevelt told White House reporters, "The crowds were so tremendous, and you felt that they would do anything—if only someone would tell them what to do." Roosevelt's inaugural address heartened the nation. Finally, after a tumultuous and finally disastrous decade, a leader had emerged who might really "tell them what to do" and lead them out of the worst depression in the country's history.

The Great Collapse

The Crash. Herbert Hoover became President on March 4, 1929. On October 24 the stock market, which had soared during the twenties, collapsed. Within two weeks the value of securities shrank by $25 billion; within three years, one hundred and ten thousand businesses closed their doors, five thousand banks failed, and national income toppled from $88 billion to $42 billion. Prices hit bottom: cotton, for example, dropped from 16 cents a pound to 5 cents. More than ten million workers joined the unemployment lines.

Wages for those fortunate enough to have jobs fell 55 percent. New investments in business dropped from $10 billion in 1929 to $1 billion in 1932, not even enough to maintain existing plants. On the farm crops rotted and farmers dumped their milk; in the cities breadlines and souplines grew longer.

Dispossessed and adrift, the penniless and hungry congregated in shantytowns called "Hoovervilles" and "hobo jungles," in which patchwork shambles served as shelter. Desperate veterans formed a "bonus army" to demand full payment on their service certificates and then marched on Washington, where they established headquarters on Anacostia Flats along the Potomac.

At first the nation was stunned by this tragedy of poverty in the midst of plenty, of hunger in the midst of surplus. Then protesting voices were raised—from churchmen, industrialists like Gerard Swope, labor unions, radicals, men and women in the street. Agonized voices demanded that someone "do something."

"Prosperity Is Just Around the Corner." Herbert Hoover, too, was baffled. He had no experience with the many indicators of a coming collapse: chronic agricultural depression; limited depression in coal, textiles, and railroads; unequal distribution of income leading to wild speculation; widespread underconsumption caused by one half the income receivers getting less than subsistence earnings; large withdrawals of foreign funds; an unusual "bull" or inflated market; a rigid, overmonopolized economy; and large numbers of unemployed in the midst of apparent prosperity. Today such signs would stimulate immediate government action. Hoover, however, firmly believed that "natural laws" should operate without government interference. In his view, the nation's economy was sound; prosperity was "just around the corner." Thus, initially Hoover believed that if the government requested business to maintain wages and prices, not only would they do so voluntarily, but this response would stop the slide. Hoover also relied on voluntary relief efforts to assist the unemployed. They quickly proved ineffective, and within a few months wages and prices fell even more sharply. When it became impossible to ignore the full impact of the collapse, Hoover finally moved beyond volunteerism, inaugurating what was subsequently called the "Little New Deal."

Hoover's Little New Deal (1929–32). Hoover's program for recovery was based on his belief that government must first rescue the capitalist from distress. In 1932 the government launched the huge Reconstruction Finance Corporation (RFC) to loan money to the banks, railroads, building-and-loan companies, and other businesses in danger of bankruptcy. The Glass-Steagall Banking Act of 1932 eased the tight credit situation by permit-

ting the issue of Federal Reserve notes with only government bonds and commercial paper as backing. A Federal Home Loan Bank attempted to halt the flood of foreclosures on mortgages. To bolster relief to the unemployed, the RFC was empowered to lend up to $300 million to states whose treasuries were exhausted. Farmers received additional aid through the Agricultural Marketing Act (1929), which permitted the government to purchase surpluses in an effort to prop up farm prices.

Despite these aids to business, Hoover still opposed direct relief. Americans became increasingly angry with his efforts, as millions of workers could find no jobs and breadlines stretched even longer. By 1932 the situation reached its lowest ebb. Only about one quarter of the unemployed received any aid. Families who had been evicted lived in communities of lean-tos made of scrap metal and packing boxes. Many existed on soup and beans or garbage. Thousands of homeless men, women, and children rode the railroads or roamed the countryside looking for work or begging for food. Everybody was affected.

As would be expected, those on the lowest rung of the economic ladder—blacks and Mexican Americans—lost their jobs first. Many middle-class professionals and white-collar workers who lost their jobs often were too proud to ask for charity. Even the rich were affected, and many lost everything in the stock market crash and collapse of businesses. In the summer of 1932, Hoover's image was irrevocably damaged after he ordered troops to clear out the two thousand veterans who had settled down in shanties at Anacostia Flats.

The Election of 1932. In his speech accepting the Democratic nomination for president, Franklin Delano Roosevelt, then governor of New York, created the slogan for his administration. "I pledge you," he said, "I pledge myself, to a new deal for the American people." Not much of this "New Deal" appeared in the Democratic platform, which promised to balance the budget, reduce federal expenditures, remove government from fields of private enterprise except for public works and conservation, maintain a sound currency, reform the banking system, lend relief money to the states, and control crop surpluses. (All these promises were in fact echoed in the Republican platform.) Outright repeal of the Eighteenth Amendment was purely a political issue. Only an endorsement for unemployment and old-age insurance sounded new.

Renominated by the Republicans, Hoover exuded an air of pessimism and petulance, a combination that alienated voters even more. In contrast, Roosevelt waged a confident campaign, and, as it progressed, he became much more specific in discussing his reform program (although few noticed it), including crop control for the farmer, hydroelectric projects, full production, and full employment. In other words, Roosevelt was prepared to do whatever seemed necessary to end the depression.

But even more forceful than his program was his magnetic personality, which inspired immense confidence. His heroic struggle against polio (an attack in 1921 left him crippled in both legs) caused the public to applaud his courage and feel that even though Roosevelt came from a background of wealth and privilege, he not only understood human suffering but also could overcome it. To some critics, the Democratic standard-bearer appeared to be an intellectual lightweight. Indeed, little in his previous history showed a commitment to the drastic reform that many observers deemed necessary. Nevertheless, Roosevelt won the election in a near landslide; the electoral vote was 472 to 59.

The General Staff. When Roosevelt took the oath of office on March 4, 1933, thirteen million Americans were unemployed. In his inaugural address, the new President proclaimed that "the only thing we have to fear is fear itself." What the nation needed was leadership. Roosevelt flayed the "rulers of the exchange of mankind's goods," the "unscrupulous money changers" and "self-seekers." He called for a spiritual rebirth—and for jobs. Congress was to be called into session to grant him "broad executive power to wage a war against the emergency . . ."

Roosevelt appointed strong administrators to Cabinet posts: Cordell Hull as Secretary of State, Henry Morgenthau, Jr., to head the Treasury, Henry A. Wallace in charge of Agriculture, Harold L. Ickes in the position of Secretary of the Interior, Frances Perkins as head of Labor—the first woman cabinet member in American history—and as Postmaster General, James Farley. Then, from the nation's universities and other intellectual centers, Roosevelt gathered a "brain trust" consisting of Raymond Moley, Thomas Corcoran, Benjamin Cohen, Jerome Frank, Rexford G. Tugwell, Robert Sherwood, Hugh Johnson, Louis McHenry Howe, Samuel Rosenman, and others. While far from unanimous in opinion (in fact, the New Deal lacked a consistent ideology), this group brought to the administration a high level of idealism and intellectual gifts. Soon the middle ranks of government, too, were filled with college professors, young lawyers, and a variety of experts. A number of these were women, mainly through the efforts of Roosevelt's wife, Eleanor, and Molly Dewson of the Democratic National Committee.

New Deal Measures.   Congressional legislation passed during this period fell into four categories: emergency legislation, which became inoperative when the emergency had passed; trial-and-error legislation, which was abandoned when it produced failure; reform legislation, which redesigned existing laws to eliminate weaknesses exposed during the onset of the Great Depression; and legislation creating new structures, which protected the physical resources of the country, redistributed the wealth of its citizens, and extended the government protection to new groups.

During Roosevelt's first one hundred days in office, Congress approved fifteen out of fifteen major pieces of legislation proposed by the President. Although they did not end the depression (it lasted six more years), these measures and the President's optimism turned the tide psychologically for the nation.

Emergency Legislation

Opening the Banks.   By March 4, 1933, virtually every bank in the country was closed as a result of state-ordered "bank holidays." Invoking the "Trading with the Enemy Act of 1917," Roosevelt immediately proclaimed a four-day national bank holiday. He coupled this with an embargo on the export of gold, silver, and currency. Congress then passed an Emergency Banking Relief Act (March 9) under which the Treasury officials and the RFC could begin to reopen sound banks and to liquidate insolvent ones. On March 12 the President held his first "fireside chat" (via the radio) with the American public and informed them in simple language of what the government had done and what they must do, namely, return to normal banking habits. The people did so, and by April 1 one billion dollars in currency and gold was returned to the banks. By these measures Roosevelt saved the banks.

The Unemployed.   With each passing month thousands of young people were entering the labor market, swelling the total of the unemployed. With private, municipal, and state relief funds exhausted, emergency measures were required to stave off hunger. On March 31 Congress enacted the Civilian Conservation Corps Reforestation Relief Act to give jobs to 250 thousand unemployed men between eighteen and twenty-five years of age. These young people were housed and fed in work camps, given $30 a month (part of which went to their dependents), and set to work under Army supervision planting trees, draining swamps, and combating soil erosion, poison ivy, and hay fever–causing weeds.

The Federal Emergency Relief Act (May 12) provided a half-billion dollar allotment to states and municipalities for the creation of work-relief projects. When a temporary business revival in mid-1933 collapsed, the Civil Works Administration (CWA) under Harry Hopkins was created (November 1933) to provide federal employment for four million jobless persons. Almost a billion dollars was spent on CWA for one hundred and eighty thousand work projects before this phase of relief was abandoned (March 1934).

The WPA. In 1935 Congress produced the Works Progress Administration (WPA) in response to the need for work-relief programs. The WPA lasted until 1943 and, during its existence, spent $11 billion and found work for over eight million people. The bulk of the money went for employing adults on projects that would not compete with private industry or require large expenditures on capital equipment. Such projects included construction of schools, playgrounds, and airports; maintenance of roads, water mains, and sewers; flood relief, snow removal, and similar public services.

The WPA devoted special attention to unemployed artists, actors, writers, and scholars, who, under its aegis, produced hundreds of murals and statuary for public buildings. The Federal Theatre Project employed thousands of directors, actors, and stagehands and in the process educated millions in great drama. The Federal Writers' Project did research that produced guidebooks, dictionaries, and a thousand pamphlets. And the National Youth Administration created part-time jobs for two million high school and college students, thus removing them from the labor market.

Like other relief efforts, the WPA failed to end the depression, although it helped many of the unemployed. Critics charged that it was too costly and that it smacked of socialism. In fact, however, the WPA did not go far enough because of Roosevelt's fear of an unbalanced budget.

Foreclosures on Farm Mortgages. With surpluses on their hands and prices at rock bottom, farmers were unable to meet their debts. Foreclosures multiplied; 25 percent of farm families went on relief, and a large number were reduced to tenancy or to grubbing a bare subsistence from unproductive lands. Congress acted to halt further foreclosures. It extended funds to Federal Farm Loan agencies, enabling them to refinance mortgage payments that had come due but could not be met. Congress also enacted a foreclosure act, permitting farmers to renegotiate mortgages that had already been foreclosed. But the most radical approach to foreclosure was the Frazier-Lemke Act (1934), which placed a five-year moratorium on foreclosures and provided a method for repurchase of lost properties. Enraged creditors went to the Supreme Court and, in 1935, won their case on the unconstitutionality of the law (*Louisville Joint Stock Land Bank v. Radford*).

Congress struck back at the Supreme Court with the Farm Mortgage Moratorium Act (1935). Under this law (which was upheld by the Court), the courts could grant to farmers three years' grace against foreclosure if they paid rent or repossessed their property. Creditors could force a sale at auction, but the farmers might then redeem their farm at auction price. Finally, for those who had been permanently displaced and were now tenants or agricultural laborers, Congress experimented with creating subsistence homesteads and resettlement projects. The Bankhead-Jones Farm Tenancy Act (1937) consolidated a number of these efforts.

The government also established the Federal Security Administration (FSA) to make loans to help tenants buy land, build camps for migratory workers, and construct subsistence homestead projects. Like the WPA, FSA measures met hostile criticism from conservatives who charged it with "paternalism," "socialism," and "demoralization." Few men in public life received more abuse than Rexford G. Tugwell, head of the Resettlement Administration, as he sought to establish "Greenbelt Towns" (subsistence homestead communities in suburban areas) and promote cooperative farming and soil-conservation projects.

"Priming the Pump." America's business revival hinged on the ability of solvent enterprises to make short-term and long-term loans. The banks were unable to do so, and the savings banks, insurance companies, trust companies, title, and mortgage companies were unwilling to do so. Therefore, the New Deal began to "prime the pump." It shot funds into sick industries. The RFC was expanded and granted the right to loan directly to private businesses, municipalities, and public corporations for housing projects, electric-power projects, and the like. Title II of the National Industrial Recovery Act (June 1938) created a Public Works Administration (PWA). Secretary of the Interior Ickes was placed at its head and given $3.3 billion to spend on projects to put private contractors back into business. They, in turn (it was hoped), would begin to employ labor, and thus the pump would be primed through an increase in consumption power. Unfortunately more money was consumed in purchase of capital goods than in employment of labor.

The NIRA. The greatest failure of the New Deal was the National Industrial Recovery Act (NIRA), passed during the first one hundred days (in June 1933), which created a National Recovery Administration (NRA) under General Hugh Johnson. The NIRA's stated aims were all-embracing: to free commerce; secure cooperative action among trade groups; achieve united action of labor and management; eliminate unfair competition; promote full production; increase purchasing power; reduce unemployment; improve labor standards; rehabilitate industry; and conserve resources—in a word, to end the depression.

How was this omnibus goal to be achieved? Antitrust laws were suspended for the duration of NIRA; employers of good will in all industries were to submit voluntarily to "codes of fair competition," which they themselves would draw up. Volunteerism and cooperation were the keynotes; but, if any group proved stubborn in refusing to agree to a code, then the government might impose a code upon it. The codes provided for self-regulation through production controls, minimum prices, assigned quotas, quality controls, minimum wages, and maximum hours. In the highly significant Section 7A, it specifically recognized labor's right to organize and to bargain collectively. Employers who submitted to the code (thousands did) received a "Blue Eagle," (symbol of NIRA) and those who did not were publicly condemned by Johnson and prosecuted in the federal courts.

These agreements achieved some long-sought reformist goals, such as the elimination of child labor, the establishment in principle of governmental regulation of wages and hours, and a huge increase in union membership. Critics attacked these codes furiously from their inception.

Large producers sought to dominate or destroy them; small businessmen charged that the codes simply legalized monopolistic practices; certain labor leaders complained that employers had only been driven to more ingenious methods of destroying unions and that minimum wages were fast becoming maximum and maximum hours minimum; and consumers complained that restricted production resulted in price increases without compensating wage increases.

Noncompliance became the rule, and by March 1934 Congress was seething with discontent. Relief was general when the Supreme Court declared NIRA unconstitutional in the Schechter Poultry Case (1933), arguing that it constituted an improper extension of Congress's power over interstate commerce. NIRA was the widest deviation of the federal government from traditional American free enterprise. In declaring it unconstitutional, the Supreme Court ended the first major effort of the federal government to dominate industry completely.

Reform Through Regulation

Transport and Coal. During the New Deal the Interstate Commerce Commission (ICC) expanded its powers as government economists strove to eliminate the weakness in government regulation of basic industries. The plight of the railroads, for example, was pitiful. They were harassed by accumulated fixed debts that could not be reduced, duplication and waste of services, and competition from autos, buses, water transport, pipelines, and planes. An epidemic of bankruptcy threatened the entire industry in 1931.

In 1933, therefore, Congress passed the Emergency Railroad Transportation Act, creating a Federal Coordinator of Transportation whose task was to aid the roads by consolidating them into three major systems. The ICC was also given control over railroad holding companies to prevent their corrupt "milking" operations. But the Federal Coordinator had little success, for he was powerless to overcome the railways' inability to compete with cheaper means of transport.

To counteract this defect, in 1935 Congress extended the power of the ICC over the rates and finances of airlines as well as motor carriers and then, in 1940, over water transport. The commission now could distribute government aid impartially to the weakest sectors of transport. Rate-making was separated from the value of the investment and designed to make all traffic profitable.

As in railroads, so in coal. The coal industry, too, suffered from reduced demand, overcompetition, heavy fixed costs, and so forth. The Guffey-Vinson Act (1937) created a code of fair competition for the entire industry and sought to improve its position by restricting output.

Monopoly Price-Fixing and Quality Control. Few issues so preoccupied the New Deal theoreticians as monopoly. In 1938 Congress decided to begin a massive inquiry into American monopoly and set up a Temporary National Economic Committee (TNEC) for this purpose. The committee conducted a three-year inquiry, heard more than 550 witnesses from every walk of life, and collected seventeen thousand pages of testimony plus forty-three volumes of special monographs by outstanding economists, sociologists, and political scientists. In convening the investigation Roosevelt had declared that there "is a concentration of private power without equal in history" in America; the TNEC proved there was. The mountain of research produced a mouse of remedial legislation. The Department of Justice proceeded with enforcement of antitrust prosecutions. But many Americans considered the antitrust laws antiquated.

The New Deal itself established rigid prices in an effort to prevent cutthroat competition that drove out the small businesses. In the Miller-Tydings Act (1937), it sanctioned state laws enforcing the monopolistic practice of price-fixing to protect small retailers against chain stores; in the Robinson-Patman Act it amended the Clayton Antitrust Act (1914) to protect wholesalers against the buying power of chain stores and mail-order houses by again maintaining retail prices and eliminating discounts for large-scale purchases. The FTC was empowered to enforce uniform discounts. In other words, price-fixing was not the evil; the destruction of competition was, and if fixed prices protected a competitor—then government would fix them.

Was uncontrolled competition the answer? Certainly not where the health of the public was concerned. The New Deal was particularly active on the consumer front, and this required severe control over quality. Under the Commodity Exchange Act (1936), the Secretary of Agriculture could set standards for agricultural produce traded on the Exchange. In 1938 the Food, Drugs and Cosmetics Act empowered a Food and Drugs Administrator to enforce standards for all three kinds of products—food, drugs and cosmetics. The Administration could subject them to inspection; prohibit the sale of new drugs until they had been tested and found harmless; and make accurate labeling of all drugs and cosmetics mandatory. In the same year, the Wheeler-Lea Act expanded the power of the FTC to include advertisements of drugs, cosmetics, and therapeutic devices. In 1939 quality standards and mandatory labeling were extended to wool products; manufacturers had to indicate whether the wool was new, reprocessed, reused, or adulterated.

In practice, then, the New Deal found no overall approach to the problem of monopolies. In some cases (coal, railroads), they proved desirable; in others, they could be limited by monopolistic government practices (price-fixing, quality controls). Monopolies were enmeshed in the total economy; they had to be balanced with the needs of consumers, workers, and small businessmen. Perhaps the best answer lay in regulated coexistence.

Public Utilities.   Unregulated monopoly had produced extraordinary evils in the area of public utilities. Holding companies milked their operating subsidiaries; magnates focused on stock manipulation instead of services; subsidiaries refused to expand electric facilities to low-income groups; outrageous rates could be forced upon helpless consumers. In 1935 Congress passed the Wheeler-Rayburn Public Utility Holding Company Act outlawing the pyramiding of control of gas and electricity companies. The act gave the Securities and Exchange Commission (SEC) the power to regulate the service, sales, construction contracts, loans, and dividends of the public utilities. The SEC also was given the task of simplifying the sprawling pyramids of holding-company control by lopping off subsidiaries that were neither economically nor geographically justified. (Utilities called this provision of the act the "death sentence" clause.)

The act also broadened the power of the government to control interstate commerce in power. Utilities now had to file their rate schedules, and the government could suspend unwarranted rate charges. New power projects on public lands and navigable rivers required the consent of the government. In 1938 similar government controls were extended to the natural gas industry. Federal control over these varied utilities worked well: more realistic values of their properties were established, and consumers paid lower rates.

Securities and Exchanges. The most obvious areas for extension of government control were the stock and commodity exchanges. The rise and fall of economic values had been most sensational in these areas. One of the earliest measures passed by the New Deal Congress was the Truth-in-Securities Act of 1933. It allowed the FTC to require every corporation offering new securities for sale through the mails or in interstate commerce to register them with the Commission. This function was transferred in 1934 to the SEC. Besides requiring registration of securities, the SEC had the power to license exchanges; define the function of members, dealers and brokers; require annual reports; and investigate unfair market practices. The Federal Reserve Board (FRB), however, was given the power to regulate margin requirements (such as buying stocks on the installment plan with a down payment), although the SEC could investigate excessive trading on margin. The SEC soon acquired other powers: control over

unlisted securities; regulation of corporate bankruptcies involving more than $3 million; enforcing the "death sentence"; and investigation of investment trusts.

New Legislation

Protecting the Physical Resources.   Besides being great avenues of transport, rivers are sources of hydroelectric power. At appropriate water sites huge dams can be constructed to supply the water to power plants; power plants can then generate and distribute electricity. In the Federal Water Power Act of 1920, the government announced its ownership of all water-power sites on public lands and navigable rivers. The act also created the Federal Power Commission (FPC) to license private power companies, state governments, or municipalities for the use of these sites.

In the 1920s George W. Norris had sponsored bills for the complete development of the Tennessee River Valley. Norris argued that the demands of the nation for cheap electricity and the conservation of natural resources could best be met by a legitimate extension of the federal authority. Even earlier, in 1917, the government constructed a hydroelectric plant at Muscle Shoals to generate the power to produce synthetic nitrate explosives. But a considerable informal barrier existed to having the government operate the plant: it was generally held that federally generated power was a venture into socialism, that is, government ownership and operation of industry. Because of such fears, Presidents Coolidge and Hoover had vetoed Norris's bills.

But conservation loomed large in New Deal thought. Electricity and flood control were vital needs in the Tennessee Valley, as were electricity and irrigation along the Columbia and Colorado rivers. Therefore, in May 1933, at Roosevelt's urging, Congress created the Tennessee Valley Authority (TVA), empowering it to construct dams, reservoirs, powerhouses, and transmission lines; manufacture, distribute, and sell electric power; produce nitrates for military and agricultural purposes; control floods; make rivers more navigable; and engage in soil conservation by extensive reforestation.

Private companies, which had opposed the TVA, hoped that the government could be stopped in the courts. But in *Ashwander v. TVA* (1936), the Supreme Court found that federal sale of power to municipalities was constitutional; in 1939, in *Tennessee Electric Power Co. v. TVA*, it supported government competition with private power provided the primary purposes were navigation, flood control, national defense, or conservation. Having launched public ownership along the Tennessee Valley with construction of the Norris and Wilson dams and seven others, the New Deal extended its program to the Columbia River (Grand Coulee and Bonneville dams) and to the Colorado River (Hoover Dam). Opposition to these extensions was fierce and, consequently, regional planning remained limited during the New Deal.

Soil Conservation. New Deal agricultural programs also contained conservation features. One of the most pressing problems was the appearance in the thirties of huge "dust bowls"—eroded areas with their topsoil washed or blown away. The Soil Conservation and Domestic Allot-

ment Act (1936) offered farmers benefits for planting soil-restoring crops; the CCC and TVA engaged in large reforestation programs; the Resettlement Administration concerned itself with reclamation as a measure of conservation; the Department of Agriculture organized technical assistance teams that toured the farm country to teach new methods of contour and terrace farming to farmers. Throughout the period, then, the war on ecological waste was many-sided.

Redistributing the Wealth. In the Revenue Acts of 1935, 1936, and 1937 the New Deal undertook to tap more heavily the large incomes in the country. Revenue laws, Roosevelt said, "have operated in many ways to the unfair advantage of the few." These acts increased surtaxes on high incomes; more steeply graduated normal taxes; raised gift and estate taxes; taxed undistributed profits; and plugged loopholes in the tax laws. One purpose of this legislation was to redistribute wealth to raise purchasing power, thus priming the pump; another was humanitarian—to ameliorate conditions for the "one-third of the nation" who were "ill-fed, ill-clothed and ill-housed."

The New Dealers adopted relief measures costing millions to provide food and work for the unemployed. Yet there were many others whose plight did not originate in the depression, many who suffered loss of income even in the best of times and who, even then, were forced to live in unhealthy environments. These included the widowed, the orphaned, the discarded elderly, the underfed, the illiterate, and the slum-dwellers. The humanitarian impulse in the New Deal resulted in legislation that became a permanent feature of American life to aid the needy even in times of prosperity.

Social Security. The Social Security Act (1935) made federal aid available to needy, dependent children (e.g., crippled or blind children) and the needy widowed. It also offered federal funds to states that matched the funds for the launching of large-scale programs in public health, child care, and assistance for the blind. Needy persons sixty-five years old or older were able to secure old-age pensions if they proved that they had no dependents. This, too, was a matching program, with federal aid limited to $15 per person per month.

The heart of the New Deal social security scheme, however, was an old-age insurance program. The insured included the aged who had worked during their lifetime and paid insurance taxes out of their earnings; the amount of the tax on wages was matched by employers. When workers reached sixty-five, they were entitled to retirement benefits (not pensions). If they died before retirement, their widow received the benefits. Other features of the law included the establishment of minimum and maximum benefits and minimum periods of work before benefits could be secured.

The act also provided for a state-federal unemployment insurance plan. The federal government collected a special payroll tax from each state. If it enacted an unemployment insurance law, a state could receive back 90 percent of this tax. The fund for unemployment insurance benefits was to be contributed solely by employers. Any workers who became unemployed could draw certain minimum and maximum amounts, depending on the length of time they had worked (states differed in the amount of their payments). To secure payment workers had to be available for another job, if it met certain prescribed standards. Government planners were somewhat uncertain of the constitutionality of this law, but the Supreme Court upheld it, stating that the federal government may tax for the purposes of social welfare.

Housing. During the depression hundreds of thousands of Americans were either in danger of losing their homes or of being forced by loss of jobs to dwell in the slums. President Hoover had already acted to save homeowners with a Home Loan Bank System. But its capitalization at $125 million was nothing compared to the $3 billion expended by the Home Owners' Loan Corporation (HOLC), established by the Home Owners' Refinancing Act (June 15) in the first hundred days of the New Deal. The full extent of this humanitarian effort was revealed in the final report of the HOLC in 1951. Approximately 800,000 foreclosures had been staved off and 1,017,321 mortgages refinanced. The psychological gains of this cannot be overestimated.

For the "ill-housed," the National Housing Act (1934) created the Federal Housing Authority with power to stimulate residential housing construction. In 1937 the New Deal began a direct assault on the slums. For every substandard building torn down, the Housing Authority promised to build a new tenement project, with occupancy limited to low-income groups. "Housing projects" soon began to appear everywhere on the urban landscape.

Minimum Wages—Maximum Hours. In 1938 the concept of an established minimum wage and maximum hour load—first forecast in the NIRA—was written into law as the Fair Labor Standards Act (FLSA). Forty hours became the limit beyond which employers were compelled to pay time-and-a-half, and the minimum wage was set at 40 cents an hour. The FLSA also limited child labor.

The Farm Problem. By 1933 violence had flared up in the Midwest as commercial farmers struck out against shrinking farm income and land values, mounting surpluses, and foreclosed homesteads. Vigilante committees helped farmers withhold food from the market, dumped milk, frightened purchasers away from forced auction sales, intimidated judges about to foreclose on homesteads, marched on state capitals, and assaulted agents of insurance and mortgage companies. To halt this violence, the New Deal resorted to stopgap measures.

Private banks were clearly unable to finance farmers for any extended period. Congress, therefore, created a public bank, the Farm Credit Administration (FCA), which paid off the farmers' creditors and then took over their mortgages. The FCA then made loans to farmers unable to offer any kind of security. But the number of mortgages threatened with foreclosure was so great that Congress enacted moratoriums on mortgage payments. (The Frazier-Lemke Act, initially declared unconstitutional, was upheld in 1935.) The government also provided aid to farmers stricken by natural disaster. Even those not threatened with collapse were protected by liberal extensions of credit from this government bank.

Control of the Surplus and Parity Prices. Although hunger existed throughout the land, farmers had a surplus of all the basic crops. To deal with this old dilemma of overproduction and help farmers raise prices by limiting output, the New Deal paid farmers in 1933–34 to plow under cotton and to slaughter six million pigs. This policy caused widespread moral revulsion. The government also tried to store the surplus and give it away, while granting farmers loans on their storage. The Commodity Credit Corporation (CCC) was established for this purpose in 1933.

But it quickly became clear to New Deal planners that the only solution to the problem of surplus was nonproduction. Thus the Agricultural Adjustment Act of May 1933 allocated acreage among individual farmers and used government subsidies to encourage them to remove land from production. After the Supreme Court struck down the act in 1936, Congress reconstituted it in modified form in the same year and remodified it in 1938.

The final act had three goals. The first was to attain for the farmer a "parity price," that is, a price that would give agricultural products the same purchasing power with respect to the goods farmers bought as they had in the years from 1909 to 1914. Thus, when farmers sold their crops, the prices they set would enable them to buy all they needed and to discharge their debts.

This relationship of goods sold to goods bought was reestablished by curtailed production paid for by the government, in other words, farmers deliberately did not plant a surplus and got paid for not planting it. The Agricultural Adjustment Administration (AAA) paid a benefit to farmers who removed a basic crop from production and substituted soil-conserving crops like hay or alfalfa. Others obtained benefits if they accepted acreage quotas, that is, if they limited the number of acres they would plant. Intensive farming of limited acreage might still produce a surplus, so two other measures coped with this possibility: surpluses could be stored in a government granary to be sold in the market whenever shortages appeared; or surpluses could be prevented from reaching the market by marketing quotas. Such marketing quotas could be set up if two thirds of the farmers voted for them. Those violating their quota would be punished by a tax on all excess sales. If prices still remained below parity, the government would dip into the national treasury and pay the difference. Finally, if natural disasters destroyed the wheat crop, a Federal Crop Insurance Corporation would make up the losses.

Government warehouses now had the problem of what to do with the surpluses. They experimented in giveaway programs; foreign markets were sought out in reciprocal trade agreements; food was distributed in direct relief, with a large amount of it going to school lunch programs.

Criticism. These restrictive measures registered some significant gains. Farm incomes rose considerably, farm mortgages decreased moderately, and thousands of farmers were helped. The program also provoked sharp criticism. Observers charged that it was immoral to curtail crops while millions of Americans went hungry. Others claimed that farmers were being made into a privileged class supported by all other sectors of the economy. Another criticism was that not every farmer benefited. The program focused on the commercial farmer—but what of ten-ant farmers, migratory "Okies" and "Arkies" who were victims of the dust bowl, and marginal backcountry farmers? What of sharecroppers and farm laborers, many of whom were dispossessed when owners removed land from production? There were at least 5 million in these underprivileged rural groups in 1935. In 1934, 3.5 million rural families were on relief.

The War on Rural Poverty. The rural underprivileged had either no land or land too poor to farm profitably. Government-donated seeds and tools were of no use to them. The obvious solution seemed to be to resettle them on better lands. The Resettlement Administration (1935) and the Farm Security Administration (1937) wrestled with this problem, for resettlement projects would create a new set of producers at a time when curtailment was the order of the day. But they proceeded. Submarginal lands were bought up; cooperative farms were established on fertile lands and the farmers were given money, seeds, tools, and instruction in agricultural techniques; subsistence (noncommercial) farms were created in "Greenbelts" located in the suburbs of large cities; camps for migratory workers were built; and farm tenants were encouraged to borrow for land purchases. Under the guidance of Rexford G. Tugwell, valiant but uncoordinated efforts that ran counter to the main farm programs were instituted to save the rural poor.

Native Americans. In 1924 all Native Americans were made citizens, and those living on reservations were now special beneficiaries of the policy of resettlement. Attempts to individualize landholdings had failed utterly. Therefore, in 1934, the

Wheeler-Howard Act permitted a tribe to buy land and engage in business as a corporate body. Severe restrictions were placed on the resale of land by the tribes. The total value of the land so assigned was estimated to be worth about $2 billion. Some of it was rich in oil, minerals, and timber, but most of it was poor. Thus, the state and the federal governments had to give considerable supplemental aid to the Indians.

Labor and the New Deal.   Union leaders felt that labor had been lost in this new shuffle. Roosevelt was more humanitarian, they felt, than Hoover. Many New Deal acts (the CCC, the Emergency Relief Act, the Public Works Program of Title II of the NIRA, and the Civil Works Administration) took care of workers' immediate needs. The housing measures, too, offered them long-term benefits. Yet union leaders charged that the NIRA favored the employer over the worker; that few changes in wages and hours resulted despite grandiose "code" provisions; and that Section 7A, recognizing labor's right to organize, guaranteed nothing since employers began to outmaneuver workers with every known antiunion tactic. To emphasize these grievances, labor inaugurated a series of bloody strikes immediately following the adoption of the codes. To cope with the problems created by such strikes, New York's Senator Robert F. Wagner, Sr., concluded that government must ally itself directly with the cause of labor. The result was the Wagner-Connery National Labor Relations Act (NLRA) of 1935—commonly known as the Wagner Act.

The NLRA.   The law firmly established the right of employees to organize and bargain collectively through representatives of their own choosing. It also outlawed interference by employers with efforts to unionize and the establishment of company unions; discrimination in the hiring and firing of union labor; and refusal to bargain collectively. A National Labor Relations Board (NLRB) was established to supervise labor-management relations and assign unions as bargaining agents. To determine who the bargaining representatives were, the NLRB was empowered to hold elections in the plants concerned. And to insure that the law was obeyed, it could investigate complaints and hold hearings on them. Decisions of the NLRB were enforceable in the courts.

The AFL and the CIO.   Employers did not accommodate to this new emphasis in government easily. From 1935 to 1940 the NLRB handled more than thirty thousand cases and reinstated twenty-one thousand fired workers. Some leaders in the AFL pressured their president, William Green, to organize the unskilled workers in mass-production industries. But the conservative Green moved warily. While he hesitated, John L. Lewis took over this issue. His United Mine Workers were organized fully on an industrial union basis; in other words, not according to what each worker did, but according to the industry in which he or she worked. In his fight against Green, Lewis advocated industrial unionism, more militant strikes, mass picketing, and intensified political activity. To achieve these goals, he formed the Committee for Industrial Organizations (CIO) within the AFL in 1936. After the AFL expelled the CIO, it became the Congress of Industrial Organizations in 1938. Lewis became the CIO's first president, remaining in office until 1940, when he quarreled with Roosevelt and resigned. Phillip Murray of the Steelworker's Union took his place.

From 1936 to 1938 the CIO conducted a series of sensational "sit-down" strikes in which strikers ousted management and locked themselves inside plants. Fearing that machinery would be destroyed, employers hesitated to request police or military help. Sit-down strikes brought the new CIO unions tremendous victories: Goodyear Tire & Rubber, General Motors, and "Big Steel" were the first to capitulate. ("Little Steel" was far more resistant; efforts to organize this part of the industry resulted in the "Memorial Day Massacre," in which Chicago police fired upon and killed a number of picnicking picketers and their wives who were on strike against Republic Steel. Loss of Little Steel was a serious blow to the CIO; even Roosevelt's sympathy began to wane.)

But the sit-down had served labor's purpose: in two years the number of unionized workers soared from three to nine million, with the AFL having a slight edge, for it, too, had begun organizing workers on an industrial basis. The CIO also woke organized workers out of their political lethargy. In many large cities it organized "Non-Partisan Leagues," which generally supported the Democratic Party. In New York City these leagues put the American Labor Party in the field and ran their own candidates when dissatisfied with the choices offered by the Republicans or Democrats. Thus, the New Deal worked a profound revolution in labor's relation to capital and to American society. But it left America with two huge, bitterly antagonistic national labor organizations, a situation that eventually worked against labor and led in 1955 to a merger of the two groups.

The Opposition to the New Deal. Of those who felt that the New Deal had gone too far, the Supreme Court (composed of nine elderly men) was the leader. In the early years of the New Deal, the Court struck down the NIRA, the AAA, the Railroad Pensions Act, the Bituminous Coal Act, the Municipal Bankruptcy Act, and the Frazier-Lemke Farm Bankruptcy Act. In 1937 Roosevelt decided on what proved to be a rash plan—in view of the American tradition of separation of powers—to "democratize" the Court. To his opponents, it smacked of "packing" the Court.

His plan involved forcing judges to retire at age seventy by permitting the president to appoint one judge (up to a maximum of six justices) for each member of the Court over 70 who did not retire. Roosevelt justified this plan by saying it was part of a general reorganization of the court system. The bill became deadlocked in Congress because of a serious split in Democratic ranks. Even liberals opposed it, seeing the measure as a change in precedent. The Supreme Court, too, confused the issue by suddenly upholding a minimum-wage law for women, the second Frazier-Lemke Act, the Social Security Act, and the Wagner Act. Consequently, Roosevelt's Supreme Court Reform Bill died in committee. In the end, it didn't much matter, for during the remainder of the New Deal Roosevelt filled seven vacancies on the Court, and no important New Deal law was subsequently overruled.

The Election of 1936. As Andrew Jackson had done, FDR was able to weld a tremendous coalition of potentially hostile elements around the Democratic Party. At its peak, the New Deal contained the "Solid South" as well as northern blacks (blacks had been staunchly Republican since the Civil War), conservative farmers, the usually liberal urban workers, members of the "white-collar" middle class, intellectuals in the universities and the arts, and city and state political bosses. This coalition held solidly during the election of 1936. To oppose FDR the Republicans chose Alfred M. Landon of Kansas. The Democrats stood on their record. Powerfully supported by elements of big business, Al Smith, and a majority of the press, Landon hammered at the theme that the New Deal was destroying the American way of life and depriving the people of their freedom as individuals. FDR carried every state but two—Maine and Vermont.

Culture and Science

Population and Family Life. During the thirties the nation's population continued to rise, but more slowly—it grew a mere 7 percent as compared with 16 percent during the twenties. No large-scale immigration occurred; in fact, between 1931 and 1935, 103,654 more people left the United States than came into it. (Hitler's persecutions, however, brought to America Thomas Mann, Franz Werfel, George Grosz, Walter Gropius, Paul Hindemith, Bruno Walter, Albert Einstein, and other distinguished European intellectuals and artists.) The decline in the death rate helped swell the population. The depression, apparently, put a heavy premium on raising a family, leading to a lower

birth rate, and since it was too expensive to get married or divorced, those rates declined in the thirties as well. Within the home, tensions mounted as wives were discharged from jobs so that unemployed men might be hired in their place. Unemployed husbands suffered anxiety and injured pride. Overcrowding became commonplace as hungry, unemployed relations moved in to reduce the cost of living. The added tension in people's lives showed in the mounting number of mental patients and in the increased sale, when money was so scarce, of cigarettes.

Education. Schools bore a heavy load during the depression. They existed in continual financial straits; their plants and equipment deteriorated; pupil loads increased as boards of education reduced hiring; total school population increased as the labor market was forced to reject child labor. Secondary schools were now faced with the problem of educating all these children. Uniform methods and standards had to be dropped in favor of differentiated programs, homogeneous groupings based on intelligence testing, and other steps to facilitate the education of masses of students.

Vocational education expanded at the high school and college levels as students needed skills that would help them obtain jobs. As colleges adjusted to this demand, a profound controversy erupted over the nature of a college education. Robert Hutchins and Mortimer Adler led their colleagues at the University of Chicago in a battle for the traditional disciplines; St. John's introduced a "Great Books" approach to the humanities; most colleges, however, watered down their curricula to meet the need for employment skills.

Periodicals and Popular Reading. The immediate popularity of Henry R. Luce's *Life* indicated that many Americans saw the picture story as a substitute for reading. Yet other Luce publications such as *Time* and *Fortune* emphasized text, not pictures, and *The New Yorker* provided an outlet for some of America's best short-story writers and cartoonists. Magazine circulation held up well during the depression, as magazines represented one of the cheapest means of escape from despair.

Newspapers, on the other hand, were hard-hit as advertising declined. At the end of the decade, an interesting but short-lived experiment in "highbrow" tabloidism appeared. Marshall Field II's *PM* tried to operate, under Ralph Ingersoll's editorship, without advertising or sensationalism.

In popular reading, American literary preferences ran to detective stories, westerns, Dale Carnegie's *How to Win Friends and Influence People,* and to historical novels of awesome length.

Literature. Novels portraying the plight of the working class made their appearance in the thirties. Most were simple tracts about "bad guys" (capitalists and their agents) and had small literary value. Far superior work came from John Dos Passos (*USA,* a trilogy composed of *The 42nd Parallel,* 1930; *1919,* 1932; and *The Big Money,* 1936), Erskine Caldwell (*Tobacco Road,* 1932), William Faulkner (*Light in August,* 1932), James Farrell (*The Studs Lonigan Trilogy,* 1932–35), and John Steinbeck (*The Grapes of Wrath,* 1939). While unsparing in their criticism of a society capable of producing the human wreckage caused by the depression, these

men continued the search begun in the twenties for American values and the meaning of the American past. Thomas Wolfe fulfilled himself in the thirties. Novels such as *Of Time and the River* (1938) were formless, but no readers could miss his deep, abiding love for America. Willa Cather and Ellen Glasgow continued in their familiar vein; and Sinclair Lewis, Eugene O'Neill, and Pearl Buck won Nobel Prizes.

Among poets, Edna St. Vincent Millay, Archibald MacLeish, and Carl Sandburg affirmed their faith in the American people. Robert Frost wrote with deep irony and pathos of the New England "common man."

Theater, Film, and Radio. The American theater experienced a renaissance as a result of works by Maxwell Anderson, Clifford Odets, Elmer Rice, Robert Sherwood, Paul Green, Sidney Kingsley, and Thornton Wilder. Eugene O'Neill also continued to write until 1934. (He was then silent until 1946). These playwrights (with the exception of O'Neill) wrote mostly in the traditional vein but did not neglect the theatrical innovations of the twenties. They subordinated folklore, contemporary problems, and historical events to the creation of living characters. The Federal Theatre Project proved a valuable medium for producing the classics and experimenting with new dramatic forms. One of its most controversial experiments was the "living newspaper"—dramatic presentations of the topical themes.

Hollywood made great efforts to create vital films that grappled with real problems, such as hunger, the dispossessed, racial intolerance, slums, and old age. Poetic documentaries like *The River* and *The*

Plow that Broke the Plains were produced. But the escapist element predominated in the usual run of penthouse frolics, song-and-dance flicks, and slapstick comedies. Walt Disney's rise to fame on the basis of the animated cartoon was spectacular; more Americans knew the names of his Seven Dwarfs than those of the President's cabinet.

Radio, too, had its more intellectual and artistic moments in the thirties, though it was still dominated by soap operas, murder tales, sports events, and the comedy shows. Broadcasters experimented with serious forums, highbrow quiz programs, symphonic concerts, and operas.

Music. Jazz gave way to swing and to the swingmasters like Benny Goodman, Tommy Dorsey, and Artie Shaw. In classical music America produced an excellent modernist in Aaron Copland; Roy Harris, Virgil Thomson, and others made key contributions to the modern musical idiom. Native artistic talent became internationally renowned.

Painting. Three painting trends characterized the thirties: some artists began the rediscovery of American regionalism and history—the most publicized were Thomas Hart Benton and Grant Wood; others depicted the social scene—outstanding among these were William Gropper, Raphael Soyer, Jack Levine, and Ben Shahn. A third group continued in the modernist manner—the better known included Marsden Hartley, Walt Kuhn, and Stuart Davis. Not all of their works were uniformly excellent, but many are still widely exhibited today.

Sculpture. Sculpture in the thirties became more abstract, the artists more concerned with their medium than with representation. For example, Alexander Calder's "mobiles" were metal shapes that were delicately balanced in space.

Architecture. Raymond Hood constructed the clean art deco lines of the Daily News and McGraw-Hill buildings and collaborated in the construction of Rockefeller Center. Function was more nearly related to form in these structures. Prodded by Lewis Mumford and Frank Lloyd Wright, however, architects were still struggling for some synthesis between a building and its surroundings and for ways to integrate the interior and the exterior of a structure.

Science. Americans made major contributions in the field of atomic research. Irving Langmuir investigated the chemical activity of an element; Ernest Lawrence constructed the first cyclotron; Harold Urey discovered heavy hydrogen. This caliber of work brought Americans six Nobel Prizes.

CHAPTER TWENTY-ONE

The New Deal and World Affairs

On December 7, 1941, Franklin Roosevelt was talking with his aide Harry Hopkins when he received a telephone call from his navy secretary telling him that the Japanese had just launched a surprise attack on Pearl Harbor. The shocked Hopkins exclaimed that there must be some mistake, but Roosevelt disagreed. The Japanese were, he felt, capable of doing something exactly like that. The surprise dawn attack pushed the United States into World War II, and the nation's energies turned from waging war on the depression to defeating the Japanese in the Pacific and the Germans and Italians in Europe.

Foreign Policy

The Reciprocal Tariff Program. Determined to shape America's foreign policy to the nation's depression needs, Roosevelt kept Hoover's pledge to attend the 1933 World Economic Conference. The President instructed Secretary of State Cordell Hull to discuss nothing but bilateral tariff treaties to increase foreign trade. In June of 1934 Congress passed the Trade Agreements Act, permitting the President to cut American tariffs by 50 percent if other nations would do likewise. Hull began to negotiate bilateral treaties almost immediately, thus revolutionizing America's tariff policy.

Recognition of the Soviet Union. For seventeen years America had refused to recognize Russia for many reasons. For example, the Soviets had refused to pay Tsarist debts, pressing instead their own claims for damages incurred during the American military intervention of 1917–20, in which American troops joined those of Britain and France in Arctic Russia ostensibly to keep the Germans sufficiently busy to prevent the transfer of troops to the western front. However, while in Siberia, the American forces became involved in the civil war of 1918–20 between the Bolsheviks and their opponents, the anti-Bolsheviks, who were helped by the presence of western troops. Russian willingness to negotiate these matters and American hopes that a new understanding might result in a mutual trade boom led to the Roosevelt-Litvinov Agreement in 1933, in which the United States formally recognized the Soviet Union.

The Good Neighbor Policy. In his inaugural address President Roosevelt had said: "In the field of world policy, I would dedicate this nation to the policy of the good neighbor." At the Inter-American Conference at Montevideo in 1933, Secretary of State Hull spelled out the meaning of "good neighbor." "No state has the right to intervene in the internal or external affairs of another."

Cuba, Haiti, Panama. Cuba was torn by a revolt. The American ambassador, Sumner Welles, proposed "limited intervention," but Hull refused to intervene. When a temporary government took over, Hull granted it immediate de facto recognition. He then negotiated a treaty with Cuba to abrogate the Platt Amendment, thus removing America's legal right to intervene. Next, the two countries agreed to a tariff treaty favorable to Cuba. Hull had concretely shown Latin America that the United States had every intention of living up to her "good neighbor" pledge. Yet since little economic aid was offered to the region, resentment against the powerful northern neighbor remained.

In 1934, the United States withdrew all American troops from Haiti. And after a prolonged battle, the Senate modified the Hay–Bunau-Varilla Treaty to give Panama the commercial rights of a sovereign state in the Canal Zone.

Mexico. Mexico put the Good Neighbor Policy to a severe test. Under Lázaro Cardenas, in 1936 it adopted a six-year plan calling for nationalization of American oil companies, redistribution of the land, and complete secularization of the state. Despite heavy pressure to intervene, Hull openly acknowledged Mexico's right to expropriate properties worth half a billion dollars, although insisting on fair compensation. To secure the latter, he cut Mexico off from America's silver-support policy. Negotiations as equals followed, with Mexico eventually paying for the expropriated properties. The United States, in turn, supported Mexican silver prices and made large loans to her through the Export-Import Bank.

Montevideo, 1933. When the Inter-American powers met at Montevideo to consider matters of Hemispheric peace and trade, Hull made a firm commitment not to intervene in the affairs of the Latin American nations. He led the conference to approve tariff reductions, conciliation treaties, and other matters of significance to the Latin Americans. This change in policy came none too soon, for Inter-Americanism was taking on new meaning as the fascist powers of Germany and Italy were beginning an economic and propaganda assault on Latin America.

Buenos Aires, 1936. The direct link between South America and Europe were the French, Dutch, and British Guianas. Should the three European powers fall into German or Italian hands, their South American holdings would become overseas bases for the German and Italian armies. By 1935 Italy and Germany had made their aggressive intentions known. In 1935 the Italians attacked Ethiopia, and in 1936 Spanish Fascists rebelled, with military assistance from Hitler and Mussolini, against their country's republican government. These ominous events raised the specter of another world war. Aware of the rising danger, Roosevelt suggested in 1936 that a conference be held to consider the maintenance of peace in the Western Hemisphere. At Argentina's request the conferees met in Buenos Aires. There the Inter-American powers agreed to consult in the event of an international war that might menace the peace of the Americas. They also stipulated that they would not recognize territorial acquisitions by force, or support intervention, forcible collection of debts, or violent settlement of Inter-American disputes.

The Long Road to War

The Inter-American Response to War. The Buenos Aires agreement was implemented at Lima, Peru, in 1938. There the Inter-American powers also agreed that if European hostilities commenced, the foreign ministers of the twenty-one republics would devise methods of countering any attempt to "invade" the Western Hemisphere. After war erupted in Europe in 1939, the foreign ministers met in Panama and took several measures: they drew sea-safety zones around the Western Hemisphere, warned belligerent vessels to stay out of the proscribed waters, and announced (in Havana in 1940) that American republics would take over the administration of any endangered European possession in the New World. After the United States became a belligerent in 1941, it was recommended that all the Americas break diplomatic relations with the Axis powers (all except Chile and Argentina did so immediately; Chile followed in 1943; Argentina, in 1944), and that materials, bases, and manpower be supplied in behalf of the common cause.

Isolation: Neutrality. Isolationism took the form of neutrality. Though fully aware of the fascist threat, America chose a policy designed to keep herself out of war. In deciding what neutral course to take, Congress followed the lead of North Dakota's Senator Gerald Nye and his congressional investigation (1934–36) into the causes for American entry into World War I. Nye's committee had concluded that trading in munitions by firms such as Du-Pont, loans to belligerents, travel by United States citizens in war zones, and machinations by American and international munitions makers were the primary causes. Although no proof was offered, the public readily accepted Nye's version of events. Therefore, in 1935 Congress drew up a Neutrality Act that banned the President from selling arms to any belligerent and warned American citizens that they traveled on belligerent ships at their own risk.

The Test of Neutrality. In 1936 the outbreak of the Italo-Ethiopian War and the Spanish Civil War put these provisions to the test. Roosevelt invoked the Neutrality Act in response to the war in Ethiopia. But Italy, under its Fascist Prime Minister Benito Mussolini, needed oil, not guns, and oil was not classified as an "article of war." Roosevelt called upon American producers for a "moral embargo" on oil, but exporters ignored his plea.

With respect to Spain, Roosevelt feared interference might provoke world war, and so he did not even invoke the Neutrality Act. Both conflicts also strengthened congressional resolve to "stay out of war," and in 1936 the Neutrality Act of 1935 was strengthened by a new provision forbidding all loans to belligerents.

"Permanent" Neutrality. In 1937 American isolationism reached its zenith as Congress attempted to achieve "permanent" neutrality. It extended provisions of the acts of 1935 and 1936 to apply to civil as well as international wars, forbade American citizens to sail on belligerent ships, and required that all trade other than munitions be carried out temporarily on a cash-and-carry basis. The United States in effect served notice on Italy, Germany, and Japan (which had overrun Manchuria in 1931 and invaded China in 1937) that it would do nothing to oppose their plans of conquest. Yet, one year later, the permanent neutrality laws began to unravel.

"Quarantine the Aggressor!" In 1936 Japan and Germany signed the Anti-Comintern Pact, and in 1937 Italy joined as well. In the same year Japan conquered China's coastal regions and main railways. During its assault, Japan bombed open cities, closed the Open Door, established a puppet Chinese government, sank an American gunboat (though Japan apologized and paid damages), and bombed and strafed American and foreign schools, hospitals, and churches in China. Roosevelt refrained from proclaiming a state of war so that China might be able to buy war goods, but he did label Japan a treaty violator, and Japanese-American relations deteriorated. In October 1937, the President asked all peace-loving powers for a "quarantine of aggressors," who were "creating a state of international anarchy and instability from which there is no escape through mere isolation or neutrality." Japan was told flatly that the United States would not recognize her "New Order in Asia" in areas over which the Japanese had no sovereign right. Instead, the government continued to insist on enforcement of the Open Door Policy. Yet America cautiously continued to sell copper, steel, oil, and machinery to the Japanese. And Roosevelt refrained from imposing an embargo, fearful that it would motivate further military conquests in Asia by Japan as it sought these products elsewhere.

From "Appeasement" to War. Prime Minister Neville Chamberlain of England and Premier Edouard Daladier of France were determined to purchase peace at any price, and so adopted a policy of appeasement toward Germany. They did not oppose Hitler's policy of rearmament, his occupation of the Rhineland (1936), or the German annexation of Austria (1938). In September 1938 Hitler demanded that Czechoslovakia return the German-speaking Sudetenland, which had been lost to Germany in World War I. Chamberlain and Daladier met with the Nazi leader at Munich (1938) and agreed to persuade Czechoslovakia to surrender the contested region in return for Hitler's promise to leave the rest of that nation alone. Such was the policy of "appeasement"—a policy of submission with the primary aim of detering the fascist powers from seeing the western powers as their enemy and thus instigating a mutually destructive German-Russian war, and thereby eliminating each of these powers as a military threat. But this policy began to unravel with alarming swiftness. In March 1939

Hitler swallowed up the rest of Czechoslovakia, and three weeks later Mussolini seized Albania. Then in August 1939 Russia and Germany shocked the world by signing a "nonaggression" pact and a secret protocol to partition Poland. England, suddenly awakened to the failure of appeasement, warned Germany that an attack on Poland would mean war. The invasion came on September 1, 1939, and two days later France and England declared war.

From Neutrality to Nonbelligerency. When Germany threatened Poland, Roosevelt asked Congress, in January 1939, to repeal the Neutrality Laws so that, in the event of war, America could sell arms to Britain and France. Congress refused. After the invasion of Poland, Roosevelt immediately summoned Congress into special session and asked for the repeal of the embargo on war goods. In November Congress permitted these sales on a cash-and-carry basis, yet American ships were prohibited from transporting products to belligerents.

Following the blitzkrieg attack on the Low Countries and Scandinavia (between April 9 and June 22, 1940), and the fall of France in June, Hitler controlled most of western Europe. Roosevelt responded by promising all-out aid to France and England. The mood of Congress now shifted. It passed the first peacetime draft (1940), and American rearmament began in earnest. A "destroyer-base" deal was then concluded with England in which fifty old destroyers were exchanged for eight Atlantic military bases, thereby evading a direct sale of the vessels, which would have violated American and international laws. This deal helped England stave off German submarine attacks on shipping. Then, in September, Japan signed a mutual assistance pact with Italy and Germany, and the war became a global conflict.

The Election of 1940. Roosevelt decided to run for a record third term in 1940 and easily won renomination. The Republicans chose Wendell L. Wilkie of Indiana to oppose him. Roosevelt's charisma, the split in Republican ranks between isolationists and interventionalists, the lack of any real differences in policy between the two candidates, and the fear of "changing horses in midstream" with war raging in Europe, led to an easy Democratic triumph.

The Road to War. His victory permitted Roosevelt to move more boldly away from neutrality. In March 1941 Congress adopted the Lend-Lease Act, which made America into an "arsenal of democracy" and permitted the President to make available to any country vital to the defense of the United States all war materials on a loan or lease basis. (America eventually shipped $50 billion in supplies to her beleaguered allies, receiving about $10 billion in "return" lend-lease.) The passage of the Lend-Lease Act opened the way for deeper American involvement short of war. In April American troops occupied Greenland; in May Roosevelt declared an unlimited national emergency, and after the German invasion of Russia in June, he was even able to persuade Congress, despite its hostility to the Soviets, to grant them $1 billion in aid.

Pearl Harbor. In 1939 Japan took several steps hostile to the United States' interests: it seized Pacific islands close to the Philippines; created a "Greater East Asia Co-Prosperity Sphere" that excluded the United States from all of the Far East; seized French Indochina from its Vichy French rulers; and concluded a tripartite military pact with Germany and Italy aimed directly at the United States. American policy toward Japan toughened. Congress embargoed the export of petroleum, scrap metal, and aviation gasoline to Japan; the government recalled Americans in the Far East; loans to China were increased; Japanese funds in America were seized; and Japan was warned to end her aggressions. The United States ordered the Japanese to withdraw from French Indochina, China, and the Tripartite Pact. Following this ultimatum, the Japanese warlords decided to attack the United States. Japan sent a decoy envoy to Washington to negotiate the ultimatum. But the negotiations broke down. Several days later, on December 7, 1941, which Roosevelt was to call "a date which will live in infamy," the Japanese bombed the American Naval Base at Pearl Harbor, Hawaii, crippling the American Pacific fleet and killing more than 2,400 American sailors. Two hours before the attack Japan had declared war on the United States; on December 8 Congress declared war against Japan. Three days later Germany and Italy declared war against the United States.

World War II

When the United States entered the war, the Axis powers were near the height of their power. German submarines dominated the Atlantic; England was reeling under a murderous air bombardment; all of continental Western Europe was a Nazi fortress; German armies were slicing into Russia and heading eastward to India; Japanese armies, now dominating all of southeast Asia, were advancing westward on India to make a decisive link with the Nazis.

In a Declaration of the United Nations, signed on January 1, 1942, twenty-six nations formed a Grand Alliance to fight under joint command "to preserve human rights and justice in their own lands as well as in other lands."

First Phase. The lowest ebb in the fortunes of the Allies came in the spring-summer of 1942. The Japanese captured Guam, Wake, Hong Kong, the Philippines, the Dutch East Indies, and (after annihilating an Allied naval force in the Battle of the Java Sea) New Britain and the Solomon Islands; now they threatened southern New Guinea and Australia.

The Americans tried to set the stage for an offensive. A Japanese convoy was sunk in the Battle of Macassar Strait; Admiral William F. Halsey bombed the Marshall and Gilbert islands; General James Doolittle bombed Tokyo itself in a daring raid. In the European sector Allied planes began to bomb German cities.

On May 7–8, 1942, Americans sank a Japanese task force bound for Australia. This was followed by the Battle of Midway (June 1942)—which resulted in a catastrophic defeat for the Japanese Navy. The way was now paved for an American offensive around Guadalcanal (one of the Solomon islands), which began in August 1942.

In 1942, Nazi subs sank eight million tons of Allied shipping in the North Atlantic; General Erwin Rommel drove the British to El Alamein in Egypt, seventy-five miles from Alexandria; Nazi armies swung south into the Caucasus and entered Stalingrad.

Second Phase. In October 1942 the British broke through Rommel's siege of El Alamein, forcing him to retreat; in November Allied forces, commanded by General Dwight D. Eisenhower, landed in French North Africa and won important victories. At the Casablanca Conference in January 1943, the Allies decided to invade Sicily and demand the enemies' unconditional surrender.

In the Pacific American armed forces captured the Solomon and Admiralty islands (Guadalcanal fell in February 1943); moved into the Marshall Islands in the Central Pacific; cleaned the Japanese forces from the Aleutians; and began the attack on the Mariana Islands.

Third Phase. In January 1943 the Russians captured the Nazi army besieging Stalingrad. The Allies crushed the submarine menace in the Atlantic; attacked Sicily from Africa (July 1943) and then the mainland of Italy (September 1943). Rome finally fell to the Allies in June 1944, and an armistice was concluded with Italy.

Victory in Europe. On June 6, 1944, D Day, Allied forces under Eisenhower's command landed on the Normandy coast. Then, on August 25, Free French troops organized by Charles de Gaulle from London liberated Paris, and by March 7, 1945, the Allies were poised for a breakthrough to Berlin. General Eisenhower arranged to meet the Russian forces at the Elbe River to the south of Berlin. This would permit the Soviets to take all of East Germany.

On April 12, 1945, Roosevelt who had won easy reelection to a fourth term in 1944, died of a cerebral hemorrhage. The new President, Harry S Truman, agreed with Eisenhower's plan of attack; the Allied forces moved south into Bavaria while the Russians moved east through Czechoslovakia. On April 27 Soviet and Allied forces made contact; on April 28, Mussolini was killed by Italian partisans; on the next day Hitler committed suicide in his Berlin air-raid shelter. The German surrender came on May 8, 1945, known as V-E Day, for Victory in Europe.

Pacific Theater. In the summer of 1944 the Mariana Islands fell to the Americans. In the Battle of the Philippine Sea, the United States destroyed the Japanese fleet. On October 20, 1944, the counterattack on the Philippines began, and by July 5, 1945, the islands were in American hands, followed by the fall of Iwo Jima and Okinawa. On July 26, at their meeting in Potsdam, outside of Berlin, British Prime Minister Winston Churchill, Russian Premier Joseph Stalin, and President Truman demanded Japan's unconditional surrender; their ultimatum was rejected. Days later the situation was to dramatically change with the dropping of the atomic bomb.

In the spring of 1939 Roosevelt had authorized the secret development of an atomic bomb. Since then, under the leadership of the physicist J. Robert Oppenheimer, American and British scientists together with European refugee scientists, had been working feverishly in Los Alamos, New Mexico, on the plan, dubbed the Manhattan Project. On July 16,

1945, they successfully detonated the first A-bomb over the New Mexican desert.

Less than a month later, on August 6, Americans dropped the first wartime atomic bomb on the Japanese city of Hiroshima. About 75,000 Japanese were killed instantly and 100,000 injured out of a population of 344,000. (Many more were to die of radiation poisoning.) Two days later the Russians entered the Pacific war and overcame the Japanese troops in Manchuria. But hearing no word of Japanese surrender, the United States dropped a second bomb, this time over the city of Nagasaki, on August 9. On September 2, 1945, the stunned Japanese formally surrendered.

Postscript. The destruction and death wrought by World War II cannot be calculated; statistics are only cold indicators. It was a global war, the most lethal in history—probably 20 million soldiers and civilians were killed. The brutalities surpassed anything previously imaginable—6 million Jews were gassed and cremated or died in other ways in Nazi concentration camps; the Japanese forced their prisoners on "death marches" in the Philippines; and well over 100 thousand Japanese died as a result of the two atomic bombs. Damages were astronomical—whole cities were reduced to rubble and desert. Americans paid heavily for their participation—1.120 million casualties, 300 thousand of them dead. War costs in the United States alone were $341 billion.

The decision to drop the bomb aroused controversy in the United States and throughout the world. Supporters argued that it saved the lives of hundreds of thousands of Americans by bringing a quick end to the war. Critics countered that Japan had been on the brink of surrender and that dropping the bomb was unnecessary. But with the end of the war most Americans felt that an immense evil—world enslavement by fascist powers—had been prevented.

The Home Front

The Armed Forces. Just as he had been a symbol of confidence and optimism during the depression, so Roosevelt boosted the spirit of the nation now that it was at war. Under the Selective Service Act, 15 million men and women were recruited for military service. In 1944 Congress passed the "GI Bill of Rights," providing veterans with educational and other benefits.

Production. In the midst of confusion and inefficiency as the nation switched to a war economy under a president who was better at inspiring than administrating. The government poured billions into the construction of new factories. Antitrust laws were suspended for the duration of the war and total manufacturing output nearly doubled. Farmers also increased production by 22 percent.

Labor. A War Manpower Board moved millions of workers from civilian to defense jobs. A National War Labor Board kept the number of strikes down, wartime strikes involved only 1 percent of all the workers employed. In the early stages of the war effort, devices like the "Little Steel Formula"—that is, linking wage rises to cost-of-living indexes—failed; some strikes then erupted, forcing

Congress to pass the Smith-Connally Act (1943), which required a thirty-day notice before a strike, permitted the government to seize strikebound factories, and made fomenting strikes in war plants a criminal offense. The war also essentially solved the unemployment problem created by the depression. In 1940 approximately eight million Americans were still unemployed; by 1945, the civilian work force had grown by seven million. Many of these new workers were women; millions of them found jobs in the defense industry.

Inflation. Shortages of goods and increased income and credit sent prices sky-high. The government responded by launching eight bond drives; enforcing wage ceilings; creating the Office of Price Administration (OPA), which placed ceilings on rents and retail prices; rationing goods by a stamp system; and eliminating installment buying. Widespread "black-marketing," however, enabled many to evade these regulations.

The Treatment of Japanese-Americans. Civil liberties were fully protected during the war for all Americans except Japanese-Americans on the West Coast, which was declared a "theater of war." About one hundred and ten thousand Japanese-Americans (the Isei, or Japanese-Americans who had immigrated from Japan, and the Nisei, or people of Japanese ancestry born in the United States and, therefore, American citizens) were forced into "relocation centers" in Arkansas and California. Here they were treated as prisoners and guarded by armed soldiers. The Supreme Court upheld relocation in *Korematsu v. U.S.* (1944), but later in the same year, in *Ex parte Endo*, it prohibited the internment of loyal Japanese-Americans. Still, the camps were not closed until January 1945.

Blacks During the War. The war occasioned great population shifts. Millions of soldiers were sent to training camps across the country before being sent abroad; millions of workers found themselves at defense plants in states like Washington and Tennessee. In this wartime environment, the condition of blacks improved. The one million blacks in the service generally fared better than blacks in the armed forces had in World War I. The armed forces were still segregated, but blacks were allowed to join the air force and the marines. They also could be found higher up in the ranks of the army and the navy. On the home front, too, blacks advanced. The shortage of labor meant full black employment. A threatened March on Washington by A. Philip Randolph of the Brotherhood of Sleeping Car Porters was called off when Roosevelt agreed to prohibit discrimination in defense plants. Despite these gains, race riots continued to occur in many cities, and black soldiers often suffered discrimination from white soldiers.

Marriage and Divorce. More people married and more children were born during the war period. Perhaps these statistics reflected confidence in prosperity, the anxiety of soldiers facing war and leaving loved ones, and the instability of the times. Some of these stresses also led to a sharp increase in the rate of divorce.

The Postwar World

The Grand Design. President Truman inherited the herculean task of completing the work begun by Roosevelt. The Grand Alliance of major powers now worked within a broader alliance called the United Nations. Unity was achieved through "summit meetings" of the heads of states. At these meetings Roosevelt had committed the United States to a number of pledges to be carried out after the war. At Moscow (1943) the United States accepted the Moscow Declaration, which proclaimed the "necessity of establishing a general international organization . . . for the maintenance of peace and security"; at Cairo (1943) it agreed to stripping Japan of all Pacific islands; restoring to China all the territories seized from her; and granting Korea independence; at Yalta (1945) it consented to grant Russia the Kurile Islands, southern Sakhalin, an occupation zone in Korea, privileges in Manchuria, recognition of Outer Mongolia, and occupation of eastern Poland. In exchange for these concessions, the Soviets agreed to enter the Pacific War, and support postwar "free and unfettered elections as soon as possible" in Poland.

Truman strove faithfully to fulfill these many commitments and undertook others. At the Potsdam Conference (July–August 1945), he agreed to the division of Germany into four occupation zones, the eradication of Nazism, and the bringing to justice of Nazi war criminals; the complete demilitarization of Germany and the destruction of her war industries; reparation plans that heavily favored the Russians; the future unification of Germany on an undefined "democratic basis"; a Council of Ministers to draft peace treaties with Italy, Rumania, Bulgaria, Austria, Hungary, and Finland; and a mandatory transfer of 6.5 million Germans out of Hungary, Czechoslovakia, and Poland into Germany.

By 1947 peace treaties with Italy, Hungary, Bulgaria, and Rumania were submitted to the Senate, which ratified them but rejected a short draft treaty providing for the independence of Austria. As a result, Austria remained divided into four zones until February 1955 when, in a sudden policy reversal, Russia proposed a treaty that restored her independence.

War Crimes.   An International Military Tribunal was established in Nuremberg, Germany, with Supreme Court Justice Robert H. Jackson as chief American prosecutor. As a result of the Nuremberg trials, twelve Nazis were sentenced to be hanged. In twelve additional trials in the German zone under United States control, 503,360 Germans were convicted of various war crimes. Of these, 430,890 were given light fines, 27,413 sentenced to "community work," and 7,768 sent to "labor camps." In a series of Tokyo trials, 4,200 people were convicted (1949) and 720 were executed.

The United Nations.   A United Nations organization had been projected by Churchill and Roosevelt as early as 1941 in the Atlantic Charter. At the Moscow Conference the need for such an organization was officially proclaimed and the basic principle of the equality of states announced. At Teheran, Iran, (December 1943) a planning committee was projected; it met at Dumbarton Oaks, Virginia (1944) and consisted of the Big Four—the United States, Great Britain, the Soviet Union, and China.

Ninety percent of the charter of the United Nations was hammered out at

Dumbarton Oaks. The remainder was completed in three phases. At Bretton Woods, New Hampshire an International Bank for Reconstruction and Development and an International Monetary Fund to stabilize world currencies were set up. At Yalta the formula on voting procedures in the Security Council was worked out, and each of the great powers was given an absolute veto on all matters except procedure. In San Francisco (April–June 1945) the important addition of Article 51 was made. This article provided for regional pacts for individual or collective self-defense pending action by the Security Council. To avoid the error committed at Versailles in 1919, all the American delegations to these meetings were bipartisan. The Senate approved the United Nations Charter in July 1945, by a vote of eighty-nine to two.

The Western Hemisphere. The framework of a united Western Hemisphere was designed between 1945 and 1948. In the Act of Chapultepec (1945) the American nations agreed that any act or threat of aggression against one American nation would be considered a threat to all. The Treaty of Rio de Janeiro (1947) provided that an attack on one nation would be considered an attack on all and that appropriate steps would be taken if the representatives of two thirds of the American nations voted it. (The United States, however, required congressional approval for the use of armed forces.) At Bogotá (1948) this collective security pact was transformed into the Organization of American States (OAS) and defined by a written constitution that created four organs: an Inter-American Conference to meet at least once every five years; a Consultation of Foreign Ministers to meet as the occasion required; a Council, consisting of one representative from each of the twenty-one states to be in permanent session; and a Secretariat (the old Pan-American Union) also to be in permanent session.

From its inception the OAS faced a number of major problems including the political and economic instability of member nations and the problem of American dominance in the hemisphere. These problems continue today.

CHAPTER TWENTY-TWO

Postwar America (1945–60)

Explaining the effect on the press of the red-baiting senator from Wisconsin, Joseph McCarthy, newspaperman George Ready commented, "We had to take what McCarthy said at face value. Joe couldn't find a Communist in Red Square—he didn't know Karl Marx from Groucho—but he was a United States Senator." In the Cold War period following World War II, American fears of Soviet aggression were skillfully exploited by right-wing extremists such as McCarthy.

The "Cold War"

Less than two years after the end of World War II, the ideal of a Grand Alliance of great powers that would make "One World" was shattered. In its place arose the "Cold War" between the two most powerful nations to emerge from the conflict—the United States and the Soviet Union. The Cold War originated in a postwar conflict of interests between the United States and Russia.

Soviet Imperialism. Soviet imperialism had begun in 1940 with the annexation of Lithuania, Latvia, and Estonia. In 1945 the Red Army occupied Poland, Rumania, and Yugoslavia. At Yalta Stalin had promised self-determination and free elections for these countries, and, briefly, he permitted the formation of coalitions of "governments-in-exile" and Communist parties. But within these coalitions the Communists invariably controlled the police apparatus. This power enabled them to destroy non-Communist opposition. With electoral victory thus assured, satellite "people's republics" were created. In this way Eastern Europe became sovietized. Elsewhere in the world, Communist influence also increased substantially.

The Truman Doctrine. Determined that Communism should make no further advances, President Truman announced on March 12, 1947, what became known as the Truman Doctrine. "It must be the policy of the United States," he told a joint session of Congress, "to support free peoples who are resisting attempted subjugation by armed minorities." Truman went on to say that if Greece or Turkey became Communist, the entire Middle East might fall into Communist hands. To prevent this "unspeakable tragedy," he asked Congress for $300 million to help the Greek government put down a Communist-led rebellion and for $100 million to assist Turkey's resistance to Russia's territorial demands. A bipartisan majority approved the request, and men and materials began to flow into these threatened areas. America thereby inherited the British mantle in the Balkans, and made it clear to the Soviet Union that she would act to "contain" Communist expansion.

The Marshall Plan. Military aid was followed by the Marshall Plan to finance European recovery. Behind the proposal lay the assumption that Communism fed upon "hunger, poverty, devastation, and chaos." Moreover, Europe should be discouraged from returning to the ruinous prewar policy of economic nationalism. Humanitarianism dictated that the hungry be fed and the uprooted sheltered. Europe was America's best customer; its postwar economic collapse had already caused a mild recession in the United States; European revival might have the opposite effect. Thus, in a commencement speech at Harvard on June 5, 1947, General George C. Marshall, now the Secretary of State, proposed that the Europeans meet and decide what their chief economic needs were. The United States, he declared, was prepared to supply the funds and goods to satisfy these needs. Within six weeks sixteen European nations had met and requested $22.4 billion in American money. In April 1948 Congress (made

anxious by the Communist coup in Czechoslovakia in February) voted the Foreign Assistance Act that launched the European Recovery Program. The measure granted $13 billion for the program.

Results. The Marshall Plan, as the program was called, was a great success. It hastened Western Europe's recovery, while helping to maintain American prosperity. Industrial production in Europe rose significantly; inter-European trade increased; and European agriculture revived and expanded. By 1951 Western Europe was not only economically healthy, it was prosperous.

The Marshall Plan fostered European integration. Belgium, the Netherlands, Luxembourg (the Benelux nations), France, Italy, and West Germany united in a European Payments Union designed to alleviate currency and exchange difficulties; the Schuman Plan Community pooled coal and iron resources; the Euromarket was formed to gradually abolish all tariffs within the community; Euratom fostered shared nuclear-energy construction; and the Council of Europe, an advisory political group, aimed to resolve differences among the partners. The United States supported this community of continental nations. England opposed it and began to organize a European Free Trade Area aimed at abolishing tariffs among Britain, Norway, Sweden, Denmark, Portugal, Switzerland, and Austria. This community was also supported by the United States, but reconciling the hostilities between the two plans became a vital element in United States foreign policy.

A New Foreign Aid Policy. The Marshall Plan initiated an American policy of foreign aid, and over the years this policy became quite complex. Truman's "Point Four" Program offered technical assistance to backward areas; the Mutual Security Agency concentrated on military assistance to all nations opposing the Soviet bloc; an Agricultural Trade and Development Act authorized the sale of surplus farm products for foreign currencies; and friendly nations were permitted to suspend payments on loans. New loans were extended through a Development Fund created in 1957, the International Bank for Reconstruction and Development, and the Export-Import Bank. The government bestowed outright grants on many countries whose economies could not support large military establishments. Additionally, the United States participated actively in financing projects originating outside its boundaries. For example, it supported the British-sponsored Colombo Plan for aid to southeastern and southern Asia, regional development agencies in Latin America and the Middle East, and United Nation's agencies such as the Technical Assistance Program and the Special Fund for a survey of resources. In the earlier stages of this foreign-aid program, European nations received the bulk of the aid. But as the Sino-Soviet bloc launched its own programs of foreign aid to compete with those of the United States, America gave increasing amounts of aid to the Far East, Middle East, and Pacific regions.

The Arms Race.   Throughout his presidency Eisenhower was keenly aware of the dangers of a nuclear holocaust and sought ways to end the atomic arms race that had been motivated by the Cold War. In April 1953, after Stalin's death, Eisenhower asked the new Soviet government to cooperate in a disarmament effort. When the Soviets ignored this request, he proposed an "atoms for peace" plan, in which the two superpowers would donate nuclear material for peaceful purposes. Then, at a summit meeting in Geneva in 1955, he suggested "open skies," or mutual aerial surveillance. The Soviets turned down both ideas, but he kept on trying. In 1958 he and Soviet Premier Khrushchev agreed to voluntarily suspend future atomic testing until a formal test-ban treaty could be concluded. Although such a treaty was not worked out between the two leaders, neither country resumed testing during the rest of Eisenhower's presidency.

Military Pacts

NATO.   The North Atlantic Treaty Organization (NATO) originated in response to fears in Western Europe of Russian military aggression. These nations wanted the assurance of American military support to protect them against attack. Thus, in April 1949, twelve nations (Belgium, Canada, Denmark, France, Iceland, Italy, Luxembourg, the Netherlands, Norway, Portugal, the United States, and the United Kingdom) signed the North Atlantic Treaty. It provided that for twenty years the signatories would keep peace among themselves; give each other military and economic aid; and, according to Article 5, consider "an armed attack against one or more of them . . . an attack against all of them." If such an attack occurred, each would avail itself, under Article 51 of the United Nations Charter, of the right of individual and collective self-defense and would take such action as it deemed necessary. The Senate approved this treaty in July 1949. In 1950 Truman appointed General Eisenhower as NATO's supreme commander, and agreed to send four American divisions to be stationed in Europe. Greece and Turkey joined the alliance only after strenuous objection from the most northerly members. After these two countries and West Germany joined NATO, the "North Atlantic" area embraced more than four hundred million people, with a potential army of seven million.

An effort to form a united European armed force (the European Defense Community) failed when the French Parliament vetoed the proposal. More successful was the creation in the United States of the Mutual Security Agency (1951) to replace the Marshall Plan. This agency, part of the Foreign Operations Administration, provided funds for military assistance to NATO members and other powers.

The Soviet Response. Reacting to the creation of NATO, the Soviet bloc joined together in the Warsaw Pact, a military alliance that distributed thermonuclear warheads and ballistic missiles to each of its member countries (the East European satellites). A huge military balance of power was thus effected: NATO versus the Warsaw Pact. The creation of NATO had clearly led to increased tension between the two superpowers.

The United States in the Far East

The Far East in Disarray. President Truman had made Europe his first objective in the struggle against Communism, but the situation in Asia also demanded his attention. World War II had left the Far East in disarray. Large parts of Japan were destroyed, and the political and social situation in China was chaotic, with nationalist forces under Chiang Kai-shek in control of the South, the Communists under Mao Tse-tung in control of the northern countryside, and the Japanese holding most of the northern cities. Lacking confidence in Chiang, Truman decided to concentrate on restoring Japan, which would then, he believed, act as a stabilizing force in the Far East.

Japan. Truman assigned General Douglas MacArthur and his occupation army the task of democratizing, demilitarizing, and decartelizing Japan. In pursuing these objectives, MacArthur had to override opposition from a four-power Allied Council in Japan (Truman, nevertheless, effectively excluded the Soviets from any role in Japan's recovery), from the Russians, Filipinos, and Koreans demanding huge reparations, and from the Australians and New Zealanders who sought to cripple the Japanese forever. To rehabilitate the defeated nation, MacArthur halted reparation payments, granted Japan economic aid, helped it recapture some former overseas markets, and prohibited strikes. To democratize his former enemy, he pushed through a new constitution, which provided for a bicameral parliament based on universal suffrage, lowered the voting age from twenty-five to twenty and granted women the right to vote, made the Emperor a figurehead, gave the Japanese a Bill of Rights, and separated church and state. Other reforms included the abolition of conscription and the renunciation of war as the right of the nation. War criminals were tried and executed, and former military officers excluded from holding political office.

To decartelize Japan, the Zaibatsu (a vast holding company dominated by five families) was dissolved and its shares of stock sold to the public; large landed estates were redistributed; and free enterprise was encouraged through a program of loans to small businesses. Because the Japanese adapted to these changes swiftly, MacArthur lifted certain restrictions on economic development, and Japan began to reemerge as a political and economic power.

China.   The situation in China was far more difficult. At Cairo, Yalta, and Potsdam, the United States had envisioned the formation of a strong Chinese state under Chiang Kai-shek within which the Chinese Communists would have the status of a minority party. The Stalin-Chiang treaty of "friendship and alliance" signed in 1945 gave substance to this vision. In October 1945 American Ambassador Patrick Hurley induced Chiang and Mao to settle some of their differences. The conflict between them, however, was fundamental, and clashes became more frequent. Efforts by special ambassador George Marshall, sent by Truman to China to secure a settlement failed. Mao was confident that the Communists could win militarily in China, while, Chiang, overestimating his popularity, believed he would emerge the victor.

Realizing the futility of Marshall's mission, Truman recalled him in January 1947, and shortly afterwards, civil war broke out. In 1949 the Communist forces completed the mainland conquest of China. Chiang was forced to flee to the island of Formosa (now called Taiwan) in December 1949. A Communist "people's republic" was established on the mainland, and the Soviet bloc promptly recognized the new government. In February 1950, Russia and China agreed to an alliance against "aggression" by Japan "or states allied with it."

The American Response.   President Truman's response to these provocations consisted of nonrecognition of Communist China and active opposition to its admission into the United Nations. Yet he stepped back from all-out support of the nationalists on Formosa, informing Congress that the United States would not establish bases there or provide Chiang with military aid. And, in defining the American "defensive perimeter" in the Far East, Secretary of State Dean Acheson deliberately omitted Formosa and Korea. Truman's actions signified the decision by the United States to put most of its efforts in Asia toward building up Japan. Such a policy angered right-wing Republicans, who charged that the United States should have supported the nationalists more strongly.

The Korean War.   Korea had been divided at the thirty-eighth parallel by Russian and American troops in 1945. This military separation became a political division when Russia instituted a "people's republic" in industrial North Korea, while the United Nations sponsored free elections in the South, resulting in the creation of the Republic of Korea. By 1949 Soviet and American forces had departed from Korea. After a number of border incidents, the North Koreans attacked across the thirty-eighth parallel on June 25, 1950, in a gamble for conquest. Seeing this as an example of Soviet-supported aggression, Truman instantaneously reversed American policy. He requested that the United Nations Security Council meet, and when it did the United States (during Russia's temporary absence) secured a resolution passed by a vote of nine to zero declaring North Korea guilty of aggression, demanding that it withdraw behind the thirty-eighth parallel, and calling on all members of the United Nations to render every assistance in carrying out this resolution. Truman then ordered the American navy and air force into a "police action" and gave cover and support to South Korean forces south of the thirty-eighth parallel. On June 27 the Security Council endorsed the President's military actions and appointed General Douglas MacArthur commander-in-chief of United Nations forces in Korea. Although the response was ostensibly a United Nations police action, the war was clearly between America and North Korea.

Initially, the North Koreans achieved some success. But then counteroffensives carried the war to the northern border of Korea (the Yalu River). Despite predictions to the contrary by MacArthur and Secretary of State Dean Acheson, China joined the conflict. By December the Chinese had pushed the United Nations troops out of North Korea. After stabilizing the front south of the thirty-eighth parallel in the spring of 1951, MacArthur urged the President to let him bomb the Chinese installations north of the Yalu and pushed for a naval blockade of China. Fearing that such moves would lead to World War III, Truman rejected MacArthur's proposals. The angry general openly criticized his commander in chief, and when he continued speaking out in violation of Truman's orders, the President fired MacArthur. Frustrated at the inconclusive struggle, a majority of Americans backed the popular general. But after the Communists agreed to discuss a truce in June 1951, his strategy lost support. Two years later President Dwight D. Eisenhower negotiated a peace treaty that ended the fighting and divided the country into two parts, North and South Korea. Peace finally came to embattled Korea on July 2, 1953, when the Communists agreed to an armistice, but the country remained divided.

The Cold War in Asia. The Korean War caused the United States to extend its European anti-Communist policy into the Far East (and eventually into the Near East). And, as Germany became the pivot of the American policy in Europe, so did Japan become pivotal in Asia.

On September 8, 1951, the United States together with forty-eight other states concluded a peace treaty with Japan that reduced Japan to four main islands, ended the occupation, returned Japanese prisoners of war, relieved the country of the burden of reparations, and permitted it to join regional security pacts to redevelop an armaments industry and to assist in her defense.

Defense Pacts. This "peace of reconciliation" with Japan disturbed the Filipinos, Australians, and New Zealanders because Japan was now free to rearm. To reassure them, the United States signed two defense treaties: a bilateral pact with the Philippines (August 1951) and the ANZUS treaty with Australia and New Zealand. These treaties were less clear-cut than that of NATO: an armed attack on one of the signees would be "considered dangerous to the peace and safety" of the others; each would act, in the face of common danger, "in accordance with its constitutional processes."

The United States eventually signed defense pacts with South Korea, Iran, Thailand, Pakistan, Saudi Arabia, India, Israel, Japan, and Iraq. The various treaties allowed American forces to be stationed inside the Philippines and South Korea. The pact with the Japanese permitted the United States to deploy its armed forces inside Japan.

Military Assistance. Japan was thus converted into an American military bastion. In return, the United States continued to grant its former enemy large sums in economic and military aid, strengthened Japan's naval defenses, and returned the Amani Islands in 1953. Formosa also became a large American base. Chiang's half-million-man army was brought to full strength and serviced by the American Navy.

Meanwhile, the situation in Indochina demanded United States attention. Since 1950 America had supplied military and economic aid to France in her war in Indochina against Communist forces led by Ho Chi Minh and supported by Chinese arms. Yet when the Communists besieged twenty thousand French troops at Dien Bien Phu early in 1954, Eisenhower refused France's request for an American air strike to break the siege. Eisenhower feared further involvement, in which American troops would have no chance against a guerrilla army well-versed in jungle warfare. His decision doomed the French garrison at Dien Bien Phu, which

surrendered in May. At Russia's suggestion a truce was negotiated, and at Geneva in 1954 the country was divided at the seventeenth parallel. The northern part, under the control of Ho Chi Minh, became Communist, while the southern part continued under the rule of the Emperor, Bao Dai. The two leaders agreed to elections in 1956 to decide the future of the country. But in the meantime, conservatives deposed the Emperor, and the election was not held.

SEATO. For some time Eisenhower's Secretary of State, John Foster Dulles, had been urging a Southeast Asia Treaty Organization based on the model of NATO. The unresolved situation in Vietnam stirred eight governments into action (the United States, the United Kingdom, France, Australia, New Zealand, Pakistan, the Philippines, and Thailand). In the Manila Pact (September 1954), they adopted the formula of the United States' previous bilateral agreements with Asian countries. The absence of India, Burma, and Indonesia ("neutralist" nations), however, made the pact considerably weaker than NATO.

Ongoing Far Eastern Difficulties. As the postwar period drew to a close, the growing strength of Communist China, persisting border raids between Communist and free countries, and widespread neutralism were the focus of United States concern in Asia. For example, Communist China showed its power in the 1954 bombardment of the offshore islands of Quemoy and Matsu, which were occupied by the nationalists. The Chinese situation was a particular thorn in America's side. Until 1972 the United States refused to recognize the People's Republic of China and opposed its entry into the UN, viewing Chiang Kai-shek's government in Taiwan as China's legitimate government.

The United States in the Middle East

U.S. Interests in the Middle East.   During the Truman and Eisenhower years, American policy in the Middle East was guided by attempts to prevent Soviet expansion, maintain access to oil-producing regions, and restrain conflict between the new Jewish state of Israel, which had declared independence in 1948, and its Arab neighbors. Truman quickly recognized Israel, but the Arabs tried to crush it militarily. Primarily concerned with the increasing Soviet influence in the region, Eisenhower was less ardent in his support of Israel. After Egyptian King Farouk was overthrown in 1952, Dulles offered the new leader, Colonel Gamal Abdel Nasser, economic aid. But while Nasser accepted this offer, he also bought arms from the Soviets. Distressed by Nasser's drift toward the Communists, Secretary of State John Foster Dulles withdrew America's offer of support for the building of the giant Aswan Dam in 1956.

The Suez Crisis.   In retaliation, Nasser seized the Suez Canal, thereby precipitating a great crisis. Dependent on the Canal for their shipments of mideastern oil, England and France, without informing the United States, attacked Egypt. Simultaneously Israel also launched an invasion, quickly defeating the Egyptian army in the Sinai Peninsula. The United States introduced a resolution in the United Nations, calling for a cease-fire. While Russia supported the resolution, Britain and France vetoed it. Soviet leader Nikita Khrushchev then threatened to launch a missile attack against the two European nations if they did not withdraw, and Eisenhower also demanded their withdrawal. On November 6 British Prime Minister Anthony Eden declared a cease-fire and Israeli troops departed from Egypt. The Nine-Days War was over, but the cost of peace was an embarrassing defeat to America's two allies and bad feelings between them and the United States.

To repair some of the damage, the President announced the "Eisenhower Doctrine" in January 1957. Approved by Congress, it authorized United States armed assistance, if requested by a Middle Eastern nation, to repel aggression by a Soviet-bloc nation. Thus, after Iraq underwent a military coup in July 1958, Lebanon requested the presence of United States marines to prevent the spread of revolt. When it became apparent that Karim Kassim, the new leader of Iraq, would not permit a Communist-backed government to be established in his country, the marines withdrew. Moreover, as Nasser himself became disillusioned with Soviet-bloc aid and apprehensive of Russian moves throughout the Middle East, the United States resumed its former policy of large-scale economic aid to Egypt and other Arab nations.

Policymakers faced continuing problems in the Middle East, including how to curb the more violent aspects of Arab nationalism, the need to diminish Soviet infiltration, and the challenge of raising the standard of living in the region.

Domestic Affairs (1945–60)

Demobilization and Reconversion to a Peacetime Economy. The American economy immediately after World War II was characterized by deflationary tendencies. The armed forces were so rapidly reduced that on the eve of the Korean War in 1950 they numbered only six hundred thousand men; military expenditures dropped to $13 billion, taxes were reduced by $6 billion, and the government sold $15 billion worth of government war plants and surplus goods to make up the loss. To head off an anticipated postwar recession, Congress passed the Employment Act (1946), which created a Council of Economic Advisers to study the economy, analyze weaknesses, and propose measures for stabilization.

The President and Congress. Truman's annual message to Congress in 1945 set the stage for a bitter struggle with that body. The new President—spirited but modest, idealistic but commonsensical, stubborn but capable—offered the American people what came to be known as the Fair Deal, an attempt to complete the New Deal. He proposed an increased minimum wage, public housing, medical insurance, extension of social security, aid to education, more public power projects, and more agricultural aid. But Congress, reacting to the mood of the American people (who wanted to enjoy their prosperity), and to the President's combative style, rejected most of his program. Republicans and Democrats in Congress joined together to force the abandonment of price controls, pass the Taft-Hartley Act of 1947 (curbing "unfair union practices" and outlawing the union shop) over Truman's veto, cripple his anti-inflation program, reduce his housing program, and, in the agricultural arena, changed Truman's proposed "fixed parity" of 90 percent to "flexible parities" ranging from 60 percent to 90 percent.

The Election of 1948. Optimism prevailed in the Republican convention, which nominated New York's Governor Thomas E. Dewey for president. Truman's Fair Deal had been stopped, and the Roosevelt coalition was irrevocably broken when Secretary of the Interior Harold Ickes and former Vice President (now Secretary of Agriculture) Henry Wallace resigned from the Cabinet. Wallace had organized the Progressive Party, which would draw voters from the Democrats; conservative southern Democrats, upset by Truman's support of civil rights, seceded from Democratic ranks and organized the "Dixiecrats" or States' Rights Party, nominating Governor Strom Thurmond of South Carolina for the presidency.

Defying all those who had predicted his defeat, Truman triumphed, having barnstormed the country while the overconfident Dewey carried on a lackluster campaign. The old Roosevelt coalition was frayed, but it still held together.

The Fair Deal. Truman regarded his "miracle election" as a popular mandate to enact a Fair Deal program consisting of repeal of the Taft-Hartley Act; sweeping civil rights legislation (including anti-lynching laws; anti–poll tax laws, and fair employment practices); expanded and more generous social security; minimum-wage and housing legislation; compulsory federal health insurance; federal aid to education; increased protection of natural resources; authority for the government to build industrial plants to overcome national commodity shortages; effective enforcement of the antitrust laws to protect small business; high farm subsidies; and a sweeping anti-inflation program.

The Election of 1952. It seemed to be time for a change. The Korean War was stalemated, and some of Truman's aides were involved in scandals involving the acceptance of private gifts from influence peddlers. To add to the troubles of the Democrats, Senator Joseph McCarthy of Wisconsin was investigating the State Department, which he claimed had been infiltrated by Communists. Although no such evidence was found, the charges made good campaign material. The Republican ticket of Dwight D. Eisenhower and Richard M. Nixon easily defeated the Democratic slate of Governor Adlai E. Stevenson of Illinois and John Sparkman by an electoral vote of 442 to 89.

The "New Republicanism." The American people believed that Eisenhower possessed the ability to lead them to peace, unity, and prosperity. The "New Republicanism," as exemplified by Eisenhower and other moderates, was characterized chiefly by acceptance of the main features of the New Deal as part of the American way of life. Eisenhower continued many of the policies of his Democratic predecessors, including billion-dollar foreign aid; liberalized immigration laws; reciprocal trade agreements; increased Social Security benefits; minimum-wage laws; increased unemployment insurance payments; and federal aid to housing.

Concentrating on foreign policy during his two terms in office, Eisenhower delegated much of his domestic authority to top aides. This fact, plus his dislike of lobbying Congress, led to only moderate legislative results for his domestic program. He obtained a raise in the minimum wage, an extension of social security benefits, and he pushed through the Highway Act of 1956, which appropriated money to construct a forty-one-thousand-mile interstate highway system connecting all of the nation's major cities. Completed after twenty years, the interstate system shortened travel time, increased the country's dependence on the automobile, and led to the growth of industries, food and recreational facilities, and residential housing near these new highways.

The Communist Issue. The Cold War heightened domestic fears of Communist subversion from abroad. Revelations of Soviet espionage activities heightened these fears. In 1946 the House Un-American Activities Committee (HUAC) held hearings that suggested Communist agents had infiltrated the government during the 1930s. In the ensuing panic, Truman reluctantly instituted security checks on government employees, and thousands of government workers lost their jobs. The political climate worsened in 1948 when ex-Communist Whittaker Chambers accused Alger Hiss, a former State Department official, of copying classified documents for the Soviets. Because the statute of limitations had expired, Hiss was subsequently tried for perjury, not espionage. In January 1950 he was convicted and received a five-year jail term. As a member of HUAC, before which Hiss testified two days after Chambers's charges, Richard Nixon had zealously pursued the former

State Department official, arranging a confrontation between him and his accuser and pouncing on inconsistencies and gaps in Hiss's testimony. Nixon's performance was to earn him many enemies among liberal Americans.

Shortly afterward, British scientist Klaus Fuchs admitted that he had given atomic secrets to the Russians. His admission, and the arrest and conviction on the same charge of his American associate Harry Gold and two other Americans, Julius and Ethel Rosenberg, fueled the "Red Scare." In 1951 the Rosenbergs were found guilty of treason, and, despite appeals from around the world, they were executed two years later.

In this charged atmosphere, the relatively unknown Senator Joseph McCarthy of Wisconsin charged in a speech in February 1950 that the State Department was "infested" with Communists. Although he never substantiated his charge, he engaged in a four-and-a-half-year crusade to weed out alleged Communists from the government. Skillfully exploiting the press, the public's fears about Communism, and congressional fears concerning chances of reelection if they opposed him, McCarthy—and McCarthyism—became a major force in American life as people from all walks of life who were thought to be Communists faced blacklisting and the loss of their careers. McCarthy drew his support from working-class Catholics and ethnic groups who usually voted Democratic and from conservative Midwestern Republicans.

Having grown too confident of his powers, he finally overreached himself in 1954, when he attacked high army officers. The ensuing Army-McCarthy hearings were televised. Millions of viewers watched, ap-palled, as the senator bullied witnesses whom he viewed as hostile. The public's response encouraged moderate Republicans to join with Democrats and censure him in the Senate in December 1954. After the vote, McCarthy's political demise was complete. Yet his legacy remained in the cultural conformity that characterized the rest of the decade.

Civil Rights. Although blacks had gained economically from World War II, they still endured economic and social discrimination. They fared worse in the South than in the North; in every sphere of activity they were almost completely segregated from whites. Southern blacks attended separate schools and were denied the use of public facilities. They had to ride in the rear of buses, drink water from separate fountains, and use separate rest rooms.

Truman strengthened the Civil Rights division of the Department of Justice and, in 1948, banned segregation in the armed forces. Eisenhower completed the integration of blacks into the military. But the greatest advances in civil rights during his term originated in a landmark decision by the liberal Supreme Court. In 1954 the Court heard the NAACP-sponsored case of *Brown v. Board of Education of Topeka.* In a unanimous decision, the judges reversed the Court's 1896 decision (*Plessy v. Ferguson*) upholding the constitutionality of "separate but equal" facilities. Chief Justice Earl Warren (an Eisenhower appointee) declared in his opinion that "separate educational facilities are inherently unequal." In 1955 the Court ordered the states to proceed "with all deliberate speed" in integrating schools.

Southern states made little effort to

obey the Court. Believing that laws did not change people, Eisenhower, though hardly a racist, did not press for desegregation. Yet in 1954 he felt compelled to act, sending in federal troops to ensure integration of Central High School in Little Rock, Arkansas. But, by the end of the 1950s, less than 1 percent of black children attended integrated schools.

Despite the slow pace of school desegregation, the Brown decision set the stage for other advances. The Civil Rights Act of 1957 authorized the Attorney General to obtain injunctions against southern white officials who prevented blacks from registering and voting. The law also established a Civil Rights Commission and a Civil Rights Division in the Department of Justice.

The Emergence of Black Activism. Blacks began to realize that if change were to occur, they would have to push for it themselves. On December 1, 1955, a black seamstress, Rosa Parks, was arrested in Montgomery, Alabama, for refusing to give up her bus seat to a white. Led by a young minister, Martin Luther King, Jr., Montgomery's blacks supported Parks by boycotting city buses. Walking and organizing themselves into car pools, they kept the boycott going, vowing it would end only when segregated seating was eliminated. A year later, the Supreme Court declared Alabama's segregated seating law unconstitutional. Southern blacks realized that they had found a new strategy to overturn racially restrictive laws and policies: passive, or nonviolent, resistance. Soon after, King founded the Southern Christian Leadership Conference (SCLC) to direct the effort against segregation.

Literature. Two of the best novels to come out of World War II were Norman Mailer's *The Naked and the Dead* (1948) and James Jones's *From Here to Eternity* (1951). If these realistic novels were in the mainstream literary tradition, they also reflected the emergence of new spiritual and moral issues. The works of Beat novelists, such as Jack Kerouac (*On the Road*, 1957), and poets, such as Allen Ginsberg (*Howl*, 1956) rejected traditional values, seeing American society as materialistic and empty. The beat writers encouraged Americans to explore alternative lifestyles, including drugs, Eastern religions, and sexual freedom. In his extremely popular *The Catcher in the Rye* (1951), J. D. Salinger depicted a young man engaged in a more personal rebellion. Another great popular success was Joseph Heller's *Catch-22* (1955) which exposed the absurdity of war. The novels of Saul Bellow, including *The Victim* (1947) and *The Adventures of Augie March* (1953), described the attempts of urban Americans to define their roles and responsibilities in the modern world.

Painting. After the war, American artists no longer took their direction from Europe. Led by Jackson Pollock, the New York School of abstract expressionists, or action painters, painted large, energetic canvasses in which artistic spontaneity, and a freewheeling technique were essential. Other notable abstract expressionists included Mark Rothko, Robert Motherwell, Lee Krasner, and Franz Kline. The break from the past signalled by abstract expressionism encouraged other experimentation, such as pop art, which mocked American violence, emptiness, and materialism; and later, op art, which used the combination of pure complementary colors to produce eye-popping optical effects. Painters like Jasper Johns, Andy Warhol, and Robert Rauschenberg made Americans look more closely at the symbols of their culture, such as comics, flags, soup cans, movie stars, and dollar bills. The line between art and society narrowed, and it is not surprising that this period marked the emergence of the artist as celebrity.

The Space Race. In October 1957 the Russian Sputnik, the first unmanned space satellite, successfully orbited the earth, sending shock waves across America. Fearing that the United States had lost its scientific edge, the President and Congress reacted quickly. In 1958 Congress established the National Aeronautics and Space Administration (NASA) and generously allocated funds to make it competitive in the space race. Public concern that American education was lagging behind that of the Soviets, especially in the sciences, led Congress to pass the National Defense Education Act (1958), initiating federally supported scientific and foreign-language programs in schools and colleges. Thus the loss of confidence momentarily engendered by Sputnik had led by the end of the 1950s to a reassertion of American competitiveness and a renewed sense of national pride.

CHAPTER TWENTY-THREE

The Sixties

Many blacks felt President John F. Kennedy was moving too slowly to end racial discrimination. In New York his brother, Attorney General Robert Kennedy, met with black artists, intellectuals, and activists. The civil rights activist Jerome Smith attacked the Attorney General, saying he was "nauseated" at being in the same room with him and that he was unsure how much longer he could remain nonviolent. Afterward Kennedy, stung by these remarks, acknowledged that such expressions of anger on the part of blacks "made no sense, but in a way they made all sense," that is, they were illogical yet justified.

In the sixties the United States was swept by the furious forces of change led by protestors confronting a variety of social ills. Among the most significant protests was that of the Civil Rights Movement, which prodded the government into increasing activism on behalf of blacks.

John F. Kennedy (1961–63)

The Election of 1960. During the presidential primaries of 1960 Senator John F. Kennedy of Massachusetts seemed handicapped by his youth—he was forty-three years old—and his religion. He was a Catholic, and no Catholic had ever been elected president. Yet his victories in the Wisconsin and West Virginia primaries showed that Kennedy could win in Protestant regions, and he captured the Democratic nomination on the first ballot. Lyndon B. Johnson, the Senate majority leader from Texas, was nominated for the vice presidency. The Republicans nominated Vice President Richard M. Nixon as their presidential candidate and Henry Cabot Lodge, Jr., as his running mate.

During the campaign Kennedy vowed that under his leadership the United States would win the Cold War, strengthen national defense, and speed economic growth. Aware of his conservative image, Nixon ran on the popular Eisenhower's record. For the first time, presidential candidates faced each other in a series of televised debates. While Nixon appeared uneasy before the cameras, Kennedy projected warmth, wit, self-confidence, and enough knowledge of the issues to convince Americans that, despite his youth, he would be a capable president. Seen by over seventy million viewers, the debates helped swing the electorate to Kennedy.

The popular vote was extraordinarily close: out of 68,836,000 ballots cast, Kennedy received 49.7 percent and Nixon 49.5 percent. The spread in the electoral college was wider, however: 303 to 219. Kennedy's religion helped him in eastern cities, but hurt him in rural areas and the West. The Democrats retained their Congressional domination, but the effective voting bloc remained that of the southern Democrats and the Republicans, confronting President Kennedy from the start with a bumptious, conservative coalition.

Inauguration. The new President ignored these political realities in his inspiring inaugural address. Hoping to move the nation in a new direction, he called for personal commitment: "Ask not what your country can do for you," he said, "Ask what you can do for your country."

Cabinet and Consensus. A superb politician, Kennedy understood the politics of consensus. He realized that it had to be built on the coalition of liberals and conservatives, labor and management, ethnic groupings, religious groupings, and so forth. Consensus dictated that some members of each of these groups be permitted to share in the government, regardless of party label, and Kennedy's Cabinet choices reflected this pragmatic approach. The liberals were represented by Dean Acheson as Secretary of State, and Adlai Stevenson as Ambassador to the UN, although many observers felt that they received relatively minor posts. The conservative group was pleased with the

appointment of Douglas Dillon, a Republican banker, as Secretary of the Treasury, and Robert McNamara, President of the Ford Motor Company, as Secretary of Defense. Kennedy appointed the neutral, noncontroversial Dean Rusk as Secretary of State. The appointment of Arthur Goldberg, the AFL-CIO general counsel, as Secretary of Labor, pleased the Jewish and organized-labor blocs. An offer of the Postmaster Generalship to a black undoubtedly excited that community, although the offer was eventually rejected. The Catholic bloc got an additional boost when the President appointed his brother, Robert, as Attorney General. Although he was the most controversial of the appointees, Robert Kennedy overcame objections with his brilliant exposure of the corruption of James Hoffa of the Teamsters Union. The President also called on a "Kitchen Cabinet" of prominent intellectuals—Arthur Schlesinger, Jr., Theodore Sorensen, McGeorge Bundy, and others—to help shape the New Frontier.

Setting the Stage. In his message to Congress, Kennedy spelled out the details of the New Frontier. His cautious demands did not exceed those of Truman's Fair Deal. Kennedy emphasized, however, the need for governmental planning to achieve a steady and high rate of economic growth. He called for medical care for the aged, federal aid to education, better use of natural resources, housing and community development, highway construction, expanded national defense expenditures, and increased foreign military and economic aid.

Legislative Achievements. The legislative achievement of the Kennedy administration was spotty. Two major bills, one for Medicare and the other for federal aid to education, were defeated, creating the impression that Congress had shelved the entire program. Actually, it did pass some important new legislation. To accomplish even this, however, Kennedy had to overcome his own distaste for legislative infighting and the opposition of the conservative coalition of southern Democrats and northern Republicans. One particularly difficult obstacle was the extremely conservative Congressman Howard Smith, chairman of the House Rules Committee, where so much of the progressive legislation had been delayed. Kennedy allied himself with House Speaker Sam Rayburn to break Smith's power by adding three members to the committee, putting control into the hands of the moderates. This done, Congress passed a minimum-wage law that raised the hourly rate from $1 to $1.25 over a period of four years and added more than 3.5 million workers to the list of those covered. It increased Social Security benefits, provided for children of needy unemployed, permitted men as well as women to retire at age sixty-two, and created a retirement fund for the self-employed. Congress also allocated slightly less than $5 billion over a four-year period for slum clearance, FHA housing projects for middle-income families, urban renewal projects, student housing, housing for the elderly, and loans for repairs.

Other major accomplishments included the establishment of area redevelopment and manpower training programs to retrain workers whose skills had become obsolete and who had joined the new army of the permanently unemployed that existed even though overall employment had increased. Other bills provided for the allocation of money for the relief of businessmen and unemployed persons in depressed areas; aid for the mentally retarded; tightening of controls over the manufacture and distribution of drugs; and expansion of trade by giving the President power to reduce tariffs 50 percent over five years and to eliminate some tariffs altogether. Congress also approved measures to provide for medical education, college construction, relief of areas affected by federal projects, and defense education. Kennedy also obtained legislation prohibiting racial discrimination in the sale or rental of federal housing projects built since 1961.

Planning. Behind Kennedy's legislative requests was his desire to revive the sluggish economy. According to one of his closest economic advisers, Paul Samuelson, this could be accomplished by direct intervention of the federal government to stimulate economic growth with heavy aid for distressed areas and residential construction, by raising unemployment compensation allotments, securing lower interest rates to encourage mortgage investments, and, if these steps failed, by cutting taxes to increase effective demand. These expenditures, Kennedy realized, would create inflationary pressures. To counteract them he thought he could ask unions to keep their wage demands low. But when the steel industry raised its prices, in April 1962, after Kennedy had persuaded the United Steel Workers to accept a new contract without wage increases, he angrily threatened to cut off Pentagon purchases to compel a retraction. He succeeded, but at the cost of losing his popularity with big business. Finally, however, the continued slowness of the economy prompted Kennedy to suggest a $13 billion income-tax reduction to stimulate consumer spending in 1964. By the early 1960s, personal incomes had increased by 13 percent and corporate profits by 67 percent.

The Surge to Freedom.   The Civil Rights Movement posed a dilemma for Kennedy. On the one hand, during the 1960 campaign, he had won the support of blacks and liberal whites when he helped Martin Luther King win release from a southern jail. On the other hand, Kennedy feared alienating the southern Democrats who dominated Congress.

Kennedy's administration saw blacks and their white supporters adopt numerous tactics to break the power structure that upheld racial discrimination and segregation. New black organizations appeared to reinforce the contingents from Roy Wilkins's NAACP. In addition to Martin Luther King's SCLC, the Urban League, the Congress of Racial Equality (CORE), the Black Muslims, and the Student Nonviolent Coordinating Committee (SNCC) launched nonviolent integrationist actions: "sit-ins" to integrate restaurants and parks; "pray-ins" to integrate churches; "freedom rides" to integrate transportation facilities and to supply the South with workers to get out the black vote; and picketing and boycotting of de facto segregated neighborhood schools. The movement reached its high point in the celebrated March on Washington (August 1963) in support of pending civil rights legislation.

Southern white supremacists fought back. They formed White Citizens' Councils, joined the Ku Klux Klan, attacked demonstrators, murdered northern civil rights workers, and intimidated liberal southern newspaper editors and owners of radio stations. Pressured by black activists on one side and white racists on the other, Kennedy abandoned his cautious strategy. At the Justice Department, Robert Kennedy moved to compel desegregation of interstate transportation, obedience to civil rights laws, and school integration. In 1962, when James Meredith sought admission to the University of Mississippi, the President sent in the National Guard to protect him against angry mobs.

Then, in 1963, Police Commissioner Eugene "Bull" Connor ordered his police to crush a massive protest led by Martin Luther King, Jr., to desegrate public facilities in Birmingham, Alabama. The nation watched on TV as policemen used clubs and police dogs against the unarmed demonstrators. The administration quickly negotiated a settlement with the city's business community, granting the blacks their demands.

The events in Birmingham galvanized the President. In 1963 he sponsored a civil rights bill, making discrimination in public places illegal, giving the Justice Department the right to bring suits against those resisting school desegregation, and authorizing federal agencies to withhold funds from state programs that discriminated. In August 1963 two hundred thousand marchers rallied in Washington to support the bill. At this event Martin Luther King delivered his famous "I Have a Dream" speech. (In a typical American irony, following all this action the conservative Congress failed to pass the comprehensive Civil Rights Act. After Kennedy's death the bill was passed during the administration of Lyndon Johnson.)

Despite these actions, critics contended that Kennedy had moved too cautiously in the arena of civil rights. Others believed that by waiting for a consensus to develop, he was able to design legislation that would help blacks achieve their goals.

A Political Revolution.   In *Baker v. Carr* (1962), the Supreme Court ordered the Federal District Court of Tennessee to re-apportion the Tennessee state legislature if it found that the Constitutional require-ment of representation according to popu-lation was being violated. In most states of the Union fewer than 40 percent of the voters chose the majority of representa-tives of the legislature as a result of the unequal size of legislative districts. An-other reapportionment case then extended this principle of "one man–one vote" to congressional districts. Most states re-vised their apportionment formulas to eliminate the imbalance between the vot-ing strength exercised by rural and urban dwellers.

Defense.   Secretary of Defense McNa-mara modernized the Department of De-fense with computers and cost-analysis techniques to eliminate any missile gap between the United States and the U.S.S.R. and provide a firmer foundation to the new politics of "the balance of ter-ror," which theorized that nuclear war could be avoided as long as each side feared the others' nuclear arsenals. Ken-nedy also authorized construction of one thousand Minuteman Intercontinental Ballistic Missiles (ICBMs), which gave the United States the capacity to carry out a successful first nuclear strike. The Presi-dent and his advisers also realized that if the balance of terror held, new wars

could assume guerrilla as well as conven-tional forms; therefore, much of the mili-tary was trained in "counterinsurgency" tactics. The emphasis on military pre-paredness and the beginning of American involvement in Vietnam pushed annual military expenditures close to the $50 bil-lion mark. To an increasing extent, the prosperous economy became linked with expenditures on armaments.

The Space Race.   In 1957 the Russians had orbited the satellite Sputnik around the earth. Having taken the lead in the space race, they held it through 1963, the year that Colonel John Glenn, Jr., became the first American to orbit the earth. The Soviets' rocket booster was more power-ful; they orbited the first cosmonaut; they established a long-distance record in or-biting the earth; and they launched two cosmonauts on succeeding days who then brought their vehicles close together in space. To overcome the space gap, Ken-nedy recommended the $20 billion Apollo project, designed to land an American on the moon. Congress enthusiastically voted billions of dollars annually for this program.

The Dallas Bullets.   On the afternoon of Friday, November 22, 1963, while riding in a motorcade through Dallas, Texas, Kennedy was shot in the head by Lee Har-vey Oswald. The President died instantly. Two days later, while Oswald was being transferred from one jail to another, Jack Ruby, a Dallas restaurant owner, shot and killed him in full view of the police and millions of television watchers. Many peo-ple believed that the two murders were part of a wider conspiracy, but an investi-gation by a special commission headed by Chief Justice Earl Warren identified Oswald as the lone assassin. Yet even today, doubts still persist. President Kennedy was buried in Arlington National Cemetery on November 25, in a funeral attended by officials of almost every country in the world.

Lyndon B. Johnson (1963–68)

The Interim President.   Two hours after John F. Kennedy's death, Lyndon B. Johnson was sworn in as thirty-sixth president. A master in the art of practical politics, canny, energetic, and hugely ambitious, the larger-than-life Johnson quickly acted to make the painful transition as smooth as possible. He asked Congress to fulfill the Kennedy program by passing civil rights and economic legislation. (Although a Southerner, Johnson had consistently supported racial equality ever since he had become a prominent legislator.) Then he added something of his own: a program to conduct a "war on poverty." Johnson also announced that he would retain the Kennedy Cabinet and those advisers who wanted to remain. The nation's tension abated as the public witnessed their new President's assurance, born out of long political experience. Aided by a willingness on the part of Congress to move, and by his own great political know-how, the energetic and ambitious new President accomplished in his first hundred days what his predecessor could not achieve in three years: a tax cut, passage of Kennedy's 1963 foreign-aid bill, several education laws, and a broad-based Civil Rights Act.

The Civil Rights Act of 1964.   The act that finally passed both houses accom-

plished five things: (1) it prohibited racial discrimination in restaurants, theaters, hotels, and other places of "public accommodation"; (2) it authorized the Attorney General to initiate suits or otherwise intervene on behalf of victims of discrimination, including schoolchildren; (3) it prohibited discrimination by employers or labor unions; (4) it withheld funds from federally supported projects practicing racial discrimination; and (5) it compelled uniform standards for voting for whites and blacks.

Reactions to these legislative proposals varied. Many parts of the South integrated public accommodations without fuss or protest. Fewer undertook to integrate schools. Two southern blacks defeated their white opponents in a city council race. The white supremacists embarked on a reign of terror: they bombed black homes and churches and murdered civil rights volunteers. Southern juries even acquitted self-confessed killers of blacks.

In the North, blacks responded to these outrages with racial riots in the ghetto areas of New York City, Rochester, Philadelphia, and Jersey City. Millions of dollars' worth of property was damaged, and when local police proved unable to curb the riots, the National Guard had to be called in. Now it was the turn of the northern whites to experience racist "backlash." They fiercely protested proposals to integrate segregated neighborhood schools by bussing children from one school district to another.

Tax Planning.   Early in 1964 Congress provided for more than $9 billion in tax reductions on individual incomes and $2.4 billion on corporate profits. At the same time, federal revenues fell $8.4 billion short of expenditures, thus adding even more to the $300-billion public debt. The tax cut, however, was deliberately designed to shore up the lagging economy with a large injection of spending power. And it worked, for the next year the gross national product rose sharply again.

The War on Poverty.   Emboldened by his early successes, Johnson declared war on poverty and set out to shape what he called a "Great Society," one in which poverty would not exist. Was there any need for such an ambitious program? Many critics of American society thought so. In support of their argument, they pointed to the 20 to 25 percent of Americans (about forty million people) living below the poverty line in 1960. (The poverty line was the government's estimate of minimum subsistence level.) Johnson's war on poverty had two goals: to help the poor help themselves and to offer them direct assistance. Thus, the Economic Opportunity Act of 1964 established the Job Corps to aid school dropouts in obtaining job training. An education program, Project Head Start, was established for poor preschoolers. Part-time employment was provided for students so that they would be less inclined to quit school. Local communities with their own antipoverty programs received federal aid. Farmers received grants to improve their productivity, and small businesses were given incentives to employ the so-called "chronically disemployed." Heads of families receiving public assistance were also offered job training.

The Great Society.   Before the election of 1964, Congress followed Johnson's leadership by establishing a nine-million-acre wilderness preserve for conservation and recreation; passing a housing act for construction of thirty-five thousand units of low-rent dwellings to aid the poor and clear the slums; providing cities with federal aid to solve their transit problems; helping school districts whose population had increased because of federal facilities in the area; and extending the National Defense Education Act to improve instruction. But Congress refused to act on Johnson's proposal for Medicare to provide medical aid to the elderly under Social Security and on his request for $1 billion to abolish poverty in Appalachia.

The Election of 1964.   In a convention dominated by their conservative wing, the Republicans nominated Senator Barry M. Goldwater and Congressman William Miller of New York to run against President Johnson and Senator Hubert Humphrey of Minnesota, the Democratic vice presidential choice. Goldwater was defeated by the largest margin in the history of presidential elections. The popular vote was 43,126,584 to 27,177,838. The Republicans received 52 electoral votes from the South, which voted Republican to register its protest against the Civil Rights Movement. But thousands of moderate Republicans who were not threatened by Johnson's liberal reforms crossed party lines to vote for him. These crossovers also deserted the Republican candidates in protest over the tactics of the right-wingers, who had gained control over their party. Many of Goldwater's supporters were extremists who wanted to end Social Security, make America withdraw from the United Nations, allow field commanders in Vietnam to use nuclear weapons, put civil rights legislation exclusively in the hands of the states, sell the TVA to private interests, and end farm-price supports.

The Elected President.　President Johnson saw his massive victory as a mandate to push ahead with the Great Society. He quickly brought to the Eighty-ninth Congress a legislative program that made it the most revolutionary Congress since Franklin D. Roosevelt's time.

Immigration.　The Immigration Act of 1965 returned America to what it had been originally, a land open to immigrants without regard to country of origin. While Congress retained a limit on total immigration, and even extended it to Latin America, immigration was separated from the discriminatory system of "national origins" to which it had been attached since 1921. Under the new law, the classification of immigrants by national origins was to be abolished beginning in 1968. Until then the unused quotas could be assigned to low-quota countries. No nation was permitted more than twenty thousand emigrants to America. Total immigration per year was fixed at one hundred and seventy thousand for all countries outside the Western Hemisphere and one hundred and twenty thousand for those within. Admission was on a first come–first served basis, with the exception of close relatives of American citizens and scientists, artists, professional people, and workers who could fill shortages. Up to sixty thousand close relatives could come in, even if a country's quota had been reached.

Education.　One of Johnson's main goals was to improve the quality of education in the post-Sputnik world and to ensure that everyone could receive its benefits.

The Elementary and Secondary Education Act of 1965 contained more than $1 billion dollars in aid to education. It supplied funds to improve the schooling of poor children who were thought to be "educationally deprived."

Health.　In January 1965 Johnson proposed a compulsory hospital insurance program for elderly people. Known as Medicare, it included payment for hospitalization, nursing homes, and post-hospital care. A voluntary medical insurance plan for doctors' fees and surgical costs (the government paid part of them) was made available for $3 a month. Congress also passed a bill to control air and water pollution through the scientific disposal of waste.

Appalachia.　To revive this poverty-stricken area economically (it extends over eleven states in the Southeast), Congress voted $1 billion for roads, construction of health centers, and land improvement.

Cities.　Urban problems received much attention under Johnson's program. He created a Department of Housing and Urban Development and appointed Robert Weaver, a black housing expert, to head the department. Additionally, Congress passed a housing act that included the radical feature of having the federal government pay the rent of families who could not afford to live in low-income housing projects. The real objective of Johnson's program was to lessen the high human costs of intensive urbanization. This goal, however, had to wait for the second session of the Eighty-ninth Congress.

Minimum Wages.　Johnson proposed that the base pay of workers should increase to $1.40 by February 1967 and then to $1.60 by February 1968. A major break-through occurred when farm laborers, workers in small retail shops, and hospital workers, who had been systematically ex-cluded from all previous wage legislation, were brought under the umbrella of mini-mum-wage guarantees.

Food for Freedom.   The war on poverty caused a significant reversal in farm pol-icy. The government now encouraged farmers to increase their planted acreage. It also sharply reduced price supports and supported the planning of production with an eye to all domestic and foreign demands.

Civil Rights.   After the comprehensive bill of 1964, the Civil Rights Act of 1965 implemented an important part of voting rights. In those areas where 50 percent or more of the adults were unregistered or had not voted in the 1964 elections, all literacy tests and other voting qualifi-cations were suspended. A sixth-grade ed-ucation was considered a presumption of literacy, and the Attorney General could now send federal examiners into these areas to register qualified voters. Meanwhile, the Supreme Court held that the imposition of poll taxes was unconstitutional.

The Lesser Eighty-ninth.   A sharp change in the congressional attitude to-ward the Great Society occurred between 1965 and 1966. The off-year elections were looming in November 1966, and congress-men began to be concerned with the effects of their radical welfare programs. Presi-dent Johnson seemed to share their mood. He had become so focused on the war in

Vietnam that he could not work up his old enthusiasm for domestic reform, espe-cially for a program that had, along with the conflict, unleashed an inflation that destroyed the guidelines he himself had set for advances in prices and wages.

Defeated Legislation.   The result of this loss of heart was that the most far-reach-ing civil rights act yet conceived went down to defeat after considerable debate. The measure would have attacked the heart of the ghetto problem by making illegal racial discrimination in the sale or rental of dwellings in large housing and apartment developments. It would also have outlawed discriminatory juries.

Congress backed away from other re-forms as well. It refused to support labor's plea for abolition of section 14b from the Taft-Hartley Act (permitting states to pass "right-to-work" laws which opposed or banned the closed or union shop). Nor did it act on the President's requests for streamlining Congress, lengthening repre-sentatives' terms of office to four years, eliminating the electoral college, creating new machinery to deal with labor-man-agement disputes, and controlling the sale of firearms.

The Congressional Election of 1966. The results of the November election clearly supported Congress's reluctance to enact much of Johnson's program in the second session of the Eighty-ninth Con-gress. The Republicans enjoyed a resur-gence of power, gaining a number of con-gressional seats, winning twenty-three of the thirty-four contested governorships, and regaining control of several state leg-islatures that they had lost in 1964. More-over, the party seemed to have put aside the feelings of despair caused by Goldwater's defeat two years earlier; indeed, the Republicans optimistically talked of winning back the presidency. There were a number of reasons for the Democrats' defeat: "white backlash," the feeling by a large segment of the white population that too much was being done for blacks (in 1967 Johnson appointed the first black to the Supreme Court, Thurgood Marshall); the perception by many middle-class people that Johnson's program was moving the country too close to a welfare state; and growing concern over the Vietnam War, especially fears that the United States was becoming increasingly involved in a long-term military commitment with no foreseeable victory.

Foreign Policy

Latin America. In 1959 rebels led by Fidel Castro overthrew the Cuban dictator Fulgencio Batista. As Castro's left-wing program became apparent, the United States severed diplomatic and economic relations because of the disquieting prospect of a Communist state located only ninety miles from its own shore. The desire to prevent a similar occurrence elsewhere became the touchstone of United States policy in Latin America. Supplied with American weapons, a force of Cuban exiles attempted to invade Cuba, landing at the Bay of Pigs on the island's southern coast in April 1961. The operation was a disaster, and the invaders were forced to surrender. Their defeat dealt a serious blow to American prestige throughout the world, and President Kennedy accepted full responsibility. He did not, however,

soften his attitude toward Cuba, asserting that the United States would continue to resist "Communist penetration" in the hemisphere.

The nadir in American-Cuban relations during Kennedy's presidency came in October 1962 with the disclosure that the Russians were building missile bases in Cuba. The President ordered a blockade to prevent Soviet ships from entering the island's waters and demanded that the missile bases be dismantled and all weaponry capable of striking the United States removed. Kennedy threatened nuclear retaliation in the event of a nuclear-based attack from Cuba. After a few tense days, Soviet Premier Khrushchev retreated, announcing that he would dismantle the bases. By standing tough, Kennedy had won a striking victory. On the one hand, the resolution of the crisis led to a decrease in Cold War tensions. A "hot line" was established to permit the two leaders to communicate directly. Stalled nuclear-arms negotiations resumed, resulting in the Nuclear Test Ban Treaty of 1963, in which Britain, the United States, and the Soviet Union agreed to outlaw nuclear-weapons tests in the atmosphere. On the other hand, military hawks in the United States became more vocal, arguing that the showdown in Cuba showed the need for the United States to maintain its nuclear superiority. The hawks won a victory when Kennedy agreed to authorize the construction of one thousand Minuteman Intercontinental Ballistic Missiles (ICBMs), which gave the United States first-strike capability.

As President, Johnson continued Kennedy's policy of containing Communism in Latin America. Fearing a Castro-type takeover in the Dominican Republic, Johnson rushed a contingent of United States marines there, ostensibly to protect United States civilians. What resulted was a crude occupation by American forces who were unable to find the Communist revolutionaries supposedly preparing for the coup. In 1966 American troops were withdrawn, but not before Johnson lost some liberal support over his aggressive anti-Communism in Latin America.

Vietnam. A major encounter between the United States and Communist China seemed to be developing in Vietnam. With the defeat of the French at Dien Bien Phu in 1954, the Geneva Accord had divided Vietnam (formerly French Indochina) into northern (Communist) and southern (non-Communist) territories and called for national elections under neutral supervision. The United States had already intervened in this war by lending France millions of dollars and giving her special advisers, but Eisenhower, having foreseen where military intervention might lead, had wisely refrained from it. After the French left, America provided assistance to President Ngo Dinh Diem, who repudiated the elections and established himself as dictator. In response, the pro-Communist army in the south, the Vietcong, began an assault on Diem's government. They were aided by the Buddhists, who had also been alienated by Diem. President Kennedy then increased the military aid and dispatched the first United States combat troops to serve as "advisers." By the time of his assassination, the number of American military in Vietnam had risen from 3,200 to over 16,000. Shortly before Kennedy's death, Diem was also assassinated.

In August 1964 President Johnson disclosed that North Vietnamese torpedo boats had fired on an American destroyer in the Gulf of Tonkin. He demanded and easily obtained from the angry Congress authorization, in the Tonkin Gulf Resolution, to take "all necessary measures to repel any armed attack against the United States and to prevent further aggression." Having been given a blank check, Johnson sent in combat troops, assumed command of what was essentially a civil war, and permitted bombing of both South and North Vietnam. The American battle techniques included widespread napalm assaults, defoliation procedures, and tear gas attacks. By the end of 1965, 184,000 American troops were in Vietnam, and by 1968, 538,000. But the undeclared war persisted as American troops found it difficult to counter the guerrilla tactics of the Communists.

Domestic Reaction to the War. The Vietnam War profoundly divided the nation. On one side were the hawks, who saw American military involvement as necessary if all of Asia was to be saved from Communism. (According to the "domino theory," if Vietnam fell, the Communists would take over its neighbors, one by one.) On the other side were the doves, who believed that America had no business meddling in another country's civil war. The doves also argued that the corrupt South Vietnamese government hardly constituted a democracy, opposed American military actions from the enormous aerial bombardment of Vietnam to the use of defoliants like napalm (which harmed civilians and combatants alike) and to the murder of civilians by American troops. By 1970, with over 40,000 Americans dead, protests over the war reached their peak. As the war dragged on, it became clear to many that victory was impossible. But Johnson, following his generals and advisers, pressed on until he was almost totally obsessed by what was happening on the front.

The 1968 Election.   In November 1967 Minnesota's Senator Eugene McCarthy, a dove, announced his candidacy for the Democratic presidential nomination. But even he knew that if Johnson were in the running, there would be no way to wrest the nomination from him. Despite his unpopularity over the war, the President still retained to some degree the prestige of his domestic achievements. Now, however, events intervened to change the presidential race. Early in 1968 the North Vietnamese and Vietcong launched a surprise offensive, penetrating deep within South Vietnam. The situation became so desperate that American troops claimed they had to destroy towns and cities to save them from the Communists. The shock waves caused by the Tet Offensive reached America, arousing most people to resist the idea of any further escalation of United States involvement. In the New Hampshire primary, 42 percent of the Democratic voters chose McCarthy. Encouraged by these results, Robert F. Kennedy, the brother of President Kennedy, declared his candidacy. The political situation now swiftly changed. Johnson, sensing which way the wind was blowing, announced he would not run. Vice President Humphrey then declared his candidacy, although it was too late for him to enter the primaries. McCarthy and Kennedy each won several. But immediately after delivering a victory speech following the California race, Kennedy was assassinated by Sirhan Sirhan, a Palestinian immigrant. Kennedy's death

worked to Humphrey's advantage, and he easily defeated McCarthy at the Chicago Democratic Convention. Outside the convention hall, unarmed protesters were brutally attacked by Mayor Richard Daley's police. With most of the nation watching these events on TV, Humphrey's "politics of joy" evaporated.

In a far calmer atmosphere, the Republicans nominated Richard M. Nixon for president and Maryland Governor Spiro T. Agnew as his running mate. During the campaign Nixon reaped the benefits of the war's unpopularity while avoiding controversy. Humphrey, however, had to walk a fine line: he had to avoid alienating Johnson by disavowing the war, yet appease the antiwar demonstrators. The third-party candidacy of the anti–civil rights politician George Wallace presented another obstacle for him. Finally, in late September, Humphrey announced that if elected he would end the bombing of North Vietnam. Afterwards, Nixon's lead diminished. Nevertheless, he won narrowly in the popular vote. His victory margin was just five hundred thousand votes, but in the electoral college he scored a clear victory. The American people obviously wanted an end to war and a return to domestic peace.

Social Change

A Decade of Ferment.   The sixties were a time of great social ferment and turmoil. This period was characterized by the idealism of American youth attempting to re-create their values and form a just and ethical society. Yet it was also a time of violence, with the assassination of several major public figures, occasional violence by revolutionary sects, and the sometimes brutal acts of police and local militia to put down the demonstrations that were so widespread throughout the decade.

Many far-reaching movements for social change were initiated in the sixties: the women's rights movement has its roots there; blacks became more militant in their quest for full equality; the sexual revolution brought about a change in mores. It was students who were often at the forefront of these movements.

The Student Revolt. Between 1965 and 1968, as the Vietnam War escalated, students began to protest America's involvement in the war. The first student outburst occurred at the University of California at Berkeley in the fall of 1964. Forming the Free Speech Movement (FSM), small groups of students occupied university buildings to protest a prohibition on soliciting funds and volunteers for political causes on the campus. For two months the school remained in turmoil, as hundreds of angry students were arrested. Finally, the university capitulated, and the FSM won the right to free speech.

What caused student unrest, initially at Berkeley, then in colleges across the country? First, many students believed that American participation in the Vietnam War was immoral. Second, feeling frustrated by their inability to exert much influence on the outside power structure, they tried to stop any further university involvement with war-related research projects. Third, many of the protesting students were aware of being relatively affluent and able to avoid the draft, while millions of Americans were poor and burdened by the injustices of racism and had

to serve in Vietnam. Fourth, many of the more radical students had been initially involved with the Civil Rights Movement, but as blacks began to assume leadership of it, they looked for a new cause, and found one in the Vietnam War. These radical white students, sometimes joined by black peers, organized into groups like Students for a Democratic Society (SDS), and incited large groups of more moderate students to join teach-ins, sit-ins, and other tactics designed to disrupt university life. Protest over Vietnam led to actions over broader issues of university behavior.

The climax of student unrest came at Columbia University in 1968. Members of SDS and black students seized five university buildings, refusing to leave unless their "nonnegotiable" demands concerning the university's participation in secret military research and relations with neighborhood minorities were met. After eight days Columbia's President, Grayson Kirk, called in the police to clear out the students occupying the buildings. In the ensuing riot, the police clubbed the protesters as well as innocent bystanders, arresting seven hundred. After Columbia, students throughout the country escalated their confrontations with university authorities. Although in the end student protest alone did not end the war, it did change the way universities were run. Students were given a greater voice in the curriculum and in shaping their social and political life on campus.

The Cultural Revolution. During the sixties, young people's rebellion did not involve only political issues. They also challenged adult values in sex, clothing, hairstyles, and music. In an attempt to create a new life-style, members of the sixties counterculture experimented with communal living, used drugs such as marijuana and LSD, wore jeans, favored long hair, and listened to music by the Beatles, the Grateful Dead, and other groups. Led by Abbie Hoffman and Jerry Rubin, a movement called the "Yippies" (Youth International Party) ridiculed the materialism of American society as a way of motivating America's youth to become involved in political and social protest. In Woodstock, New York, over four hundred thousand young people attended a giant three-day rock concert that, according to observers, was the climax of the sixties Youth Movement and its commitment to peace, music, love, and sexual and drug experimentation.

Women's Liberation.   The climate of political and social protest encouraged American women to speak out with greater urgency for their rights. Radical women who joined the Civil Rights and student movements quickly learned that they were expected to be subordinate to the men. On the job, too, women faced discrimination: lower pay than men for the same work, less chance of rising to the top, and fewer occupations open to them. One of the earliest leaders of the women's movement was Betty Friedan. In her 1963 book *The Feminine Mystique*, she attempted to raise female consciousness by arguing that the limited, selfless role of housewife was filling American women with a dissatisfaction they couldn't even name. In 1966 Friedan and other feminists founded the National Organization for Women (NOW). The new group called for equal pay and equal employment for women, legalized abortion,

day-care centers, and an Equal Rights Amendment. NOW and other women's groups fought for the neutral word "Ms." to separate women's identity from their marital status. Not all women supported these efforts, however. Many felt that the women's liberation movement looked down on the housewife. But whatever their position or ideology, Americans of both sexes were affected directly or indirectly by the women's movement, both at home and in the workplace. It is due to the work of feminists, for example, that the Civil Rights Act of 1964 prohibited job discrimination on the basis of sex.

"Black Power."   The political gains of the Civil Rights Movement raised black expectations but frustration rose when their economic condition failed to improve significantly. Young blacks vented their anger in a series of devastating urban riots. One of the worst occurred in the Los Angeles ghetto of Watts in 1965, where for six days rioters looted and set fire to buildings. The summer of that year saw a wave of similar riots in New York, Chicago, Newark, and other cities. Black anger also led to a rift between the militant Student Nonviolent Coordinating Committee (SNCC) and the moderate SCLC. Stokely Carmichael, SNCC's new leader, called for black power (not white help) and advocated violence, if necessary, to obtain it. H. Rapp Brown, who succeeded Carmichael in 1967, suggested that a black crowd burn down Cambridge, Maryland. Huey Newton, a founder of another militant group, the Black Panthers, claimed that "political power comes through the barrel of a gun." The presence of such black militants on the scene caused the nonviolent King's prestige to decline somewhat among blacks who were impatient for change. Moreover, his opposition to the Vietnam War caused Johnson and conservative organizations like the NAACP to withdraw their support from him. King thereupon switched his focus from racism to poverty. But before he could lead a poor people's march to Washington, he was killed, in April 1968, by a white man, James Earl Ray, in Memphis, Tennessee. In over one hundred cities, blacks exploded in a frenzy of looting and burning. In the wake of these riots, American society became increasingly polarized according to race. Yet blacks emerged from the sixties with greater self-respect and a stronger racial identity. Black pride was more than a slogan as they reclaimed their cultural heritage and continued to press for full equality.

The Effect of Technology. Although the use of atomic energy for peaceful purposes was relatively rare compared to other energy sources such as oil, scientists recognized its enormous potential. By 1951 nuclear fuels had been used to produce electricity. Meanwhile, the development of the computer was beginning to revolutionize American society. Computers could collect and store huge amounts of data, solve complex mathematical prob-

lems, and speed up work in the factory and the office.

But the side effects of these and other technological advances were also starting to be felt. The use of nuclear energy raised the question of the possible effects of radiation. Many scientists said the danger was virtually nonexistent, but none could rule out entirely the possibility of nuclear accidents. Nor was anyone sure how to dispose safely of nuclear wastes. Another problem of which the public was only vaguely aware (if at all) was the proliferation of plastics and paper used in packaging products. These produced a veritable mountain of trash—much of it nonbiodegradable—that somehow had to be disposed of. Still another problem was that Americans relied heavily on petroleum to produce power, but burning it released pollutants into the atmosphere. In some cities like Los Angeles smog from industries and cars caused a variety of health problems ranging from minor eye and skin irritations to serious breathing difficulties. Chemical pollution of the waters was also a growing problem, and Rachel Carson's *Silent Spring* alerted Americans to the dangers of insecticides. Future generations of Americans were to pay a high price for the continued absence of a coordinated policy to deal with environmental issues.

CHAPTER TWENTY-FOUR

From Vietnam to Watergate

On August 9, 1974, Richard Nixon, his wife Pat, and their two daughters Julie and Tricia walked to a helicopter that would take them to the presidential plane waiting for them at Andrews Air Force Base. Before boarding the helicopter, Nixon turned to wave at the crowd. Then the door shut and the Nixons were off on the first leg of their journey to their home in San Clemente, California. While they were flying across the continent, Gerald Ford was being sworn in as president. The events leading to Nixon's disgraced departure from the White House were to affect deeply the moral tone of American politics in the following decade.

The Nixon Presidency

The "New" Nixon. In January 1969 Richard Nixon took office. Observers noted that the "new Nixon" seemed more moderate than the "old Nixon." The highly ambitious political animal had been replaced, they suggested, by the statesman. Nixon assembled a strong cab-

inet, leaving domestic affairs primarily in the hands of his top aides, H. R. Haldeman and John Ehrlichman, while devoting himself to foreign policy.

Triumph in Space. The Nixon administration opened on a triumphant note that increased national pride and optimism. Six months after the new President's inauguration, on July 16, 1969, astronaut Neil Armstrong became the first human being to set foot on the moon. Stepping onto its surface, he prophetically remarked, "That's one small step for man, one giant leap for mankind."

A Middle Course. In domestic affairs, Nixon, like Eisenhower, steered a middle course, seeking not to dismantle Johnson's programs, but to make them more efficient. In his Family Assistance Plan, he sought a minimum annual wage of $1600 for each poor family to be paid by the federal government. The Democratically controlled Congress, however, defeated the measure, citing the low level of payments. In other social areas, however, Nixon attempted to shift responsibility from the federal government to local authorities. He introduced the idea of revenue sharing, in which the federal government would give funds to state, county, and city agencies for local needs. In 1972 Congress allocated $30.1 billion for these purposes to be distributed over a five-year period.

Nixon refused to use his powers to enforce school desegregation unless ordered to by the courts. Meanwhile, he tried to shape a more conservative Court, appointing Warren Burger to replace the retiring Chief Justice Earl Warren. But Congress rejected two other Nixon nominees to fill another court vacancy, Clement Haynesworth of South Carolina and G. Harold Carswell of Florida. Nixon's third appointee, the more moderate Harry Blackmun, won confirmation. These and other appointments did accomplish Nixon's goal, although the Nixon court still supported desegregation and protected the rights of women to have abortions in its landmark *Roe v. Wade* decision of 1973.

Controlling Inflation. The inflationary economy, caused largely by Johnson's attempt to wage war without raising prices, was Nixon's most pressing domestic problem. To solve it, he cut government spending and balanced the budget while encouraging the Federal Reserve Board to force up interest rates to slow industrial expansion. Prices continued to rise, however, as did the trade deficit. In 1971 Nixon announced a ninety-day wage-and-price freeze and set a 10-percent surtax on all imports. These actions slowed inflation, and the surcharge, combined with a devaluation of the dollar, made American goods more competitive.

Foreign Policy

Ending the War. Nixon focused his attention mainly on ending the Vietnam conflict. Initially he proposed a phased withdrawal of Americans to be followed by internationally supervised elections. But the North Vietnamese responded by insisting on unconditional withdrawal. Nixon then decided to build up the South Vietnamese, so they could continue to conduct the war as Americans left. This strategy was called Vietnamization. In June 1969 the President announced the withdrawal of twenty-five thousand soldiers. Two months later he added twenty-five thousand more to be phased out by mid-December.

Nixon and the Protesters. American war protesters responded by keeping the pressure on Nixon. On October 15 demonstrators in cities across the nation participated in student-led antiwar demonstrations; in a second Moratorium Day, over two hundred and fifty thousand people gathered in Washington to protest the war. Nixon apparently remained unmoved. Troop withdrawal continued, but the war did also. In 1970 Americans learned to their horror of the 1968 massacre of nearly 350 civilians by American troops in the hamlet of My Lai 4. In April 1970 Nixon announced more troop reductions: within a year one hundred and fifty thousand Americans would be withdrawn. Yet a week later he stated that, because the Vietcong was consolidating its supply bases in neutral Cambodia, he was sending troops to destroy these bases. (The United States actually had widened the war into Cambodia in 1969 by secretly bombing supply lines there, but neither

Congress nor the public was aware of this until 1973.) Americans reacted to this escalation with massive antiwar protests. At Kent State University in Ohio, National Guardsmen fired on taunting students on May 4, killing four and wounding eleven. Two days later two black students were killed as a result of riots and protests at Jackson State University in Mississippi. Again the outcry stiffened Nixon's resolve to ignore the swelling criticism of what opponents called his unconstitutional and irresponsible actions in Vietnam. Both domestically and in Vietnam, the situation remained at a tense standstill until 1971.

Students and the Antiwar Movement. As they had in the Johnson years, young people assumed the leadership of the antiwar movement. Some students objected to any war, but the majority were opposed to a war waged against a small country on the other side of the world. As the war continued and more American soldiers returned home in body bags—with the horrifying images flashed across TV screens—student opposition grew, as did that of other Americans of all ages, classes, and races. Thousands of middle-class students continued to avoid the draft by remaining in college, while a smaller number fled to Canada to escape induction. Still others burned their draft cards in a more direct challenge to the war.

Détente. Nixon and National Security Adviser Henry Kissinger now seized the diplomatic initiative. In February 1972 they met with Chinese leaders in Peking. The Americans agreed to support Chinese admission to the United Nations and to begin cultural and economic exchanges between the two powers. Nixon's bold recognition of China received widespread support domestically and internationally. Then, in May, he and Kissinger negotiated a Strategic Arms Limitation Treaty (SALT) with the Russians in Moscow. The superpowers agreed to halt the production of nuclear missiles and reduce the size of their antinuclear missile arsenals to two hundred.

This new policy, called détente, or the relaxing of international tension, had its desired effect on North Vietnam. Realizing that it might be possible to negotiate with America and that they had failed to overrun South Vietnam, they agreed finally to make some concessions to get the United States out of the war. By October the participants had drafted a cease-fire and agreed to a plan for withdrawal of American troops and the return of American prisoners of war. With perfect timing, Kissinger announced before the 1972 presidential election that peace was "at hand."

Aftermath

The Election of 1972. Nixon defeated the Democratic candidate, the pro-peace Senator George McGovern of South Dakota, by a landslide, winning 60.8 percent of the popular vote. McGovern's campaign had been badly hurt by the revelation that his running mate Senator Thomas Eagleton of Missouri, had received electric shock treatments for emotional problems. The public subsequently questioned McGovern's judgment, and, by implication, his ability to run the country. The Democrat's liberal platform, including his advocacy of abortion, also hurt him with many voters who perceived him as too left-wing. Nor did Nixon's foreign policy triumphs help McGovern, who was inexperienced in that area.

To crown Nixon's triumph, in January 1973 an agreement was finally reached to end the Vietnam War. The North Vietnamese received a large portion of South Vietnam, and American prisoners of war were to be released in sixty days. Almost forty-six thousand Americans had died, and over three hundred thousand were wounded; $109 billion had been spent on the first war the United States had lost. Nevertheless, Nixon's prestige was at its height. He had gotten Americans out of the Vietnam quagmire.

Watergate. During the 1972 election campaign, Nixon, fearing further leaks about the United States' bombing of Cambodia, ordered the telephones of reporters and the staff of Kissinger's National Security Council to be wiretapped. Nevertheless, the *New York Times* and the *Washington Post* started to publish the Classified Defense Department Study of the Vietnam War (which the press dubbed the Pentagon Papers). The President went even further in trying to plug the leak. His aides created a "plumbers" unit, directed inside the White House by former FBI agent G. Gordon Liddy and CIA veteran E. Howard Hunt. In an unsuccessful attempt to embarrass Daniel Ellsberg, the former Defense Department official who had leaked the Pentagon Papers, they broke into the office of his psychiatrist. Unsure that Nixon would win reelection, White House staffers used whatever means they could muster, some of them illegal, to defeat McGovern. Forming the Committee to Reelect the President (headed by Attorney

General John Mitchell), specialists in dirty tricks harassed the Democrats. Then Liddy decided to bug the Democratic National Convention headquarters in the Watergate complex in Washington. On June 17 James McCord and several other "burglars" were caught by police during their break-in. When Nixon denied any responsibility in the matter, most people believed him. They did not know that he had previously ordered that the FBI be kept out of the case and had instructed his aides to lie under oath if the situation called for it.

Nixon and the Cover-up. Initially there seemed no need for such elaborate measures. Although convicted for their part in the burglary, Hunt and Liddy did not talk. But everything changed when Judge John Sirica imposed long prison terms on the burglars. One of them, James McCord, wrote a note to Sirica, claiming that the White House had paid him and promised a pardon if he kept silent. A subsequent string of embarrassing revelations led Nixon to dismiss White House Counsel John Dean. His dismissal was followed by the resignations of Haldeman, Erlichman, and Attorney General Richard Kleindienst (his predecessor, John Mitchell, had also resigned as a result of related revelations).

Next, the Senate appointed a special committee, under the chairmanship of Sam Erwin, Jr., of North Carolina, to investigate the scandal. During his week-long testimony, Dean implicated the President in the cover-up. Nixon's position became even more vulnerable when it was revealed that he had systematically taped White House conversations and phone calls. The committee requested the tapes, hoping they would reveal the extent of the President's knowledge. At first Nixon, invoking executive privilege, refused to release them. Some people began to call for his resignation.

Nixon now made his situation worse by refusing to turn over the tapes to Archibald Cox, whom he had appointed to the office of Special Prosecutor to investigate the affair. Cox got a subpoena from Judge Sirica ordering Nixon to comply with his request. While the case was going through the courts, the beleaguered President ordered Attorney General Elliot Richardson to fire Cox, but Richardson refused and resigned instead. Solicitor General Robert Bork then dismissed the special prosecutor on Saturday, October 20. The Saturday Night Massacre, as it was called, outraged the public, and many demanded Nixon's impeachment. With no other options left, he handed over the tapes, although later it was revealed that some were missing and a critical section of one had been erased.

Resignation. In the summer of 1974, the House Judiciary Committee (led by Peter Rodino of New Jersey), which had been empowered to investigate the affair, decided to conduct public meetings. Afterwards, the committee adopted three articles of impeachment. Rather than face this process, Nixon resigned on August 8. The next day Vice President Gerald Ford became the new president of the United States. The Michigan congressman and House minority leader had been selected by Nixon to replace Vice President Spiro Agnew, who, charged with federal income-tax evasion for accepting payoffs from construction companies while governor of Maryland and during his vice presidency, had resigned in October 1973, to secure immunity from further criminal prosecution and a possible jail term. Bowed but unrepentant, Nixon left the White House. The President was gone, but the system he had attempted to circumvent had survived.

CHAPTER TWENTY-FIVE

America at the End of the Century

When Republican Senator Pete Domenici urged Ronald Reagan to raise taxes, the President replied, "I'm just not going to accept this. This is just more of the same kind of talk we've heard for forty years." During his presidency, Reagan tried to alter the economic course of the United States, and to a large extent succeeded, moving it away from the policies of the New Deal. The effects of the Reagan Revolution are still with us today.

The Ford Presidency (1974–77)

Ford and Congress. Solid and unimaginative, Ford nevertheless lacked Nixon's fatal flaws of secrecy, insecurity, and mistrust. Amiable, open, and unafraid of public scrutiny, he also believed, as a former congressman from Michigan, that the executive must cooperate with the legislative branch of government. Yet the new President got off to a bad start when, in an effort to end the bitterness of Watergate, he pardoned Nixon "for any crime he may have committed in office." Since

Nixon had not even admitted any guilt, Ford's action after only one month in office made it seem to many as if a deal had been worked out before Nixon's resignation. Many Americans also found it hard to accept that the former President could "get off" while his three closest advisers (Haldeman, Erlichman, and Mitchell) were being tried for their part in the scandal. Resentment flared even higher when the three were convicted and imprisoned.

Ford's dealings with Congress did little to redeem his image of ineptitude. More conservative than Nixon, he vetoed over thirty-nine bills. His record on the economy was similarly weak. His method of dealing with inflation was to ask people to wear buttons expressing their desire to combat it. Afterwards, when unemployment rose sharply by 9 percent and production declined, Ford had to ask for tax cuts to stimulate business.

The Democrats reacted with glee when Ford announced that he would seek the presidency in 1976. His weak record and Republican vulnerability over Watergate made him an easy target. In the Republican primaries, former movie actor and

California governor Ronald Reagan, the candidate of the party's right wing, mounted a strong campaign. The Republicans nominated Ford by a narrow margin at their convention in August.

To oppose him the Democrats chose former Georgia governor Jimmy Carter. A former naval officer and peanut grower, Carter ran as an outsider who, unlike Ford, was untainted by Washington politics. Open and candid, he constantly referred to his honesty and deep religious convictions. It did not hurt him either that as a Southerner, he had accorded blacks respect during his governorship. Carter won the election by a slim margin, 297 electoral votes to 241. While Ford won easily in the West, Carter carried most of the South and key industrial states. An overwhelming majority of blacks also voted for him rather than Ford, whom they perceived as unsympathetic to the poor.

The Carter Presidency (1977–81)

Foreign and Domestic Policy. In foreign affairs Carter advocated "the defense of basic human rights," and he scored several diplomatic triumphs. He negotiated treaties with Panama to gradually turn over the Canal to that country. After a lengthy debate (conservatives disliked the idea of "giving up" the canal), the Senate approved the treaties in 1978. Carter also ended recognition of Taiwan and began the exchange of ambassadors with mainland China. He then negotiated another Strategic Arms Limitation Treaty (SALT II) with the Soviets, limiting the two superpowers to twenty-four hundred nuclear warheads apiece.

In an effort to bring peace to the troubled Middle East, he invited Egyptian President Anwar Sadat and Israeli Prime Minister Menachem Begin to come to negotiate a peace treaty at Camp David, the presidential retreat. Due largely to Carter's patience, the two nations signed a document (the so-called Camp David Agreement) in which Israel agreed to withdraw from Egyptian land it had captured in the Six-Day War of 1967. In return, Egypt became the first Arab country to recognize Israel.

Domestically Carter fared more poorly. Surrounding himself with fellow Georgians who, like himself, were inexperienced in the ways of Washington, he proved ineffective in pushing his legislation through Congress. If Congress opposed a particular domestic policy, Carter often dropped it. The President was not the only one who was frustrated. Many Americans were concerned about the deterioration of cities. Rising crime rates, in the older cities especially, decaying public transportation, and overcrowded schools contributed to a sense of hopelessness that the government seemingly did nothing to alleviate. Nor did Carter appear to be able to deal with the double-digit inflation that was gripping the country. When Congress raised the minimum wage to help workers at the lowest rung, the benefits were offset because the inflation continued to rise. To check the inflationary spiral, Carter named the fiscally conservative banker Paul A. Volcker as chairman of the Federal Reserve Board. Volcker believed that by tightening the money supply, he could stop the upward spiral. His tight-money policy caused interest rates, which were already high, to rise even higher. The

Board's policies led to a recession. By July 1980 unemployment was at 7.8 percent.

The Iranian Hostage Crisis. Carter's fortunes reached their lowest ebb with the Iranian crisis. The Shah of Iran, Mohamad Reza Pahlavi, was a strong American ally, but disliked by his people for his attempts to introduce western ideas and practices as well as for his despotism. When the exiled religious leader the Ayatollah Khomeini led a successful fundamentalist Moslem revolt in 1979 against the Shah, the deposed ruler fled the country. A month after Carter permitted him to enter the United States for medical treatment in October, angry Iranian mobs besieged the embassy of the "Great Satan," as they called the United States, and held fifty-eight Americans hostage. The Iranians promised to release the prisoners only if the United States returned the Shah to Iran (to be tried for his crimes) and released his assets in American banks. Carter refused to return the Shah, froze Iranian assets, and prohibited trade with Iran until the hostages were freed. The United States found itself virtually helpless in breaking the stalemate, a fact that some observers saw as a sign of the decline in American power during the 1970s. In April 1980 Carter decided to fly commandos into Iran by helicopter to rescuc the hostages, but the raid failed dismally. The hostage crisis was still unresolved by the time of the 1980 elections.

The Failure of Détente. Carter's support for human rights added to the friction between Russia and America. The Soviets were angered by his criticism of their treatment of dissidents and their refusal to let Russian Jews leave the country. They believed that Carter was singling them out while ignoring the repressive policies of American allies such as South Korea and the Philippines. A second blow to détente came in December 1979, when Russian troops entered Afghanistan to aid rebels in overthrowing the government. Carter responded by barring the shipment of grain and advanced technology to the Soviets and by withdrawing the SALT II treaty from Senate consideration. In another show of protest, the United States boycotted the 1980 Olympics in Moscow.

Détente also received a cool reception from some powerful people within the administration, such as National Security Adviser Zbigniew Brzezinski. He persuaded Carter to press for the new MX missile system to replace the existing Minuteman missiles, which Brzezinski believed were vulnerable to a Soviet first strike. The MX (together with the planned Trident submarine) advanced the arms race.

The Election of 1980. During the primaries Carter defeated his main rival, President Kennedy's youngest brother Senator Edward Kennedy of Massachusetts. At their convention the Republicans nominated sixty-nine-year-old Ronald Reagan. Originally a New Deal Democrat, the ex-actor had moved increasingly to the right. As president of the Screen Actors Guild from 1947 to 1952, he waged a bitter fight against alleged Communist influence in the film industry. During his two terms as California governor, he delegated authority, preferring to let others handle the nitty gritty while he set the ideological tone of his administrations. (He was to do the same as president.) During the campaign Reagan's optimism, charm, good humor, and unflappability appealed to voters in comparison with Carter's more driven personality. The Californian won the election handily, carrying forty-four states and 51 percent of the popular vote. Reagan did especially well in the Sunbelt and stole some voters from the old Democratic coalition: Jews and blue-collar workers. During Carter's last weeks in office, the hostage crisis was finally resolved. War with Iraq had severely strained Iran's economy, making the need for its frozen assets urgent. Using Algeria as an intermediary, Iran agreed to release the hostages in exchange for the return of these assets. On the day of Reagan's inauguration, January 20, the fifty-two hostages were freed after 444 days in captivity.

The Reagan Presidency (1981–89)

Reagan's First Term (1981–85). Once in office Reagan acted decisively to end inflation, cut Federal involvement in social welfare programs, and beef up America militarily. The implementation of these policies came to be dubbed "Reaganomics." Early in his first term the President persuaded Congress to lower taxes by 215 percent over three years and to reduce social services such as food stamps and welfare "handouts." Reagan was simply following "supply-side economics," his advisers explained. According to supporters of this theory, the public would invest the money saved from taxes in business rather than in consumer items, and this would then lead to increased production, more jobs, prosperity, and more tax-

able incomes. Support for the new President and his programs rose after a deranged young man, John W. Hinckley, Jr., shot him in Washington on March 30, 1981. Reagan's calmness and humor throughout his ordeal impressed many Americans as did his ability to recover swiftly at his age. So great was his popularity that he came to be known as the "Teflon" president—no criticism could stick to him or mar his popularity.

Most economists felt that Reaganomics was a modern version of Hooverism, and just as unworkable. Their predictions seemed to be validated by the depression which hit the country at the end of 1982, leaving 10 percent of the workers unemployed. Another discouraging sign was that the annual budget deficit was rising. In 1980 it was $59 billion; in 1983, $195 billion. Yet, just as criticism began to mount, the economy began to show signs of recovery. Inflation decreased to 4 percent, permitting the Federal Reserve Board to relax its tight-money policy a bit. The resulting lower interest rates encouraged increased consumption. By 1984 unemployment declined to below 8 percent.

But if Americans were spending money on consumer items, this also meant that they were not, as Reagan had predicted, investing in business. This and the escalating military budget prevented interest rates from falling further and caused economists to still worry about inflation. Therefore, even Reagan's advisers tried to persuade him to cut military spending and increase taxes. He refused. In his view the Soviet Union was an "evil empire" to be stopped at any cost. The Communists, he claimed, were supplying arms and money to Nicaragua's leftist government and to rebels in El Salvador. Acting on his belief that Communists respected the use or show of force, Reagan sent troops into the Caribbean island of Grenada to topple its military government in October 1983. After the humiliations of Vietnam and Iran, the American public approved Reagan's decision and its triumphant outcome.

Women in Government. Throughout his first term (and his second), Reagan opposed both legalized abortion and the Equal Rights Amendment to the Constitution, which would ban discrimination based on sex. His opposition did not prevent him from appointing women to positions within the government. His biggest achievement in this area was the nomination of Sandra Day O'Connor to the Supreme Court in 1981—she became the first woman to sit on the Court. But the number of women and minority appointees was still lower than it had been during Carter's presidency.

The Election of 1984. After a lengthy and hard-fought series of primaries, the Democrats chose Carter's Vice President, Walter Mondale of Minnesota, as their nominee and, in a bold move, New York Congresswoman Geraldine Ferraro as his running mate, the first woman to run on a national ticket. The Democrats criticized Reagan for creating an enormous deficit and risking war with Russia by his aggressive stance, but his immense popularity, coupled with the sense of most voters, that the country was prosperous, made him unbeatable. In his bid for reelection Reagan received even greater popular support than in his first campaign, winning almost 60 percent of the popular vote and 525 of the electoral votes.

Reagan's Second Term (1985–89). Despite Reagan's aggressive anti-Communism, Soviet-American relations began to improve slowly, mostly due to the influence of Russia's new premier, Mikhail S. Gorbachev, who assumed office in March of 1985. Impelled by the need to revitalize his nation's economy, the innovative and vigorous Gorbachev originated the policies of *glasnost* (openness) and *perestroika* (restructuring) and declared his intention to honor SALT II although it had never been ratified by Congress. Reagan belligerently replied that the Russians had not previously honored it and he did not trust them to start doing so now. He then asked Congress for funds to develop a computerized, space-based defense system, which critics ironically called Star Wars (after a space adventure movie of the same name), to defend against a first strike by Soviet missiles. The immense costs involved in creating such a program and its questionable usefulness caused Star Wars to remain an idea rather than a reality during his presidency.

Political terrorism, which had grown around the world in recent decades, was on Reagan's agenda. He adopted a tough policy in dealing with terrorists.

In October 1985 several Arab terrorists seized the Italian cruise ship *Achille Lauro* in the Eastern Mediterranean, killing an American tourist and demanding that Israel free fifty jailed Palestinians. They surrendered to Egypt when that country promised to fly them to Libya, whose prime minister, Muammar Qaddafi, was an outspoken enemy of Israel and the United States as well as a supporter of terrorists. Reagan ordered navy jets to intercept the Egyptian airliner transporting the terrorists and force the pilot to land in Italy, and the terrorists were arrested there. Reagan again flexed America's muscles after the bombing of a West German club where American servicemen congregated. Suspecting that Libya was behind the attack, he ordered an air strike against Libyan bases to show the United States' resolve to retaliate against terrorism. The April 1986 bombings succeeded in their military objective. (A young child of Qaddafi's was also killed in the raid.) Tired of and frustrated by terrorism, Americans supported Reagan's show of force, although the nation's European allies worried about where his aggressiveness might lead.

Reagan now focused on events in the Soviet Union and began to realize that the Russians might be sincere in their stated desire for arms reduction. In October 1986 he and Gorbachev met in Iceland to discuss these issues. The meeting ended in failure, after Reagan stubbornly adhered to his plans for Star Wars. But, at a second Icelandic summit in 1988, the two leaders signed a treaty eliminating medium-range missiles.

On the domestic front, Reagan supported the Income Tax Act of 1986, reducing the highest levy on personal incomes from 50 to 28 percent and on corporate profits from 46 to 34 percent. The bill also removed most tax shelters used by corporations and the wealthy, while allowing six million people with low incomes not to pay any taxes. Nevertheless, the bill essentially aided the wealthy by being the first income tax to depart from the principle of progressive taxation in which people with higher incomes were required to pay a greater percentage of their income than those with lower incomes.

Reagan also attempted, by appointing conservatives to federal judgeships, to reduce the federal government's intervention in social welfare issues. After Chief Justice Burger resigned in 1986, the President appointed an extremely conservative associate justice, William H. Rehnquist, to the position of chief justice, and the equally conservative Antonin Scalia as associate justice. A year later, however, the Senate rejected Reagan's ultra-conservative nominee Robert Bork, (a somewhat controversial figure who had, as Nixon's Solicitor General, discharged Archibald Cox, the Watergate special prosecutor) to replace retiring Justice Lewis F. Powell. Finally, the less controversial but still conservative Anthony Kennedy was confirmed without opposition.

The New Immigrants. During the 1970s four million immigrants, mainly from Latin America and Asia, had entered the United States. Throughout the 1980s this influx continued unabated. Many immigrants entered illegally (they were called "undocumented aliens"), primarily by crossing the Mexican border. Some of these refugees were fleeing for their lives from countries such as El Salvador, Haiti, Colombia, and Vietnam where government repression or revolutionary violence endangered many people. In cities across the country, these new immigrants crowded together in ethnic ghettos. Those who were illegal worried constantly about being deported back to their country of origin. To help them and to simplify an almost impossible bureaucratic tangle, in 1986 Congress passed a law granting amnesty to illegal aliens who had resided in the country before a certain date. The measure also penalized employers who hired illegals after the law went into effect.

Social and Economic Problems. The Reagan era saw a rise in crime rates, largely as the result of an increase in drug-related offenses. A cheap form of cocaine called crack became widely used, with devastating social and economic consequences. Hospitals and social workers, for instance, began to see crack-addicted babies born to addicted mothers. The government responded by pressuring drug-producing countries such as Peru and Colombia to stop growing such crops and to jail the leaders of drug cartels. Critics argued that fighting crime and the drug cartels was not the answer, that the government was not doing enough to prevent drug abuse.

The same criticism was leveled against the administration because of its tardy, and many felt inadequate, efforts to deal with the crisis engendered by the spread of a new and deadly disease, the acquired immune deficiency syndrome (AIDS). Caused by a virus that destroys the body's immune system, AIDS was inevitably fatal. In the beginning of the AIDS crisis, which reached epidemic proportions in the eighties, the majority of victims were homosexuals, but since the virus is transmitted by the exchange of bodily fluids, intravenous drug users (who frequently share needles) and their sexual partners have become increasingly at risk. Children born to a mother with AIDS are also at great risk of being born with the disease.

Still another problem during the eighties was the growing number of homeless people who roamed the streets of American cities. Again, critics charged that there

was no coherent government policy to deal with the problem, which stemmed partially from a lack of affordable housing. Nor did Reagan offer any solutions to other poverty-related problems such as regional decline, the continued deterioration of inner cities, and the existence of large pockets of entrenched poverty.

Changes in Business and the Workplace. In the financial world, Reagan's deregulatory policies and nonsupport of antitrust laws spurred another kind of epidemic, that of mergers and acquisitions. Using borrowed funds, a company was able to buy other companies; a smaller company could even buy a larger one. Unfortunately the new, combined company often had to shoulder the heavy debts incurred in financing the takeover. (Even if a company successfully fought off a takeover, it would be left with the burden of having to pay the enormous legal and advisory costs involved.) Another trend throughout the decade was the increased reliance on advanced technology, including computers and automatic machinery, in the workplace. In a number of fields, this resulted in a need for fewer workers and, consequently, a decline in union membership. The unions also suffered a major defeat at the hands of the President when air traffic controllers illegally walked off their jobs to press their demands for wages and benefits. Reagan ordered them back to work and, following their refusal, filled more than 1,100 of their jobs, establishing programs to train the replacements. Reagan's firmness caused the strike to collapse, and he subsequently refused to rehire any of the strikers. The union never recovered, and labor's power was seen as diminished during the rest of his time in office.

These changes continued the shift in the United States from a manufacturing to a service- and information-based economy. Finally, Reagan's tax reductions, coupled with his resistance to raising taxes, helped create a national debt nearing $3 trillion.

The Environment. The previous administrations had moved toward tougher enforcement of environmental protection. Reagan reversed these policies, easing industrial antipollution laws, allowing greater private development of resources on public lands, and appointing top officials to the Environmental Protection Agency who, environmentalists charged, were lax in enforcing hazardous-waste laws and were too close to polluters. Increasing attacks of this nature prompted the resignation of Secretary of the Interior James Watt in 1985, and his replacement by a more neutral Republican, William Clark.

The Iran-Contra Affair. In 1979 Nicaraguan rebels called Sandinistas overthrew dictator Anastasio Somoza, replacing him with a Sandinista-led leftist government. The existence of such a government in Latin America moved Reagan to support the Contras, a group of insurgents seeking to depose the new regime. In 1981 Congress allowed the President to provide arms to the Contras, whom he called "freedom fighters." But even with this support, the Contras made virtually no headway in Nicaragua, where they lacked popular support. Moreover, many Americans, remembering Vietnam, did not want to assist them for fear that the outcome might be full-scale United States involvement. As these feelings mounted, Congress

passed the Boland Amendment in 1984, prohibiting further military assistance to the Contras. The President, so critics charged, then tried to solicit private funds to keep them going.

Marine Colonel Oliver North, an aide to National Security Adviser Admiral John Poindexter, directed the administration's effort to raise arms for the Contras. The war between Iran and Iraq, begun in 1980, offered some possibility of obtaining money to buy weapons for the Contras and to gain the release as well of Americans held hostage in Lebanon by terrorists. Desperate for arms, the Iranians were willing to do business even with the hated Americans. Thus, Reagan decided to permit an indirect shipment of weapons to Iran via Israel. When no hostages were released, he went so far as to authorize the secret sale of arms directly to Iran. The reason for the secrecy was the knowledge that the American public, still outraged over the hostage crisis during Carter's administration, would refuse to condone bargaining with terrorists or Iran. Colonel North used $12 million of the profits from the Iranian weapons sale to provide arms for the Contras, thereby violating the Boland Amendment; but he kept Poindexter advised of his activities. In November 1989 news of these dealings leaked out. Poindexter resigned, North was dismissed, and a special prosecutor, Lawrence E. Walsh, was appointed to investigate the affair. Reagan denied any knowledge about such aid to the Contras, but most Americans didn't believe him. Nevertheless, his great personal popularity remained untouched until he left office.

The Election of 1988. The Republicans nominated Vice President George Bush as their presidential candidate, and he picked the young and extremely conservative Senator Dan Quayle of Indiana, who he thought would appeal to young voters and those concerned that Bush was not a true conservative, as his running mate. After a series of primary battles, the Democratic race narrowed to a contest between Governor Michael Dukakis of Massachusetts and black leader Jesse Jackson, who was running for a second time. Although Jackson, the first black to try to win the presidential nomination of a major party, was the more charismatic candidate, his very progressive politics frightened many Democrats and Dukakis, a liberal in the more traditional Democratic mold, emerged the victor. Still, Jackson's "rainbow coalition"—his attempt to attract voters across all racial and social boundaries—gained more white votes this time than it had in 1984. As his vice president, the liberal Dukakis chose the Senator from Texas, Lloyd Bentsen to balance the ticket between North and South and liberal and conservative. In a dirty campaign which kept Dukakis on the defensive, Bush forces charged him with being unpatriotic and weak on crime. Dukakis's attempts to capitalize on his administrative efficiency failed to excite the voters. Bush won easily, with 426 electoral votes and 54 percent of the popular vote.

The Bush Presidency (1989–   )

A Changing World. The Bush presidency has been dominated by a stunning change in international affairs. Because of Gorbachev's refusal to intervene militarily—as his predecessors had done—in their affairs, the nations of Eastern Europe deposed their Communist leaders with seemingly dizzying speed and began to move toward democratization and free-market economies. (The Soviets have been tougher with the Baltic republics, who have pressed for their own independence.) With the exception of Romania, these revolutions were accomplished peacefully. Moreover, the two Germanys, divided since the end of World War II, have started the process of unification.

These astonishing changes were allowed to come about primarily because the Soviet leadership recognized that their economy was in terrible shape and that the huge expenditures involved in keeping up the Cold War could be better used to shore the nation up. The Soviet Union, too, appears to be moving toward a free-market economy.

In China, the situation was quite different. The conservative members of the ruling elite were able to exert their power over more liberal voices. Government troops crushed the huge student-led pro-democracy demonstrations in Beijing's Tiananmen Square in June 1989. Bush responded to the government's actions by removing China from most-favored trade status and publicly condemning the repression. Critics contended that these steps were too mild.

One of Bush's major challenges has been in the Persian Gulf. Faced with the invasion of Kuwait by Iraq, under the leadership of President Saddam Hussein, the United States created an international alliance to launch a military offensive, which resulted in Iraq's withdrawal from Kuwait.

On the domestic front, the Bush administration has reaped some benefits from the thawing of the Cold War. The President's popularity has soared. Even the reversal of his campaign pledge not to raise taxes has failed to erode his popularity. The need to trim the deficit is not the only explanation of this reversal on taxes. The enormous savings-and-loan scandal (the nation's most costly financial debacle) is another. The roots of the scandal lie in the deregulation by Carter and Reagan of the nation's savings-and-loan institutions. This permitted Wall Street junk bonders (those who sold high-risk bonds) and money brokers to combine with Sunbelt savings-and-loans to provide a privileged elite with huge sums of easy money. A tidal wave of speculative excess and greed ended in the bankruptcy of many of these institutions. Since all money in such banks is federally insured, the government must now pay back the losses to people with accounts in those that failed. It is estimated that the savings-and-loan bailout will cost at least $500 billion, or $2000 each for every American man, woman, and child. Finally, a number of other domestic issues confront the American people as they near the end of the century. The struggle over the rights of women to legal abortions has intensified during the Bush presidency, as has that over the controversial "right to die" issue, which involves the question of whether terminally ill patients may choose to end life-sustaining medical support and, if they are mentally incapacitated, whether others may make that choice for them.

As the Western European countries move closer to uniting into one economic community, as Eastern Europe continues to move toward democracy, and as Japan continues its ascendancy in the East, the United States will be faced with the challenge of dealing with this new international, political, and economic order.

Presidents of the United States

1. George Washington—1789–1797
2. John Adams—1797–1801
3. Thomas Jefferson—1801–1809
4. James Madison—1809–1817
5. James Monroe—1817–1825
6. John Quincy Adams—1825–1829
7. Andrew Jackson—1829–1837
8. Martin Van Buren—1837–1841
9. William Henry Harrison—1841
10. John Tyler—1841–1845
11. James Knox Polk—1845–1849
12. Zachary Taylor—1849–1850
13. Millard Fillmore—1850–1853
14. Franklin Pierce—1853–1857
15. James Buchanan—1857–1861
16. Abraham Lincoln—1861–1865
17. Andrew Johnson—1865–1869
18. Ulysses Simpson Grant—1869–1877
19. Rutherford Birchard Hayes—1877–1881
20. James Abram Garfield—1881
21. Chester Alan Arthur—1881–1885
22. Grover Cleveland—1885–1889
23. Benjamin Harrison—1889–1893
24. Grover Cleveland—1893–1897
25. William McKinley—1897–1901
26. Theodore Roosevelt—1901–1909
27. William Howard Taft—1909–1913
28. Woodrow Wilson—1913–1921
29. Warren Gamaliel Harding—1921–1923
30. Calvin Coolidge—1923–1929
31. Herbert Clark Hoover—1929–1933
32. Franklin Delano Roosevelt—1933–1945
33. Harry S Truman—1945–1953
34. Dwight David Eisenhower—1953–1961
35. John Fitzgerald Kennedy—1961–1963
36. Lyndon Baines Johnson—1963–1969
37. Richard Milhous Nixon—1969–1974
38. Gerald Rudolph Ford—1974–1977
39. Jimmy Carter—1977–1981
40. Ronald Wilson Reagan—1981–1989
41. George Bush—1989–

The Constitution of the United States

We the People of the United States, in Order to form a more perfect Union, establish Justice, insure domestic Tranquility, provide for the common defence, promote the general Welfare, and secure the Blessings of Liberty to ourselves and our Posterity, do ordain and establish this CONSTITUTION for the United States of America.

Article I

Section 1. All legislative Powers herein granted shall be vested in a Congress of the United States, which shall consist of a Senate and House of Representatives.
Section 2. The House of Representatives shall be composed of Members chosen every second Year by the People of the several States, and the Electors in each State shall have the Qualifications requisite for Electors of the most numerous Branch of the State Legislature.

No Person shall be a Representative who shall not have attained to the Age of twenty-five Years, and been seven Years a Citizen of the United States, and who shall not, when elected, be an Inhabitant of that State in which he shall be chosen.

Representatives and direct Taxes shall be apportioned among the several States which may be included within this Union, according to their respective Numbers, which shall be determined by adding to the whole Number of free Persons, including those bound to Service for a Term of Years, and excluding Indians not taxed, three fifths of all other Persons. The actual Enumeration shall be made within three Years after the first Meeting of the Congress of the United States, and within every subsequent Term of ten Years, in such Manner as they shall by Law direct. The Number of Representatives shall not exceed one for every thirty Thousand, but each State shall have at Least one Representative; and until such enumeration shall be made, the State of New Hampshire shall be entitled to chuse three, Massachusetts eight, Rhode-Island and Providence Plantations one, Connecticut five, New York six, New Jersey four, Pennsylvania eight, Delaware one, Maryland six,

Virginia ten, North Carolina five, South Carolina five, and Georgia three.

When vacancies happen in the Representation from any State, the Executive Authority thereof shall issue Writs of Election to fill such Vacancies.

The House of Representatives shall chuse their Speaker and other Officers, and shall have the sole Power of Impeachment.

Section 3. The Senate of the United States shall be composed of two Senators from each State, chosen by the Legislature thereof, for six Years; and each Senator shall have one Vote.

Immediately after they shall be assembled in Consequence of the first Election, they shall be divided as equally as may be into three Classes. The Seats of the Senators of the first Class shall be vacated at the Expiration of the second Year, of the second Class at the Expiration of the fourth Year, and of the third Class at the Expiration of the sixth Year, so that one-third may be chosen every second Year; and if Vacancies happen by Resignation, or otherwise, during the Recess of the Legislature of any State, the Executive thereof may make temporary Appointments until the next Meeting of the Legislature, which shall then fill such Vacancies.

No Person shall be a Senator who shall not have attained to the Age of thirty Years, and been nine Years a Citizen of the United States, and who shall not, when elected, be an Inhabitant of that State in which he shall be chosen.

The Vice President of the United States shall be President of the Senate, but shall have no vote, unless they be equally divided.

The Senate shall chuse their other Officers, and also a President pro tempore, in the absence of the Vice President, or when he shall exercise the Office of the President of the United States.

The Senate shall have the sole Power to try all Impeachments. When sitting for that purpose, they shall be on Oath or Affirmation. When the President of the United States is tried, the Chief Justice shall preside: And no person shall be convicted without the Concurrence of two thirds of the Members present.

Judgment in Cases of Impeachment shall not extend further than to removal from Office, and disqualification to hold and enjoy any Office of honor, Trust, or Profit under the United States: but the Party convicted shall nevertheless be liable and subject to Indictment, Trial, Judgment, and Punishment, according to Law.

Section 4. The Times, Places and Manner of holding Elections for Senators and Representatives, shall be prescribed in each state by the Legislature thereof; but the Congress may at any time by Law make or alter such Regulations, except as to the Places of Chusing Senators.

The Congress shall assemble at least once in every Year, and such Meeting shall be on the first Monday in December, unless they shall by Law appoint a different Day.

Section 5. Each House shall be the Judge of the Elections, Returns and Qualifications of its own Members, and a Majority of each shall constitute a Quorum to do Business; but a smaller number may adjourn from day to day, and may be authorized to compel the Attendance of absent Members, in such Manner, and under such Penalties, as each House may provide.

Each House may determine the Rules of its Proceedings, punish its Members for disorderly Behavior, and, with the Concurrence of two thirds, expel a Member.

Each House shall keep a Journal of its Proceedings, and from time to time publish the same, excepting such Parts as may in their Judgment require Secrecy; and the Yeas and Nays of the Members of either House on any question shall, at the Desire of one fifth of those Present, be entered on the Journal.

Neither House, during the Session of Congress, shall, without the Consent of the other, adjourn for more than three days, nor to any other Place than that in which the two Houses shall be sitting.

Section 6. The Senators and Representatives shall receive a Compensation for their Services, to be ascertained by Law, and paid out of the Treasury of the United States. They shall in all Cases, except Treason, Felony, and Breach of the Peace, be privileged from arrest during their Attendance at the Session of their respective Houses, and in going to and returning from the same; and for any Speech or Debate in either House, they shall not be questioned in any other Place.

No Senator or Representative shall, during the Time for which he was elected, be appointed to any civil Office under the Authority of the United States, which shall have been created, or the Emoluments whereof shall have been increased, during such time; and no Person holding any Office under the United States shall be a Member of either House during his continuance in Office.

Section 7. All Bills for raising Revenue shall originate in the House of Representatives; but the Senate may propose or concur with Amendments as on other bills.

Every Bill which shall have passed the House of Representatives and the Senate, shall, before it become a Law, be presented to the President of the United States; If he approve he shall sign it, but if not he shall return it, with his Objections, to that House in which it shall have originated, who shall enter the Objections at large on their Journal, and proceed to reconsider it. If after such Reconsideration two thirds of that House shall agree to pass the bill, it shall be sent, together with the objections, to the other House, by which it shall likewise be reconsidered, and if approved by two thirds of that House, it shall become a Law. But in all such Cases the Votes of both Houses shall be determined by Yeas and Nays, and the Names of the Persons voting for and against the Bill shall be entered on the Journal of each House respectively. If any Bill shall not be returned by the President within ten Days (Sundays excepted) after it shall have been presented to him, the Same shall be a Law, in like Manner as if he had signed it, unless the Congress by their Adjournment prevent its Return, in which Case it shall not be a Law.

Every Order, Resolution, or Vote to which the Concurrence of the Senate and House of Representatives may be necessary (except on a question of Adjournment) shall be presented to the President of the United States; and before the Same shall take Effect, shall be approved by him, or being disapproved by him, shall be repassed by two thirds of the Senate and House of Representatives, according to the Rules and Limitations prescribed in the Case of a Bill.

Section 8. The Congress shall have Power To lay and collect Taxes, Duties, Imposts and Excises, to pay the Debts and provide for the common Defence and general Welfare of the United States; but all Duties,

Imposts and Excises shall be uniform throughout the United States;

To borrow money on the credit of the United States;

To regulate Commerce with foreign Nations, and among the several States, and with the Indian Tribes;

To establish an uniform Rule of Naturalization, and uniform Laws on the subject of Bankruptcies throughout the United States;

To coin Money, regulate the Value thereof, and of foreign Coin, and fix the Standard of Weights and Measures;

To provide for the Punishment of counterfeiting the Securities and current Coin of the United States;

To establish Post Offices and post Roads;

To promote the Progress of Science and useful Arts, by securing for limited Times to Authors and Inventors the exclusive Right to their respective Writings and Discoveries;

To constitute Tribunals inferior to the Supreme Court;

To define and punish Piracies and Felonies committed on the high Seas, and Offences against the Law of Nations;

To declare War, grant Letters of Marque and Reprisal, and make Rules concerning Captures on Land and Water;

To raise and support Armies, but no Appropriation of Money to that Use shall be for a longer Term than two Years;

To provide and maintain a Navy;

To make Rules for the Government and Regulation of the land and naval forces;

To provide for calling forth the Militia to execute the Laws of the Union, suppress Insurrections and repel Invasions;

To provide for organizing, arming, and disciplining the Militia, and for governing such Part of them as may be employed in the Service of the United States, reserving to the States respectively, the Appointment of the Officers, and the Authority of training the Militia according to the discipline prescribed by Congress;

To exercise exclusive Legislation in all Cases whatsoever, over such District (not exceeding ten Miles square) as may, by Cession of particular States, and the acceptance of Congress, become the Seat of Government of the United States, and to exercise like Authority over all Places purchased by the Consent of the Legislature of the State in which the Same shall be, for the Erection of Forts, Magazines, Arsenals, dock-Yards, and other needful Buildings;—And

To make all Laws which shall be necessary and proper for carrying into Execution the foregoing Powers, and all other Powers vested by this Constitution in the government of the United States, or in any Department or Officer thereof.

Section 9. The Migration or Importation of such Persons as any of the States now existing shall think proper to admit, shall not be prohibited by the Congress prior to the Year one thousand eight hundred and eight, but a tax or duty may be imposed on such Importation, not exceeding ten dollars for each Person.

The privilege of the Writ of Habeas Corpus shall not be suspended, unless when in Cases of Rebellion or Invasion the public Safety may require it.

No Bill of Attainder or ex post facto Law shall be passed.

No capitation, or other direct, Tax shall be laid unless in Proportion to the Census or Enumeration herein before directed to be taken.

No Tax or Duty shall be laid on Articles exported from any State.

No Preference shall be given by any Regulation of Revenue to the Ports of one State over those of another: nor shall Vessels bound to, or from, one State, be obliged to enter, clear, or pay Duties in another.

No Money shall be drawn from the Treasury, but in Consequence of Appropriations made by Law; and a regular Statement and Account of the Receipts and Expenditures of all public Money shall be published from time to time.

No Title of Nobility shall be granted by the United States: And no Person holding any Office of Profit or Trust under them, shall, without the Consent of the Congress, accept of any present, Emolument, Office, or Title, of any kind whatever, from any King, Prince, or foreign State.

Section 10. No State shall enter into any Treaty, Alliance, or Confederation; grant Letters of Marque and Reprisal; coin Money; emit Bills of Credit; make any Thing but gold and silver Coin a Tender in Payment of Debts; pass any Bill of Attainder, ex post facto Law, or Law impairing the Obligation of Contracts, or grant any Title of Nobility.

No State shall, without the Consent of the Congress, lay any Imposts or Duties on Imports or Exports, except what may be absolutely necessary for executing its inspection Laws: and the net Produce of all Duties and Imposts, laid by any State on Imports or Exports, shall be for the Use of the Treasury of the United States; and all such Laws shall be subject to the Revision and Control of the Congress.

No State shall, without the Consent of Congress, lay any duty of Tonnage, keep Troops, or Ships of War in time of Peace, enter into any Agreement or Compact with another State, or with a foreign Power, or engage in War, unless actually invaded, or in such imminent Danger as will not admit of delay.

Article II

Section 1. The executive Power shall be vested in a President of the United States of America. He shall hold his Office during the Term of four years, and, together with the Vice President, chosen for the same Term, be elected, as follows:

Each State shall appoint, in such Manner as the Legislature thereof may direct, a Number of Electors, equal to the whole Number of Senators and Representatives to which the State may be entitled in the Congress; but no Senator or Representative, or Person holding an Office of Trust or Profit under the United States, shall be appointed an Elector.

The Electors shall meet in their respective States, and vote by Ballot for two persons, of whom one at least shall not be an Inhabitant of the same State with themselves. And they shall make a List of all the Persons voted for, and of the Number of Votes for each; which List they shall sign and certify, and transmit sealed to the Seat of the Government of the United States, directed to the President of the Senate. The President of the Senate shall, in the Presence of the Senate and House of Representatives, open all the Certificates, and the Votes shall then be counted. The Person having the greatest Number of Votes shall be the President, if such Number be a Majority of the whole Number of Electors appointed; and if there be more than one who have such Majority, and have an equal Number of Votes, then the House of Representatives shall immediately chuse by Ballot one of them for President; and if no Person have a Majority, then from the five highest on the List the said House shall in like Manner chuse the President. But in chusing the President, the votes shall be taken by States, the Representation from each State having one Vote; a quorum for this Purpose shall consist of a Member or Members from two-thirds of the States, and a Majority of all the States shall be necessary to a Choice. In every Case, after the Choice of the President, the Person having the greatest Number of Votes of the Electors shall be the Vice President. But if there should remain two or more who have equal votes, the Senate shall chuse from them by Ballot the Vice President.

The Congress may determine the time of chusing the Electors, and the Day on which they shall give their Votes; which Day shall be the same throughout the United States.

No person except a natural-born Citizen, or a Citizen of the United States, at the time of the Adoption of this Constitution, shall be eligible to the Office of President; neither shall any Person be eligible to that Office who shall not have attained to the Age of thirty-five years, and been fourteen Years a Resident within the United States.

In Case of the Removal of the President from Office, or of his Death, Resignation, or Inability to discharge the Powers and Duties of the said Office, the same shall devolve on the Vice President, and the Congress may by Law provide for the Case of Removal, Death, Resignation, or Inability, both of the President and Vice President, declaring what Officer shall then act as President, and such Officer shall act accordingly, until the disability be removed, or a President shall be elected.

The President shall, at stated Times, receive for his Services a Compensation, which shall neither be increased nor diminished during the Period for which he shall have been elected, and he shall not receive within that Period any other Emolument from the United States, or any of them.

Before he enter on the execution of his Office, he shall take the following Oath or Affirmation:—"I do solemnly swear (or affirm) that I will faithfully execute the Office of President of the United States, and will, to the best of my Ability, preserve, protect, and defend the Constitution of the United States."

Section 2. The President shall be Commander in Chief of the Army and Navy of the United States, and of the Militia of the several States, when called into the actual Service of the United States; he may require the Opinion, in writing, of the principal Officer in each of the executive Departments, upon any subject relating to the Duties of their respective Offices, and he shall have Power to Grant Reprieves and Pardons for Offences against the United States, except in Cases of Impeachment.

He shall have Power, by and with the Advice and Consent of the Senate, to make Treaties, provided two thirds of the Senators present concur; and he shall nominate, and by and with the Advice and Consent of the Senate, shall appoint Ambassadors, other public Ministers and Consuls, Judges of the supreme Court, and all other Officers of the United States, whose Appointments are not herein otherwise provided for, and which shall be established by Law: but the Congress may by Law vest the Appointment of such inferior Officers, as they think proper, in the President alone, in the Courts of Law, or in the Heads of Departments.

The President shall have Power to fill up all Vacancies that may happen during the Recess of the Senate, by granting Commissions which shall expire at the End of their next Session.

Section 3. He shall from time to time give to the Congress Information of the State of the Union, and recommend to their Consideration such Measures as he shall judge necessary and expedient; he may, on extraordinary occasions, convene both Houses, or either of them, and in Case of Disagreement between them, with respect to the Time of Adjournment, he may adjourn them to such Time as he shall think proper; he shall receive Ambassadors and other public Ministers; he shall take Care that the Laws be faithfully executed, and shall Commission all the Officers of the United States.

Section 4. The President, Vice President and all civil Officers of the United States, shall be removed from Office on Impeachment for, and Conviction of, Treason, Bribery, or other high Crimes and Misdemeanors.

Article III

Section 1. The judicial Power of the United States shall be vested in one supreme Court, and in such inferior Courts as the Congress may from time to time ordain and establish. The Judges, both of the supreme and inferior Courts, shall hold their Offices during good Behaviour, and shall, at stated Times, receive for their Services, a Compensation, which shall not be diminished during their Continuance in Office.

Section 2. The judicial Power shall extend to all Cases, in Law and Equity, arising under this Constitution, the Laws of the United States, and treaties made, or which shall be made, under their Authority;—to all Cases affecting ambassadors, other public ministers and consuls;—to all cases of admiralty and maritime Jurisdiction;—to Controversies to which the United States shall be a Party;—to Controversies between two or more States;—between a State and Citizens of another State;—between Citizens of different States,—between Citizens of the same State claiming Lands under Grants of different States, and between a State, or the Citizens thereof, and foreign States, Citizens or Subjects.

In all Cases affecting Ambassadors, other public Ministers and Consuls, and those in which a State shall be Party, the supreme Court shall have original Jurisdiction. In all the other Cases before mentioned, the supreme Court shall have appellate Jurisdiction, both as to Law and Fact, with such Exceptions, and under such Regulations as the Congress shall make.

The trial of all Crimes, except in Cases of Impeachment, shall be by Jury; and such Trial shall be held in the State where the said Crimes shall have been committed; but when not committed within any State, the Trial shall be at such Place or Places as the Congress may by Law have directed.

Section 3. Treason against the United States, shall consist only in levying War against them, or in adhering to their Enemies, giving them Aid and Comfort. No

Person shall be convicted of Treason unless on the testimony of two Witnesses to the same overt Act, or on Confession in open Court.

The Congress shall have power to declare the Punishment of Treason, but no Attainder of Treason shall work Corruption of Blood, or Forfeiture except during the Life of the Person attained.

Article IV

Section 1. Full Faith and Credit shall be given in each State to the public Acts, Records, and judicial Proceedings of every other State. And the Congress may by general Laws prescribe the Manner in which such Acts, Records and Proceedings shall be proved, and the Effect thereof.

Section 2. The Citizens of each State shall be entitled to all Privileges and Immunities of Citizens in the several States.

A Person charged in any State with Treason, Felony, or other Crime, who shall flee from Justice, and be found in another State, shall on demand of the executive Authority of the State from which he fled, be delivered up, to be removed to the State having Jurisdiction of the crime.

No Person held to Service or Labour in one State, under the Laws thereof, escaping into another, shall, in Consequence of any Law or Regulation therein, be discharged from such Service or Labour, but shall be delivered up on Claim of the Party to whom such Service or Labour may be due.

Section 3. New States may be admitted by the Congress into this Union; but no new State shall be formed or erected within the Jurisdiction of any other State; nor any State be formed by the Junction of two or more States, or parts of States, without the Consent of the Legislatures of the States concerned as well as of the Congress.

The Congress shall have Power to dispose of and make all needful Rules and Regulations respecting the Territory or other Property belonging to the United States; and nothing in this Constitution shall be so construed as to Prejudice any Claims of the United States, or of any particular State.

Section 4. The United States shall guarantee to every State in this Union a Republican Form of Government, and shall protect each of them against Invasion; and on Application of the Legislature, or the Executive (when the Legislature cannot be convened) against domestic Violence.

Article V

The Congress, whenever two-thirds of both Houses shall deem it necessary, shall propose Amendments to this Constitution, or, on the Application of the Legislatures of two-thirds of the several States, shall call a Convention for proposing Amendments, which, in either Case, shall be valid to all Intents and Purposes, as part of this Constitution, when ratified by the Legislatures of three-fourths of the several States, or by Conventions in three-fourths thereof, as the one or the other Mode of Ratification may be proposed by the Congress; Provided that no Amendment which may be made prior to the Year One thousand eight hundred and eight shall in any Manner affect the first and fourth Clauses in the Ninth Section of the first Article; and that no State, without its Consent, shall be deprived of its equal Suffrage in the Senate.

Article VI

All Debts contracted and Engagements entered into, before the Adoption of this Constitution, shall be as valid against the United States under this Constitution, as under the Confederation.

This Constitution, and the Laws of the United States which shall be made in Pursuance thereof; and all Treaties made, or which shall be made, under the Authority of the United States, shall be the supreme Law of the Land; and the Judges in every State shall be bound thereby, any Thing in the Constitution or Laws of any State to the Contrary notwithstanding.

The Senators and Representatives before mentioned, and the Members of the several State Legislatures, and all executive and judicial Officers, both of the United States and of the several States, shall be bound by Oath or Affirmation to support this Constitution; but no religious Test shall ever be required as a qualification to any Office or public Trust under the United States.

Article VII

The Ratification of the Conventions of nine States shall be sufficient for the Establishment of this Constitution between the States so ratifying the same.

Done in Convention by the Unanimous Consent of the States present the Seventeenth Day of September in the Year of our Lord one thousand seven hundred and Eighty seven, and of the Independence of the United States of America the Twelfth. In Witness whereof We have hereunto subscribed our Names.

Go. Washington, *President and deputy from Virginia; Attest* William Jackson, *Secretary; Delaware:* Geo. Read, Gunning Bedford, Jr., John Dickinson, Richard Bassett, Jaco. Broom; *Maryland:* James McHenry, Daniel of St. Thomas' Jenifer, Danl. Carroll; *Virginia:* John Blair, James Madison, Jr.; *North Carolina:* Wm. Blount, Richd. Dobbs Spaight, Hu Williamson; *South Carolina:* J. Rutledge, Charles Cotesworth Pinckney, Charles Pinckney, Pierce Butler; *Georgia:* William Few, Abr. Baldwin; *New Hampshire:* John Langdon, Nicholas Gilman; *Massachusetts:* Nathaniel Gorham, Rufus King; *Connecticut:* Wm. Saml. Johnson, Roger Sherman; *New York:* Alexander Hamilton; *New Jersey:* Wil. Livingston, David Brearley, Wm. Paterson, Jona. Dayton; *Pennsylvania:* B. Franklin, Thomas Mifflin, Robt. Morris, Geo. Clymer, Thos. FitzSimons, Jared Ingersoll, James Wilson, Gouv. Morris.

Articles in Addition to, and Amendment of, the Constitution of the United States of America, Proposed by Congress, and Ratified by the Legislatures of the Several States, Pursuant to the Fifth Article of the Original Constitution.

Amendment I [1791]

Congress shall make no law respecting an establishment of religion, or prohibiting the free exercise thereof; or abridging the freedom of speech, or of the press; or the right of the people peaceably to assemble, and to petition the Government for a redress of grievances.

Amendment II [1791]

A well regulated Militia, being necessary to the security of a free State, the right of the people to keep and bear Arms shall not be infringed.

Amendment III [1791]

No Soldier shall, in time of peace, be quartered in any house, without the consent of the Owner, nor in time of war, but in a manner to be prescribed by law.

Amendment IV [1791]

The right of the people to be secure in their persons, houses, papers, and effects, against unreasonable searches and seizures, shall not be violated, and no Warrants shall issue, but upon probable cause, supported by Oath or affirmation, and particularly describing the place to be searched, and the persons or things to be seized.

Amendment V [1791]

No person shall be held to answer for a capital or otherwise infamous crime, unless on a presentment or indictment of a Grand Jury, except in cases arising in the land or naval forces, or in the Militia, when in actual service in time of War or public danger; nor shall any person be subject for the same offence to be twice put in jeopardy of life or limb; nor shall be compelled in any criminal case to be a witness against himself, nor be deprived of life, liberty, or property, without due process of law; nor shall private property be taken for public use, without just compensation.

Amendment VI [1791]

In all criminal prosecutions, the accused shall enjoy the right to a speedy and public trial, by an impartial jury of the State and district wherein the crime shall have been committed, which district shall have been previously ascertained by law, and to be informed of the nature and cause of the accusation; to be confronted with the witnesses against him; to have compulsory process for obtaining witnesses in his favor, and to have the Assistance of Counsel for his defence.

Amendment VII [1791]

In suits at common law, where the value in controversy shall exceed twenty dollars, the right of trial by jury shall be preserved, and no fact tried by a jury, shall be otherwise reexamined in any Court of the United States, than according to the rules of the common law.

Amendment VIII [1791]

Excessive bail shall not be required, nor excessive fines imposed, nor cruel and unusual punishments inflicted.

Amendment IX [1791]

The enumeration in the Constitution, of certain rights, shall not be construed to deny or disparage others retained by the people.

Amendment X [1791]

The powers not delegated to the United States by the Constitution, nor prohibited by it to the States, are reserved to the States respectively, or to the people.

Amendment XI [1798]

The Judicial power of the United States shall not be construed to extend to any suit in law or equity, commenced or prosecuted against one of the United States by Citizens of another State, or by Citizens or Subjects of any Foreign State.

Amendment XII [1804]

The Electors shall meet in their respective States and vote by ballot for President and Vice-President, one of whom, at least, shall not be an inhabitant of the same State with themselves; they shall name in their ballots the person voted for as President, and in distinct ballots the person voted for as Vice-President, and they shall make distinct lists of all persons voted for as President, and of all persons voted for as Vice-President, and of the number of votes for each, which lists they shall sign and certify, and transmit sealed to the seat of the government of the United States, directed to the President of the Senate;— The President of the Senate shall, in the presence of the Senate and House of Representatives, open all the certificates and the votes shall then be counted;—The person having the greatest number of votes for President, shall be the President, if such number be a majority of the whole number of Electors appointed; and if no person have such majority, then from the persons having the highest numbers not exceeding three on the list of those voted for as President, the House of Representatives shall choose immediately, by ballot, the President. But in choosing the President, the votes shall be taken by states, the representation from each state having one vote; a quorum for this purpose shall consist of a member or members from two-thirds of the states, and a majority of all the states shall be necessary to a choice. And if the House of Representatives shall not choose a President whenever the right of choice shall devolve upon them, before the fourth day of March next following, then the Vice-President shall act as President, as in the case of the death or other constitutional disability of the President.—The person having the greatest number of votes as Vice-President, shall be the Vice-President, if such number be a majority of the whole number of Electors appointed, and if no person have a majority, then from the two highest numbers on the list, the Senate shall choose the Vice-President; a quorum for the purpose shall consist of two-thirds of the whole number of Senators, and a majority of the whole number shall be necessary to a choice. But no person constitutionally ineligible to the office of President shall be eligible to that of Vice-President of the United States.

Amendment XIII [1865]

Section 1. Neither slavery nor involuntary servitude, except as a punishment for crime whereof the party shall have been duly convicted, shall exist within the United States, or any place subject to their jurisdiction.

Section 2. Congress shall have power to enforce this article by appropriate legislation.

Amendment XIV [1868]

Section 1. All persons born or naturalized in the United States, and subject to the jurisdiction thereof, are citizens of the United States and of the State wherein they reside. No State shall make or enforce any law which shall abridge the privileges or immunities of citizens of the United States; nor shall any State deprive any person of life, liberty, or property, without due process of law; nor deny to any person within its jurisdiction the equal protection of the laws.

Section 2. Representatives shall be apportioned among the several States according to their respective numbers, counting the whole number of persons in each State, excluding Indians not taxed. But when the right to vote at any election for the choice of electors for President and Vice-President of the United States, Rep-

resentatives in Congress, the Executive and Judicial officers of a State, or the members of the Legislature thereof, is denied to any of the male inhabitants of such State, being twenty-one years of age, and citizens of the United States, or in any way abridged, except for participation in rebellion, or other crime, the basis of representation therein shall be reduced in the proportion which the number of such male citizens shall bear to the whole number of male citizens twenty-one years of age in such State.

Section 3. No person shall be a Senator or Representative in Congress, or elector of President and Vice-President, or hold any office, civil or military, under the United States, or under any State, who, having previously taken an oath, as a member of Congress, or as an officer of the United States, or as a member of any State legislature, or as an executive or judicial officer of any State, to support the Constitution of the United States, shall have engaged in insurrection or rebellion against the same, or given aid or comfort to the enemies thereof. But Congress may by a vote of two-thirds of each House, remove such disability.

Section 4. The validity of the public debt of the United States, authorized by law, including debts incurred for payment of pensions and bounties for services in suppressing insurrection or rebellion, shall not be questioned. But neither the United States nor any State shall assume or pay any debt or obligation incurred in aid of insurrection or rebellion against the United States, or any claim for the loss or emancipation of any slave; but all such debts, obligations, and claims shall be held illegal and void.

Section 5. The Congress shall have the power to enforce, by appropriate legislation, the provisions of this article.

Amendment XV [1870]

Section 1. The right of citizens of the United States to vote shall not be denied or abridged by the United States or by any State on account of race, color, or previous condition of servitude—

Section 2. The Congress shall have power to enforce this article by appropriate legislation.

Amendment XVI [1913]

The Congress shall have power to lay and collect taxes on incomes, from whatever source derived, without apportionment among the several States, and without regard to any census or enumeration.

Amendment XVII [1913]

The Senate of the United States shall be composed of two Senators from each State, elected by the people thereof, for six years; and each Senator shall have one vote. The electors in each State shall have the qualifications requisite for electors of the most numerous branch of the State legislatures.

When vacancies happen in the representation of any State in the Senate, the executive authority of such State shall issue writs of election to fill such vacancies: *Provided*, That the legislature of any State may empower the executive thereof to make temporary appointments until the people fill the vacancies by election as the legislature may direct.

This amendment shall not be so construed as to affect the election or term of any Senator chosen before it becomes valid as part of the Constitution.

Amendment XVIII [1919]

Section 1. After one year from the ratification of this article the manufacture, sale, or transportation of intoxicating liquors within, the importation thereof into, or the exportation thereof from the United States and all territory subject to the jurisdiction thereof for beverage purposes is hereby prohibited.

Section 2. The Congress and the several States shall have concurrent power to enforce this article by appropriate legislation.

Section 3. This article shall be inoperative unless it shall have been ratified as an amendment to the Constitution by the legislatures of the several States, as provided in the Constitution, within seven years from the date of the submission hereof to the States by the Congress.

Amendment XIX [1920]

The right of citizens of the United States to vote shall not be denied or abridged by the United States or by any State on account of sex.

Congress shall have power to enforce this article by appropriate legislation.

Amendment XX [1933]

Section 1. The terms of the President and Vice-President shall end at noon on the 20th day of January, and the terms of Senators and Representatives at noon on the 3d day of January, of the years in which such terms would have ended if this article had not been ratified; and the terms of their successors shall then begin.

Section 2. The Congress shall assemble at least once in every year, and such meeting shall begin at noon on the 3d day of January, unless they shall by law appoint a different day.

Section 3. If, at the time fixed for the beginning of the term of the President, the President elect shall have died, the Vice-President elect shall become President. If a President shall not have been chosen before the time fixed for the beginning of his term, or if the President elect shall have failed to qualify, then the Vice-President elect shall act as President until a President shall have qualified; and the Congress may by law provide for the case wherein neither a President elect nor a Vice-President elect shall have qualified, declaring who shall then act as President, or the manner in which one who is to act shall be selected, and such person shall act accordingly until a President or Vice-President shall have qualified.

Section 4. The Congress may by law provide for the case of the death of any of the persons from whom the House of Representatives may choose a President whenever the right of choice shall have devolved upon them, and for the case of the death of any of the persons from whom the Senate may choose a Vice-President whenever the right of choice shall have devolved upon them.

Section 5. Sections 1 and 2 shall take effect on the 15th day of October following the ratification of this article.

Section 6. This article shall be inoperative unless it shall have been ratified as an amendment to the Constitution by the legislatures of three-fourths of the several States within seven years from the date of its submission.

Amendment XXI [1933]

Section 1. The eighteenth article of amendment to the Constitution of the United States is hereby repealed.

Section 2. The transportation or importation into any State, Territory, or possession of the United States for delivery or use therein of intoxicating liquors, in violation of the laws thereof, is hereby prohibited.

Section 3. This article shall be inoperative unless it shall have been ratified as an amendment to the Constitution by conventions in the several States, as provided in the Constitution, within seven years from the date of the submission hereof to the States by the Congress.

Amendment XXII [1951]

No person shall be elected to the office of the President more than twice, and no person who has held the office of President, or acted as President, for more than two years of a term to which some other person was elected President shall be elected to the office of the President more than once.

But this Article shall not apply to any person holding the office of President when this Article was proposed by the Congress, and shall not prevent any person who may be holding the office of President, or acting as President, during the term within which this Article becomes operative from holding the office of President or acting as President during the remainder of such term.

Amendment XXIII [1961]

Section 1. The District constituting the seat of Government of the United States shall appoint in such manner as the Congress may direct:

A number of electors of President and Vice President equal to the whole number of Senators and Representatives in Congress to which the District would be entitled if it were a State, but in no event more than the least populous State; they shall be in addition to those appointed by the States, but they shall be considered, for the purposes of the election of President and Vice President, to be electors appointed by a State; and they shall meet in the District and perform such duties as provided by the twelfth article of amendment.

Section 2. The Congress shall have power to enforce this article by appropriate legislation.

Amendment XXIV [1964]

Section 1. The right of citizens of the United States to vote in any primary or other election for President or Vice President, for electors for President or Vice President, or for Senator or Representative in Congress, shall not be denied or abridged by the United States or any State by reason of failure to pay any poll tax or other tax.

Section 2. The Congress shall have the power to enforce this article by appropriate legislation.

Amendment XXV [1967]

Section 1. In case of the removal of the President from office or his death or resignation, the Vice President shall become President.

Section 2. Whenever there is a vacancy in the office of the Vice President, the President shall nominate a Vice President who shall take the office upon confirmation by a majority vote of both houses of Congress.

Section 3. Whenever the President transmits to the President pro tempore of the Senate and the Speaker of the House of Representatives his written declaration that he is unable to discharge the powers and duties of his office, and until he transmits to them a written declaration to the contrary, such powers and duties shall be discharged by the Vice President as Acting President.

Section 4. Whenever the Vice President and a majority of either the principal officers of the executive departments, or of such other body as Congress may by law provide, transmit to the President pro tempore of the Senate and the Speaker of the House of Representatives their written declaration that the President is unable to discharge the powers and duties of his office, the Vice President shall immediately assume the powers and duties of the office as Acting President.

Thereafter, when the President transmits to the President pro tempore of the Senate and the Speaker of the House of Representatives his written declaration that no inability exists, he shall resume the powers and duties of his office unless the Vice President and a majority of either the principal officers of the executive departments, or of such other body as Congress may by law provide, transmit within four days to the President pro tempore of the Senate and the Speaker of the House of Representatives their written declaration that the President is unable to discharge the powers and duties of his office. Thereupon Congress shall decide the issue, assembling within 48 hours for that purpose if not in session. If the Congress, within 21 days after receipt of the latter written declaration, or, if Congress is not in session, within 21 days after Congress is required to assemble, determines by two-thirds vote of both houses that the President is unable to discharge the powers and duties of his office, the Vice President shall continue to discharge the same as Acting President; otherwise, the President shall resume the powers and duties of his office.

Amendment XXVI [1971]

Section 1. The right of citizens of the United States, who are 18 years of age or older, to vote shall not be denied or abridged by the United States or any state on account of age.

Section 2. The Congress shall have the power to enforce this article by appropriate legislation.

INDEX